Contents

List of Figures		v
List of Tables		vii
Preface		ix
1	Why Images, and What Do We Know about Them?	1
2	Cognitive Foundations for Image Processing	7
3	Organizing and Providing Access to Images	69
4	Machine Processing of Images	139
5	Image Attributes: The Research Framework	203
6	Towards the Future	241
Bibliography		277
Subject Index		321
Author Index		329
About the Author		341

Figures

Figure 2.1	Gestalt principles	22
Figure 3.1	Example of MARC record with relevant visual fields	106
Figure 5.1	The Pyramid	230

Image Retrieval

Theory and Research

Corinne Jörgensen

The Scarecrow Press, Inc.
Lanham, Maryland, and Oxford
2003

SCARECROW PRESS, INC.

Published in the United States of America
by Scarecrow Press, Inc.
A Member of the Rowman & Littlefield Publishing Group
4501 Forbes Boulevard, Suite 200, Lanham, MD 20706
www.scarecrowpress.com

PO Box 317
Oxford
OX2 9RU, UK

British Library Cataloguing in Publication Information Available

Library of Congress Cataloging-in-Publication Data

Library of Congress Cataloging-in-Publication Data

Jèorgensen, Corinne, 1947–
Image retrieval : theory and research / Corinne Jèorgensen.
p. cm.
Includes bibliographical references and index.
ISBN 0-8108-4734-5 (alk. paper)
1. Information storage and retrieval systems—Image files. 2. Image files—Abstracting and indexing. 3. Image processing. I. Title.
Z699.5.P53J67 2003
025.04—dc21

2003000002

∞™ The paper used in this publication meets the minimum requirements of American National Standard for Information Sciences—Permanence of Paper for Printed Library Materials, ANSI/NISO Z39.48-1992.
Manufactured in the United States of America.

Tables

Table 3.1	Percentage distribution of subjects from a sample of the *TGM I*	80
Table 3.2	Attributes occurring at a frequency above 2% in the *TGM I*	81
Table 3.3	Distributions of attribute codes across the facets in the *AAT*	87
Table 3.4	Distribution of attributes in the *AAT*	87
Table 3.5	Distribution of sample of headings from *Thesaurus iconographique*	90
Table 3.6	*Thesaurus iconographique* attributes ranked by frequency	91
Table 3.7	Fields containing descriptive information in different metadata schemas	117
Table 5.1	Two sample records from descriptive Viewing Task	205
Table 5.2	Statistics for the descriptive Viewing, Search, and Memory Tasks	206
Table 5.3	Most frequently occurring attributes averaged across the describing tasks	206
Table 5.4	Distribution of Classes by average percentage across three describing tasks	207
Table 5.5	Image presentation order and number of images remembered	209
Table 5.6	Sample of data sorted by participant, term, and attribute for Viewing Task	211
Table 5.7	Repeat rate for three describing tasks by individual term, by attribute, and by Class	212
Table 5.8	Descriptive Viewing Task: Total number of attributes in Class, and number and percentage of attributes above median by Class.	213

Table 5.9 Percentage of terms in each level for describing tasks 220

Table 5.10 Attribute Classes by percentage for Sorting Task 216

Table 5.11 Comparison of Class frequency by percentage for the describing tasks and the Sorting Task 217

Table 5.12 Class distributions, by percentage, for the same six images for the Sorting Task and describing tasks (averaged across three describing tasks) 218

Table 5.13 Comparison of describing tasks' images (illustrations) with pretest images (fine arts) 220

Table 5.14 Frequency of selected Classes for images of decreasing realism 221

Table 5.15 Attributes grouped by generic, specific, and abstract levels 228

Table 5.16 Recursive attributes (VISUAL ELEMENTS) and Gestalt attributes 229

Table 6.1 Schema for CHILDREN PLAYING IN SAND 252

Table 6.2 Current methods of representation using textual and machine processing and future approaches, by attribute Classes 258

Preface

Humankind has a deep-seated affinity with images. Speaking of the discovery of the visually compelling cave paintings in France, Cutting and Massironi eloquently summarize this:

> Clearly, pictures have been with us a long time and, with the Chauvet discoveries, much longer than previously thought. Pictures can no longer be seen as an artifact of the development of a particular culture. They now seem likely to be a defining characteristic of our species. The antiquity and ubiquity of pictures suggests the ability to understand pictures is deeply embedded in the human mind, even the genome (Cutting and Massironi 1998, 137–138).

Our earliest evidence of human communication is in the form of visual images, not texts (Hall 1979). Indeed, images (e.g., pictograms, ideograms) were the *only* form of written communication for 25,000 out of the 30,000 years of human recorded experience (Davies, Bathurst, and Bathurst 1990). The invention of the phonetic alphabet began to change this, and it is only during the last 500 years, with the invention of printing, that pictures as serious "messengers" receded well into the background. One reason for this was the sheer difficulty in producing images. Pictures of faraway places, people, or news events had to be created by hand, preferably by someone with artistic capabilities. Even with the invention of automatic recording devices such as cameras, there was no way to easily distribute images. Thus, during the last few centuries, words dominated images as the privileged form of communication and the preferred means of education.

In the last few decades, with the development of such technologies as television, video recording, and computer-based graphics packages, tools for the creation of images have become widely accessible. Furthermore, advances in technology have made possible not only the digitization of images and the creation of large imagebases but also the transmission of images over long distances using both network and satellite technology. These factors have combined to produce a growing number of both images and collections of images stored in digital format. Images have become ubiquitous, woven into our daily lives in such a way that we are often barely conscious of them. They are valued not only for their aesthetic nature but also for their instructional, informational, and commercial applications, and their persuasive capacities are recognized and applied in both obvious and subtle ways. This shift towards a visual culture was noted by authors such as Gattegno and later Dondis, who noted the movement of a language-dominated culture toward the iconic (Dondis 1973; Gattegno 1969).

Thus we are, it appears, on the hinge of an important historical swing back towards what may be called the primacy of the image. A seismic shift has taken place, and within the last several decades images have been reasserting their role as immediate and influential messengers. Additionally, the widespread use and acceptance of graphical user interfaces (GUIs) in computer systems and the development of iconic programming languages demonstrate that visual mechanisms appeal to a broader range of cognitive abilities than text alone. In a sense, then, images *are* the hinge between textual representation and a heightened level of direct experience.

Davies, writing of the shift from words to images, also called attention to the primitive state of the codification, indexing, and retrieval of images (Davies, Bathurst, and Bathurst 1990). Given the fact that visual materials are being created at astonishing rates and are being incorporated into vast manual and electronic collections, access to these image collections becomes more critical daily. Fortunately, with the exponential growth in digitized collections of images, indexing and retrieval of images have become important research areas over the last ten years as well.

This book is intended to introduce the interested reader to the relevant literatures associated with image access and retrieval, including investigations of theory and practice across several disciplines. The research review presented within began as a prelude to the author's dissertation research, which focused on discovering the range of attributes or features named by humans when they describe images. The expanded discussion presented here is intended not only to further research efforts aimed towards answering these questions but also towards facilitating intelligent system design based upon a broad integration of what we already know.

The literatures necessary for a full understanding of the theoretical issues involved in providing access to images are many, and range from cognitive psychology to computer science and artificial intelligence, the psychology of art and aesthetics, cultural anthropology, information retrieval and systems design research, knowledge representation, semiotics, and communication and mass media. The purpose of this book is to review relevant literatures in several areas: human perception and cognition, the psychology of art, library and information science (LIS), and computer science and related fields. This book is motivated by the need to link these research communities and heighten awareness of projects utilizing an expanded theoretical base and new techniques for representation.

It is my hope that this greatly expanded and updated work will serve as a foundation for others who are at the beginning stages of exploration into the issues of image access and retrieval. By presenting multiple perspectives, the goal is to introduce researchers to (perhaps) unfamiliar disciplines and encourage researchers to explore beyond their own intellectual traditions and enter into collaborative multidisciplinary research projects. I have also, throughout the chapters, attempted to explain concepts and material to an audience that may be unfamiliar with the source discipline. While this may be of less pertinence to those already familiar with the subject area, I felt that to do otherwise might contribute further to problems of disciplinary isolation or interdisciplinary *mis*understanding. The issues within each discipline are decidedly complex, and an appreciation of that complexity could hopefully inspire new approaches to solving some of the problems faced in image access.

Acknowledgments

This book has been long in the making, and has benefited from the input of too many people to acknowledge each one individually. It also represents the cumulation of a great deal of information gained through participation in a number of research projects. Therefore, a few short words of thanks to my major supporters, with the caveat that this is only a tiny fraction of those who have contributed in any number of ways to this project.

First (and last), thanks to my husband, Peter, for his unfailing support (including housecleaning, dinner preparation, and library pickups, as well as technical assistance with recalcitrant software and hardware) during the writing of this book. All this while he was working on his own dissertation, and I was supposed to be helping him.

Secondly, thanks to Sue Easun at Scarecrow Press for her unfailing confidence in me, and for her understanding of the realities of trying to write a book while one is carrying out other professional responsibilities. Thanks also go to Crystal Clifton and other members of the editorial staff for their assistance and quick replies to my formatting questions. Thanks especially goes to Karen Gray, the production editor, whose steadfast assistance during the process greatly alleviated the stress of some unexpected roadblocks. To the anonymous proofreader: heartfelt appreciation for the detailed and perceptive proofreading and editing of the manuscript, which helped shape it into a much more polished final work.

One community that both educated and listened to me is the MPEG-7 standards group, composed of computer scientists and electrical engineers from many countries working to make images and multimedia more accessible. Participation in this initiative helped me understand different disciplinary and professional perspectives, and was invaluable for this project. Thanks are owed to the Department of Library and Information Studies, School of Informatics, University at Buffalo (and to George Bobinski, dean during my participation) for making my attendance at MPEG-7 meetings possible.

Thanks also to a number of Ph.D. students in LIS, computer science and electrical engineering, geography, art, and other disciplines for stimulating ideas and conversations. Special thanks to research assistants Trevor Oakley and Susan Mitchell for all their help in searching and retrieving hard-to-find articles. The efforts of Jill Ortner and her assistants in interlibrary loan services at Lockwood Memorial Library in tracking down and obtaining some of the less readily available materials are also acknowledged and greatly appreciated. Thanks also to Aimee Reist and Claudia Montague and their team of student assistants at the Goldstein Library, School of Information Studies, Florida State University, for help with last minute details.

While somewhat unusual, a heartfelt thank-you goes to the creators of the Google search engine, which enabled me to access more information than imaginable on the topics covered in this book, and quickly, and in my own office. From tracking down page numbers in a citation to finding a definition to getting fulltext of an esoteric conference proceeding to verifying a quotation, it did it all. While the print literature retains its authority and reliability and provided the foundation for the work (yes, many hours spent browsing in the stacks, and still nothing is as satisfying as bringing home an armload of books), electronic access provided breadth and depth that couldn't have been gained without much more time, energy, and money. The goal of this book is to make access to images similarly efficient and productive.

Chapter 1

Why Images, and What Do We Know about Them?

Vast collections of both analog and digital images now exist in many types of organizations and institutions: libraries, museums, archives, information centers, research centers, hospitals, educational institutions, and newspapers, as well as in personal archives. While some image collections may be of interest only to researchers in a narrow field (such as those being created for medical diagnoses), other image collections are being created that will be of interest to many, including the artist, the scientist, the educator, the historian, the journalist, the student, and the leisure seeker. Collections at the University of California at Berkeley exemplify the diversity of visual resources which can potentially be made available; they include original materials housed in museums of art, paleontology, anthropology, and vertebrate zoology, as well as more replicable materials including botanical specimens, satellite images, motion picture film, insect specimens, slides of art and architecture, maps, and architectural images (Besser and Snow 1990). Many organizations are concerned with access to visual resources that may be too large, too small, too valuable, or too fragile to access directly. Adding these concerns to the long-existing barrier of distance, the impetus for digitization projects is overwhelming.

With the advent of a large number of digital library projects, stimulated by funding from a number of sources, Lew notes:

> Digital visual information is here to stay. The major world nations are converting their cultural heritage into digital libraries. The era of digital video has also arrived for television, movies, and even home video. Tying it together, the World Wide Web gives us the ability to communicate and share the

> information. Visual information permeates every facet of our life in the twenty-first century. Finding it is the next step (Lew 2001, vii).

In the last several decades, there has also been an increasing interest in the cognitive approach to information retrieval (Allen 1991). Studies have investigated such areas as the cognitive and affective aspects of the information search, the components of browsing behavior, and the meaning and utility of the concept of relevance to information retrieval; a number of models are proposed which incorporate these frameworks. Information science has broadened its scope of inquiry to include the burgeoning amount of spatial and visual information stored in digital formats.

In so doing, it continues the work by the European documentalists of the 1930s, especially Paul Otlet and Suzanne Briet, who were concerned with the issue of the extension of information retrieval beyond text (Buckland 1991, 586–587). Otlet insisted that a document can be three-dimensional and that objects themselves can be regarded as documents if one is informed by observation of them. Briet proposed that information retrieval is concerned with "access to evidence," and a star, a pebble, and an antelope become documents when there is a photograph of a star, a specimen of a pebble, or an antelope in a zoo as a research and educational exhibit. By 1933 the definitions of "document" were beginning to include museum objects explicitly.

The applicability and utility of images in information representation and retrieval are also being explored. Images serve not only as direct sources of information but, with the development of visualization techniques, they can also be used to enhance understanding of that information, conveying multidimensional concepts and aspects of data that are difficult or incomprehensible in their textual or numeric forms.

Those who are working today in the field of information retrieval have at their disposal a staggering number of techniques with which to approach the problems associated with accessing information resources. The last thirty years have seen the development of computerized retrieval technologies and text-processing algorithms that seemed to herald the solutions to many text-based retrieval problems. However, humans continue to be demanding, creative, and unpredictable in their use of information retrieval systems. Systems have not yet been able to accommodate all of the human needs and behaviors involved in document retrieval, much less facilitate other endeavors beyond information retrieval, such as exploration and creativity.

This overview of research draws from the major disciplines involved in the study of the perception, representation, and retrieval of images: cognitive psychology, library and information science, and computer science.

Scope and Organization of the Book

As noted in the preface, the research review presented within began as a prelude to the author's dissertation research. In searching various literatures for guidance as to what features or attributes image indexing can most usefully focus upon, a broad, fundamental, but unanswered question emerged:

What is the range of attributes of images that are typically noted and described by humans in performing various tasks with images?

Related to this question is the notion of how these attributes may relate to each other.

The definition of an "attribute" used in the current work is drawn from my dissertation research, and follows that of Medin and Barsalou: "any kind of feature, component, or property of a stimulus that can be represented by an information processing system." They continue: "We make no assumptions about the format of these representations . . . nor do we assume that the attributes correspond to innate detectors" (Medin and Barsalou 1987, 485). In this definition, "information processing system" includes both organizational and retrieval systems. An image attribute is therefore a feature, component, or property of a stimulus (an image) that can be represented by an information processing system. An image attribute is thus not limited to purely visual characteristics, but includes other cognitive, affective, or interpretive responses to the image such as those describing spatial, semantic, or emotional characteristics.

The review presented herein is concerned with the still image in all formats and disciplines. The definition of image is taken from the Random House Unabridged Dictionary: "a physical likeness or representation of a person, animal, or thing, photographed, painted, sculptured, or otherwise made visible" (Flexner 1993). This is understood as being a likeness of any form that can be captured by some method and is not limited to purely realistic, pictorial images. "Image" refers to concrete external representations rather than to mental or internal imagery (although the author recognizes that in some cognitive processes—such as rotation—it is theorized that the form of an external image is held internally for processing). The term "picture" is also frequently used in the literature, especially in relation to human memory. Therefore, the terms "picture" and "image" will both be used in appropriate contexts to refer to items meeting the above definition of image. Depending on the specific domain of discussion, images may also be described by their format, such as photograph or painting; these are also considered synonymous with image.

Given the approach discussed above, a caveat is that many of the topics presented in the book are, of course, worthy of a book in and of themselves. Many of the topics require much more in-depth discussion to do them full justice; the many sources cited should, however, provide a jumping-off point for further investigation into any of the areas discussed. While I have attempted to cover the various areas of interest with the same level of detail and inclusion, nevertheless the selection of sources is also, undoubtedly, somewhat subjective, perhaps slanted towards those areas that I personally find more of interest or that I think point to new and interesting (or heretofore underutilized) methods and directions. There are also, of course, far too many individual works to cover them all, and this also necessitates selectivity in coverage. Any omissions, however, are solely my responsibility.

This review cannot cover all areas. It does not cover image attributes associated with their production, encoding, transmission, or migration (e.g., technical metadata such as file format or size, resolution, or encryption), although these can also have an effect on image access and use. It does not cover the area of moving-image processing and retrieval (a topic with a large and growing body of literature and worthy of several books in itself) or the larger issues of multimedia (text, images, graphics, video, audio). While it does not cover the semiotics or aesthetics of images in any depth, this is touched upon in several discussions.

Other more complex philosophical and epistemological questions also exist, such as the multiple interpretations of images and the relationship of images to text (Barthes 1977; Wittgenstein 1958). The book does not address these, nor does it cover the mass media perspective of images related to such issues as visual persuasion or rhetoric. There are a number of worthy books on these subjects, among them Barry's (1997) *Visual Intelligence*, Solso's (1994) *Cognition and the Visual Arts*, Aumont's (1997) *The Image*, and *Visual Persuasion* by Messaris (1997). Other references for further reading are included throughout the text.

Another caveat is, of course, that this book will be quickly out of date (indeed, writing it has most certainly been pursuing a moving target). Research thankfully continues to build new knowledge, and newly minted researchers bring more energy and fresh ideas to the disciplines covered herein. Nevertheless, the highly sourced information within this work will hopefully provide one foundation from which this new knowledge can be built.

Chapters Two through Four provide background material from the perspectives of cognitive psychology, library and information science, and computer science. Chapter Five reframes the discussion in terms of a personal research perspective and presents some of the author's research in more detail. Chapter Six discusses the implications of this research, informed by the material in the first three chapters, and suggests a research agenda for the future. It summarizes theoretical considerations relating to the insights of the previous chapters and presents some new perspectives within which to consider the problems of image access.

Approaches to Image Access

Before moving on to the more detailed information presented in the following chapters, a general overview of the approaches and issues related to image indexing introduces the reader to several topics which will frame the forthcoming discussions.

There are currently two main areas of research aimed at solving the problems of image access, one relying on textual indexing and human intelligence and one drawing primarily on the new power that machine intelligence offers. Additionally, both of these approaches draw upon fundamental knowledge in human perception and cognitive science for models and methods. The two general areas of research both focus on image indexing but concentrate on either *manual* or *automated* methods. Manual ("human-based") indexing assigns textual indexing terms (free-text or controlled vocabulary) to visual materials; some systems include numeric representations as well, but these are not derived automatically from the image content. Automated (often referred to as "content-based" retrieval, CBR, or machine processing) indexing produces primarily numeric representations of image content and permits retrieval by image features such as color, texture, and shape which map to the output of lower-level perceptual processes.

Content-based research generally focuses on algorithms and procedures to represent lower-level features, while traditional indexing research looks at the types of attributes to be indexed, creation of indexing vocabularies, and the needs of particular user groups. LIS contributes theoretical discussions of both structure and process in indexing images; these discussions can serve as a foundation for advances in understanding both the essential components of images and their gestalt, both of which need to be addressed in the process of image indexing and retrieval. However, LIS contributes relatively little empirical work in image retrieval, compared to computer science and its associated disciplines. Both research communities look for new methods for deriving, organizing, and representing visual content descriptors.[1] Thus, there is currently a wide range of values (numeric, text, or a combination) which can be used to represent a variety of image attributes, from low-level perceptual attributes such as color, to the objects in an image, to abstract concepts such as symbolism or affective dimensions. However, very few systems attempt to integrate the two approaches.

While each community can bring complementary strengths to the problems of image indexing and retrieval, analyses of citation interconnections between these two suggest that there has been and continues to be little communication between the two groups of researchers (Cawkell 1993; Chu 2001). This points out the dichotomy between the two major research areas of "image processing" and "image indexing." These two communities have generally been focused on their own established methodologies, and researchers rarely communicate outside their particular disciplines or participate in collaborative efforts. While the CBR community is beginning to realize the need for higher-level "semantic" or conceptual retrieval, and the LIS community has experimented with integrating CBR into some systems, efforts at continuing collaboration remain infrequent.

This lack of communication also highlights a central problem in image access research: much development is "system-driven" rather than user-driven. Both groups derive solutions to the problem of image access drawing upon a single narrow dynamic, and this has resulted in a somewhat narrow theoretical base for their respective research agendas. While this would seem to be partly the result of each group's reliance on its own traditional techniques of information processing, it also suggests that both groups of researchers are generally ignoring more fundamental questions, of which one of the most basic is an understanding of the needs of the users of these image access systems. "Needs" as used in this overview denotes not simply subject matter requirements but a full understanding of the range of visual-perceptual, interpretive, and affective responses describing those image attributes typically noticed and to which people desire access.

In addition to disciplinary and theoretical limits, other boundaries that have constrained this research are geographical and professional. Additionally, the diversity of existing image indexing systems and the dichotomy in approaches means that image storage and access systems are being designed without a clear understanding of how users search for images or those image attributes that users typically note in this process. A parallel situation to that of text retrieval exists today with these types of information: large amounts of resources (human, technical, and financial) are being devoted to creating storage and access systems, but without a basic understanding of the cognitive processes or contextual factors involved in retrieving these kinds of information or the human behaviors involved in these types of retrieval tasks.

This is not to say that there has not been progress. Some are recognizing the need for more collaboration and are issuing calls for the alliance of the concept-based and content-based paradigms (Enser 2000). The results of the last decade of research have produced well-established techniques and tools for both automatic and manual indexing, yet both communities acknowledge that meeting the needs of users remains challenging. Researchers in both communities have begun to realize the scope of the problem, and a maturing of the research agenda is evident, as the chapter discussions demonstrate. However, solving the fundamental problems of image searching calls for a broader scope and understanding than that provided by a single discipline. It is towards this end that this book is dedicated.

Notes

1. For a recent review, see Rasmussen (1997).

Chapter 2

Cognitive Foundations for Image Processing

There is a large body of research concerned with the cognitive aspects of human image perception and understanding, both within the more general area of cognitive psychology and within a more specialized area of psychology focusing on the psychology of art. Cognitive psychology focuses on the general processes of human image perception, recognition, and memory and seeks to establish an understanding of these, while research in the psychology of art seeks to understand the cognitive foundations for the "aesthetic experience," considered a component of both the production and appreciation of art. Thus, a knowledge of human perception, understanding, and memory of images provides insights to those image elements which are typically perceived, attended to, and retained by humans. Knowledge of theories of visual pattern and object recognition and understanding also provide models for image retrieval system design.

Image perception and understanding have been studied within psychology from a number of different perspectives: cognitive, neurophysiological, developmental, and cultural, among others. A review of the psychological literature reveals many gaps in our understanding of the cognitive processes involved in image perception and understanding. Ultimately, current research methods are unable to reveal the "black box" of the human mind, as a single piece of evidence can be used to support arguments for several different and conflicting theories as to the essential nature of such processes. Nevertheless, empirical studies concerning human image perception, understanding, and memory provide a basis from which to explore the range and types of image attributes typically noted in these processes.

Within the literature of cognitive science itself there are a number of different perspectives. Vision begins with sensory detection (conversion of light into nerve impulses) and pattern recognition. A large body of literature reports physiological responses associated with the perception of specific visual elements, such as line, color, shape, and motion. Research in neuropsychology has established the existence of both specific types of cells and different areas of the brain which respond selectively to different varieties of visual stimuli. Current research in image perception, understanding, and memory is using more sophisticated research instrumentation (such as positron emission tomography) to enable the study of functional anatomy and the mapping of brain areas activated during low-level visual and perceptual semantic processing and memory (Buckner and others 1996; Murtha and others 1999). Work is also being done to develop models of higher-level processes that are better grounded in a basic understanding of neural processing; much of this work is based on theories of neural computation (Anderson 1990). However, there remains a large gap in knowledge at the level at which physiological responses and synaptic interactions map onto specific psychological and computational functions (Uttal 1988).

Furthermore, a common thread running through discussions of these perceptual and cognitive activities is that of classification (Bruner 1973). Classification is seen as an organizational process underlying perception, generalization, and memory (Bjorklund 1989; Carnine 1990; Edelman 1987). Additionally, in investigations of the basic processes of visual psychophysics such as contour or pattern perception, other processes such as memory for shape, experiences, and environmental conditions may determine the types of shapes and perceptual organizations that are experienced (Caelli 1981, 137–138).

Studies also provide evidence that culture may have an impact on perception of pictorial materials (Deregowski 1980). For instance, numerous studies with African peoples show that cultural influences play a part in image perception (Deregowski 1999). Picture interpretation skills of South African children are affected by schooling and achievement in home language, but the effects are generally in the opposite direction from those reported for children in Western European countries. This suggests that children from different cultures may use pictures in rather different ways (Liddell 1997).

There is also an "ecological" view towards the evolution of vision and perception (Gibson 1979). This view suggests that vision evolved to enhance the chances of survival; thus the eye can rapidly perceive motion and anomalies in the environment to answer questions such as "what is that?" and "where is it going?" related to potential dangers (or dinners or dates). Recent empirical evidence seems to support this evolutionary basis. For instance, it is known that facial muscle reactions in general reflect emotional activity, but the reactions are more intensively evoked when people are exposed to certain evolutionary biological relevant stimuli (Dimberg and Karlsson 1997).

There is also a long-standing, intertwined relationship between art and psychology. As Machamer describes it:

> Historically one can find clear instances of the influences of perceptual theory on art theorizing. The relations between the writings of thirteenth- and fourteenth-century opticians and the development of Renaissance artistic theory is one such case. But even where the historical connections concerning individuals or movements is lacking, there still exists the basic connection: *It is impossible to hold a well developed or coherent theory of art or art criticism without at the same time holding a theory of perception* (Machamer 1980, 14).

While there are areas of overlap in the research interests of these two groups, there has been a tension between the two research communities, stemming partially from their different perspectives and also from the methodological approaches of each field's research traditions. A useful scientific strategy in cognitive psychology is to decompose a stimulus into its elements and to study the impact of these individual elements, hoping at some point for a sufficient aggregation of data to accomplish a larger synthesis. However, when the stimulus is a complex pictorial phenomenon, researchers in the psychology of art regard the scientific method as being limiting, and a common sentiment has been that "traditional approaches to the study of art often reveal more about the workings of psychological investigations than they do about art" (Kose 1984). Thus, the research agendas and literatures have remained somewhat separate.

There are many interweaving factors influencing the relationship between the physiological processes of visual perception and the cognitive and contextual processes which produce image comprehension and understanding. Given the theoretical uncertainties remaining in the field, the following discussion focuses on data that provides evidence for *awareness* of the products of the processes of perception and understanding. This discussion focuses on higher-level visual and organizational processes and the manner in which people actively engage with pictures. This chapter will not discuss details of the physical structure or the physiological processes of the visual system nor short-term or sensory memory of images.[1] Although a fascinating topic, it does not delve into the related literature on visual illusions or allusions, which are strikingly covered in many other texts (Coren and Girgus 1978; Rothenstein and Gooding 2000; Wade 1990). Other relevant work is covered in Chapter Four, in relation to the use of cognitive models as foundations for systems design and implementation.

The first section provides a broad overview of how human vision and perception work. Following sections review cognitive theories of human visual organizational processes and understanding in more detail. Evidence supports different theories of visual processing, and data from eye-tracking research provide tantalizing glimpses into human attentive processes during pictorial perception. It should be noted that there is also a fundamental assumption that visual perception of an image and of the "real" world are *functionally* equivalent.[2] Classification processes are discussed as a cognitive foundation for perception and understanding. Pertinent evidence concerning what information human image memory retains is reviewed. The final section presents perspectives on these issues from the study of the psychology of art. Although a vast body of research exists, cognitive psychologists are still in the theory-building stage, and much remains open to discussion.

Overview of Human Vision and Perception

Theories of Human Perception

Much of the theory concerning human vision has held that the eye and the brain process and translate, through reflected light, a direct and stable internal representation of the external world exactly as it is. Many eye fixations build up this representation, and it is held in some sort of buffer, available for use. Indeed, it is these ideas which have seemingly confirmed a "mind's-eye" image of the world. Much work has thus been done based upon single fixations of the eye and the resulting retinotopic representations. During the last half of the twentieth century, vision physiology concentrated largely on single-neuron studies, and this trend continues today.

There are four broad theories of how human perception achieves this representation: Bruner's theory of *constructive perception*, Gibson's theory of *direct perception*, *Gestalt theory* (discussed in detail below), and Marr's *computational theory of perception*.[3] Explanations of the stages and mechanisms of visual perception will vary depending upon which theoretical basis is adopted. Briefly, *constructive perception* holds that sensory information is used as a foundation for perception of a stimulus, but other sources of information are used as well, such as knowledge stored in memory and higher-level cognitive and inferential processes (Bruner 1957; Gombrich, Hochberg, and Black 1972). A shortcoming of the theory is that it underestimates the importance of the sensory data. In contrast, *direct perception* holds that information in our sensory receptors, including the sensory context, is all that is needed for perception (Gibson 1971). Motion (optical flow) provides another important source of information; as an observer moves around, some objects will remain relatively constant, while changes in relationships among objects signal movement. Higher cognitive processes, previous experiences, or other sources of information and knowledge are unnecessary. While research testing this theory has yielded mixed results, it prompted researchers to pay more attention to the characteristics of the sensory stimulus. Cutting and Massironi (1998) offer a synthesis of these two theories, arguing that constructive perception is more typical of pictures, while direct perception applies to everyday viewing. The *computational theory of perception* proposes a three-stage model accounting for complexity in the cognitive processes required for perception based on sensory data (Marr 1982). The first stage utilizes edges, contours, and regions to map out a 2-D primal sketch within the brain; other features (shading, orientation, motion, spatial relationships) enable a progression from 2-D to 2 1/2-D to 3-D. This model lends itself to computational implementation, but the one-way flow of information is considered limiting.'

There is, as Walsh notes, an interplay between notions and processes of visual constancy and plasticity, and he notes that "the visual system does not trouble itself to give a perfect description of the world," but rather a "useful" description, as too precise constancy would in fact risk losing valuable information (Walsh and Kulikowski 1998, 3). Other authors such as Rensink reinforce the idea that vision must be studied not only over multiple fixations but at different levels, including processes of perception beyond the retina (Rensink 2000; Rensink, O'Regan, and Clark 1997). Rensink suggests that (just as in other research areas such as high-energy physics) for there to be a complete understanding of human vision, there is a need for a "grand unified theory" to bring disparate empirical observations and multiple processes and structures into harmony. Nevertheless, some basic processes occur which are well understood, although a theoretical understanding of such aspects as the temporal and dependency relations among these processes might not be.

Human Vision

Rock (1975) characterizes human visual perception as a data processing and reduction procedure involving three types of data, processed by different structures: 1) *image data* received from the eye; 2) *problem-oriented signal features* transferred through the optic nerve to the brain; and 3) a *responding signal* from the brain which is used in decision making. The image data received by the eye is limited to the number of receptors in the retina. Information transmitted in the second step is further reduced by the problem-oriented focus of the human visual system. The brain then attempts to match the information to stored models.

Thus, vision begins with light reflected from objects in the environment entering the eye. This light is focused by the cornea and lens onto the rods and cones of the retina, which then transforms the information produced by these into electrical impulses which reach the brain through the optic nerve. The portion of the retina most sensitive to pattern is the fovea, a small area at the back of the eye containing only cones. As visual angle increases, cones decrease and rods increase. The fovea produces a finer representation of input from a fixation, while the rest of the retina produces a coarser representation.

The assumed model for visual processing is that in the very early stages, a sensory representation is produced which is closely linked to the physical properties of the stimulus; then information must be obtained from this representation for further processing. In these early stages, it appears that intertwined sensory and information-acquisition processes are undertaken without regard to the complexity of the stimulus or to the eventual tasks for which the acquired information is to be used (Loftus and McLean 1999). Specialized brain cells (the lateral geniculate nucleus or LGN) process color, contrast, spatial resolution, movement, and depth. A great deal of research has focused on these low-level visual processes driven by sensory perception of edges, specific geometric or text forms, depth, or differences in wavelengths. Within the LGN, there is specialization in processing between the magnocellular layers (magno system) and the parvocellular layers (parvo system). The magno system quickly detects motion and visual events through sensitivity to luminance contrast and depth. It is not sensitive to color and handles spatial resolution in a limited manner. The parvo system responds to factors such as spatial resolution and color more slowly than the magno system, but does not respond to motion and depth. Furthermore, within the parvo system separate cells process color or orientation. This specialization suggests that a visual image is decomposed into primitive elements such as color, motion, orientation, depth, and movement.

While it is by no means clear exactly how this early preconceptual vision works, this preattentive or low-level vision has been conceptualized as rapid, automatic, parallel, and unable to be affected by an observer's changing goals. It is a feature extraction process, where physical properties such as depth, color, and texture are extracted in parallel from the visual field. From these properties, edges and surfaces are generated. Tasks such as searching for items with a specific feature, or estimating their number and identifying boundaries can be completed in less time than it takes to initiate an eye movement. Another theory (*Visual Indexing*) proposes that before a stimulus can be recognized, the visual system must first "individuate" a small number of what are called "primitive visual objects" and must keep track of them, without necessarily encoding what properties they have (shape or momentary location), where they are, or what changes they are undergoing, and proposes that focal attention can shift among these objects (Pylyshyn 1998).

From here, information is passed to the visual cortex, whose components further process color, motion, and form. There appears to be specialization within the visual cortex also, with the parietal lobe primarily responsible for processing the "where" and the inferior temporal lobe processing the "what." Corballis explains this distinction within an evolutionary framework:

> The "what" system presumably evolved to enable us to recognize objects independently of where they are located in space. This would surely have survival value to a foraging animal, because prey, predators, or other objects of interest might appear in any location. Conversely, the "where" system presumably has to do with navigation and reaching, allowing us to know where things are independently of what they are. This system would enable us to walk around in an environment in which nothing was familiar, and to pick things up and examine

them (Corballis 1994, 88–89).

This information is then sent on to many other areas of the brain for further processing. There is evidence suggesting that there may also be cerebral hemispheric specialization, with a left hemisphere/verbal/analytic versus right hemisphere/nonverbal/perceptual/holistic dichotomy.[4] This model of hemispheric lateralization suggests that different functions of cognitive processing become consolidated over time primarily in the left or right hemispheres of the brain (Jaynes 1976; Levy 1974; Penfield and Roberts 1959). The brain's left hemisphere seems to be linked to speech acts, analytic functioning, attention to details, sequential and temporalized processing, and seems to reflect the structures which have been attributed to verbal language by linguists and semanticists (Saint-Martin 1990, 90). The brain's right hemisphere, with attention to gestalts or totalities, handles spatial reasoning, symbolic processing, and pictorial interpretation. Work with split-brain patients with viewing restricted to one or the other hemisphere reinforces the specialization, with the left hemisphere functioning in object identification ("what") and the right hemisphere in location ("where") (Zaidel 1990).

Attentive or mid-level processing is thought to be a serial process whereby shape and spatial relations are extracted and primitive features are assembled into larger objects and scenes, building up detailed descriptions of objects and scenes over time. High-level vision concerns the mapping from visual representations to meaning. Cognitive and perceptive processes interact to create representations and identification of objects and scenes. This stage includes active acquisition of information and is presumed to include short-term memory for visual information.

It should also be noted that the terminology in the literature is not always consistent when talking about levels of processing. While low-level processing generally refers to perception of basic features such as edges, texture, and color, the lines between mid-level and high-level processing are not clear. Object perception may be referred to on both these levels, while sometimes high-level also refers to "meaning" or identification. This confusion reflects the uncertainties in the relationships among these levels as well, and the lack of understanding of the effect of other factors such as attention.

Much empirical work has focused on the early and mid-stages of vision, following the process of building up a coherent representation from the many subfunctions. However, there are also many "failures" of vision, such as evidence of the unreliability of eyewitness accounts. Vision is an interactive process, a translation from environmental signals and also a result of a long process of evolution and conditioning from past experiences. In the words of Jacques Aumont, "an image, like any visual scene observed over time, is seen not only in time, but through a form of exploration that is rarely innocent" (Aumont 1997, 39).

Perception of Low-Level Features

Preattentive processing takes place before the eye has time to initiate a movement to a different location; tasks that can be performed in less than 250 msec are considered preattentive.[5] Typical tasks are target detection (detecting an item in a field of similar items), boundary detection, and counting. Reported low-level features which can be detected preattentively include orientation, size, curvature, intersection, closure, color, flicker, and direction of motion. Visual properties that are processed preattentively can be used to highlight higher-level image characteristics.

An understanding of perception of lower-level features such as color and texture provides background information for understanding these in relation to other topics such as machine processing, discussed in later chapters. Following brief descriptions of neurophysiological processes, discussion focuses on the relevance of these processes for higher-level understanding of these features. These features and relevant representational theories are discussed further in relation to image processing (Chapter Four). For more detailed information on visual perception, the reader is referred to the excellent chapter for the lay reader, "Light, Color, and Shape: The Science of Vision," in *In the Eye of the Beholder* (Bruce and Young 1998).

Color

Human color vision comes from the cones of the retina, specifically three types which respond to different spectral sensitivities. The human visual system is able to distinguish small differences in stimulation of these three, allowing millions of distinguishable color sensations. However, since there are three types of photoreceptors responding, it is also possible that two different colors (or more technically, two different spectral power distributions) can appear to be the same color.

In spite of the ability to specify colors mathematically, there is still difficulty in specifying human perception of color, as many factors can affect this perception (including the display device). Hendee (1993) notes that the perception of color is a property of the observer and is strongly influenced by the observer's perceptual characteristics. Color vision cannot be transcribed into absolute physical properties that are demonstrable through an "ideal color observer" who can be considered in isolation. Itten refers to this process as "optic and cerebral perception" and notes that the eye and the mind achieve distinct perception through comparison and contrast (Itten 1973, 19).

Color description is complex (see also Chapter Four), and there are a number of systems of color description and nomenclature that have been developed according to certain needs or pragmatic hypotheses (e.g., Birren 1969; Goethe 1976; Itten 1970; Munsell 1969). However, as Saint-Martin (1990) explains, regardless of the detail of these systems one could never be assured that an identity existed between the physical reality of a color and the color which an observer perceived. Color undergoes a process of a holistic or Gestaltian type of adaptation; an isolated color cannot exist. The colored aspect of a section of material perceived depends on the visual field in which it is situated and not on its own chromatic constitution. Color is affected by the composition of rays reflected by matter but also by interactions between a colored area and surrounding colors. The reader is encouraged to peruse Itten's *The Art of Color* for lovely examples of these phenomena (Itten 1973).

In addition to the effects of context, human eyes do not see colors in isolation in the same way either, and the excitation produced by a continuous stimulus does not remain constant over time. Memory of colors is one of the most difficult to achieve within the whole family of percepts, and there is a very great difficulty in relating a perceived color to an ideal scale. While humans can, in general, distinguish approximately 10,000 nuances of color, research demonstrates that humans recognize and name only about a dozen color terms, even across different cultures and societies (Berlin and Kay 1969; Bornstein 1987; Kueppers 1982).

These hypotheses concerning human color perception are supported by the most recent hypothesis of the neurophysiology of color vision, which defines the receptor cones of color activating not one color but a range of colors, and introduces the idea of chromatic poles, limiting notions of color with "fuzzy" rather than discrete boundaries (Saint-Martin 1990). Color receptors have been shown to react to a range of colors (e.g., red receptors react to vermilion, carmine, minium, and so forth), leading to the idea of a "red" chromatic pole. This also supports the research previously mentioned, establishing approximately a dozen colors named and recognized universally.

Echoing the limitations described above concerning true color perception, one author (writing in the area of color matching by automatic methods) predicts "the future emphasis of color will be in models of human vision that calculate the color appearance, rather than the color match. All the technologies listed above work one pixel at a time. . . . Humans are different. The color they see at a pixel is controlled by that pixel and all the other pixels in the field of view. Human color vision is a spatial calculation involving the whole image" (McCann 1998, 38).

Texture

Considerable work has been done with human perception and descriptions of texture, in both the fields of cognitive science and within machine vision research (Chapter Four).[6] Texture research has been conducted with both artificial stimuli (patterns composed of letters or geometric components) and natural textures. Work with artificial stimuli uses very short (milliseconds) exposure times, and is assumed to capture preattentive processes. Formal definitions of texture include the individual texture elements or "particles" and the spatial organization of these elements. The ability of preattentive vision to perform segmentation spontaneously is assumed to rely on these two components. Julesz (1981) provided one of the most complete statistical models of texture. He identified "textons," three textural features: color, elongated quasi-rectangular blobs, and terminator (end of line segment) number. These are detected at the preattentive level, and it is the presence of these textons which permits analysis of image texture. Textons can be further described. For instance, elongated blobs can be described by orientation, length, and aspect ratio, and texton densities appear to be computed over small areas.

There are two other theories of texture perception, Beck's theory of texture segmentation, which placed emphasis on the grouping of units rather than the segregation of regions, and Treisman's feature-integration theory, which emphasizes the role of attention in binding units together (Beck 1966; Treisman 1986). In a review of these, Kehrer and Meinecke (1996) note that these theories all assume that local texture properties are detected by feature detectors, and that different distributions of texture properties determine how well perceptual segmentation can proceed.[7] However, the critical features for texture perception (such as orientation) are defined on different levels among the theories, and they all share a weakness in that most supporting evidence presented relies on artificial and binary (black and white) textures into which specific features have been built, rather than on natural textures, which present much greater challenges.

More recent work by Rao and Lohse (1993) using natural textures focuses on texture features at the attentive level. Using sorting experiments, Rao and Lohse found that the variables which work for artificial textures were not adequate to describe similarity of natural textures. They found three attributes that were responsible for identifying and classifying the natural textures. Two (repetitiveness and orientation) were similar to other findings, but a third, called complexity (degree of difficulty of producing a verbal description of the texture), differed.

Heaps and Handel explain the interrelationship of texture elements and their spatial organization:

> The focus on texture elements has led to two primary levels of analysis that reflect the imposition of successively greater levels of structure or organization in the process of visual perception. Texture elements, referred to as *microtexture*, represent the first level, and the organization and pattern of those elements, referred to as *macrotexture*, represent the second level. Thus, the more the microtexture elements of a texture lend themselves to segregation or grouping, the more macrotexture, and consequently structure, is present in the texture. When a great deal of structure is present in a texture, aspects of the macrotexture can themselves be seen as elements (Heaps and Handel 1999, 299–300).

The two major approaches for modeling texture also use the distinction between microtexture (statistical approaches) and macrotexture (structural approaches which focus on aspects such as orientation).

Other models attempt to unify the two approaches to explain the relationship between the preattentive and attentive levels of processing, but recent research with attentive texture features demonstrates that this may be difficult. Building upon the work of Rao and Lohse, Heaps and Handel (1999) investigated attentive texture features that emerge across sets of natural textures. The results demonstrated that similarity between pairs and the emergence of perceptually salient features in the set are based upon the characteristics of *all* the textures in the set.[8] These researchers conclude that a generalizable dimensional model of natural texture features does not exist, that attentively available similarities emerge in large part due to the *contexts* in which the textures are considered, and that there is no fixed set of dimensions that characterize natural textures. Thus, the preattentive texture processes may produce output which attentive processing then interprets in a contextually-dependent manner.

For more in-depth discussion, Landy and Graham (forthcoming) provide a much more detailed overview of visual texture perception.

Shape

Shape perception depends upon a combination of other features, such as color, edges, shading, and depth, which are the products of preattentive processing. In order to segment an image, the visual system depends not so much on finding homogeneous regions but rather on looking for regions of dramatic change in color or intensity which can signal contours. Black and Panchanathan (2000) note that humans perceive line drawings to be similar to natural images and suggest that this indicates the ability of the human visual system to translate natural images into "line drawings" in the brain. In fact, the visual system does just this by using separate channels to process changes in intensity, texture, color, spatial frequency, stereo disparity, and motion, then adding these together to provide robust contour detection. However, the two most important sources for segmentation in natural scenes, binocular vision and motion parallax, are lacking for 2-D still images. One compensation for this is the presence of specialized detectors for line termination (noted as an important feature for texture), which also compensate for lack of color or contrast. In addition, incomplete line segments can be "filled in" by the human visual process to produce the perception of a continuous contour. The human visual system makes certain assumptions regarding shading which help in the determination of shape: lighting comes from above, there is only one light source, and, other things being equal, shapes are convex rather than concave (Anstis and Ramachandran 1995).

While shape's exact position in a processing continuum from low to midlevel processing can depend upon the specific visual processing model, shape is assumed to be a fundamental input to higher levels of processing. There are multiple theories of shape recognition, which generally propose some form of internal representation of an object, including its shape, and other properties such as a label (Caelli and Bischof 1997). Barry groups models of shape recognition into four broad categories: recognition of the whole shape; recognition of geometric shape components such as vertical and horizontal lines, curves, or angles; Fourier models which decompose the optic array into trigonometric components sensitive to intensity, orientation, and spatial frequency; and structural or symbolic representations (Barry 1997, 40). There may also be multiple representations, and these are not necessarily direct replicas of retinal stimulation (as different objects can produce the same retinal shape stimulation). Caelli and Bischof summarize a number of these theories:

> Each theory may make different assumptions regarding the type of representation used (e.g., feature space, geons, predicates, graph), the number of representations per object (e.g., store one composite 3D representation or multiple 2D representations obtained from different viewing positions), the breakup of objects into classes for mapping into representations, the inclusion of spatial relationships between objects and their component parts (relational or propositional representations), the amount and type of pre-processing given to the initial retinal image (e.g., various forms of edge detection, filtering, and contrast enhancement), how the matching is to be performed (e.g., sub-graph isomorphism, decision trees, feed-forward neural net, and so forth), or a suitable metric for similarity matching (Caelli and Bischof 1997, 316–317).

For the interested reader, these authors also offer a critique of existing models from the computational, epistemological, and physiological and biological standpoints. One major point is that many models of human and vertebrate vision do not address the whole problem, but assume input from lower-level, as yet unspecified processes. Another problem is the assumption of a one-way flow of information from early to later processes. For more details of human visual processes, the reader is referred to books such as Gregory's *Eye and Brain* and Hendee's *The Perception of Visual Information* (Gregory 1997; Hendee and Wells 1997). A good nontechnical introduction can also be found in Hoffman's *Visual Intelligence* (Hoffman 2000).

Theories of Mid-Level Processing

The following sections discuss perception at the point when physical processes have operated to produce some input into the visual system (a percept). A percept is defined as "the mental result or product of perceiving, as distinguished from the act of perceiving; an impression or sensation of something perceived."[9] This term is contrasted to "concept," a purely mental idea with does not require an external physical stimulus. In terms of mid-level visual processing, the first question that arises is which comes first: recognition of larger patterns (global or "top-down" processing) or local elements ("bottom-up" processing), or if these two interact in ways not yet understood. This question of "global or local precedence" is a major unresolved debate in visual processing, and mirrors debate across all levels of visual perception concerning the relationship between holistic versus analytical processing as the basis for visual understanding.

Local Processes

The structuralists proposed that primitive features are first extracted and then combined to become recognized patterns or objects (percepts) through local, bottom-up processes. Some researchers hold that understanding at a global level can be activated only *after* physical relations among local features are specified and objects are identified. One theory of object perception holds that it may involve processes in which an object can be seen as a configuration of simple components oriented along major axes in which relative spatial arrangements are preserved (Marr 1982; Marr and Nishihara 1978). For instance, Marr proposed an analytical model in which a "primal sketch" is first composed of edges and blobs, then refined by texture and depth, and finally culminates in a 3-D model.

Biederman's (1987) theory of *Recognition-by-Components*, one of the most well-known of these theories, proposes three stages in the recognition of an object. First, the object is segmented into a set of basic subobjects, which are defined by their line contours. Second, once an object has been segmented into basic subobjects, these are classified into categories. He describes thirty-six categories of subobjects, which he calls *geons* (geometric ions, basic forms such as cubes, cylinders, cones, and so on), invariant over different views, which can serve as an alphabet for composing objects. Only edges are needed to define geons, and certain properties of edges, such as collinearity, curvilinearity, symmetry, parallelism, and cotermination serve as reliable cues to related properties of edges in the world. Third, having identified the pieces out of which the object is composed and their configuration, one quickly recognizes the object as the pattern composed from these pieces. The subobjects become features; small variations of these are not critical for recognition and such attributes as color, texture, and small detail should not matter. Earlier work supports this theory. For instance, Hoffman and Richards (1985) propose that certain configurations, such as concave creases, can be used to partition an outline representation of an object into its component subobjects.

Anderson (1990, 72) notes that the critical assumption for this theory is that object recognition is mediated by recognition of the components of the object. One test of this theory is whether schematic line drawings of complex objects are recognized as quickly as detailed color photographs of such objects. Biederman and Ju (1988) present results supporting this. Earlier research by these authors and others asked subjects to identify objects degraded in one of two ways, either by removal of lines at midsegments or by removal of whole components (Biederman and others 1985). Subjects made significantly more errors with component deletion than with midsegment deletion.

Feature-based models are supported by much physiological research demonstrating selective response of cells in the visual cortex to features in specific orientations. Feature analysis and abstraction specifies relationships among the features that are most important to the pattern. Thus patterns can vary, yet still match on critical local features. Feature-based processing allows the recognition of many varying images of an item to be recognized as a member of a class. *Prototypes* (Rosch 1978) or *schemata* (Bartlett 1932) define the extent and boundaries of variation among critical features for inclusion (see discussion below). In the constructivist approach, perception and recognition are considered an active process in which the viewer forms and accepts or rejects hypotheses about the object's identification, based upon visual features and past experience. These models are used as the basis for computational approaches to object recognition (Chapter Four). These feature-based models are in contrast to template based recognition models, in which matching relies on nearly identical shape.

There are a number of problems associated with these models (Caelli and Bischof 1997). Many models tend to address only one part of the problem, often assuming primitives which are supplied by a lower-level but unspecified process. Objects are also too dynamic in nonstationary viewing to be represented only by a shape or its components. Vision must be a process of confirmation rather than repeated recognition, as recognition and recall times decrease with repeated exposures and increasing selectivity in picking up relevant information. Additionally, output from the system should move beyond simply producing a "label" to some appropriate behavior.

Global Processes

Another major theory proposes that perceptual processes proceed top-down from global to local. Navon (1977), building upon the work of the early Gestalt psychologists, proposed the "global precedence hypothesis," which holds that perceptual processing proceeds from more general to more detailed information. Local patterns are organized into objects or figures according to the Gestalt principles of perceptual organization, which holds that the perceptual whole is perceived first. In contrast to the *Recognition-by-Components* theory, an object in a *Gestalt* possesses features which are *not* inherent in the smaller features of which it is composed.

These whole figures or *Gestalts* were first studied by the Gestalt psychologists of the 1920s (led by Max Wertheimer, Kurt Koffka, and Wolfgang Kohler) and represent a top-down, holistic approach. Experimental work asking subjects to view various patterns at short exposure times and describe what they saw produced a number of important principles explaining various visual phenomena. Of particular interest was the "figure–ground" problem, in which an observer can see one of two possible images but never both at the same time (Rubin 1958). Arnheim, drawing upon these principles, later explained how a picture is organized into the two major components of figure and ground: "(a) The enclosed surface tends to be figure, the enclosing, ground. (b) Inner articulation, such as the dotted texture of a circle, makes for 'figure.' An empty circle would show the effect less clearly. (c) Convexity makes for figure, concavity for ground" (Arnheim 1966, 248–249). Additionally, the relatively smaller elements tend to be figure.

In any image depicting objects such as human beings, houses, or other objects in front of a background, figure–ground relationships help create pictorial space. The general rule can be summarized as follows: the figure–ground version that produces the simpler total pattern will prevail (Arnheim 1974, 185). To explain this phenomenon, Gestalt theorists such as Wertheimer (1958) proposed that "form" is the fundamental unit of perception and that, most importantly, its origin is *mental* rather than *sensory*. Recent research suggests that figure–ground relations are assessed in parallel across the elements present before attention is allocated to spatial regions (Humphreys and Mueller 2000).

Wertheimer (1958) describes some of the major organizing principles which give rise to form:

- PROXIMITY: Elements which are near each other tend to become grouped into units. Thus otherwise uniformly spaced dots may organize into rows or columns depending on whether the horizontal or vertical space is greater.
- SIMILARITY: Objects that are similar tend to be grouped together. In the above example, if an area of dots is the same color or texture, they will be grouped and perceived as a whole.
- GOOD CONTINUATION: Elements are organized in a manner which, to the extent that it is possible, preserves continuity of line. For example, when a line is intersected by another line, the lines are perceived as crossing rather than touching; general orientation of the line is preserved.
- CLOSURE: Elements tend to be formed into simple, closed figures, independent of their other continuation, similarity, or proximity. These figures are referred to as "Good Forms." A nearly complete circle will be called a "circle" even though it is technically a closed curve.
- COMMON FATE: Elements subjected to the same process, such as directional movement, become grouped.

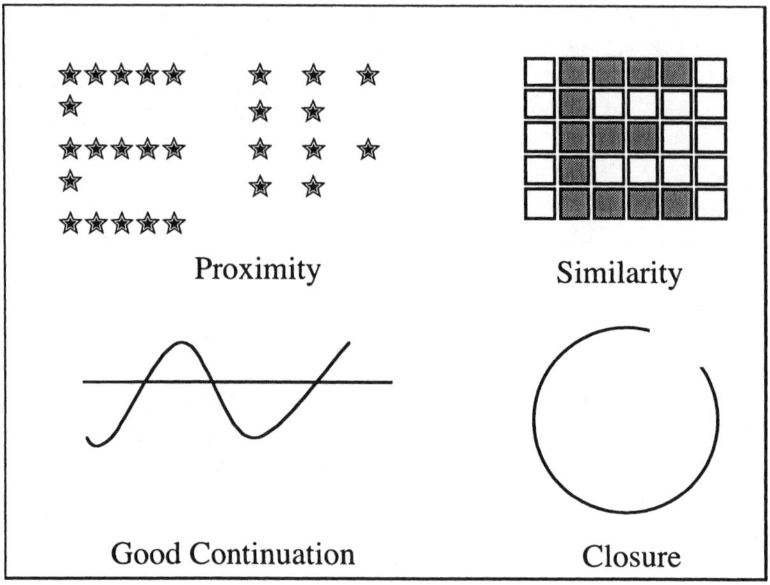

Figure 2.1. Gestalt principles.

Other principles concern element segregation, important in distinguishing between background and figure:

- AREA: When two figures overlap, the smaller will be viewed as the figure and the larger as the ground.
- SYMMETRY: The more symmetrical a figure is, the more likely it is to be perceived as a closed figure.[10]

Spoehr and Lehmkuhle (1982) placed the Gestalt principles within an information theory account, in which one of the goals is to specify which aspects of a stimulus convey information about the identity of that stimulus. If few cues are provided about a stimulus, then the viewer has little information with which to identify it. On the other hand, a stimulus that contains much information is easier to identify. Considered in the light of information theory, each Gestalt principle refers to a situation of high redundancy whereby elements that share the same information are grouped together perceptually. Spoehr and Lehmkuhle believe that "good figures" are defined by high redundancy *and* few points of high informational content. For instance, Attneave (1954) demonstrated that information is concentrated at points of maximum curvature and that areas of homogeneous color or direction or slope contain redundant information. Others argue that visual processing uses Gestalt principles to organize input into the *simplest* interpretation possible (Hochberg and McAlister 1953; Koffka 1935; Werner 1935). Hochberg (1998) proposes that the Gestalt laws of organization are opportunistic guides as to what will afford desired visual information, and that they may vary widely in level, speed, and power.'

A number of researchers have sought to verify and quantify these principles over the years by testing their applicability and organization, and researchers addressing other issues have also found supporting evidence (Beck 1966; Hochberg and McAlister 1953; Hochberg and Silverstein 1956; Olson and Attneave 1970). More recent work with motion demonstrates that multiple factors may combine to produce percepts (Fidopiastis and others 2000). In this work, perceived motion in color-from-motion displays using dots could not be accounted for by nearest-neighbor mechanisms alone. Rather, a combination of three measures was necessary to model human performance in the construction of visual curves and surfaces: (1) mean largest-dot radius, (2) largest dot variance, and (3) linear nearest-neighbor distance. Other work demonstrates that under certain conditions one factor may take precedence; for instance, texture takes precedence over motion in depth perception of planar surface slant (O'Brien and Johnston 2000).

Palmer and Rock (1994) later proposed the additional principle of uniform connectedness (UC), as a necessary but not sufficient condition for unit perception. This principle states that closed regions of homogeneous properties, such as luminance, dots, lines, and so on, are perceived initially as single units and are the entry-level units for visual perception. It is not a form of grouping at all, as there may be no units to connect, but rather becomes a matter of detecting a uniform region. UC can even overpower the powerful grouping principles of proximity and similarity. As can be seen in the example below, despite proximity and similarity, grouping occurs because of the uniform connectedness of the circles:

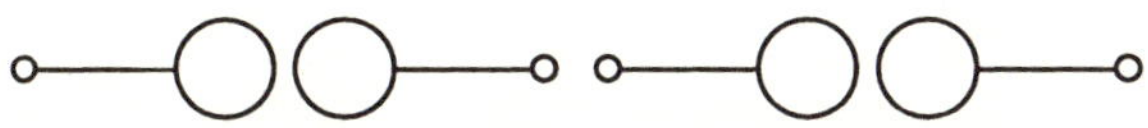

UC accounts for the lack of explanation within Gestalt theory of the perception of elementary units as such.

While Gestalt phenomena have been demonstrated and elaborated upon through much experimental research, as yet there remains no adequate theory of vision to explain them, and they remain poorly understood. Work by a number of researchers over the years suggests that an interactive hierarchical process occurs, with certain principles operating to analyze and organize the overall configuration first, then the smaller elements (Kahn and Foster 1981; Lupker 1979; Navon 1977; Palmer and Rock 1994; Townsend and Ashby 1982). While it has been assumed that physical information is processed before access to higher-level semantic information can take place, evidence indicates that semantic access may take place before the physical processing is complete. Boucart and

Humphreys (1997) propose that processing of the global configuration of an object activates stored representations of that object and related objects, and then physical processing continues until a perceptual decision is reached. Other work demonstrates that, even when attending to local features such as color, texture, and motion, processing the form of an object (or associated properties such as shape, size, or orientation) produces semantic effects, and suggests that it is attention to global information, whatever the physical dimensions processed, that activates the stored representations of objects (Boucart, Humphreys, and Lorenceau 1995). This is also supported by work in analyzing the role of color (rather than object recognition) in recognizing scene gists (Oliva and Schyns 2000). Results suggest that colored blobs at a coarse spatial scale, along with luminance cues, form a relevant spatial layout that mediates express scene recognition.

More recently, the psychophysics of scale perception supports this by suggesting that recognition uses coarse blobs before fine-scale edges, because the former are perceptually available before the latter. Global spatial information is effectively represented by low spatial frequencies, and a global precedence potentially implies a low-frequency dominance, producing a coarse-to-fine temporal order in visual spatial perception (Hughes, Nozawa, and Kitterle 1996).[11] Noting that this perceptually determined scenario neglects the nature of the task the recognition system must solve, other researchers provide empirical evidence that different spatial scales transmit different information about the input (Oliva and Schyns 1997). Thus, an identical scene might be flexibly encoded and perceived at the scale that optimizes information for the task at hand. Lindeberg explains the overall problem of scale succinctly:

> The problem falls back on a basic scale problem, namely that objects in the world and details in images, [*sic*] only exist as meaningful entities over limited ranges of scale. . . . A simple example is the concept of a branch of a tree, which makes sense only at a scale from, say, a few centimeters to at most a few meters. It is meaningless to discuss the tree concept at the nanometer or the kilometer level. At those scales it is more relevant to talk about the molecules that form the leaves of the tree, or the forest in which the tree grows (Lindeberg 1992, 8–9).

In summary, both bottom-up, feature-based processes and top-down, global processes appear to be operating in visual recognition. Lasaga's examination of numerous studies on this issue reveals "many remaining gaps in our understanding of the microgenesis of the perceived whole" (Lasaga 1989, 200). The critical theoretical problem in visual perception remains arriving at an understanding of the relationship between the processing of local properties and the global, contextual processes that combine these properties to form features which are understood as objects. While grouping mechanisms and order of these processes is still not fully understood, the Gestalt principles may be suggestive of the types of image attributes typically perceived by humans. Grouping mechanisms tie together close or similar elements or those subjected to a process such as movement, and the percepts so created override their individual constituents, whether of shape, size, color, or motion. Closure and symmetry operate to complete those figures that are incomplete.

The Role of Context and Semantics

The question arises of how smaller elements can be organized into larger wholes without their prior or simultaneous processing. There are at least four modern theories which propose to explain how such holistic contextual effects occur (Palmer 1992). The overall content and organization of a picture influence the processing and interpretation of local elements (Biederman 1972; Loftus and Mackworth 1978; Pezdek and others 1988). Hochberg demonstrated the power of global expectations in the perception of "impossible" figures, such as many M. C. Escher drawings. Contradictions are not immediately recognized; several fixations are necessary to recognize the depth or spatial contradictions within such pictures (Hochberg 1968).

Biederman (1972) found that object identification, even when cued, was poor in "jumbled" pictures, scenes that had been cut apart and reassembled randomly. In the rearranged pictures predictable organizational expectations are disrupted, and this suggests that overall organization of the picture exerts an influence in object perception. Biederman, Glass, and Stacy (1973), using negative trials with probable and improbable objects, demonstrated that subjects recruited context in a visual scene to help with their identification of an object. Thus subjects used both organizational and contextual expectations. Biederman (1981) later demonstrated that one effect of jumbling was to make it difficult to identify the theme of a picture.

Biederman (1981) proposes that three separate factors are necessary to comprehend a picture's content: 1) perception of the objects present; 2) an understanding of the functional relations among the objects; and 3) an understanding of the spatial relations among objects. He suggests that the context or schema of a picture (see discussion below) serves to integrate these separate aspects. Such a schema also imposes constraints on the content and organization of a picture and thus can also limit expectations. Gould proposes that a person constructs a representation heavily influenced by expectancies; meaning is actively extracted and this extraction does not await the complete mental composition of the picture (Gould 1976, 332).

Biederman proposes five classes of relations that may be needed to characterize a well-formed scene, and his data show that their violation interferes with both perception of objects and understanding of functional and spatial relationships (Biederman 1981, 213, 217). The first two constraints are physical laws of placement: 1) *support* requires that objects be supported; and 2) *interposition* requires that a superimposed object block the contours of the objects behind it.

The latter three refer to the identity of the object: 3) *probability* relates to appropriateness of objects given the overall schema; 4) *position* and 5) *size* refer to the appropriate spatial and form relationships of objects. Support and interposition are syntactic constraints and can be specified without knowing what the object is, but the other relations require access to the referential meaning or semantics of the object and its context. He reports experimental results which indicate that the semantic relations of a scene are accessed at least as fast as the physical relations, and he argues that physical and semantic relations are available simultaneously and do not appear to be processed independently (Biederman 1981, 224).

Other early work provided evidence that object detection is facilitated by consistent scene context (Biederman, Mezzanotte, and Rabinowitz 1982). However, recent work replicating this experiment suggests that object identification processes are functionally isolated from scene contextual information (Hollingworth 1998; Hollingworth and Henderson 1999). This data is consistent with a functional architecture of the visual system in which object perception is isolated from stored information about objects likely to appear in a scene. This is necessary because of the "frame problem," which suggests that it would be too time consuming in daily life to have to access and to discriminate between large amounts of relevant and irrelevant information. Once an object representation has been formed, however, the semantic status of the object with the scene may influence memory for that object or may influence the allocation of visual/spatial attention, leading to an enhanced representation of an object inconsistent with the scene.

Therefore, the role and weighting of context in visual processing is still uncertain. Recent results in face recognition experiments related to this issue suggest that both featural and configural processing make important contributions to face recognition, and that their effects are dissociable (Cabeza and Kato 2000). Other work indicates that while facial expressions are recognized as descriptions of parts and part relations, these descriptions are recognized holistically in that they are encoded with a description of the face as a "basic-level object" (see discussion below), together, as an undecomposed whole (White 1999; White 2000).

Role of Attention and Emotion

Attention and emotion also play a part in visual processing and recognition. Attention may enable visual processing in a variety of ways: binding features together, selecting stimuli to process, event or object recognition, enhancement of a stimulus, and reduction of uncertainty (Wolfe 2000). The interested reader is encouraged to read Wolfe's chapter for further details. Ballesteros explains there are several unresolved questions concerning attention and its relation to perceptual organization. Two questions which researchers have focused on are the problem of the limited capacity of attention (the attentional bottleneck), and whether selection in the information processing system occurs early or later (where the bottleneck may occur) (Ballesteros 1994, 4). For example, work by Rensink implies that visual perception of change in objects occurs only when that object is given focused attention. An absence of attention causes the contents of visual memory to be simply overwritten by subsequent stimuli, whereas attention allows entering the objects into visual short-term memory (Rensink, O'Regan, and Clark 1997).

Based on their research on grouping, texture segregation, and pop-out, Rock and Mack (1994) argue that when perceptual patterns are viewed without attention, perceptual grouping does not seem to take place; therefore shape cannot be perceived without attention. They propose three levels of attentional processing: 1) the nonattentional level, at which colorless, shapeless blobs are perceived; 2) the distributed-attention level, in which voluntary attention to the array allows detection of multiple elements and features in parallel, and in which Gestalt grouping mechanisms operate; and 3) the focused attention level, where focused attention to individual items requires serial processing. Another question being researched is whether visual attention selects objects or locations. While the mechanisms of attention remain uncertain, nevertheless it appears that attention plays an important, if not well understood, role in processing visual information.

Much biopsychological and neurophysiological research conducted with picture viewing also demonstrates affective responses to images; these responses are assumed to be similar (although perhaps less intense) to those occurring in a real environment. Human attention is viewed by some as "information processing that involves procedures of selection and evaluation of *motivationally* relevant input" (italics added) (Lang, Bradley, and Cuthbert 1997, 98–99). Attention changes the viewer from a passive receiver to an active processor of information and guides actions or redirects attention itself. As Kinsbourne explains, this selective attention is necessary to survival:

> In species such as humans, which are generously equipped with sense receptors, the environment offers so many concurrent opportunities for information processing that rigorous selection is required to safeguard the individual from being immobilized into helplessness by a flood of competing response demands. Selective attention and response mechanisms systematically assure definitive decision and action and avoid behavioral impasse (Kinsbourne 1994, 105).

Historically, psychology has separated emotion from higher-level cognitive processes. As Barry (1997) explains, until the mid-1980s, when neurobiologists began mapping the role of the limbic system, emotion was viewed as resulting from conscious and unconscious thought processing. This mapping revealed dual pathways of sensory perceptual processing: one with sensory signals traveling to the thalamus and to the amygdala (the proposed seat of human emotional response) before traveling to the neocortex, and the other with a direct route to the neocortex, which performs perceptual analysis. The significance of stimuli can be assessed in either route before conscious processing. Barry continues, "This neural independence also explains the internal emotional response that is derived from such simple stimuli as color alone, and how the emotional 'coloring' of a situation—as in light and shadow in photographs, for example—can create emotional bias before conscious judgment is formed. Perceptual processing of color and movement appear to be neurologically preprogrammed and therefore particularly susceptible to subliminal affect" (Barry 1997, 21).

Affective responses to images can be viewed as supporting Gibson's ecological theory of the evolution of vision, in which attention is motivated in relation to potential threats from the environment and to appetitive drives, such as food or mating. These two types of affective responses are characterized as aversive and attractive, together referred to as *valence* (Dickinson and Dearing 1979). Valence is also correlated to varying levels of arousal or interest, and valence and arousal are considered the two dimensions of emotion. Evidence demonstrates that negative pictures are named faster than positive ones, but affect does not influence reading of negative words (De Houwer and Hermans 1994). This research also showed that the affective evaluation of pictures was much faster than the evaluation of words. Interestingly, unpleasant pictures are not viewed for shorter time periods than pleasant ones, unless they happen to be phobic objects for subjects, such as spiders and snakes (Hamm and others 1991).

Findings from other experimental work where subjects viewed emotional picture sets of varying valence under different levels of attentiveness support a hypothesis that interest and attention modulate both early and late stages of visual processing (Lane, Chua, and Dolan 1999). Attentive processing may also be correlated with the informativeness of an object. Neurophysiological evidence suggests that different areas of the brain are activated during picture viewing, depending on whether subjects are attending to their subjective emotional responses or to spatial aspects of identical emotional picture sets (Lane and others 1997).

There are theorized to be six basic emotions: happiness, disgust, surprise, fear, anger, and sadness (Ekman and Friesen 1975). Davis and others suggest that these six basic emotions could represent most human affective states, with more complex states represented by various combinations such as fear/happiness for "exhilaration" (Davis and others 1995). Similarity of affective response to images is the basis for several well-known picture tests used as diagnostic aids and as stimulus material for a variety of experiments. For instance, the International Affective Picture System (IAPS, University of Florida, Center for the Study of Emotion and Attention)[12] consists of approximately 700 color slides (also available as digitized images) that have been widely used in the experimental study of affect and 720 colored pictures standardized on large normative subject samples for judged pleasure and arousal. Work using the IAPS demonstrates that, in spite of individual differences, these slides elicit means of self-reported affect that are highly replicable (Davis and others 1995).

Lang defines emotion as a "motivationally tuned state of readiness" and reports experimental results using responses to the IAPS demonstrating that most affective responses to images are either somewhat neutral or high-arousal pleasant or high-arousal unpleasant (Lang, Bradley, and Cuthbert 1997, 101). This organization is consistent with the aversive/attractive responses modulated by interest, and a number of physiological responses also covary along these dimensions. Attempts to force responses into the low-arousal/pleasant or low-arousal/unpleasant dimensions have not been successful. These two dimensions of pleasantness–unpleasantness and attention–rejection have also been established cross-culturally (Triandis and Lambert 1958).

One area of active research related to affective responses is in the area of understanding facial expressions and the emotions conveyed by them. Of interest is whether facial expressions could be accurately judged and used as index points. In her research, Katsikis (1997) used seventeen judges to rate 161 photographs (posed "peak" facial expressions created specifically as test stimuli) on six emotions and one neutral expression. Results indicate that happiness was the most easily distinguished and most reliable; disgust was also easily distinguished. Judges achieved moderate agreement between surprise and fear, and anger and sadness. Judges had more difficulty distinguishing among sadness and fear and a neutral expression. Katsikis also used a multidimensional scaling procedure to reveal the two dimensions underlying these six emotions: the pleasantness–unpleasantness dimension and a new one relevant to facial expressions, upper-face–lower-face dominance. On the pleasant–unpleasant dimension, happiness and surprise are at one end while disgust, anger, and sadness are at the other.

Results from other studies have been mixed. In a study of adults' freely produced emotion labels for babies' spontaneous facial expressions, only facial expressions taken during the "happy" condition showed agreement by a majority across three cultural samples: Canadian, Japanese, and Chinese (Yik, Meng, and Russell 1998). Agreement on the pleasant–unpleasant quality of the baby's expressions was higher, but still varied with culture. Subjects have accurately discriminated between photographs showing an expression of anxiety on a photo anxiety questionnaire and ranked the photographs from "relaxed" to "very anxious." Agreement between subjects was not good, however, and females in photographs were judged to be more anxious (Schouwstra and others 1996). In summary, while there are six emotions which seem to be cross-culturally recognized, distinguishing among these solely on the basis of facial expressions is not always reliable.

Results from research with caricature effects on facial expressions shows that the perceptual representation of facial expression appears to be coded independently of the perceptual representation of what is "face-like" (Calder and others 2000). These results also support categorical perception (see below), in that there is an abrupt category boundary between expressions. Thus, there may be "special status regions" for expressions encountered frequently. Supporting this is research demonstrating that facial-emotion-matching tasks activate specific parts of the brain (Narumoto and others 2000; Whalen and others 1998).

In addition to the dual roles of playing a part in focusing attention and being a personal response to viewing, there is further evidence that emotion may impact cognitive processing. Thus, it may also have an effect on the perceptual process itself (Clore, Schwarz, and Conway 1994). Kuhl's theory of functional meaning of emotions (1983) proposes that emotions can affect the mode of processing. Emotions which signal some danger (fear, shyness, guilt) facilitate an analytic mode of processing, and emotions which are oriented to remove obstacles or unpleasant states (interest, joy, anger) facilitate a holistic mode of information processing. Research also indicates that cognitive anxiety may affect performance completing a perceptual task; these findings also indicate marked differences in the dynamics of people's interpretation of small and gradual changes in the perceptual field (Stuchlikova, Kindlman, and Man 1996).

Eye-Tracking Experiments

Eye-tracking experiments, in which specialized equipment monitors eye movements, have been widely used to provide data on the sequences of movements of the human eye as it moves over a text or an image. The assumption underlying eye-tracking experiments is that in a visual experience the center of the fixation of the eyes is the center of attention at a given time, and data from eye tracking provides fascinating glimpses into just what elements humans appear to attend to in an image.

There are two components of eye movements: *fixations*, during which the eye is stationary for a few hundreds of milliseconds (msec) and focused on only one part of the picture; and *saccades*, quick (10 msec to 100 msec) movements of the eye to another part of the picture. Research has established several parameters of eye movements, with the average number of eye fixations being approximately three per second, or 258 msec per fixation (Yarbus 1967). Saccades are unnoticed by the perceiver, and during these eye movements incoming visual information is suppressed. These movements only occupy about 5–10% of the scanning time, and rarely move the eye more than fifteen degrees of visual angle. These two components appear to support different tasks, with a fixation allowing analysis of the foveated area and saccades providing new areas for analysis. Studies of human and primate brains demonstrating specialization of the temporal (response to complex shapes such as faces and hands, related to identification of objects) and parietal (analysis of spatial relationships) lobes of the visual cortex also support this what/where distinction (Swain and Ballard 1991).

Buswell (1935) conducted some of the earliest eye movement research to determine how people look at pictures. He asked 200 subjects of varying ages to look at a set of large colored pictures as they would if they were selecting one of the pictures for their own, and he recorded photographic records of their eye movements. The pictures included a variety of visual images: paintings; vases and dishes; furniture and design; statuary and museum pieces; tapestries and designs on cloth; architecture and interior design; posters; outlines, silhouettes, and geometric figures. There were 1,877 total completed records.

Buswell used a number of different techniques to analyze the data, including density plots of a number of subjects' eye fixations for one picture to show areas of greatest interest; comparisons of earlier and later eye fixations; and analysis of duration of eye fixations. Buswell proposed that his data supports the following hypothesis: a long fixation pause is indicative of a central thought process, whereas shorter fixations are typical characteristics of normal visual perception where there are no particular thought difficulties involved. Buswell found that the average duration of fixations increases as one continues to look at a picture, and analysis of the pictures shows that the main centers of interest, as judged by the number of fixations, also receive the fixations that are longest in duration (Buswell 1935, 87–90).

Buswell's and later Antes' analyses revealed two general patterns of perception: a general survey in which the eye moves over the main portions of a picture in a series of relatively short pauses, and a series of fixations longer in duration that concentrate on small areas of the picture (Antes 1974). The survey type generally characterizes the early part of the examination of a picture, while detailed study appears later. Other work demonstrated that overall knowledge about a scene and the main objects in it are obtained in the first fixation (Potter 1976). Papin (1984) noted the same scanning patterns in student pilots while they are learning the instrument panel, where longer saccades (movements of the eye) to a new region do not appear random. Another theory suggests that peripheral vision guides subsequent eye movements (Gould and Dill 1969).

Buswell (based on data for three pictures) notes that horizontal and vertical movements of the eyes are in accord with expectations that the eye will follow strong compositional elements (such as the vertical lines of columns or spires or the lines of spiral motifs) but may not necessarily follow them in the direction predicted by writings on art aesthetics (up or down or in a circular motion). Repetitive designs were first examined with a left-to-right series of eye movements. Yarbus's data reveal similar patterns.

Buswell found that when the pictures were divided into sixteen rectangles, the center four rectangles receive the greatest amount of attention as determined by the number of fixations, then the two center rectangles at the top, while others receive much less attention. For one abstract picture, the percentage of deviation differed little from more realistic pictures.

Buswell also compared finished and unfinished pictures; attention increased for portions of the picture that had been enriched in detail in the finished product. In his work, Yarbus notes that many fixations occur in areas that are defined as being "highly informative;" he defines the concept of informativeness loosely, as being of use or essential to perception, either in reality or in the opinion of the viewer. In his work, subjects focused on textured areas and areas showing details of decoration, but details receive relatively few fixations unless they follow the principle of informativeness. Mackworth and Morandi (1967) asked subjects to rate images by informativeness of region, then asked other subjects to view these; the density of fixations in each region was related to the judgments of informativeness of the regions. The correlation between informativeness and density of fixations (and hence length of viewing) was supported by later research (Henderson, Weeks, and Hollingworth 1999; Loftus and Mackworth 1978).

Buswell and Yarbus observe that human heads or faces receive a great amount of attention, as do other body parts, especially eyes, nose, mouth, and hands. Yarbus found that fixations tend to occur on similar features in a cyclic manner, such as on an eye and then on a mouth. Animals also receive attention. Eye fixations do not appear to follow contour, unless in regions of informativeness such as facial profiles, and fixations for silhouettes and pictures or paintings are similar. Motion depicted in a picture will also attract eye fixations (Gould 1976). Buswell found relatively little influence of color, while Yarbus found that fixations do not necessarily occur in either the darkest or the brightest regions. Buswell's diagrams show that areas of strong contrast, such as windows or openings, receive more attention. Buswell's data reveal that human-built structures receive more attention than natural elements such as clouds or trees.

When images and text were combined, Buswell found that only about one quarter of his subjects looked at the title of a painting. Similarly, for advertising images combining image and text, there were more fixations on the image, and fixations on the text were brief. Even when subjects were instructed that they should remember the name of an object (printed below a picture of an object) they fixated more on the object (Tversky 1974).

These findings generally fit well with Spoehr and Lehmkuhle's (1982) discussion of information theory, which suggests that high information content is equivalent to low predictability. Extending this theory to the visual perception of images suggests that highly informative regions are likely to be in regions that are not predictable. Other research supports this; Berlyne (1958) found that the less well-formed member of an image pair generates more fixations. In another experiment, Mackworth and Morandi (1967) had a separate group of raters judge predictable content in experimental pictures, and results indicated that more fixations occurred in regions rated to have less predictable content. Gould (1976) argues that processing differences or discrepancies reduces the information load.

Contours may also be highly informative regions. In contrast to Buswell and

Yarbus, Mackworth and Morandi conclude that subjects make more fixations in regions containing contours than in regions composed of largely unbounded textures. Fisher and others note that while sequence of the scan path does not reveal an underlying organization, fixations are correlated with areas of high information (Fisher and others 1983). In some cases it appears that, with Buswell's and Yarbus's data, recorded temporal saccadic paths may obscure the occurrence of other events such as detection of contours.

The above observations on informative regions were based on post hoc analysis of eye-tracking diagrams. Loftus and Mackworth, drawing upon Shannon's (1948) theory of communication, propose a definition of informativeness: "An object in a picture is informative to the extent that the object has a low a priori probability of being in the picture given the rest of the picture and the observer's past history." (Loftus and Mackworth 1978, 566). They then tested this definition by showing subjects pictures of organized scenes, half of which contained an improbable object (such as a farm scene with an octopus). The improbable objects were fixated sooner, more often, and for longer durations than the more predictable objects, supporting their definition. Pezdek refers to this as the consistency effect: subjects recall and recognize items inconsistent with expectations better than items consistent with expectations (Antes and Penland 1981; Pezdek and others 1989). Other researchers, however, were not able to replicate this result and conclude that semantic likelihood of an object has no effect on order or density of fixations (De Graef, Christiaens, and d'Ydewalle 1990; Friedman 1979; Henderson, Weeks, and Hollingworth 1999).

Other work suggests that context develops prior to the identification of objects (Metzger and Antes 1983). Pictures were rated prior to testing on three levels of informativeness at each of eight locations. Medium-informative sections were recognized better than high- or low-informative sections, and medium-informative sections were recognized better in the periphery, while highly informative areas were recognized more accurately at central locations.

Both Buswell and Yarbus found that task influences scanning patterns. Buswell found that detailed examinations of pictures and longer fixations occurred if the subjects were asked to find a particular detail. Kosslyn (1973) found that instructions to focus on particular things effectively directed scanning strategies. Yarbus had subjects try to determine the age or material wealth of people shown in a picture, tasks that resulted in increased scanning of the faces or of objects in the picture. Möckel and Heemsoth (1984) present evidence that prior knowledge and expectations about a scene affect eye fixation patterns; in the absence of a predefined task, increasing knowledge of a process results in increased eye fixations at points of maximal informativeness. Yarbus found that when he asked subjects to remember the positions of people or objects, their eyes zigzagged back and forth among parts of people or objects. This suggests that the magnitude of the saccadic movements may assist in such spatial assessment and may be related to the observation that it is difficult for subjects to reorganize a picture in memory.

Buswell found wide individual differences in the general patterns and duration of fixations and suggests that these differences are more directly related to characteristics of individuals rather than differences in pictures being observed. Characteristics which Buswell found had little effect on subjects' perceptual patterns in looking at a picture were score on an art test or experience in art school, age of subject, and nationality (American or Oriental). However, a study of artists' eye movements found that artists made longer fixations viewing familiar paintings, and nonartists made longer fixations viewing unfamiliar paintings (Kristjanson and Antes 1989). In a qualitative summary of typical scanning patterns, Yarbus found no single tendency that was characteristic of all subjects or all pictures; both individual differences and the specific effects of pictorial elements accounted for some variation. Noton and Stark found that scanpaths for familiar objects were similar for an individual, following regular pathways, and that scanpaths for different images viewed by the same individual were different (Noton and Stark 1971; Stark and Ellis 1981). They proposed that an initial scanpath becomes a "feature ring," an internal representation in memory for that object, and that this feature ring not only enables future recognition but guides an individual's subsequent scanpaths for that object. Their results support this: sixty-five percent of their subjects subsequently viewing a previously viewed object used the same learned scanpath. This also suggests that eye movements for familiar objects are not primarily based upon lower-level features but are controlled by memory and recognition processes.

Stark and Ellis (1981) provide a compelling argument but little supporting evidence for their theory that cognitive schemata determine the individual's scanning pattern. Gould notes that while eye movements would probably not *directly* reveal cognitive changes in expectancies, encoding, and synthesis, he nevertheless suggests that people search pictures for "meaning" and not for specific targets (Gould 1976, 333–334). However, other researchers believe that eye movement data suggest some interdependencies between attention and eye movements and that attention may be central to a recombination of initially independently coded properties (Humphreys and Bruce 1989). Viviani (1990) summarizes eye movement research relating to mental states and notes that fixations occur around appropriate points when subjects are trying to perceive a particular solution for a polysemous image (an image which can be interepreted correctly two ways). Similarly, when searching for a hidden target image, fixations occur on the target pattern when it is partially recognized, and experts fixate on details which are only important in a particular context (such as medical images).

Currently, eye movement research is gaining new attention after a period of less intense activity. More recent work has focused on determining the relationship of spatial frequencies to eye movements and further investigations of informativeness. Issues include discriminating between the visual informativeness of a scene and the semantic informativeness, which may have given rise to seeming inconsistencies in some earlier results, and the extent to which a proposed peripheral semantic analysis controls initial fixation placement. Henderson and others, noting that initial fixations do not occur with semantically inconsistent objects, but that semantically inconsistent objects *are* fixated more often and for longer times, propose a saliency map framework of eye movement control to explain these results (Henderson and Hollingworth 1998). A saliency map is composed of spatial position and saliency weight. In this theory, an early global view of the scene uses low-frequency (coarse) information to generate regions weighted by saliency, and thus initial fixation placement is determined by visual (luminance, contrast, texture, color, contour density) rather than semantic factors. Task may modify salience, but only if it depends upon visual features. As local regions are processed into meaningful elements, salience becomes determined by cognitive factors and viewing concentrates on semantically informative regions.

Schyns and Oliva (1994) conducted research focusing on determining the relationship of eye movements to different spatial frequencies obtained by putting an image through low-pass and high-pass filters, which reduce an image to courser or finer scales. The data suggest that recognition occurs at both coarse and fine spatial scales. By attending first to the coarse scale, the visual system can get a quick and rough estimate of the input to activate scene schemata in memory; attending to fine information allows refinement or refutation of the raw estimate. More recent work attempts to correlate eye movements with seven spatial features (luminance maxima and minima, image contrast, maxima of local positive physiological contrast, minima of local negative physiological contrast, edge density, and high spatial frequency), but found no association except for a weak effect for edge density (Mannan, Ruddock, and Wooding 1996). However, this work further confirms that fixations occur more in central regions and lends support to the notion that fixations are more dense in semantically meaningful regions. The researchers note that filtering operations do not affect the relative distribution of large-scale structures in the image and suggest that these global factors play an important role.

Other research using statistical evaluation of fixated regions suggests a hierarchy of eye movements supporting the concept of informativeness (Kreiger and others 2000). Results indicated that nonredundant features such as curved lines and edges, occlusions, or isolated spots play a role in the saccadic selection process. Specifically, regions of no change (constant signal) are fixated the least. Features such as straight lines and edges, which can be represented by a function of one variable, are fixated more, and features requiring higher-order statistics such as corners, junctions, and curved lines and edges, are fixated the most as they fulfill the need for informativeness. An example is a polygon in which the interior is fixated the least, bounding edges are next, and corners are most frequently fixated.

Although there is a body of evidence describing eye movements and their relationships to certain tasks, as yet their meaning remains uncertain. Analysis focusing on scanning patterns is inconclusive. Fisher found little visual or mathematical evidence to support correspondences in picture-viewing eye movement patterns and concludes: "at this point we can substantiate any theory of viewing pictures on the basis of scan patterns, which in effect means we can substantiate none. . . . the frequent occurrence of what appears to be a completely idiosyncratic, unrepeatable eye movement pattern delimits the availability of appropriate models to describe the data" (Fisher and others 1983, 208–210). Inconsistent empirical results may also be affected by variation in experimental factors (e.g., image size, content and type, task, viewing time per scene) across studies.[13] However, eye movement data is suggestive of theories of visual and semantic processing in which both global scene analysis and regional analysis take part. Others note that a complete theory of eye movements needs to account for viewing of dynamic scenes or observer motion. Rensink suggests that these results point to a need for tighter connections among eye movement, visual attention, visual memory, and scene perception research (Rensink, O'Regan, and Clark 1997).

Results such as those reported above for contours, anomalies, areas of contrast and detail, and specific pictorial elements such as the human face, however, are suggestive of image attributes that are typically focused upon and attended to in the viewing process. These results, which contribute to a concept of informativeness, may be usefully applied in building theory for indexing images and their attributes.

Theories of Image Understanding

It appears that perception and cognition are highly interrelated, and image understanding calls into play higher-level cognitive processes. An ongoing debate concerns the role of expectations, knowledge, and learning in the processes of conceptualization and understanding of percepts. Another major question that relates to image understanding is the question of the fundamental nature of similarity judgments in a visual environment, as similarity in a visual context has yet to be defined. The notion of similarity is related to theories of human processes of grouping and categorization, and it appears that human processes of categorization may enter into image perception and understanding. An understanding of theories related to categorization provides further insight into these processes as well as their outcomes.

Schemata

Bartlett (1932) first suggested the concept of a schema during his studies of memory. He found that subjects recalled details of stories that were not actually in the stories. This led him to theorize that memory takes the form of a schema or mental framework for understanding and remembering information. As noted above, some researchers theorize that schemata or global expectations also guide perception and understanding of scenes. Rumelhart (1980) later characterized these global expectations as units of organized knowledge (mental structures) about events, situations, objects, or people. A schema can contain several different types of information about different aspects of the percept; these can vary from very detailed perceptual information (lists of objects in a scene) to more abstract, conceptual attributes and relationships (certain types of objects are used for certain activities or functions; for instance, kitchen utensils are associated with the activity of cooking). Schemata can function at various levels of abstraction, and they can be embedded in one another. Thus, a novel situation may have several familiar schemata embedded in it, and these allow understanding to proceed.

As described by Rumelhart and Norman (1988), schemata have "slots" for different variables. For instance, a "farm" schema has the following variables: land, crops or animals, a farmer, machinery, products, and specialized buildings. The specific values that get filled in depend upon the situation: farm X may raise vegetables; farm Y may raise horses. General knowledge can be used to infer information in unspecified slots; for instance, horses require more land than vegetables. However, unspecified slots also operate under the constraints imposed by the rest of the schema; a building on a farm is more likely to be a barn than a castle.

Schemata have two important functions that lead them to play fundamental roles in perception. Moates and Schumacher (1980) characterize these roles as information-accepting systems and plans for picking up information from the environment. Information can only be meaningful to an individual who has a schema that can accommodate the information, and, conversely, schemata greatly reduce the complexity of the world by providing guidance as to where certain types of information are likely to occur.

Schemata are not fixed or static; they become modified or elaborated through processes of "assimilation" or "accommodation" during a person's interactions with the environment (Crozier and Chapman 1984b). As a schema directs perceptual processes, it makes more information available to that schema, and the schema may then be modified. Rumelhart and Norman theorize that schemata are active processing units, themselves responsible for the recognition of data that fit, and they are self-activating when this occurs. Additionally, a schema can be activated by either events in the environment or conceptually, by other schemata.

Biederman's research found that violation of semantic relations (expected schema) was disruptive of object perception (Biederman, Mezzanotte, and Rabinowitz 1982). Other work on object recognition assessed the influence of color as a surface feature (a blue apple) versus its influence as stored knowledge about a particular object (apples are red); the results indicate that stored color knowledge relative to a specific object is more influential in object recognition than apparent surface color (Joseph and Proffitt 1996).

Hochberg proposed that an abstract, schematic mental structure of space and events plays a fundamental role in perception (Hochberg 1968; Hochberg 1978). He supported his thesis by citing the ability of a viewer to understand moving pictures which include rapid shifts of the camera's view (Hochberg 1986). He suggests that "schematic maps" are generated both on the basis of previous knowledge stored in long-term memory and on the basis of what the person has just seen. He proposes that the mental schema maintains important spatial and form-related information, without being a sensory representation. Hochberg argues that in perception a schema is as important as the perceptual stimuli, providing expectations about the probable layout of the next eye fixation and providing a spatially organized storage system that incorporates perceptual information.

Strong gender stereotyping in picture interpretation supports schema-based interpretation as well. In studies with gender- and size-neutral animal pictures, child characters at play and solitary characters were viewed as boys, and adult characters involved with children were viewed as women, with males being most influenced by gender stereotypes (Arthur and White 1996; White, Morris, and Arthur 1996).

Similarity and Categorization

In information systems, similarity has traditionally been defined in a geometric model, with objects as points in some coordinate space and metric distances representing the (dis)similarities among objects; in this model, similar objects are near one another in clusters. The classical (*i.e.,* taxonomic) view of similarity holds that categories are mutually exclusive, and natural categories are held to be structured in terms of a set of necessary and sufficient features. Only if an entity has these features can it be a member of the category. Other researchers do not agree with this view and note that physical features do not predict classification performance (Lockhead 1992; Medin and Wattenmaker 1987). Medin and Wattenmaker (1987) cite, as an example, a list of seemingly unrelated objects such as children, jewelry, portable television sets, photograph albums, manuscripts, and oil paintings, which when placed in the context of "things to take out of one's home during a fire" become coherent because of their conceptual framework.

Empirical work by Goldmeier (1972) into shape similarity demonstrated that human similarity judgments depend upon more than comparing lists of shared parts or features. Rather, results suggested that individual components are not perceived as such but as part of a perceptually significant group, the gestalt of the overall figure. Furthermore, he translates the Gestalt notion of *Prägnanz* as *singularity*, meaning that certain elements, such as components of equal size or spacing or straight lines, if present, are a determining factor in perception of shape similarity. When no singularity feature is present, another type of feature, such as area, is used to determine similarity. Thus, there appears to be a hierarchy upon which shape similarity judgments are made.

Tversky's (1977) work showed that the relative weighting of a feature varies both with the stimulus context and experimental task, adding support to the argument that similarity depends upon more than matched feature sets. Tversky and others proposed a feature-theoretical approach, in which the similarity of two objects is expressed as a function of their common and distinctive features weighted for salience or importance, thereby allowing for a variety of similarity relations over the same set of objects (Tversky and Gati 1978). The goal is to model the smallest number of features or dimensions which can adequately capture the observed similarities. This type of matching of properties has been the predominant approach to similarity, and relies on the concepts of prototypes, exemplars, and graded categories (see below).

Others argue that similarity can be considered to be a *product* of a process of comparison rather then the *basis* upon which such a process takes place (Murphy and Medin 1985). However, the most serious weakness of defining similarity as a summing of features occurs because there are no constraints provided as to what should count as a feature or an attribute, and any two entities can be arbitrarily similar or dissimilar depending on the criterion of what is to count as a relevant attribute (Medin and Wattenmaker 1987). The number of attributes that two objects share can be infinite, depending upon how these attributes are defined (smaller than an elephant, not yellow, and so forth). Principles specifying relevance and importance of properties are needed; otherwise similarity becomes too flexible to account for conceptual coherence.

Common attributes can be used to represent conceptual coherence, but it is not clear whether similarity is a by-product of conceptual coherence or is its determinant. A concept is more than the sum of a set of independent features. Medin and Wattenmaker argue that "all the features that are characteristic of a bird do not make it a bird—unless these properties are held together in some kind of a 'bird structure.' This bird structure certainly consists of a large set of relational properties and not simply attributes" (Medin and Wattenmaker 1987, 31). They state that similarity-based approaches to category "goodness" are insufficient to explain fully the richness of conceptual structure, and believe that since conceptual structures significantly affect both perceptual and conceptual categories, a sharp distinction between these is probably not useful. Therefore, as Medin and Coley (1998) explain, a theory-based approach to similarity holds that conceptual behavior may be knowledge-based and driven by theories.

Lockhead cautions that these ideas may not, however, generalize to functional, man-made objects (Lockhead 1992, 112). Thus, depicted objects in a visual representation may have varying types of similarity judgments, some based on feature lists and others based on more abstract notions. If indeed there are two (or more) types of similarity judgments, it is unclear what part they each contribute or which may be more typically used in similarity judgments for pictorial stimuli.

Related to notions of similarity, a very general problem in cognitive science has to do with how humans categorize, or sort the "things" of the world into categories. Harnad characterizes the things of the world as being anything from a concrete object to an abstract idea, and notes that categorization, or "sorting," includes many differential responses to a thing, from detection to identification to verbal description (Harnad 1987b, 1). Categorization is viewed as playing a critical role in perception, thinking, language, and communication (Bruner 1973). Categorizing has implications for perceptual and cognitive processes, as it may be used both to identify an object, and then infer or predict information about that object.

Categorization processes may depend upon such factors as familiarity with the type of object to be categorized or may be influenced by items in spatial or temporal proximity. Social psychologists and cognitive psychologists have studied classification processes from different perspectives, in different cultures and contexts (social and nonsocial), using dissimilar stimuli (geometric shapes, human faces, sounds) and different types of cues (category label first or example first).[14] Differing results from these studies indicate that categorization may proceed by varying combinations of different processes, depending upon the context.

Prototypes, Exemplars, and Basic-Level Objects

There are two general classes of theories as to how categorization takes place; these are abstraction-based models and instance-based models. Prototype theory, an abstraction-based model, proposes that natural categories divide the world up into clusters of correlated attributes (*e.g.*, birds have wings and lay eggs) (Rosch and Mervis 1975). Therefore, these clusters become "prototypes," abstract summaries of the categories representing central tendencies, and classes of objects are stored not as individual objects, but as sets of the most frequently encountered (most salient) features of these objects. The summary is represented as either a "best example" of a category or as an average value of an attribute. Various types of empirical evidence support prototypes. For instance, category membership exhibits graded effects; some members of a category are "better" members than others (a robin is a "better" bird than a penguin). Those members of a category that are the best members share the most attributes with other members of that category (higher family resemblance) and the fewest attributes with members of contrasting categories. Contrary to these, poor members of a category share more features with members of contrasting categories.

Another piece of evidence for this theory is the existence of the *basic-level object*, an object that is a good member or shares a large number of attributes at that particular level (Rosch and others 1976). The basic-level is the preferred level used in describing objects, and objects at this level share a large number of perceptual features. Smith, Balzano, and Walker describe the basic-level of classification as a "compromise between a wealth of information content (e.g., Washington state Delicious apples) and an economical, abstract description (e.g., fruit)" (Smith, Balzano, and Walker 1978, 142). Thus, in this case, the basic level of description would be the term "apple." Superordinate level objects (fruit) are abstract, have fewer common attributes, and would seem to be structured by nonperceptual properties, while slightly more common attributes occur for subordinate objects (the Delicious apple). Another example of the superordinate–basic level–subordinate continuum would be furniture–chair–rocking chair.

Attribute clusters occurring in natural object categories are thus maximally correlated when the object categories occur at the basic-level, which is neither the most specific nor the most abstract level but is rather an intermediate level, such as "apple." Basic-level concepts are categorized faster, are used almost exclusively in free-naming tasks, are learned sooner than other types of concepts, and are employed similarly across different cultures (Lassaline, Wisniewski, and Medin 1992). Basic-level categories thus fulfill the principle of cognitive economy by being *both* informative and general.

Several studies of picture verification indicate that objects are first seen or recognized as basic-level objects (Rosch and others 1976; Smith, Balzano, and Walker 1978). Research demonstrates that color is also described at such a basic level (Berlin and Kay 1969). Furthermore, as Arnheim states, "Gestalt psychology suggests, instead, that perception does not consist in the mechanical recording of stimulus material, either detailed or blurred, but in the grasping of structural features, which gives the character of generality to any percept and eliminates the difference in principle between seeing an individual thing and seeing a kind of thing—the difference between percept and concept." (Arnheim 1966, 144).

Research investigating levels of object naming has used images of individual objects as stimuli. Research with more complex pictorial images used as stimuli shows that this basic-level of description holds for these types of images as well. Tversky and Hemenway (1983) demonstrated basic-level category effects in scene description: subjects labeled photographs primarily with their basic-level terms ("home," "school," "beach") rather than with subordinate ("apartment") or superordinate ("indoor") terms. Morris and Murphy (1990) found a basic level in event naming ("dinner" rather than "meals" or "family dinner"), and Jörgensen (1995b) found that the basic level can be applied to the more interpretive attributes of images as well.

In contrast to abstraction-based models are instance-based models, which hold that categorization takes place by comparing an object to other stored specific instances of that object. These instances are exemplars, or best examples of a category. Categorization proceeds by comparing features one by one; when two objects are highly similar on a sufficient number of combined features, they are considered to be members of the same class. The features used are the features of the exemplars, therefore these features may not be characteristic of the members of the category overall. Empirical evidence supporting this demonstrates that the more similar an item is to another, the more efficiently it can be classified; therefore highly similar items predict categorization better than similarity of an item to a prototypical representation.

There also appears to be a "canonical" or "best" view of an object or class, and instance-based models suggest that these canonical representations are formed through exposure to exemplars. Experimental results confirm that a canonical representation of objects exists and suggest that it is a three-quarters view of an object (Palmer, Rosch, and Chase 1981). Picture-naming studies have demonstrated that plane rotation away from a canonical upright orientation reduces the efficiency of recognition (Lawson and Jolicoeur 1998); it may be that this view best embodies or displays the important features of the object. Developmental research demonstrates that a preference for a canonical upright orientation for picture books is not present initially but develops by the age of thirty months, suggesting that development of pictorial competence is complex and multifaceted (DeLoache, Uttal, and Pierroutsakos 2000).

Related to the concept of basic-level objects is that of an "entry point level" into semantic memory, which in many cases corresponds to the basic level. However, Jolicoeur and others produce evidence that objects are not always identified first at the basic level and suggest that if an object is a very distinctive or atypical exemplar of a basic-level category, then that object may have its own entry point into semantic memory at the subordinate level (Jolicoeur, Gluck, and Kosslyn 1984). The notion of entry point applies to individual exemplars rather than the category. This is related to the finding that the entry point into semantic memory is also affected by expertise in a particular field, which also shifts it towards the subordinate level.

A review of evidence suggests that, at the conceptual level, classification is neither carried out by rigorous, nor by logical, nor by universal criteria, but rather employs more probabilistic means and may call upon unnecessary features, various stimulus dimensions, or holistic properties (Harrison 1992). There may be a progression from instance-based (exemplar) to abstract (prototype) categorization processes as one becomes more familiar with a category and its members (Zarate and Sanders 1999). Features may be learned as categorization progresses. Rosch notes that formation of categories occurs in a particular culture at a particular point in time (Rosch 1978). Keil proposes that individuals may be constrained by a communicative principle, in which the need to communicate an idiosyncratic representation of the world forces adoption of category structures that are more analytical, and therefore more stable, or consistent, across individuals (Keil 1987, 193). Categorization thus incorporates features and structural information, as well as requiring that an item to be classified have the right "explanatory relationship" to the theory which organizes the conceptual category. In other words, theory (which may not be explicit or even operate at the conscious level) helps determine which features are relevant to a particular categorization task.

There may also be physiological specialization in processing category membership decisions. For instance, recent work in picture-naming tasks demonstrates that, in addition to a dissociation between living and nonliving categories of objects, other subjects showed a finer selectivity such as differentiating animals from fruits and vegetables, tools from nonmanipulable objects, and even vehicles from furniture. These results indicate that in naming items of different semantic categories there may be different subsystems at work (Laiacona, Capitani, and Barbarotto 2000).

Beyond the role of objects in forming conceptual categories, the understanding and significance of more abstract qualities of images, such as explicit or implicit affective qualities or meaning, is also of interest, although considerably more difficult to research. However, these qualities may be distinguishing criteria for image similarity when other image facets are comparable. Recent work demonstrates a developmental shift in the focus of interest on properties found in pictures of everyday objects (Jolley, Zhi, and Thomas 1998). British and Chinese children and adults were asked to match two out of three drawings, which could be matched on color, subject matter, or visual metaphor. In both cultures, there was a significant developmental progression from matching on color to subject matter, and then from matching on subject matter to metaphor. Thus, more abstract notions may come into play for similarity judgments with increasing age and experience. Other research demonstrated that subjects as young as three years old can relate metaphorically and explain domain resemblances based on implicit and explicit criteria. Across all materials, children were better able to perceive metaphorical relations in pictures than in words.

The notion of *categorical perception* (CP) is also related to issues of category formation (Harnad 1987a). Categorical perception refers to the phenomenon that when people have learned to sort objects into categories, their perceptions of the objects change in similarity space: objects in the same category look more alike (within-category compression) and objects in different categories look more different (between-category separation). These things are thus seen as being more similar or different than would be predicted on the basis of comparing their properties. CP is exhibited by human subjects, animals, and neural net models. CP appears to operate in two ways. The first is through psychophysical means ("sensory perception") involving such phenomena as color (the color spectrum) (Berlin and Kay 1969; Bornstein 1987; Guest and Van Laar 2000) or speech sounds (acoustic continuum) (Burnham, Earnshaw, and Quinn 1987). One end result is that, given two perceptually discriminable stimuli, they are responded to as being the same. As Slater explains, "this type of organization of the perceptual input allows us to organize, make sense of, and thereby reduce the otherwise overwhelming variation in the appearance of stimuli, both people and objects" (Slater 1998, 15).

The second is through innate categories such as facial expressions (Calder and others 2000; Young and others 1997), and higher-order categories ("generic knowledge") which are semantically based (Medin and Barsalou 1987). Emotion has also been found to display category structure, and there is overwhelming evidence supporting the theory that at least the six basic facial expressions of emotion are recognized cross-culturally: happiness, surprise, fear, disgust, anger, and sadness (Izard 1994).[15] Recent work using morphed photographic stimuli, in which continua of facial expressions are used, support categorical perception along three continua: happiness–sadness, anger–fear, and anger–sadness (Calder and others 1996).

While research in the psychophysical and semantic areas of categorical perception has for the most part followed different paths, more recently scholars are recognizing the processual similarities between the two areas, in such areas as category structure and bases and use of categorization, and are attempting integrative approaches (Harnad 1987b; Livingston, Andrews, and Harnad 1998; Smith and Heise 1992). Certain theories, such as prototype theory, may be applicable in both areas.

Theories of Human Image Memory

Research describing memory for images or for specific image attributes can also contribute information to the exploration of human perception of typical image attributes, as memory processes are also involved in visual perception. There appear to be several ways in which visual memory operates. The first, iconic memory, is a transient visual memory that stores visual information briefly (a few fractions of a second). There is evidence to suggest the existence of a short-term visual memory upon which visual information can be temporarily stored, characterized as a "visuo-spatial scratch pad" (Baddeley 1986). This short-term memory requires active attention to maintain it.

Visual features are combined in a process of pattern recognition, which takes place within the context of long-term memory and involves attention. The results of pattern recognition processes can be placed in working memory for further mental processing. Theories of long-term image memory are ultimately concerned with issues of how images are represented in memory. There are currently two major theories concerning this image representation. The first is dual-coding theory, which posits two independent, but interconnected and modality-specific representational systems: nonverbal (nonlinguistic object representations or *imagens*) and verbal (linguistics word representations or *logogens*) (Federmeier and Kutas 2001; Johnson, Paivio, and Clark 1996; Paivio 1991;

Paivio, Rogers, and Smythe 1968). Supporting this is research suggesting cerebral hemispheric asymmetries in long-term memory for pictorial scenes (Nagae 1994). The second is a single amodal conceptual representation (Fodor 1975).

That several different levels of visual memory exist seems well established; the mechanisms by which they operate and interact are, however, not well understood. Researchers have long noted the "picture superiority effect," in which pictures are more easily recalled than words (Paivio, Rogers, and Smythe 1968). Recent research indicates, however, that this effect can be eliminated or reversed depending on the type of conceptual encoding task and conceptual-retrieval test (Vaidya and Gabrieli 2000). A number of experiments have sought to establish theories that explain how and how well memory for visual materials works. Long-term memory for images appears to be very good in some respects and lacking in others. While many attributes may initially be perceived, fewer receive attentive processing, and fewer still may be remembered at a later time. If there are some attributes which are more typically remembered than others, these could be usefully represented as index access points when searching for visual materials.

Several types of experiments have been used in researching memory for images. Early research focused on recognition experiments, in which subjects state whether a particular item has been seen before (usually by means of forced-recognition of pairs). Recall has been tested by asking participants to list objects or describe images. More recently, priming or speed in naming or recognizing images has been used as evidence of prior exposure to the image. Researchers currently frame recognition and recall in terms of explicit memory (knowing consciously that an image has been seen) and implicit memory (where familiarity with the image, although not conscious, is demonstrated by other effects, such as speed in naming).

Recognition Experiments

Recognition experiments indicate that memory for pictorial material is very high. Two studies used a forced-choice recognition test to determine accuracy and length of memory after viewing pictures either at a self-paced rate or for ten seconds. Shepard (1967) demonstrated excellent recognition for 612 images up to a week later, with recognition still occurring at a better than chance level four months after exposure. Standing and others used 2,560 photographs and demonstrated an immediate high recognition accuracy (90%) (Standing, Conezio, and Haber 1970).

Goldstein and Chance (1971) theorized that such good pictorial memory in these experiments was the result of two factors. The first factor concerned the complexity of the pictures: if subjects retained only a fraction of features, even a single feature would provide an adequate clue for the recognition task. The second factor suggested was that subjects used verbal descriptions to enhance memory. To test these factors, they performed an experiment using material varying on few dimensions (snow crystals, inkblots) and a more stringent recognition task. Subjects still performed at well above chance detection, although not as high as previous results, suggesting that partial learning and the multidimensional nature of the material may enhance recognition of pictures. Freedman and Haber (1974) also demonstrated that meaning enhances memory for images: images were poorly remembered when meaning could not be ascertained.

Other work demonstrated that memory is more accurate the longer subjects have to view an image, with two seconds being sufficient to give a high rate of recognition accuracy (Potter 1976; Potter and Levy 1969). It should also be noted that subjects, when asked to perform a detection task, are able to identify a particular picture at much shorter intervals, but more processing is apparently necessary for recognition. Loftus (1972) demonstrated that accuracy of recognition is a function of number of eye fixations rather than viewing time, although viewing time does correlate with number of fixations. Objects that are reported as being remembered are fixated by the third fixation and are then fixated several more times. However, Loftus did not find a difference in the number of eye fixations made by good and poor rememberers. Tversky (1974) also did not find that the correlation between eye fixations and memory held for all pictures.

Recall Experiments

Testing recall or *what* is remembered is more difficult as this can involve some degree of drawing ability; therefore recall is often tested by asking subjects to name objects seen in a picture. However, naming objects or answering questions about what features are remembered may still not provide complete information.

Bartlett attempted to test recall of simple and complex designs and pictorial materials by asking subjects to draw the image remembered after brief exposures (Bartlett 1932, 14–34, 177–185). However, some subjects experienced difficulty drawing and were allowed to use verbal descriptions. Subjects were tested drawing both a single reproduction and a series of reproductions. The testing evaluated four types of images: simple geometric figures; more detailed geometric figures; progressively complex figures; and simple concrete representations. Only form, relative size and position, and common pictorial scenes were assessed.

With very simple material, names were commonly used and there was no attempt at analytical observation. Unfamiliar features, such as a gap, were readily noticed and remembered, although their placement may have been incorrect. Interpretation leading to elaboration took place; for instance, in one case serifs were added to a letter form.

With slightly more complex geometric forms, naming took place and shaped the reproduction of the image. The name of the object seemed to fit into a preformed scheme. For an unfamiliar figure, analogy was used, having most frequently to do with shape or arrangement of lines and curves. A strong tendency to multiplication of detail with disconnected material was observed; this also occurred with some subjects' representations of geometrically complex designs. With complex designs containing a nonsymmetrical or nonordered arrangement, the technique of observation became analytical rather than unitary. With progressive figures, even slight differences were noticed, and final complete figures were evaluated as being more "simple" in construction than partial images.

With simple realistic representations, a valuing or critical judgment entered in, with images being called "bad" or "effective" compared with some "standard" or "canonical" representation. These designs were also judged simpler than the geometric ones, and Bartlett suggests that simplicity is, psychologically speaking, a matter of interest. Subjects reacted to more complex realistic representations as a unit, and certain features were consistently dominant: composition, light and shade, simple spatial references, and "meaning," with a great variety of interpretation.

Bartlett observed that the picture often stimulated a vivid visual image, and then that image would dominate and direct the perceptual observation. Bartlett comments that visual perception is exceedingly complex: "Inextricably mingled with it are imaging, valuing, and those beginnings of judging which are involved in the response to plan, order of arrangement and construction of presented material" (Bartlett 1932, 31). Although such factors, as well as "feeling," play a part, he also concludes that certain crucial features of the objects and scenes dominate. Among these are the dominance of details, the scheme or setting which makes perceiving possible, attitude factors, and inferential processes.

In spite of the prevalence and dominance of a unitary perception, there are very few perceptual situations in which some detail does not stand out and influence the perception of the rest. With structurally simple material, dominant details may be gaps, odd or disconnected features, simple spatial relationships (above, left, and so on), or light and shade. With more structurally complex material such details may be plan of construction, disposition of figures, general topic, and representational significance. He believes that these details set the stage for remembering.

Bartlett also reports interesting trends in the serial reproductions of pictorial material that may have implications for how image memory operates. The first tendency is to transform unfamiliar components in the direction of accepted conventional representations. For instance, a very abstract drawing entitled "portrait of a man" becomes much more realistic. The second trend, consistent with information reported above, was the trend towards elaboration and multiplication of features. It appears that a visual image method favors invention over a verbal method. An unfamiliar figure may be transformed into a familiar whole, at which point it becomes conventionalized and simplified. Details were elaborated in two ways, either being reduplicated, or transformed into a characteristic belonging to a new setting and perhaps stylized into a decorative motif.

Bartlett reports a different finding for detached details. When detached details appear in a decorative or nonrepresentational form they stand an especially good chance of being preserved with little change. He notes the "curious preservation of the trivial, the odd, the disconnected, the unimportant detail" (Bartlett 1932, 184).

Visual Features

Other researchers present evidence that both specific details and more general familiarity or visual–spatial information are important for picture recognition in memory tasks (Graefe and Watkins 1980; Intraub 1980; Loftus and Bell 1975; Watkins and Graefe 1981). A large body of research has produced somewhat mixed results concerning the extent to which specific visual features, such as details, color, or forms, contribute to visual memory and the performance of recognition or recall tasks.

Results testing different formats give mixed results. Nelson, Metzler, and Reed (1974) compared memory performance on four types of stimuli: black-and-white photographs, embellished line drawings, unembellished line drawings, and a brief sentence describing image content. Recognition in a two-alternative forced-choice procedure for all three types of visual stimuli was superior to the textual description. Madigan (1983) obtained similar results comparing colored or detailed object photographs, line drawings, and object names. Interestingly, size changes of pictorial stimuli across study images and test images reduces recognition memory and recall judgments (Rajaram 1996).

Mandler and Parker (1976) found that subjects have good recognition memory for objects and the object types that appear in complex pictures. However, Mandler, Seegmiller, and Day (1977) found that subjects have poor retention for the details of objects in a scene. Further research tested the assumption that detail information enhances recognition memory. In another study in which Loftus and Kallman (1979) instructed subjects to pay attention to details, subjects did significantly better in recognition. Others present additional supporting data showing that subjects recognize a great deal of sensory or attribute information in pictures (Homa and Viera 1988; Park 1980). Ritchey and Beal found better recall for detailed drawings but Ritchey found just the opposite—better recall for outline drawings (Ritchey 1982; Ritchey and Beal 1980). Other researchers reported no difference in recall for detailed drawings versus simpler versions (Coulter, Coulter, and Glover 1984; Peeck, Van Dam, and Uhlenbeck 1977). Vaina (1987) describes characteristic surface textures (such as those of "pineapples" or "sheep") which could allow recognition of an object in the absence of other components, and presents evidence from brain-damaged subjects who lose the ability to recognize objects from texture. Pezdek and others (1989) present experimental results indicating that although subjects can recognize previously seen pictures, their ability to detect missing elaborative visual details (recall) is limited. Recent work with scenes shown in either high detail (photographic) or reduced detail shows no main effect of detail on scene recognition; however, gender differences emerged, with women recognizing significantly more scenes in the photographic condition than in the reduced-detail condition (Hamel and Ryan-Jones 1997).

Research on both recall and recognition suggests that the retention of details is problematic: few subjects could identify the "real" penny on a penny recognition test (fifteen drawings of the face of a penny), and even when provided with the correct visual components, subjects were unable to accurately position them (Gernsbacher 1985; Nickerson and Adams 1979). While Standing, Conezio, and Haber's research indicated that subjects showed a high rate of accuracy (85%) in determining whether an image was reversed or not, deleterious effects of changes in left–right orientation of pictorial stimuli across study and test have been obtained for remember judgments (Rajaram 1996; Standing, Conezio, and Haber 1970).

The effects of color on memory are similarly ambiguous. In an experiment that compared detailed color drawings, detailed black-and-white drawings, schematic color drawings, and schematic black-and-white drawings, detailed color drawings were recalled better than schematic black-and-white drawings (Denis and Colonelli 1976). Paivio, Rogers, and Smythe (1968) found no difference in recall among simple black-and-white drawings and pictures colored with solid paint or pastel crayon. Madigan and Lawrence (1980) found recall better for color photographs than black-and-white outline drawings. Borges, Stepnowski, and Holt (1977) tested recall and delayed recognition of color photographs versus black-and-white photographs across three grade levels: for college-age students memory was better with color, but for the others they found no difference. Recent work showed that among ten-year-olds and adults, color pictures were recalled significantly better than both black-and-white pictures and line drawings (Shaari 1999). While these studies show the role of color to be rather ambiguous, color does play an important part in grouping operations (Kahneman 1973; Williams 1967).

Stanny and Weaver (1985) instructed subjects to use different methods (e.g., color, details) to remember pictures in a picture memory task. Their results indicate that color appears to be of little use, while details worked best; other methods (attending to large forms and multiple coding) also worked well. Recent research investigating the effectiveness of color in picture recognition memory supports this (Suzuki and Takahashi 1997). In this study, recognition performance is highest when color pictures are used in both the study and test phases, but recall for the color mode of the study pictures was not as good, suggesting that the effectiveness of color in picture recognition is not necessarily due to the memory for colors in the pictures themselves, but may be due to the distinctiveness of features highlighted by the colors. Other work suggests that changes in many physical attributes, such as color and pattern, do not affect memory except when these changes are essential to the formation of a *shape* representation which could influence the stimulus *percept* or *interpretation* (Cave, Bost, and Cobb 1996).

Recall experiments testing different formats and groupings have produced mixed results. Using a categorized list of to-be-remembered items, researchers found no differences between recall for detailed line drawings and simple outline drawings (Ritchey 1982; Ritchey and Beal 1980). Studies have shown a category superiority effect (CSE), for verbal but not for pictorial stimuli. For example, Toglia and others (1997) found no advantage for categorized or conceptually clustered versus unorganized lists of pictures. In contrast, Shaari (1999) showed that categorized lists of pictures were recalled better than the uncategorized lists. Sharps and others explain these varying results by hypothesizing that the category superiority effect depends not on the pictorial/verbal distinction but primarily on the availability of relational (generative) rather than item-specific (specific details) information in a given stimulus situation (Sharps, Wilson-Leff, and Price 1995). Names are more generative, while pictorial stimuli have a high level of item-specific detail and idiosyncratic features. CSE is therefore not to be expected with pictorial materials. The researchers varied the level of item-specific information available per pictorial or verbal item and created significant CSE for pictorial stimuli. Thus, as item-specific information available within a given pictorial representation diminishes, relational information about category membership becomes more important for successful recall.

For some of these memory tests it appears that lengthy viewing time produced a ceiling effect. Loftus and Bell (1975), repeating their test using the same stimuli but much shorter exposure times, found that subjects remembered photographs best. Subjects reported their basis of recognition; given that a detail was encoded, memory was not affected by other experimental factors. Work by Potter and other researchers demonstrated that a subject's ability to extract information and identify pictures is a function of the amount of time allowed for viewing, but also that a very brief exposure (113 msec) is enough for target detection (Intraub 1981; Potter 1976; Potter and Levy 1969).

Farley, Cohen, and Sanfeliz (1979) explored the aesthetic dimensions of memory. Their results identify one relatively pervasive dimension, "distinctiveness," encompassing most of the memorial and aesthetic variables. This supports the idea, discussed above, of informativeness as a critical determinant in both perception and perhaps memory as well. Thus details and other features may be of importance in image memory only when they are distinctive, contributing to the "informativeness" of a particular aspect of a picture. Bartlett noted that details, when detached, are retained; this may be because their detachment renders them distinctive.

Organizational and Spatial Features

Spoehr and Lehmkuhle review experimental results which reveal how the organization of a picture (as determined by Gestalt principles) and the relationships among objects in a picture affect not only the processing but the memory of an image (Spoehr and Lehmkuhle 1982, 181–184). Other researchers conducted a series of experiments using organized and unorganized pictures to determine the effect that organization has upon memory (Mandler and Johnson 1976; Mandler and Parker 1976). After viewing either organized or unorganized pictures, subjects performed an object recognition task and a reconstruction task in which they arranged the objects in the correct spatial relations on a blank background. In contrast to other experimental work, they report that memory for detail was superior to memory for either size or orientation. Memory for detail, size, and orientation did not affect performance on the tasks. However, organization did help subjects remember the spatial orientations of the objects, and subjects who viewed the organized pictures were significantly more accurate in their object placement. Placements were also more accurate in the vertical dimension than the horizontal dimension, indicating commonsense positional constraints determined by horizon. The authors propose that the organization of a picture can influence three types of information extracted from a picture: (1) an inventory of the main items in a picture; (2) the physical appearance of these items; and (3) the locations of the items, including the relative spatial relationships among them.

It appears that memory for detail and other visual features is largely independent of memory for spatial information in pictures, and organization enhances the latter. This independence has also been demonstrated for color in other experiments (Christal 1958; Cohen and Saslona 1990). Christal found that color and spatial memory have low intercorrelation and load on separate factors and are thus almost independent. Other work suggests that spatial memory is more "automatic" and less affected by voluntary effort and strategy choices (Mandler, Seegmiller, and Day 1977; Naveh-Benjamin 1987). Results from tests by Reed and others requiring the identification of parts of a pattern indicate that most retained images are highly structured, somewhat vague, and difficult to reorganize (Reed 1974; Reed and Johnson 1975).

Other researchers present experimental results that suggest that both children and adults have exceptionally good memory for the spatial location of objects positioned in an array and for the quadrant in which a picture is placed (Mandler, Seegmiller, and Day 1977; Wright, Gebhard, and Karttunnen 1975). Smith and others found that visual–spatial information can be used to support memory performance in both young and old subjects (Smith and others 1994).

Schemata in Memory

Schema expectation also influences memory, and several researchers have investigated the role that schemata play in picture memory. For instance, Palmer (1975) demonstrated that object identification was greater for objects following an appropriate context than for no prior context, but subjects had more difficulty identifying inappropriate objects shown after a specific context. Friedman (1979) reported quantitative and qualitative differences between processing details in expected and unexpected items. In a recognition memory test, subjects frequently noticed missing, new, or physical changes in inconsistent items, but rarely noticed these changes in consistent items. Friedman proposed a model that differentiates between the processes of feature detection and feature analysis. Feature detection processes usually operate on schema-consistent items and activate the appropriate scene frame for processing the entire picture (top-down processing). Schema-consistent items are processed only to the degree necessary to activate the correct frame for the scene as a whole. Feature analysis (bottom-up processing) operates on schema-inconsistent items and processes these so that the current scene can be distinguished from other scenes. The physical appearance of schema-inconsistent items is encoded in more detail than schema-consistent items. This supports Pezdek's conclusions concerning the "consistency effect": items inconsistent with expectations are better recalled and recognized than items consistent with expectations (Pezdek and others 1989).

Pezdek (1978) demonstrated that subjects organize their memory of pictures thematically, in a similar manner to extracting a theme from a number of sentences. After viewing pictures which represented components of a scene, subjects were confident that they had viewed the complete scene. Pezdek suggests that in experiments reporting high memory for pictures, such memory may be the result not of recall of specific visual details but of the ability to use thematic organizational (and perhaps linguistically based) techniques. Pezdek and others (1988) propose a model in which memory representation for both simple and complex pictures is similar to the simple form of each. Homa and Viera (1988) refute this idea, arguing that complex, nonthematic, analogue information is encoded and preserved for lengthy time periods.

Brewer and Treyens (1981) demonstrated that the "college office schema" produced a memory of books being present in an office by one-third of the subjects, even though books were not present. Similar results are reported in memories for missing exemplars (such as a beach ball in a beach scene) (Miller and Gazzaniga 1998). Saliency of an item more accurately predicts recognition of the item's addition or deletion from a scene by adults than its complexity or unnaturalness (Ando 2000). Intraub and Richardson (1989) observe that when subjects recollect photographed scenes, they tend to remember having seen informative details that were not present in the picture itself, but would have been likely to exist just outside the picture's boundaries. She argues that this "boundary extension," which occurred in 95% of the drawings, supports a schematic memory for pictures, as items included beyond the boundaries were items which would be likely to exist just outside the camera's field of view. Further research supports the view that boundary extension is a result of perceptual schema activation, rather than activation of a memory schema (normalization towards a prototypical view) or Gestalt principles of object completion (Intraub 1992). Recent work demonstrated that boundary extension also occurs soon after picture perception and when conditions mimicked a series of rapid eye fixations. The authors conclude that presentation of a picture appears to activate a perceptual schema that allows observers to understand it in a larger context, and this process distorts memory for its actual boundaries (Intraub and others 1996).[16] Similar results are obtained with perceived motion. When subjects are shown a photograph of an action scene and asked to remember it, they later choose test photos showing the action slightly forward in time, indicating that their memory had shifted forward beyond that actual representation (Futterweit and Beilin 1994).

Goodman presents evidence which suggests that when schema relevance is manipulated, high-relevance items are better recalled than low-relevance items, but low-relevance items are better recognized (Goodman 1980). Others have argued that consistency with expectation and schema relevance are orthogonal qualities (Maki and Swett 1987; Mandler 1984). Pezdek and others (1988) suggest that low-relevance items perform better on both recognition and recall.

The variety of experiments and methodologies used to evaluate human image memory have produced a variety of results and thus make drawing conclusions unwise. Much of this evidence also points to the effects of Gestalts, or holistic impressions, in image-memory processes. For instance, details are remembered better if they do not form part of a larger whole. It appears that schemas also play a part in image memory, with an item's saliency affecting its memory. There is ample room for more work in this area, including testing of image memory under more naturalistic conditions.

The Psychology of Art

Studies in the psychology of art focus on experimental aesthetics, which searches for commonalties within individual's preferences for certain types of images (Fehr 1989). As Fisher explains, researchers in experimental aesthetics believe that "the terms which designate the alleged aesthetic perceptual qualities of works of art describe observable features of the works" (Fisher 1980, 4). Crozier and Chapman (1984a) provide an overview of experimental aesthetics, initiated by Fechner in 1876 with the publication of *Vorschule der Aesthetik* (Fechner 1876). Fechner believed that the investigation of "lawful" relationships between the "formal" elements of artworks and an individual's response to those elements would produce an understanding of the aesthetic response, and he proposed the study of elements of aesthetic stimuli such as line, shape, and color. This is in contrast to a class of theories on the nature of art and of art criticism, in which the meaning of the work of art is *in* the work of art and is not dependent upon either the viewer's perception or reaction to it, nor on a constructive perception by the beholder (Machamer 1980, 17).

Fechner's studies stimulated considerable research through the next century in the area of aesthetic preferences. Much of this research, as in perceptual studies, begins with specially constructed, simplified stimuli, and not necessarily with images as complex as pictorial works. Attempts to segregate or classify essential components (aesthetic variables) complement efforts to identify systematic relationships and to produce causal explanations for qualities associated with art such as "appeal" or "meaning."[17] For instance, Berlyne (1972) investigated the relationships between aesthetic preferences (complexity, interestingness, and pleasingness) and properties of geometric forms such as repetition and number of elements in a pattern.

One assumption of many researchers in experimental aesthetics is that the origins of aesthetic preferences are biological. The ubiquity of artistic activity throughout the world's cultures suggested to authors such as Berlyne that it must grow out of some fundamental characteristic of the human nervous system (Berlyne 1971; Berlyne 1974). He equated "arousal" in the nervous system with "pleasingness" and believed that it is stimulated by such variables as novelty, complexity, "surprisingness," and "puzzlingness." However, measuring "pleasingness" and "interest" is difficult, and such responses may be dependent on sociocultural factors, reflecting an individual's exposure to the norms and values of the art world. Cross-cultural aesthetics arose out of the notion of a biological underpinning to the universality of aesthetic responses; for instance, complexity of art works has been studied in relation to child-rearing practices (Berlyne 1980; Russell, Deregowski, and Kinnear 1997).

Others suggest an evolutionary component to aesthetic preferences. Coss (1968) holds that we respond to art, and to our visual world, not just as aesthetes but as animals, creating the notion of evolutionary aesthetics. Orians and Heerwagen (1992) proposed the "savannah hypothesis," in which humans express preferences for both their own habitat and for landscape paintings such as those of John Constable based upon such criteria as the presence of water, large trees, open space, and distant views, evoking the savannah where humans evolved. Such landscapes enable the viewer to find resources and avoid danger. Furthermore, artists have been found to modify their landscapes to have more of these qualities.

In another approach, Humphrey places aesthetic preferences firmly within the human disposition towards classification:

> Considered as a biological phenomenon, aesthetic preferences stem from a predisposition among animals and men to seek out experiences through which they may learn to *classify the objects* in the world about them. Beautiful "structures" in nature or in art are those which facilitate the task of classification by presenting

> evidence of the "taxonomic" relations between things in a way which is informative and easy to grasp (Humphrey 1973, 432).

Related to this, the concept of prototypicality has been proposed as a basis for aesthetic preferences and has been the subject of investigations and much debate within the field (Brant, Marshall, and Roark 1995; Hekkert and Snelders 1995).

Historically, the relationship of cognitive psychology to the psychology of art has been an uneasy one, partly because of the separation of emotion from cognition, and partly because of a distrust of the scientific methods of psychological investigation. Indeed, researchers in aesthetics feel slighted by other disciplines, as Haig and Whitfield explain:

> Within psychology the dissociation of emotion from cognition by both Behaviourism and Cognitivism has not assisted in providing the theoretical resources for probing aesthetics. Similarly, the distinct fields that make up emotion research, complete with their own frames of reference and research paradigms, militate against coherence. After its illustrious empirical beginnings as the second published area of experimental psychology, aesthetics has suffered the same fate as research into emotion, namely, that it was ignored by behaviourists and subsequently by cognitivists. Perhaps more surprisingly, the recent emergence of emotion theories unaccountably neglect aesthetics, as do integrative theories that seek to couple emotion and cognition. Aesthetics is even ignored in areas of applied scientific research where its impact would seem self-evident (Haig and Whitfield 2001).

Machamer (1980) explains the inability of psychology to provide useful theories of art as resulting from two constraints: the limitation of scientific research which requires that the object of inquiry be kept simple so one can be sure of the variables at work, and the focus on variables that can be measured and counted. Writing on the failure of psychology in general to provide aesthetic theory with a sound basis of facts and concepts, Arnheim comments that science requires "not only the mastery of stringent method but an intuitive flair for the essentials and a keen anticipation of the truth to be verified," and science, through a lack of familiarity with the "genuine artistic experience," lacks authenticity in its approach, spending much effort on side issues, choosing poor examples, and clinging to "conventional and outmoded notions" about art (Arnheim 1966, 18). Machamer puts it more succinctly: "Works of art . . . are nightmares to the scientist" (Machamer 1980, 16).

Thus, the literature of the psychology of art remains somewhat separate from more mainstream psychology publications, not only because of the concern with affective and aesthetic responses in the process of viewing and understanding art, but also in part because of the focused language of aesthetics. Experimental aesthetics, while being firmly entrenched in the empirical approach since its inception, has also placed less emphasis on building theory than cognitive or behavioral psychology. However, an overview of recent research in this area not only demonstrates its relationship to other areas such as visual perception and categorization processes but also provides insight into the relationships of image attributes to aesthetic concerns. New approaches to research include investigating the neurobiological foundations of the aesthetic variables and generating models to test theory.

Theories of Aesthetic Perception

Three basic properties have been widely used for aesthetic evaluation: expression (capability of arousing emotion), representation (content of the work, whether physical or imagined), and form (composition and structure). There have been many attempts at formalizing these aesthetic properties, both by philosophers of art and by researchers in the psychology of art. For instance, Goldman (1995) groups descriptive aesthetic terms into eight broad groups: *broadly evaluative, formal, emotional, evocative, behavioral, representational, perceptual,* and *historical.*

Within the last half of the twentieth century, several major theorists emerged in the field and they have proposed specific psychological mechanisms for perceiving and understanding art and the aesthetic variables. Arnheim (1966) based his account of art in the perception of physical objects and the way in which perception organizes patterns within a work of art. He proposed that new understandings will come from demonstrations of the structural kinship between specific expressive effects and specific patterns in the work of art. Drawing upon the ideas of Thomas Munro, Arnheim proposes a "useful" theory of motivation based upon the concept of equilibrium (found in such diverse areas as physics, physiology, and psychology). He posited the existence of internal *form patterns* which vary not only between individuals, but within an individual at different times (Arnheim 1980, 176). These form patterns are responsible for the fact that different people see different things, that is, perceive different meanings, from the same picture. These form patterns are what the mind uses to organize the visual stimuli into meaningful concepts. He later suggested that "a systematic investigation of the dimensional scales by which works of art vary would be a laborious but worthwhile contribution to the theory of style" (Arnheim 1980, 180).

Arnheim explains that global processes, as described by the work of the Gestalt psychologists and others, are in accord with what the creative arts considers four kinds of influence upon the "normal" *non*-artistic view: a) the Gestalt laws imposing the structurally simplest view upon perception; b) the memory of the "objective" shape, color, proportion, and size of things known to the observer from past experience; c) the conception suggested by the practical functions of the objects; and d) the manner of seeing and representing that prevails in the culture, especially in its visual arts (Arnheim 1966). Arnheim notes that this "normal" or typical view of objects is something the creative thinker (the artist) strives to get away from.

E. H. Gombrich (1969) also drew upon the concepts of cognitive psychology, and based his theories on the concept of schemata. Gombrich used the concept of a schema to explain how knowledge fills the gaps in a person's perception of a representation; as in the Gestalt principles, incomplete shapes are filled in by projections, and details can be dispensed with when the proper "mental set" exists. Gombrich believes that not only the perception, but the production of a work of art and its understanding are also schema based. He argues that the expression of shapes and colors is not absolute and can only be understood when the range of alternatives is known. Therefore, expression is limited by historically determined categories and further modified by the individual's own past. The mental sets created by a particular epoch are what make works of a particular style understandable to its contemporaries, and a work of art "comes to life" by meeting the needs and expectations of the period.

Other authors have presented related theories: Hochberg (1972) argued that most or all of visual perception also involves highly skilled sequential purposive behaviors and that some large component of the perceptual process in the adult is best understood in terms of the "expectations" and "maps" that underlie these skilled behaviors. North and Hargreaves (2000) discuss the debate concerning two contemporary major aesthetic theories, known as the arousal-mediating and cognitive-variable aesthetic theories. The arousal-mediating theory suggests a key role of "collative" variables, such as novelty or complexity, in the process of aesthetic evaluation. The cognitive-variable theory equates aesthetic evaluation with information processing demands, and suggests a key role for categorical variables, such as typicality or representativeness. North notes that empirical results supporting either theory may be somewhat dependent on the experimental stimuli employed and suggests that it is impossible to distinguish between the two classes of variables, as variations in arousal-mediating factors also reflect variations in cognitive factors. He suggests that both theories can make a useful contribution to the understanding of aesthetic processes and recommends a reconciliation of the two.

Aesthetic Variables and the Visual Experience

The research program initiated by Fechner lasted throughout the next century and continues today, with researchers investigating the nature of various aesthetic variables and their role in the perception and appreciation of art. These aesthetic variables may map directly to specific image attributes or may be comprised of several of them. Image attributes, as described in the art literature, are evaluated from the perspective of the contribution which each attribute makes to the total visual experience. Most discussions of these are framed within the Gestalt theory of perception, which holds that most phenomena of nature cannot be adequately described if they are analyzed piece by piece. Arnheim describes this perspective as an "artistic look at reality" (Arnheim 1974, vii). For images, perceptual attributes such as color, shape, and location are mutually determined by each other; changing any one of these qualities will change the nature of the perception of the others as well. Researchers have attempted to tease out the impact of combinations of variables in relation to broader aesthetic qualities.

Gardner (1970) defined style as the sum of the collative qualities of color, line, texture, shape, and composition that characterize a range of works by the same artist and remain discernible regardless of subject, dominant colors, size, or medium. The aesthetic attributes and their contribution to artistic style are the focus of much of the literature of art aesthetics, and the vocabulary addressing image attributes in this context can be somewhat abstract and specialized.

Specific aesthetic qualities are also frequently discussed in the literature of art from a variety of perspectives. For instance, Arnheim (1974) describes the qualities of *balance* (weight, motion); *shape* (part–whole); *form* (orientation, perspective, occlusion, ornament); *space* (figure–ground, depth); *light*; *color* (warmth, completion); and *movement* (direction). In the descriptions of these attributes, each one is noted as affecting others and is also sometimes described in terms of the others: for instance, light creates space and movement can determine balance. Supporting this is work on specific aesthetic variables, such as that of Lazreg and Mullet (2001) evaluating the pleasantness of form–color combinations. These researchers found that participants applied a complex rule in which the weight attributed to one element depends on the value of the other element, supporting a nonequal averaging combination rule. In other recent work, Katz (1999) investigated color contrast, in which the perceived color of an area is influenced by the surrounding colors. By modeling the receptive fields of double opponent cells (neural units which respond preferentially to one of the four opponent colors: blue, yellow, red, and green), results of the model agree with observations such as preference increasing with increasing saturation and complementary colors being in maximum harmony.

Crozier and Chapman (1984a) proposed that a cognitive orientation could move experimental aesthetics away from the narrow perspective it had often taken, using such measures as preference, liking, pleasingness, and interest to introduce a broader set of attributes or variables which may represent more salient constructs with which spectators confront art works. They felt that the cognitive approach also has potential to break down what had been a compartmentalization in the investigation of the perception of art. Research into cognition as well as into affective responses and social cognition holds possibilities for more integrated theories of the perception of art. Several examples discussed in the following sections will illustrate the problems investigated and the approaches taken in the last thirty years or so.[18]

More recently, interest in automating design has resulted in attempts to describe the specific components of design variables such as shape (degree of asymmetry, size), composition (symmetry of arrangements of objects), and physical properties (color, luminance), in relation to aesthetic principles such as balance, proportion, and so on (Pham 1999).

Impact of Development and Training

The aesthetic variables have been studied from the perspective of an individual's developmental stages or training in art (Danko-McGhee 2000; Wilson 1966). For instance, Wilson (1966) investigated whether specific types of training could alter subjects' reported perception of works of art. He researched the perception of paintings in relation to the aesthetic variables, on a "customary–aspective" continuum. He defines "customary" as denoting simple recognition, whereas "aspective" denotes attention towards a number of qualities and aspects which characterize a work of art. Although Wilson drew upon responses by students to formulate some initial categories, he developed the main part of the taxonomy introspectively, "by deliberate speculation about how individuals might respond to works of art. This speculation was based on the inquirer's experience as an artist and art instructor. The establishment of one category often suggested other related categories" (Wilson 1966, 54–55). While the taxonomy was further tested with subjects, Wilson's final criterion was that it be consistent with existing theories of perception and knowledge of works of art, specifically such factors as medium, technique, design, meaning, and function.

Wilson's research resulted in the creation of a two-part classification scheme, one part of which treated "individual response mode categories," broken down into ten sublevels for the purposes of evaluating responses as aspective or customary, and one which treated "aspects of paintings categories." A somewhat judgmental approach emerges in many of Wilson's taxonomic codes: "Anecdote is considered a customary response since telling stories about what is suggested by the paintings is a generally naive mode of viewing paintings which reflects an insular approach to perception of paintings" (Wilson 1966, 62). Wilson reports coding results for verbal responses to twentieth-century paintings for subjects ranging in age from elementary school through college. He notes that there were no occurrences of many of the codes relating to "aspects of paintings." His analysis shows a strong peak at *literal*, a smaller peak at *qualitative*, and much smaller peaks at *anecdote*, *analogy*, *shape*, *color*, and *total character*. Wilson's data demonstrated an increase in *symbolic* with age of subjects. He notes that the remaining categories were either not used at all or used at about the same extent across all subjects. Overall, Wilson found that art training had little significant impact upon subjects' image descriptions, therefore presumably little impact on their perception or understanding.

Hekkert and van Wieringen (1996) investigated the effect of manipulating twelve Post-Impressionist paintings along two dimensions: degree of realism (figurative versus abstract) and color versus black-and-white. In contrast to Wilson, they found that art training lessened the negative impacts of increasing abstraction and changing a color image to black and white. Furnham and Walker (2001) also found that art education and frequency of visits to art galleries were linked to positive ratings of abstract paintings. Other research has investigated whether training can influence perceptual understanding. For instance, Miller's (1997) work demonstrates that training does not influence the magnitude of perceived depth but that experience and orientation do. When an apex of radiating perspective lines are at the top of an image, subjects perceive greater depth and size of a pictorially far stimulus.

In other work, Goude (1972) investigated factors that accounted for the majority of similarity perceived among eight works of art presented to students. Using a factor analytical method, he found six primary factors (such as "nature's lyric tranquility") which were all somewhat correlated between the groups. These six factors were grouped into three factor pairs: *emotion*, *motif*, and *composition*. A second study with children in four different age groups (using the same images and methodology) found similar results. The data suggest that the emotion and composition factor pairs remain relatively stable across age (possibly increasing somewhat) while the motif factor increases with age. Similar work by other researchers used a semantic differential based on forty-three adjective pairs to explore the dimensions upon which works of art and music are classified (Ruth and Kolehmainen 1974). Their analysis revealed six factors: 1) aesthetic–qualitative evaluation; 2) emotional tone; 3) symbolism; 4) dynamics; 5) clarity; and 6) stillness. The experimental results accorded well with the results of Goude, in particular a strong emotional tone factor and similarity of their aesthetic–qualitative evaluation factor with Goude's motif factor.

The Visual Aesthetic Sensitivity Test (VAST) is used to evaluate aesthetic sensitivity. Researchers tested children and adults and examined the influence of age, sex, personality, intelligence, and artistic training on VAST scores (Frois and Eysenck 1995). VAST scores only increased up to age fourteen; sex, IQ, personality, and artistic training had little or no effect on VAST scores, leading the researchers to conclude that the VAST is measuring an unknown "something" related to visual aesthetic sensitivity.

Freeman puts forth a framework theory of pictorial reasoning, in which relations among the picture, the artist, the world, and the beholder must be understood before children can become art critics in middle childhood, when they are able to understand the ability of the artist to realize his intentions, as well as the significance of a work of art within a social context and for individuals (Freeman 1995). Freeman and Parsons (2001) note that it takes an extended period of time for learners to work out a theory of art, and that such a theory remains intuitive and largely unarticulated for most people. In related work, Leontiev (2000) investigates nine factors in three categories involved in the perception of art: characteristics of the person viewing the art, factors relating to the work of art itself, and factors characterizing the background against which interaction between the recipient and the work takes place.

Other Factors

Other recent work related to style attempts to evaluate the relationship of personality types to reactions to specific styles of art. Furnham and Walker (2001) investigated personality and ratings of abstract art, pop art, and representational paintings. Regression analyses showed that personality and demographic variables accounted for about a fifth of the variance, and personality variables were most strongly linked to positive judgment of representational art and least related to ratings of pop art. Other work reinforces the theory that personality dimensions such as *sensation seeking* and *openness* influence aesthetic judgment (Rawlings, Barrantes Vidal, and Furnham 2000), but work investigating preference for surreal art did not find strong associations between personality dimensions and preferences, suggesting that narrower measures of personality may be better predictors (Furnham and Avison 1997).

The question of hemispheric specialization in the creation and perception of artwork is another area of research within the psychology of art. Heller reviews the effects of brain damage on artists' abilities to create spatial representations or detail (Heller 1994). In work with realistic and surrealistic paintings, Zaidel (1989) found that the left hemisphere seems to be involved in recognition and processing of surrealistic or metaphoric items, suggesting a left-hemispheric advantage in processing meaningful but incongruous arrays. Heller (1994) suggests that spatial organization of picture elements by an artist depends upon the creator's mood (and thus the active brain hemisphere) at the time of image creation.

Researchers investigating cultural effects found a significant effect of reading habits on aesthetic preference, with left-to-right readers (French) showing a preference for stimuli with a rightward directionality while right-to-left readers (Israeli) preferred stimuli with a leftward directionality (Chokron and De Agostini 2000). These effects had previously been accounted for by cerebral dominance; these findings suggest a possible interaction between this and culture.

Specific Variables

Researchers have also investigated the occurrence of specific components, such as composition, and their relation to aesthetic appeal. One area of interest to a number of researchers is the psychological investigation of the "golden ratio" (or golden section), a ratio which is supposedly more pleasing at certain values.[19] Recent research into the golden ratio has demonstrated that, in fact, among established artists and sculptors, the proportion of 1:2 and not the golden ratio was the overall ratio of choice (Macrosson and Stewart 1997). Hoge and

Konecni both found no preference for the golden section (Hoge 1997; Konecni 1997). Green (1995) suggests that there are real psychological effects associated with the golden section, but these are relatively sensitive to careless methodological practices. Other research has found overall population agreement in object placement in relation to the golden section, but wide inter-individual variability; these authors relate these results to categorization processes and propose a cognitive model of "sensory aesthetics," in which continua of any type are described categorically, with fuzzy boundaries (McManus and Weatherby 1997).

Work focusing on classical portrait composition demonstrated a significant preference for the left side of the face in single-subject portraits across media, authorship, and five centuries of portrait work (Conesa, Brunold-Conesa, and Miron 1995). This is viewed as consistent with right-hemisphere activation models in attentional bias and perception of emotion. Effects of pose have also been studied by Zaidel and Tyler (Tyler 1998; Zaidel and Fitzgerald 1994). Tyler found that data from portraits over the past 2,000 years quantify that one eye is centered with a standard deviation of less than +/– 5% relative to the canvas frame; since classical texts on composition do not mention eye positioning as such, Tyler suggests that its manifestation throughout the centuries and varieties of artistic styles must be guided by unconscious perceptual processes.

Some researchers suggest that stimuli are pleasing if they are closely tuned to the properties of the human visual system. Latto and others used Mondrian's paintings to demonstrate a stronger preference for pictures presented so that their component lines are horizontal and vertical rather than pictures presented with their component lines in an oblique orientation (Latto, Brain, and Kelly 2000). Other recent work suggests, however, that human visual preferences are determined by both objective structural regularities of image stimuli and a learned subjective interpretation of the image (Rentschler and others 1999). This research attempts to distinguish between visual recognition of image signals whose characteristics best fit innate brain and neural mechanisms and learned components (category learning) of human visual preference. The data indicate there may be two determinants of preference judgments: complexity and bilateral symmetry. The complexity factor varied with object knowledge acquired through category learning, while symmetry was unaffected by learning experience. Using computer simulations, the authors theorize that the preference for pattern complexity relies on active (top-down) processes of visual recognition, and the preference for pattern symmetry relies on automatic (bottom-up) processes.

Other work related to this investigated the effect of dimension and unpredictability on aesthetic preferences for patterns (Aks and Sprott 1996). Using mathematical measures of dimension and unpredictability, this research indicated that preferred patterns had measures that corresponded to many natural objects. A preliminary test of individual differences (creative versus scientific personality) in preferences showed further investigation may be in order.

Aesthetic Variables and Emotion

Within experimental aesthetics, other more abstract and affective concepts are also discussed in relation to the aesthetic variables: balance conveys meaning, perspective is related to symbolism, light is particularly symbolic, and color is strongly emotive (red is exciting because it connotes fire and blood; blue is cooling).[20] This literature discusses pictorial image elements (such as objects and their surroundings) extensively in terms of meaning and affect.

For instance, Takahashi (1995) investigated the relationship of line and form to specific expressive words. Subjects produced nonpictorial drawings in response to seven expressive terms (anger, joy, tranquility, depression, human energy, femininity, and illness) and to one term of their own choosing. He then had another group of subjects choose which pictures represented the terms, with a good level of agreement. Analysis of the structural characteristics found similar types of lines used for particular emotions, such as circles and circular forms for joy, curving, descending lines for depression, and horizontal lines for tranquility. Takahashi proposes that texture and rhythm, rather than shape, are responsible for the effect of the drawings, as texture provides an indication of how the line was drawn, and spatial rhythm introduces a dynamic component.

There has been a particular interest in the impact of color on emotion or arousal, beginning with Itten's color theory, which characterizes colors by objective color principles and subjective feelings (Itten 1970; Itten 1973). The objective visual principles are based on hue (the color itself), luminance (brightness of the color), and saturation ("how much" color). Twelve fundamental colors are divided into three groups: primary (yellow, red, blue); complementary (orange, green, purple); and tertiary (six colors obtained by linearly combining primary and complementary colors). Each of these fundamental colors can vary through five levels of luminance and three levels of saturation, resulting in a total of 180 colors. Subjective feelings are associated with different sets of colors, such as warm (yellow through red–purple) and cold (yellow–green through purple). Runge (1810; 1973) later arranged these into a chromatic sphere, in which perceptually contrasting colors are arranged on opposite sides of the sphere. These contrasts are of four types (warm–cold, light–dark, saturated–unsaturated, and contrasts of pure colors), and these contrasts correspond to expressive qualities of the color groups.

Itten provides many intuitively appealing illustrations supporting his ideas, and authors such as Chijiwa (1987) have utilized color combinations to express qualities such as *striking*, *feminine*, *natural*, *exciting*, *tranquil*, and *surprising*. Researchers have also attempted to provide an empirical basis for these color–emotion theories. Valdez and Mehrabian (1994) investigated emotional reactions to color hue, saturation, and brightness using the pleasure–arousal–

dominance emotion model. They found that subjects exhibited strong and consistent emotional effects for saturation and brightness. Subjects found blue, blue-green, green, red-purple, purple, and purple-blue to be the most pleasant; yellow and green-yellow were the least pleasant. Other effects were found for arousal and dominance. Hemphill (1996) showed that bright colors elicit mainly positive emotional associations, and dark colors elicit mainly negative associations, with gender differences.

Taylor (2001) found that color influenced test subjects' responses to original artworks and various types of reproductions in three ways. He found that (based upon subjects' self-reports using Likert scales), for color pictures (versus black-and-white reproductions), subjects were able to identify feelings and emotions more easily, experienced more intense feelings, and perceived the ability of the color format to convey feeling and emotion. However, his research did not find statistical differences in the mean number of terms assigned to images in different formats by the subjects.

Color preferences have been investigated in cross-cultural contexts. For instance, Saito (1996b) compared color preferences in Japan, China, and Indonesia and found that there were statistically significant differences in preferences for colors of certain hues and tones for each country, but a high preference for white for all areas. Saito (1996a) also found that color preference could be influenced by differences in age and sex, as well as geographical region.

Blank and others, using abstract paintings to remove their subjects' ability to rely on literal or content-oriented reasoning in assigning expressive dimensions to the work, found that young children perceive expression in visual art as do adults. For instance, they found that for pre-school-age children "yellow is happy, violet is sad, thick lines are loud, thin ones are quiet" (Blank and others 1984, 129–131). They propose that shapes are expressive because they are suggestive of postures associated with specific moods; therefore, a drooping form mimics a sagging posture that may be associated with sadness.

Presentation attributes have been found to affect viewers' emotional responses to pictures. In work investigating the effects of size and motion, image size positively affected the arousal of emotional responses, and large images elicited stronger feelings of arousal than the same pictures seen as small images (Detenber and Reeves 1996). Interestingly, the still versions of the images generated more arousal than the moving pictures; the authors suggest that the still images invited interpretation, and speculation and elaboration of the meaning of the picture led to greater arousal.

Affect of images has been investigated in relation to other specific types of variables as well. Avital and Cupchick (1998) had subjects rate paintings on collative (complexity, disorder) and affective (pleasingness, interestingness, tension, and power) scales. Affective ratings were tied to complexity but not to disorder. Marshall and Thornhill (1995) studied judgment of artistic quality in photographs using twenty-one combinations of pose and affect to determine the influence of novelty of pose and effect of facial expression. Subjects rated each photograph as to whether it exhibited qualities of good art and/or good photography. While subjects used the same dimensions to judge artistic and photographic merit, there were differences between the two ratings.

While the investigation of the relationships of specific aesthetic variables to the aesthetic experience continues, the field of the psychology of art is somewhat hampered by its lack of consistency in terminology, as well as by the variety of theoretical approaches and multiple goals. Nevertheless, research demonstrates that some variables such as color and line clearly have impact (although that impact may also be culturally mediated). One contribution of the psychology of art is in its elegant expression of concepts (such as "gestalt") in ways that are understandable and have direct relevance to nonspecialists. An additional contribution is the acknowledgment of the affective experience in viewing pictorial materials.

Summary

There are many unanswered questions concerning human image perception, understanding, and memory. Research is difficult to compare and evaluate not only because of the unsettled nature of theory and the number of hypotheses put forward for testing, but also because of the multiplicity of research designs and experimental methods. Theory remains fragmented and sometimes contentious and at this point offers little firm guidance or insight into the nature of human–image interactions. A visual image is decomposed into primitive elements such as color, motion, orientation, depth, contrast, and spatial resolution; then shape and spatial relations are extracted and primitive features are assembled into larger objects and scenes. Elements that share the same information are grouped together perceptually and grouping mechanisms override their individual constituents, whether of shape, size, color, or motion. Visual and contextual organizational principles appear to operate to organize parts of a picture and both seem critical in processing and understanding images, yet it is not clear what the order of precedence is, or if these visual and contextual operations can operate independently.

Eye-tracking experiments have been used to record eye movements. While results are difficult to interpret, and no hypothesis testing has occurred, fixations occur in specific areas which could be considered highly informative, and these correlate with both the Gestalt principles and experimental results supporting the roles of various image features in image memory:

- "Compositional" elements
- Humans, animals
- Areas of detail

- Areas of motion
- Areas of contrast, contours
- A "central portion" of the image
- Areas considered to be of "low predictability"

Additionally, research into image memory indicates that features which are remembered include:

- Unfamiliar features
- Detached details, if distinctive

Memory, however, degrades some aspects of images:

- Feature placement and orientation
- Picture details (schema normal)

And enhances some others:

- Object or feature elaboration
- Unfamiliar components transformed to conventional representations
- Expansion beyond the picture boundary

Color seems to be important, yet memory for colors is one of the most difficult memory tasks to achieve, and humans recognize and name only about a dozen color terms. Yet color is emotive and associated with specific affective states. Color also appears to direct attention, which increases the chance that an object will be consciously processed.

While it may be difficult to come up with inclusive definitions of phrases such as "area of motion" or "area of detail," or "distinctiveness" (determined by line, color, composition, texture, or any of a number of other factors), nevertheless these are intuitively recognizable aspects of images.

The Gestalt principles offer some guidance in assessing what areas of an image are critical, yet context, task, and meaning associated with interpretive processes also affect what is perceived by an individual when looking at a picture. In the perception of an image, both the physical and semantic relations of objects are important, and affect the interpretation. Expectations play a large role, and items inconsistent with expectations (items of low predictability) appear to be highly informative and perceived and remembered. Information theory posits that areas of high redundancy contain little information, and the experimental results discussed indicate that the most highly informative areas are at points of change.

Research indicates that spatial and schematic information also play a role in image representation and memory, with subjects displaying good memory for the spatial location of objects positioned in an array and for the quadrant in which a picture is placed. However, spatial and other relationships have been neglected in image indexing. Even when visual content is indexed, objects and attributes are generally represented only in list form, with neither structural, functional, nor semantic relationships of the objects indicated. This is similar to textual keyword indexing in which no proximity, adjacency, or other semantic relationships are specified.

Barry (1997) emphasizes the importance of motion detection, which evolved from Gibson's *ecological optics* theory and also Johansson's (1976) theory of visual motion perception as a key to "event perception." Changes in the visual field demand our attention, and movement reveals form and separates figure from ground. Motion perception is critical to survival and the visual system has evolved to alert us to the detection of events. Thus, action or implied motion in images, as well as in the environment, is detected.

This review of research in cognitive psychology presents evidence suggesting that a number of different image attributes and relationships interact in the process of perceiving, understanding, and remembering an image: the visual content, the objects represented, their functions and their relationships to each other, the overall context of the image and the viewer, and the "meanings" associated with the image. Thus, it would appear that the utility of the standard approach to image indexing—listing of specific image features in isolation both from one another and from a set of larger contexts within which these attributes operate—may be hampered by a too narrowly focused or decontextualized approach. Just as "bird features" need a "bird structure" to be recognized as belonging to a bird, so perhaps image features need a supporting "image structure" before the image can be unambiguously recognized.

The totality of an image does indeed go beyond the sum of its parts. As Barry notes:

> Neurologically all images are by nature gestalts, made up of fragments of visual experience processed modularly and then coordinated through perceptual process into what Walter Lippmann called "pictures in our heads." They are stories, always implying more than their parts, always in process and actively seeking meaning (Barry 1997, 69).

Notes

1. For reviews of these, see Hendee (1993); Humphreys (1989).
2. Again, this is another topic for which there are a number of relevant discussions; see, for instance, Gibson (1971).
3. For a detailed discussion of the first three, see Hagen (1980).
4. For a recent overview, see Springer and Deutsch (1998).
5. An interesting overview of theories of preattentive processing can be found at www.csc.ncsu.edu/faculty/healey/PP/ (accessed on May 17, 2002).
6. For an excellent historical overview of the development of theories of

texture perception, see Bergen (1991).

7. For a detailed and clear discussion of these theories, see Kehrer and Meinecke (1996).

8. Other research also shows that perceived texture density of a texture patch depends on the density of the surrounding texture (Durgin 2001).

9. Random House Unabridged Dictionary, 2nd ed., 1993.

10. These principles are beautifully illustrated at a psychology website from Macalester College in St. Paul, Minnesota: www.macalester.edu/~psych/whathap/UBNRP/aesthetics/perception.html (accessed on April 18, 2003).

11. See also the discussion in Chapter Four concerning the Fourier transform.

12. For more information, see www.hp.ufl.edu/csea/ (accessed on April 17, 2003).

13. For a detailed discussion, see Henderson and Hollingworth (1998).

14. For a discussion on the possible effects of culture on these processes, see Mishra (1997).

15. The cross-cultural study of emotional behavior is a complex topic. For an in-depth discussion, which raises a number of questions about assumptions made in this research, see Mesquita, Frijda, and Scherer (1997).

16. See Gould (1976), however, for a different set of results.

17. A second group concerned with pictorial perception treats the psychology of art and the aesthetic experience from a philosophical viewpoint. For a useful overview of both, see Takahashi (1995).

18. An excellent bibliography on visual communication by Sandra Moriarty can be found at spot.colorado.edu/~moriarts/vcbiblio.html (accessed on April 20, 2003).

19. For instance, see contents of the issues of the journal, *Empirical Studies of the Arts*, www.ume.maine.edu/~iaea/esaabstr.html (accessed on April 17, 2003).

20. Goodman (1972) makes the point that all art makes use of symbols and that the relevant question should be "When is art?" as it is the context of the artwork that determines the meaning of the symbols. This can be extended to "When is image?" with the understanding that objects can become symbols or lose their symbolic meaning depending on such factors as epoch, culture, and subjective experience.

Chapter 3

Organizing and Providing Access to Images

Throughout their history, description of visual materials has taken place largely through the traditional methods of indexing and classification within "practical" settings such as libraries, museums, and archives, where the need for access to and use of images is often immediate and tied to particular tasks of the user community, such as teaching or research. This community of practice historically has been the main arena in which indexing and classification systems for images have been developed, and the major tools used by professionals often reflect this practical orientation. Only recently have researchers conducted empirical research into users' queries and moved towards developing theoretical bases for the development of these tools.

One major impetus for this research is the immense number of digital images becoming accessible through networked access to collections. Durran notes that the average university teaching collection holds between 100,000 and 500,000 items, with digital technology holding promise for increased access of these. (Durran 1997). However, there are many barriers to this access, including the problems of conversion of materials, copyright and licensing, and intellectual access. This chapter focuses on the last of these, current approaches to intellectual access.

The standard image indexing or classification process consists of assigning a set of descriptors derived from a variety of vocabulary tools, following various guidelines for the choice and application of these terms. In addition, a uniform, standardized structure to organize these descriptors is needed. While a number of these structures have been in existence for quite some time, the term "metadata" is now widely used to refer to this type of structured information.[1] Even though this term has gained in popularity in relation to networked information (specifically the Internet and the World Wide Web), this "new" concept predates the Web environment.

Within the topic of intellectual access to images, there are several major topics discussed in this chapter. The first major section of this chapter discusses systems used to describe, organize, and facilitate access to images. The second section discusses the theoretical basis for the process of assigning descriptors to images. The third section summarizes empirical research into users, queries, and the searching process. The final section gives an overview of the image attributes addressed by these three areas.

Systems for Image Description

As alluded to above, there are three major components of image description: 1) the major tools used to derive image descriptors; 2) rules for the application of these descriptors; and 3) the metadata structures that carry them. More succinctly, these are often referred to as:

Data *value* tools, which provide the terminology used in cataloging, indexing, and documentation practice

Data *content* tools, which determine the form and choice of terminology

Data *structure* tools, which provide the structures that carry the terminology

Therefore, indexing and classification are processes in which image attributes are described. These processes employ data value tools and data content tools to produce descriptors, terms assigned to the image to describe its attributes. Data structure tools, which themselves can have an impact on indexing and classification processes, organize descriptors into a framework. An additional type of tool is a data *communication* tool, used for sharing information between data structures.

Data Value Tools: Terms for the Description of Images

According to Childress, the motivations for indexing and classification of images fall into "two not always easily separable categories: the need for physical control and the need for intellectual control" (Childress 1996, 88). Physical control (handling, storage, inventory, security) may be served by inventory-level records, while intellectual control (aimed at supporting retrieval) involves the application of one or more vocabularies or systems of subject analysis. This chapter will focus on the need for intellectual control of and access to visual materials.

There are several types of tools currently used to provide intellectual access to images. Terminology for indexing is most often derived from controlled vocabularies, lists of preferred terms. The use of such controlled vocabulary is necessary because natural language is not necessarily precise and orderly; multiple meanings for words exist, and homonyms and synonyms occur frequently. The process of indexing or classification consists of determining a subject or concept in the item to be represented and choosing an appropriate term or descriptor for this from a controlled vocabulary.

It should be noted that in the literature concerned with the retrieval of images through textual term assignment, "indexing," "classification," and cataloging may all be used informally to refer to the processes of assigning descriptors. As Chan explains, classifications, subject heading lists, and thesauri are vocabulary structuring tools which control the basic vocabulary of a subject index language by stipulating terms that may be used in the classing or indexing of documents and by displaying semantic relationships among these terms. Subject indexing is defined in a generalized sense, as "the indication of the theme or topic of any document, indeed any retrieval artifact, by any meaningful string of alphanumeric characters" (Chan, Richmond, and Svenonius 1985, xii–xiv).

The author, after Kaiser, takes as the common basis of these activities the "reduction of literature to a smaller compass," or in more modern terms, the reduction of *information* to a smaller compass (Kaiser 1985, 305).[2] While the processes of reduction can differ (elimination, selection, concentration, recapitulation, analysis), the goal remains the same, the creation of a succinct surrogate for an item. Therefore, following the literature concerned with image indexing and retrieval, the terms "index," "classify," and "catalog" will be used interchangeably, reflecting the specific document author's original language and intent. It should also be noted, however, that in a continuum from classification to indexing, the general movement is towards increased term specificity and granularity of access.

A wide range of vocabulary tools exists for generating descriptive terms for images; these include subject heading lists, thesauri, classification schemes, and controlled vocabularies. As noted above, these names are not always used with precision, and a particular tool may be referred to by more than one term. The following discussion loosely groups these tools by type (please note that these groupings are not prescriptive but are for descriptive purposes only).

Early Subject Heading Systems

Subject heading lists provide a set of controlled terms for subject access; they can be quite broad but their hierarchies are typically shallow, and their consistency, depth, and breadth can vary considerably both within and across individual systems. Historically, subject headings for images were the concern of picture librarianship and arose from the need to establish an easily understood and predictable *physical* place for each slide, photograph, or other visual item within a manual filing system. One of the earliest was *The Picture Collection: Subject Headings*, first published in 1910 as part of *The Picture Collection* by John Cotton Dana (as described by Dane 1968). Although slide collections were in existence by the 1880s, slide and picture librarians had few resources to draw upon through the first half of the twentieth century.

The motivation behind many of these cataloging schemes, as mentioned above, was purely pragmatic, and there was little reliance upon any theoretical approach to classification. Often the impetus for codifying these schemes in print form was the realization that the knowledge used to organize extensive picture collections (such as those at Newark Public Library or Hunter College) resided with one person in a particular setting and could not easily be transmitted to new personnel, should the need arise (Gilbert 1973). Subject access within a manual system is constrained by limitations on the size of the system and its components; therefore multiple access points were very limited in these early systems.

A survey of these early guides reveals a variety of approaches, even within a single system. These systems offered no or few scope notes and were an eclectic mix of subject, iconography, time period, geographical or ethnic–cultural association, and various other access points. The schemes ranged from the seemingly very simple, with only nine major headings (Evans), to more complex ones (Green) in which a heading such as "nature" (a single main heading in Evans) was broken into two main headings, depending on whether nature was "wild" or "domesticated" (Evans 1980; Green 1984). Dane (1968) noted that contemporary sociological interests also should be accommodated.

They also varied in complexity of term assignment; some required an expert level of cataloging (Green) while others required only a rough identification of the object (Hill 1975). Level and consistency of specificity was another major problem. One collection was described as containing "over 100,000 pictures under the two headings, Painters and Portraits, which may be broadly interpreted to include the homes, family, and documents relating to a particular individual," yet also contained a detailed list of "major" islands (Dane 1968, v, 52–56).

Many of these early systems were "data-up" systems, where indexing starts with the contents of the collection, and subject headings are derived from existing items. The attitude towards assigning terms in these early picture classification systems was primarily one of flexibility. In addition to the nature of the collection, the characteristics of the users were a major consideration in deciding how to catalog a picture and how to determine such factors as subdivision of topics, order of presentation of hierarchical classification structures, cross referencing, and formality or informality of nomenclature (Evans notes that an "ad hoc system" is a contradiction in terms) (Evans 1980, 63). Current systems developed for specific collections still share this pragmatic, collection- and user-centered focus (Schroeder 1998, 63).

However, even with the development of these subject heading lists, there was little to insure the consistent application of terms to pictures. Because of their variability in approaches and depth, even with the assistance of these early guides, much knowledge about access to these particular collections resided with the staff in charge of the collections, and multiple access points were an impossibility.

Many library collections, desiring to standardize access to all formats in an automated environment, have relied on the more general *Library of Congress Subject Headings* (*LCSH*) and the *Anglo-American Cataloging Rules 2* (*AACR2*, discussed below) for consistent rules by which to apply subject terms to graphic materials. However, both of these tools pose many problems for visual materials cataloging and are frequent topics of discussion at conferences held by professional societies such as the Art Libraries Society of North America (ARLIS) and the Visual Resources Association (VRA). For instance, the inadequacies of *LCSH* for subject access were discussed at the 1998 Joint VRA–ARLIS Cataloging Problems Discussion Group.[3] Depth of indexing and different levels of access, from specialized (iconography) to broad subject coverage, are consistent problems encountered in trying to use *LCSH*, as is the need to provide both collection-level and individual-item access and indicate whole–part relationships within a work. A more general problem is the limitations imposed on cataloging when record size is an immediate concern.

Classification Systems

The primary purpose of classification systems has been to organize physical collections. A classification system is similar to a subject headings list in that it provides broad subject access. It also typically uses some kind of hierarchical arrangement and employs a numeric or alphabetic notation useful in the physical arrangement of materials. Classification systems lack the explicit relationships typical of a thesaurus.

Wendell W. Simons and Luraine C. Tansey created one of the earliest generalized systems for slide classification at the University of California.[4] Developed in an academic setting, the classification was designed to be general enough to encompass the subject matter of all academic disciplines and support a historical, cultural approach to teaching, as well as to be easily browsable. The system classes all pictorial materials into three broad categories: history, art, and science.

Simons and Tansey based their system on their stated belief that "the possible range of visual content is simply not as broad as the range of verbal content in books" and that "emotions, thoughts, concepts, imagination, speculations . . . cannot become the visual content of a picture" (Simons and Tansey 1970, 3). The indexing should therefore be based on specific visual content, presumably a more objective approach, rather than on subjectively determined intellectual content. Additionally, an emphasis on historical context, or time and place, is given precedence over subject matter, reflecting a basic focus in the use of pictorial materials in an academic institution. Because of the restricted range of access provided by this system, the number of terms is limited to less than 100.

A desire for standard access, especially in a networked environment, also prompted the development and adoption of the MARC (machine readable cataloging) visual arts format (discussed below).

Art Object Information

While the cataloging of picture collections has historically been the province of librarians, the art history and museum communities focus on pictures or images as objects in their own right (as cultural heritage) or as surrogates for art or museum objects. Art/museum object cataloging serves a variety of purposes, including management of inventory and documentation of provenance (Ohlgren 1980; Stam 1989). As these objects are often fragile, images of them are often used as their surrogates to reduce wear and tear on the objects themselves. A pervasive problem for art object image description is the need to distinguish between the item depicted and the surrogate; this has been greatly exacerbated by the presence of digital items and collections.[5]

For art object description, most art-oriented classification systems have followed a basic hierarchical structure starting with medium, then subdivided by period, country, geographical or cultural area, artist, and subject or type of object. Many of these were developed in academic settings and are still used today. Some examples of institutions using these art-oriented classification systems are:

The Art Institute of Chicago[6]
Metropolitan Museum of Art[7]
Visual Resources Library, Vassar College[8]
National Gallery of Art Slide Gallery[9]
Princeton University[10]

Stam (1989) summarizes factors contributing to the difficulty of cataloging collections of images of art objects: the uniqueness of materials in art collections; the vast numbers and extremely wide variety of items to be cataloged; the dilemma of whether to catalog individual items belonging to a larger group; the lack of standards; the lack of a theoretical foundation for cataloging; the diversity in output desired; and the proprietary attitude towards research data held by many museum curators. In addition, each item may be subject to not only multiple interpretations, but the assignment of even basic access points such as "creator" can be contentious and fraught with difficulties. Durran (1997) notes that traditional classification schemes are beleaguered with recent developments broadening the scope of art history to include more emphasis on non-Western art, popular art, and visual culture, in addition to theoretical approaches encompassing feminism, Marxism, semiotics, and psychoanalysis.

Within the last several decades, the museum community has actively pursued the application of computers to the representation, storage, and retrieval of art object images and information. However, this community began its efforts lacking in some of the basic tenets of the library world, including a tradition of cooperative cataloging and a common classification scheme within which to work. Oldal (1996) comments: "No institution in the art world has the hegemony that the Library of Congress has in the book world." While the notion of shared cataloging by participating in national library-type networks appears to offer many advantages, Stam (1996) points out that the economies-of-scale argument is harder to apply to archival and museum visual resource collections.

There is also a distinct division between those who feel that images are so different from text items that there can be no similarity in methods for providing access (a school of thought that has given rise to many of the specialized indexing schemes) and those who feel that a single set of rules based on conditions of authorship can be satisfactorily applied to all materials (Shatford 1984). One attempt at solving the problem of standardized access is to use existing sets of tools such as *LCSH*, *AACR2*, and MARC format. Tools created primarily for the text world, however, create multiple problems for those attempting to describe art objects, often resulting in incomplete or imprecise description of these objects. There is no "title page," and basic information such as creator, date, and title may be missing. Even what the object *is* must often be painstakingly researched, preferably by someone with extensive scholarly knowledge of the subject area. Thus, records (especially older ones) containing art object and cultural artifact information may contain a higher level of interpretation and subjectivity than records for textual items.

For those concerned with art object information, such imprecision is not acceptable. Additionally, different types of collections, such as abstract art or medieval manuscript illuminations, also seem to require vastly different approaches. Early high hopes for interinstitutional cooperation in the creation of large shared databases of art object information decreased as the multiplicity of institutional purposes became evident. These factors resulted in a lack of motivation to communicate beyond the boundaries of a single institution with a resultant lack of interinstitutional similarity among data records. Among these records, different categories of information are recorded, different fields exist for the same type of item, and unique rules of entry and idiosyncratic choice and form of words for fields have all contributed to the insularity of such collection descriptions.

At the 1996 Visual Resources Association conference, Kessler noted:

> The notion of shared cataloging has taken on an almost talismanic value for the visual resources profession. We gather at meetings such as this, extol its virtues, urge its necessity, and then return to our own institutions to continue isolated, local cataloging practices much as we had before. The implicit redundancy of our cataloging efforts has been a chronic irritant, but as long as these efforts were applied to slides tucked away in physically discrete collections, such irritation was largely conceptual (Kessler 1996).

Another author has aptly noted that "at a very basic level, libraries have seen themselves as repositories of shared items; archives and museums, as repositories of unique items," and states that "the larger process continues to be typified by factionalism, a lack of imperative for change, and, ultimately, the absence of any entirely satisfactory solutions to the problems of access" (Taylor 1996, 17). The museum community thus came to the uncomfortable recognition that one single cataloging method could not fulfill the varied needs of the institutions concerned with art historical or object information.

More recent attempts at solving this problem have focused on the varied terminology used for description of art objects and initiatives for developing standards for the exchange of electronic data between museums. However, the quest for precision in description still hampers access in many ways. For instance, in the implementation of the Art Image Browser at the University of Michigan, categories of information which would be useful to general users (such as stylistic period) could not be applied because of disagreement among experts as to date ranges of periods and whether an art object is characteristic of a particular style (Frost 1996). In addition, verification of data was time-consuming, and such efforts would not be possible for large image collections. Frost categorized this as the conflict between "getting it perfect" and the user's simply "getting it," and notes that "it still remains to be seen if a middle ground between expert classification and no classification can be found in the process of determination of categories to enable users to browse image sets" (Frost 1996, 187). A similar sentiment is echoed by Fry, who also questions the notion of "correct form" in relation to "findability," and suggests that limited time and resources would be better spent in putting in many words and phrases rather than laboring to produce "a few properly verified and expressed ones, particularly since so many of our potential users know little except the almost random nature of cyber searching" (Fry 1998, 52).

Others, such as Stam (1996), have argued that in the networked environment of the Web, the development of a flexible front end for retrieval is more important than conformity to cataloging standards. She notes that in a borderless community, there is no homogeneity among the needs and viewpoints of users. She argues for preserving unique information in local records through collection-level cataloging rather than aspiring to a single metacatalog, with access through an overlay of metadata. This is the approach currently being adopted in projects such as Van Eyck and metadata efforts (discussed below).

However, even with advances in these projects, access to image collections will remain limited to specific user communities. Durran (1997) discusses the impact that copyright has had and will have on image libraries and notes that the emergence of the multimedia industry targeting education and the arts will lead to restrictions on access and usage (as indeed it has). Many institutions are instituting image projects which only run on local machines or which are accessible only on campus networks, protected by passwords or other means. Thus, the promise that Stam saw in the Web—that of being an efficient, cheap, and technologically powerful form of mass distribution for image collections—may be fading.

The Thesaurus Approach

Another approach to the task of classification and retrieval of images is the use of a thesaurus structure rather than a list of subject headings. As Svenonius explains, "A thesaurus is foremost a system of logical and semantic relationships" (Svenonius 1984, 35). The primary purpose of a thesaurus is to assist users in seeking information, and it does this by making explicit the relationship of a term to other terms. Standard relationships in a thesaurus include hierarchical "genus–species" relationships (the IS-A relationship, represented by broader and narrower term designations such as BT and NT), associative relationships (related terms or RT) which specify terms that may be related in any number of ways to the entry term, and synonymy (USE and USE FOR). A special type of relationship is the PART-OF relationship, which is only used in certain cases. The use of the word "thesaurus," however, is quite variable, and tools which do not follow the standard rules for thesaurus construction may be referred to as thesauri as well (for example, see the discussion on the *LCTGM*, below).

Svenonius notes that, in creating thesauri for visual materials, the language of art is particularly problematic because it is rich in synonymy, and shades of meaning are sometimes considered critical, necessitating the incorporation of linguistic diversity. Determining warrant for usage is complex; no one term may be dominant, and different specialties may prefer different terms. Another more serious problem for art thesaurus design concerns the description of objects of material culture. When thesauri are constructed from documents of a particular domain, literary warrant limits the number of terms that normally occur. However, in a thesaurus concerned with material culture, the number of objects needing description is potentially limitless. A faceted approach can limit the number of terms, but limiting compound terms can also limit hierarchical structure. Any term that recurs frequently can cause unacceptable burgeoning of the thesaurus.

Another major obstacle in the construction of such a thesaurus is agreement on how objects should be characterized. This is a problem not only in the general description of an object or an image of an object, but even more so in the area of evaluation, where imaginative, subjective, and symbolic language expressing point of view is considered both necessary and desirable. Rorvig and others observe that in the case of images, the use of thesauri to control inconsistency by guiding the choice of terms is not likely on its own to eliminate the individual responses prevalent in human reactions to visual materials (Rorvig, Turner, and Moncada 1988, 51).

Two major and widely used thesauri developed for use with images and art objects are discussed in some detail in the following sections. This discussion will highlight their development and applicability and illustrate the potential problems encountered in using these tools.

The *Library of Congress Thesaurus for Graphic Materials* (*LCTGM*), composed of two complementary parts, had its beginnings in the Prints and Photographs Division at the Library of Congress where work on picture indexing focused upon visual content or primary subject matter. In response to numerous requests for a separate list of terms to guide the subject indexing of pictures, in 1980 the Prints and Photographs Division developed a preliminary list of controlled subject headings (Betz 1980). In 1984, staff began to revise the list for use with automated cataloging and indexing systems, and in 1987 the *Library of Congress Thesaurus for Graphic Materials: Topical Terms for Subject Access (TGM I)* was published. This work "provides a substantial body of terms for subject indexing of pictures, particularly large general collections of historical images" and "offers catalogers a controlled vocabulary for describing a broad range of subjects, including activities, objects, and types of people, events, and places depicted in still pictures" (Parker 1987, viii). It does not include art historical and iconographical concepts but does supply terms for some abstract ideas such as those in allegorical prints and editorial cartoons. Its intent was to supplement the *Art and Architecture Thesaurus* (*AAT*, discussed below) by providing terms for a broader range of people, events and activities which occur as picture elements along with specific terms for the built environment found within the *AAT* (Petersen and Molholt 1990).

The main source of terminology for the first edition of the *TGM I* was the *Library of Congress Subject Headings*, but terms were also drawn from the *Art & Architecture Thesaurus* (terms for painting, drawing, architecture, and the decorative arts), and the *Legislative Indexing Vocabulary* (contemporary political and social issues).

The *TGM I* (second edition) contains approximately 6,300 authorized terms and more than 4,300 cross-reference terms.[11] New cataloging projects, along with a program to catalog single items for which orders for reproduction were received, resulted in almost 2000 new terms, and terms continue to be added. A new concept of "facilities" incorporates many terms relating to the site, structure, and activities characteristic of a particular type of facility.

The Library of Congress Thesaurus for Graphic Materials II: Genre and Physical Characteristic Terms (*TGM II*),[12] a companion work to the *TGM I*, is the second edition of the 1986 *Descriptive Terms for Graphic Materials: Genre and Physical Characteristics Headings* (*GMGPC*). This thesaurus contains over 600 terms. Postable and nonpostable terms found in *GMGPC* as of October 1994 are also included in the current *TGM I* so as to facilitate their use as subject terms as well as format terms.[13]

Within the *TGM II*, genre headings denote a variety of distinctive categories of material:

Pictorial types (e.g., Portraits)
Vantage point or projection (Bird's-eye views; Perspective projections)

Intended purpose (Advertisements; Competition drawings)
Type of creator (Student works)
Publication status or occasion (Censored works; New Year cards)

Physical characteristic headings also designate production processes and physical aspects of graphic materials:

Techniques (Albumen prints)
Results of these production processes (Proofs; Reproductions)
Instruments used (Airbrush works)
Markings (Watermarks)
Shape and size (Scrolls; Miniature works)

As *TGM I* was built initially from a base of vocabulary that was used to provide subject access to the Library of Congress Prints and Photographs Division's collections, the terminology reflects the diversity (and also the limitations) of the subject matter within the collection, which ranges from documentary photographs and architectural drawings to editorial cartoons and fine prints. Terms are added to the *TGM I* only as the topic is encountered in the course of cataloging and indexing, and thus not all possible topics are represented in the thesaurus. The varying nature of the indexing activities also gives rise to variation in the specificity of the indexing vocabulary, which is quite precise in some areas and very general in others.

As it is geared towards the indexing of single pictorial items, it follows the format of the original vocabulary drawn from the *LCSH* and contains precoordinated terms for highly specific concepts that have been found to occur frequently as subjects of images, such as CHILDREN PLAYING IN SAND, HAMMER & SICKLE, and SHIP OF STATE. Other sample precoordinated terms include HOURS OF LABOR, HEADS OF STATE, and ORDNANCE INDUSTRY. Among its precoordinated terms, the *TGM I* contains a large number of qualified nouns (e.g., "Coffee cup," "Grandpa's hat," and churches qualified by specific religion); again this is a limiting factor in the usefulness of these nouns. Because of its high degree of precoordination, the *TGM I* reflects its origins in the *LCSH* and may be more similar to a subject heading list (which names subjects) than a true thesaurus (which lists terms representing single concepts) (Greenberg 1993). It also lacks a true genus–species relationship among many parent–child terms; this contributes to an overall lack of specificity, as compared to the *AAT*.

There are several problems associated with the use of the *TGM I* for indexing images, such as the high degree of precoordination, which poses problems for indexers and searchers alike. A more detailed analysis of the *TGM I*'s breadth and term specificity serve to illustrate this problem and others.

A previous research project by the author drew a random sample (approximately 10%) of several generalized classification systems and provided a statistical description of their composition in terms of types of subject access covered (Jörgensen 1996a). This research supported the description of the *TGM I* as having a varying distribution in terminology (see Table 3.1) and as being strongly reflective of the sources from which it draws terms, especially previous *LCSH* subject headings. Terms that are strongly reflective of historical concerns such as industrial, political, and social development account for about 30% of terms; thus the *TGM I* fulfills its purpose of providing historical access to pictorial materials, especially those concerned with the history of the United States. Object and *GMGPC* terms account for another 40%. However, terms relating to such things as everyday life, activities, and events (especially within a contemporary setting) account for only about 20% of terms, making it a sparser language for indexing images outside of the historical context. It contains some terms relating to abstract concepts and some thematic and "story" elements, but again, its high degree of precoordination creates a very narrow application of many of these terms.

Table 3.1. Percentage distribution of subjects from a sample of the *TGM I*.[14]

General Subject	%	General Subject	%
Objects	19.1%	Business/Industry	20.9%
Built Environment	5.3%	GMGPC	18.6%
Government	4.5%	Activities	4.5%
Abstract Concepts	3.5%	People	4.1%
Health	3.5%	Events	3.5%
Themes	2.5%	Life in Society	2.8%
Natural History	1.7%	Settings	2.2%
Organizations	0.5%	People-Related	1.5%
State/Condition	0.2%	Visual Component	0.2%

A subsequent, more detailed analysis on a later version of the *TGM I* compared its term distribution to attributes typically named by participants in describing and sorting tasks with images (Jörgensen 1998). In this subsequent analysis, which did not rely on sampling, each term was coded as applicable to one or more of forty-one specific image attributes, rather than being placed in one of eighteen broad groups.[15] Precoordinated terms were also assigned more than one code. The results of this analysis give a slightly different picture.

The *TGM I*, because of its unique political and social historical focus, contains a very large number of terms for collective bodies such as organizations, institutions, and other groups united around a functional or ideological purpose. This required the addition of the attribute *Group* to the original attribute set, which accounted for 6.5% of the terms in the thesaurus (in the previous analysis of a sample of terms, a group name was included in the topical area to which it pertained, such as business, government, and so forth).[16]

In terms of specific attributes, Table 3.2 shows that *Objects*, *Activity*, *Setting*, *Social Status*, *Group*, *Event*, *Theme*, and *Work Type* are the most-frequently occurring attributes in the *TGM I*. Attributes accounting for less than 2% of the *TGM I* include abstract terms, time terms, and terms relating to visual components (texture, color, perspective, and so forth) of the image. Thus, according to this analysis, the *TGM I*, with a good number of attributes describing objects and the activities in an image, appears to be a good source of terminology for indexing these attributes which are also typically named in describing and sorting tasks.

Table 3.2. Attributes occurring at a frequency above 2% in the *TGM I*

Attribute	%	Attribute	%
Object	20.7	*Event*	6.2
Activity	10.6	*Theme*	5.6
Setting	10.1	*Work Type*	5.6
Social Status	8.0	*Product Type*	3.3
Group	6.5	*Emotion*	2.3

However, an analysis of terminology contained within the specific attribute groups points out some potential caveats in the use of the *TGM I* for indexing general collections of images. Within *Object* (20.7%), its historical focus is revealed in such examples as the large number of terms concerned with railroads (and far fewer referring to modern communications technologies such as fax machines and modems) and the use of outdated terms, such as "privies," but no more contemporary term, such as "restrooms." It does contain a wide variety of terms for everyday objects, from "kites" and "Keyholes" to "Kazoos" and "Ketchup," but term scattering can create problems. Precoordination again creates problems, especially in terms of applicability of terms (e.g., "Birds' eggs & nests" but no generic term "Nests"). "Empty market basket" is another striking example. Precoordination can also make it difficult to find a term such as "Household soap." This demonstrates the problems engendered from using specific collections as the source of terminology: there is no consistent method for ensuring the inclusion of both generic and specific terminology for a given object.

A large number of *Object* terms refer to *Product Type* (a particular publication type); for this research these terms were double-coded as in many cases they can function as a visual element in a picture as well (e.g., Travel, Wanted, and War posters; Comic books). A large number of objects are also precoordinated phrases, nouns bound to modifiers ("Brass instruments," "Copper ingots"). Again, "Ice buckets" appears, but no broader generic term "Buckets."

Activity terms (10.6%) include a number concerned with such everyday activities such as "Housework," yet some terms would not be familiar to a naive searcher (e.g., the more formal "Cookery"). Again, a lack of related terms for everyday activities ("Sleeping" is present but not "Napping") demonstrates the terminological gaps created by a purely bottom-up process. *Activity* terms also include those related to group work activities ("Road construction," "Search and rescue operations") and sports/recreational terms ("Skin diving" and "Sports officiating") but lacks other related and/or current terms (e.g., "Snorkeling," "Skydiving"). Terms are indeed often less than current ("Typewriting"). Interestingly, it contains a number of specific types of precoordinated hunting terms ("Coyote hunting," "Elephant hunting," "Muskox hunting," among many others, as well as the more expected "Deer hunting" and "Game bird hunting"). It contains terms relating to animal as well as human activities ("Grazing," "Animal attacks"), terms related to bodily functions ("Burping," "Coughing"), and terms related to social activities ("Dating [social custom]," "Courtship," and even "Seduction"). A large number of the *Activity* terms (over sixty) are precoordinated phrases having to do with children's activities (children sewing, smoking, stealing, swimming, and so forth).

Setting terms (10.1%) include a wide variety of environments, such as work, recreation, and home, as well as types of structures and facilities in which human activity can take place. As recent projects have focused on cataloging groups of architectural drawings and architectural photographs, more specific vocabulary applicable to settings has been added. For instance, "Houses" has been added as a narrower term under "Dwellings." *TGM I* contains general terms for "City and town life," "Country life," and so on. Agricultural production sites (various types of plantations and orchards) are covered by a large number of precoordinated terms. Terms name a large number of sites by function or business ("Air raid shelters," "Automobile dealerships") and site subunits (names of rooms), but no terms for "Art galleries" or doctor's or dentist's offices. Therefore, while a large number of terms are provided, there are some common environments that lack terminology.

The attribute *Social Status* (8%) groups terms relating to such aspects of humans and other living things as age, sex, occupation, race/ethnicity, nationality, and social class. Within the *TGM I*, proper names for ethnic, racial, and regional groups are taken from the *LCSH*. The Prints and Photographs Division uses a list of subdivisions so that files classed under names of ethnic, racial, regional groups, and classes of persons can be subarranged by broad topic, such as ARTS AND CRAFTS, CIVIL RIGHTS, POLITICAL LIFE, and so forth. Terms coded as *Social Status* in the current research include "Handicapped persons," "Illegal aliens," "Divorced women" (*TGM I* has no "Divorced men"), "Military spouses," "Middle class," and "Middle age." Terminological coverage is uneven for the sexes; "Businessmen" is included but not "Businesswomen," although "Shepherdesses" *is* included). A large number of useful terms refer to occupation, such as "Fire fighters," "Jazz musicians," "Priests," and "Radiologists." Also included are less common terms such as "Efficiency experts," "Female impersonators," "Quacks," "Ratcatchers," and "Pundits." The historical focus is exemplified in such terms as "Dervishes," "Gibson girls," and "Dandies." *TGM I* lacks terms for age, beyond broad groupings. A more finely drawn categorization, such as that available in the *ERIC Thesaurus*,[17] could be usefully included.

As noted above, the *TGM I* necessitated the addition of a code for *Group* (6.5%). Terms in this set include precoordinated terms for various industries ("Fashion industry," Food . . . , Paint . . . , Shoe . . . , and so on), and include some which may seem quaint from a contemporary perspective ("Starch industry," "Pin industry," "Vinegar industry"). Eleven precoordinated terms group people within broad industries ("People associated with health and safety"). *Group* also contains terms for educational, nonprofit, and other types of organizations such as unions ("Universities and colleges," "Music ensembles," "Printers' unions"). Terms include historical or ideological groups as well ("Pacifists," "Pioneers"), and other general group terms ("Tourists," "Runaways"). Precoordinated *Event* terms also often include *Group* references ("Airline industry strikes").

Event terms (6.2%) include activities conducted by organizations, such as strikes, and by political units, such as various kinds of warfare ("Winter warfare"), as well as other events such as "Rebellions" and "Demonstrations." While it emphasizes these terms, it also contains many terms for everyday group events such as "Birthday parties," "Flower shows," and "Rehearsals." Terms appear for disasters, accidents, and other newsworthy events such as "Prison riots," "Oil spills," and "Explosions." Sporting events are also included here.

The *Theme* (5.6%) attribute group is very broad, including terms for the overall subject or topic of a picture, including names of a specific field of study (psychology), as well as terms referring to concepts depicted within the picture. Among the terms from the *TGM I* fitting this group are "Air pollution," "Dentistry," "Good and evil," "Sociology," and "Time travel." The *TGM I* also contains a large number of terms referring to governmental and economic functions and concerns, such as "International economic assistance" and "Surplus governmental property," "Patriotism," "Peace," and "Perestroika," "Urban beautification" and "Civil service reform." Coverage of levels of government is incomplete. More abstract concepts are also incompletely covered. "Freedom" is found only in such precoordinated phrases as "Freedom of information" and "Freedom of the seas," and many of the concept terms focus on desired outcomes of a democratic form of government: "Liberty," "Honor," and "Justice." The same functional trend is seen in *Abstract* terms; the majority of these terms refer to concepts having to do with money and property ("Price regulation," "Tax cuts," "Petroleum leases"). Because of the focus on governmental and economic concerns (demonstrated in the earlier analysis by broad subject areas), most of the

Theme and *Abstract* terms would not be useful for indexing in a visual content context.

Work Type (5.6%) is a large group of terms referring to the category of work ("Drawings," "Mobiles," "Kallitypes"). Again, most of these terms are not useful for indexing visual content but are meant to classify the original work being indexed by type. Approximately 25% of the terms are precoordinated with *Product Type*, *Medium*, *Genre*, or other terms ("Patent drawings," "Ink drawings," "Cityscape drawings"). *Work Type* includes much terminology only accessible to the expert.

The distribution of attributes within the *TGM I* revealed by this research demonstrates that it accomplishes its goal of being a major source of vocabulary for indexing large general collections of historical images and providing flexible access to a variety of collections. The terms found within it, as other authors have noted, reflect both the vocabulary sources used to gather terms and the nature of the collections being indexed at the Prints and Photographs Division. The areas in which terms are lacking (for instance visual elements and art historical/iconographical terminology) are by conscious design, so as to complement other existing thesauri. However, this analysis shows that it falls short of its other goal to construct a cohesive network of terms representing commonly expressed subjects in still images. The high degree of precoordination limits the usefulness of much of the terminology. The burden of its historical focus results in a lack of much contemporary terminology, as well as overshadowing the terminology that would be useful in indexing visual content.

In order to achieve the latter goal for the *TGM I*, those developing the thesaurus would have to complement their deductive approach with a inductive one, ensuring that a true thesaurus structure exists by adding and checking broader, narrower, and related terms, both when proposing new terms for the thesaurus and retroactively. As it stands now, it is somewhat a patchwork vocabulary, and is frustrating to both indexers and searchers alike, who, rather than understanding why it is as it is, would prefer simply to be able to find the term they need and which (given the appearance of other related terms) they reasonably expect to be present. While the *TGM I* notes that the *Art and Architecture Thesaurus* has been influential in their staff's thinking through relationships among *TGM I* architectural and design terms, more of this type of activity is needed for other *TGM I* terms.

In contrast to the general approach towards which the *TGM I* aspires, other more focused thesauri are widely used to supply descriptive terminology for art, architecture, and material-culture objects and their images.

The *Art & Architecture Thesaurus* (*AAT*), begun in 1979, is the major thesaurus in the field of art and architecture and was the focus of Svenonius's remarks in 1984. During the late 1970s and throughout the 1980s there was a great deal of interest in subject indexing for visual resources. The 1978 College Art Association–Visual Resources Conference sponsored the program "Subject

Access to Visual Images," followed in 1980 by the Conference on Intellectual Access to Visual Resources (the Belmont Conference).

The Belmont Conference participants determined that there are nine requirements of a system of iconography (Fry 2000):

1. Universal, cross-disciplinary
2. Consistently applicable from one institution to another, within departments of the same institution, and by various indexers within departments
3. Addresses various levels of sophistication and complexity
4. Portable, i.e., distributable
5. Communicable, i.e., terms should elicit approximately the same visual images to persons with differing backgrounds
6. Accessible to everyone and providing comparable answers to comparable questions
7. Applicable to both visual images of objects and visual image content depicted *on* objects
8. Expandable to include additional terms
9. Include both *content* and *context* terms

These meetings stimulated academic interest in the problem of intellectual access to visual materials and culminated with the publication of the *Art & Architecture Thesaurus* in 1990. The original intent for this tool was to create a "universal access system" for architecture slides. This project evolved into the idea of an access tool in the form of a hierarchically structured thesaurus created with the collaboration of scholars in the field. Its purpose was to "form a hinge between objects and their replicas or representations and the bibliography about them" (Petersen and Molholt 1990, 5–6). While aiming to be geographically and historically comprehensive, its focus is the Western world, and it does not include terminology for iconographical themes, as these are extensively covered by other tools such as *ICONCLASS* (discussed below). It does not include terms for more general concepts.

The *AAT*, in contrast to the *TGM I*, was constructed independently of the cataloging operations of any single institution.[18] *AAT* vocabulary has been developed using the concept of "literary warrant" and inductively to a high level of specificity in constructing the hierarchies that compose it. Scholars in the field review the work at all stages. The *AAT* provides terminology for indexing the art, architecture, and material culture ("objects of significance in the discussion and analysis of cultural history") of the Western world from antiquity to contemporary culture. It is intended for use in indexing objects as well as textual and pictorial materials, and it incorporates highly specific concepts as well as the more general categories in which those concepts belong. The *AAT* includes an array of terms useful for indexing pictures of the built environment, furnishings and equipment, and manifestations of visual and verbal communication, as well as "supporting terminology" for the physical attributes, persons, and concepts that relate to the creation and appreciation of art and architecture. User communities include archives and special collections, libraries, museums, visual resources collections, and conservation agencies.

The *AAT* is arranged in seven "Facets" (categories), which progress from the abstract to the concrete: ASSOCIATED CONCEPTS, PHYSICAL ATTRIBUTES, STYLES & PERIODS, AGENTS, ACTIVITIES, MATERIALS, and OBJECTS. These are further subdivided into 33 subfacets, or "Hierarchies." The facets contain nearly 120,000 terms, and scope notes explain the usage of the particular term within the thesaurus. The great majority of terms within the *AAT* are specialized and highly technical, as can be seen from the following two examples of scope notes:[19]

> Cinquedeas
> Scope Note: Heavy civilian daggers or short swords of 15th- and 16th-century Italy, characterized by a broad, flat double-edged triangular blade measuring five fingers in width at the hilt, a pair of short, arched quillons, a grip formed of two flat pieces riveted one on each side of the tang, and a pommel that is simply an arched cap fitted over the base of the grip. The blades are fluted and often elaborately decorated on the wider parts.
>
> Dinoi
> Scope Note: Used by modern scholars to refer to ancient Greek large, round-bottomed bowls that curve into a wide, open mouth, and that often stood on a stand. Metal vessels of this shape were probably used for cooking and those made of terracotta were used for mixing wine and date from the mid-seventh through the late fifth centuries BCE. They are distinguished from "lebetes" by their larger size. Ancient literary evidence suggests that the term was originally applied to drinking cups rather than bowls, and that such bowls were at that time called "lebetes."

The *AAT* does not suffer from the high degree of precoordination that the *TGM I* does, but rather allows useful combinations of terms across the facets and hierarchies, as the following examples show:

Baroque + churches	embroidered + crib + quilts
marble + birdbaths	supermarket + coupons

As with the *TGM I*, the *AAT* was evaluated for the distribution of terms among different classes of attributes (such as objects, color terms, terms for abstract concepts, and so forth). A total of 28,116 codes were generated from 24,660 *AAT* terms (again, some double-coding was present). Analysis of *AAT* terms was fairly straightforward in many cases, as the thesaurus structure meant that most terms within a hierarchy were of the same type.

Table 3.3 shows the distributions of attribute codes across the facets in the *AAT*. Not surprisingly, hierarchies within the OBJECTS Facet account for 52.7% of the terms coded, while MATERIALS and STYLES & PERIODS follow with 14.2% and 13.8%.

Table 3.3. Distributions of attribute codes across the facets in the *AAT*

Facet	%
OBJECTS	52.7
MATERIALS	14.2
STYLES & PERIODS	13.8
ACTIVITIES	7.6
AGENTS	3.9
ASSOCIATED CONCEPTS	3.9
PHYSICAL ATTRIBUTES	3.9

This same distribution is followed quite closely in the proportions of the individual attributes themselves, as well (Table 3.4 below shows the distribution of coded attributes in the *AAT*), with *Object* attributes (roughly corresponding to the OBJECTS Facet) accounting for 37.4% of the attributes, *Style* (STYLES) accounting for 10.4% and *Time Reference* (PERIODS) accounting for 3.9%. *Theme* (3.4%) is also quite similar to ASSOCIATED CONCEPTS.

Table 3.4. Distribution of attributes in the *AAT*

Attribute	%	Attribute	%
Object	37.4	*Clothing*	2.8
Style	10.4	*Activity*	2.8
Setting	7.1	*Medium*	2.7
Time Reference	3.9	*Geographic Object**	2.2
Social Status	3.5	*Work Type*	2.1
Theme	3.4	*Color*	2.0
Text	3.3		

**Geographic Object* added for *AAT* analysis only

As described above, the class of OBJECT is largest for describing tasks; Object attributes (including *Clothing*) in the *AAT* account for about 40% of the terms analyzed. *Object* terms appear in other parts of the *AAT* as well as the OBJECTS Facet, accounting for about 50% of the terms in the MATERIALS Facet (it is useful to be reminded here that, for this analysis, terms were considered primarily for use in a visual, pictorial context). *People* terms appear in the AGENTS Facet (99.4%), but make up only a fraction (approximately 3%) of the vocabulary.

In terms of representing the story of an image, *Activity* terms and *Literary Reference* terms are used in image descriptions. *Activity* terms logically make up

100% of the Physical Activities hierarchy (ACTIVITIES Facet), and 55% of the terms in the Functions hierarchy and 40% of the Processes and Techniques hierarchy; they account for less than 3% of the total terms, however. Other story attributes well represented in the *AAT* include *Setting*, *Time Reference*, and *Theme*.

Color terms are located in the PHYSICAL ATTRIBUTES Facet and make up 90.3% of the terms in the Color hierarchy, with the rest referring to *Color Value*. *Color* terms also appear in the Materials hierarchy about 6% of the time.

The large numbers of terms within certain facets suggests extensive coverage. The numerical analysis, however, suggests that indexers searching for terms describing a particular concept must consider terms appearing across several different facets and within a number of hierarchies. For instance, while *Object* terms appear primarily in the OBJECTS Facet, they are also present in the Furnishings and Equipment, Costume, Built Environment, Groupings, Genres, and Components hierarchies.

However, analysis of the *types* of terms found within the *AAT* also suggests some caveats in its application to visual content indexing, especially when indexing visual materials to be accessed by a nonexpert audience.

Further detailed analysis by two librarians (an experienced reference librarian with a strong background in art history and a media expert) evaluated how many terms in the *AAT* are "accessible" to naive/nonexpert (in art historical/ architectural vocabulary) endusers or indexers. The results were striking: out of the 24,660 terms, only about 16% were deemed suitable in a more generalized image indexing environment. Usable terms range from a low of 2.3% in the STYLES & PERIODS Facet to a high of 73.4% in the Events hierarchy.

Several examples will illustrate the usability (or lack thereof) of terms within the thesaurus. For instance, within the Color hierarchy, only 21 terms of the 329 are considered easily enough understood to be usable without extensive training. While the Color hierarchy contains basic color terms, most indexers and users would have difficulty distinguishing among the different terms for pink, which is listed with the following modifiers: vivid, strong, deep, light, moderate, dark, pale, grayish. Then there are the combinations: pinkish white, pinkish gray, purplish pink, brilliant purplish pink, strong purplish pink, and so on.

The Physical Activities hierarchy, which includes terms for games, fares somewhat better, yet there are still problems. Some terms are more distinctly specified than others (bowling includes candlepin, duckpin, and tenpin bowling), yet there is no "snorkeling" or "diving" under water activities. In contrast, ASSOCIATED CONCEPTS is one of the more diverse facets in terms of types of words. While only having 24.5% easily "usable" terms, nevertheless it contains some of the more interesting terminology, and contains terms appropriate to thirty-five of the forty-seven codes used, the widest spread of any of the hierarchies.

This analysis confirms what many have noted about the *AAT*: it is primarily a narrowly focused indexing language containing many highly specialized terms. This is understandable given its goals and target audience and the methods used in its creation, with a high level of expertise contributing to its vocabulary. It shows good consistency in its construction, but conversely, this same hierarchical focus scatters terms as well, especially if one is seeking a generalized visual indexing language. Lying outside the *AAT*'s scope are the broader range of people, events, and activities which are important access points within more generalized picture collections.

The *AAT* in its latest edition is a complex tool which "seeks to maintain a delicate balance between providing standardization of a body of terms that is as full a representation of an area or field as possible and responding to patterns of usage and the subtleties of language" (Petersen 1994, 13). Thus, it has other goals beyond providing a means of access for a variety of resources; it also intends to provide a means of communication among the various constituents concerned with art object information.

Reflecting its complexity, there have been problems in the application of the thesaurus to indexing specific collections, and reports indicate that increased time is needed to catalog slide collections using the *AAT* (Besser and Snow 1990). The ability to formulate faceted strings provides greater specificity and precision for retrieval, yet the process of forming these strings can be difficult and time consuming. When the need for guidance and training for the users of such a complex subject vocabulary became evident, the *AAT* began a series of training workshops for indexers. The Getty Trust has also published the *Guide to Indexing and Cataloging with the Art & Architecture Thesaurus* as a companion volume (Petersen and Barnett 1994).

Work on the *AAT* continues under the auspices of the Getty Vocabulary Program (part of the Getty Standards Program), which has also produced the *Union List of Artist Names*, and the *Getty Thesaurus of Geographic Names* (see discussion on Authority Files below). Future work includes "increasing the scope, depth, and relevance of the vocabularies to the Getty, its public, and the art information community at large."[20]

The *Thesaurus iconographique, système descriptif des représentations* (*TI*) is another thesaurus claiming general applicability (Garnier 1984). It is, however, used primarily in museum and cultural heritage contexts. The *TI*, known informally as the "Garnier system" after François Garnier, who developed it, was commissioned by the French Ministry of Culture and is used in all the major French museums. The introduction explains that it is the result of "speculative reflection" and of experimentation, with progressive development of the vocabulary taking into account both theoretical and practical considerations. The thesaurus contains fourteen classes and roughly 5,500 descriptors within a hierarchical structure.

As explained in its introduction, the *TI* was developed with the goal of being a practical and efficient working tool. Therefore every attempt was made to limit the number of descriptors, avoid specialist jargon and terminology, and select natural language terms for simplicity, clarity, and precision. The *TI*'s approach is to treat the contents of an image as though it were a document, inventorying the principal visual elements and relationships within a variety of research interests. Subjects are drawn from the real world and from literary sources. The subject classes include topics such as NATURE, BIBLICAL SUBJECTS, and PSYCHOLOGICAL AND MORAL LIFE.

The *TI* was analyzed in the same manner as the *TGM I* (Jörgensen 1996a). A 10% sample consisting of 463 terms shows a distribution of terms with a somewhat different emphasis than the *TGM I* (Table 3.5). Nature, the life of man, and biblical subjects compose the most frequently occurring terms in the *TI*, followed by social and religious life. Terms relating to business and industry only account for 5.2% of the terms, whereas terms describing the body and "material life" make up close to 20% of the terms.

Table 3.5. Distribution of sample of headings from *Thesaurus iconographique*

General Subject	%
NATURE	18.4%
THE BODY AND MATERIAL LIFE	17.9%
BIBLICAL SUBJECTS	10.8%
SOCIETY AND LIFE IN SOCIETY	7.3%
RELIGIOUS LIFE	7.1%
ARTS AND PERFORMING ARTS	6.0%
ENERGY/INDUSTRY/TRADES/BUSINESS	5.2%
TRANSPORTATION/COMMUNICATION	4.5%
GENERAL CHARACTERISTICS OF IMAGES	4.1%
POLITICAL AND ADMINISTRATIVE LIFE	3.7%
AGRICULTURE/HUNTING/FISHING	3.2%
INTELLECTUAL/SCIENTIFIC LIFE	3.2%
PSYCHOLOGICAL AND MORAL LIFE	3.0%
IMAGINARY BEINGS	2.6%
ARMAMENTS/MILITARY	1.5%

A full coded analysis of the *TI* was also done in the same manner as for the *AAT* (Jörgensen 1998). The *TI* provides terminology for many of the image attributes typically noted by naive users, particularly those relating to the story of the image (Table 3.6). For instance, *Object* attributes make up 16.4% of the coded terms; additional terms in *Animal* and *Plant* bring this total up to 26.4%. It provides a large number of terms for *People*, including occupation. *Activity* terms (SOCIETY AND LIFE IN SOCIETY) account for 7.1%, with *Theme* and *Set-*

ting terms at 3.6% and 3.3% respectively. Similarly, terms for *Abstract* concepts (2.8%) and *Emotion,* (2.3%) are found in sections such as PSYCHOLOGICAL AND MORAL LIFE. While these percentages may seem low, it should be noted that the actual count numbers almost 200 terms for each of these attributes, and these terms are less specialized than those of thesauri such as the *AAT*.

In some cases, the *TI* provides more terms relating to abstract or symbolic concepts than the *TGM I* or the *AAT*. The *TI* provides more *Symbol* terms than the other two tools, as well as guidelines for how these should be used in indexing. In addition, *Emotion* terms can be used to convey abstract concepts of pictures. The *TI* also has more *Abstract* terms than the other two indexing tools, and can be a rich source of vocabulary for these more semantic aspects of images. The *TI* thus can be a rich source of vocabulary for these more semantic or meaning-based aspects of images. The limitations of the *TI* are, most obviously, the lack of an English translation, its focus on religion and religious themes, and a distinctly Western European orientation.

Table 3.6. *Thesaurus iconographique* attributes ranked by frequency

Attribute	%	Attribute	%
People	30.4	*Abstract*	2.8
Object	16.4	*Geographic Object*	2.7
Activity	7.1	*Text*	2.5
Animal	5.5	*Animal—Mythical*	2.5
Plant	4.5	*Emotion*	2.3
Theme	3.6	*Group*	1.9
Setting	3.3	*Symbol*	1.6
Social Status	3.2	*Time Reference*	1.5

ICONCLASS, begun by Professor Henri Van der Waal of the University of Leiden and carried on by Leendert Couprie and Van der Waal's staff, was developed for iconographic research (the interpretive aspects of an image, discussed more fully in "Levels of Meaning") (Couprie, 1983; Van der Waal, 1985).[21] *ICONCLASS* is a systematic classification whose classified arrangement is not always obvious. It draws upon real-world objects, persons, events, and ideas to develop the classification system. The ten primary divisions reflect its primary concerns: subjects, themes, and the iconographical interpretation of images. The divisions consist of general areas such as religion and magic, nature, human beings, society and culture, and abstract ideas and concepts, and "special" topics such as history, the Bible, and mythology. As these divisions demonstrate, it shares with the *TI* a similar approach to viewing, interpreting, and categorizing visual content.

ICONCLASS currently consists of 14,000 unique keywords and guide terms, approximately 28,000 definitions, and a bibliography of approximately 40,000 citations to items addressing topics of iconographical and cultural historical interest. A unique aspect of *ICONCLASS* is its system of notation, which uses alphanumerical classification codes. Notations always begin with a digit corresponding to one of its ten main divisions. Every notation is part of a hierarchical structure and thus it incorporates all of the iconographically broader terms in the hierarchy above it. This systematic classification has advantages over both uncontrolled and controlled vocabulary terms, as it can facilitate automatic searching up or down the hierarchy. For example, a search for paintings of flowers can return paintings of different kinds of flowers, without having to name each type individually. Additionally, the notational system is independent of language but can be approached through natural language.

Complex codes denoting elaborate indexing phrases can be built by stringing together different notations. For example, the term "fear" can be represented in a number of different contexts, from general human feelings to specific instances in visual, literary, and iconographic depiction, using different notations:

31D1(+924)	fearing, being suspicious
31A(+925)	being frightened
31E123	death struggle, inquiet death; fear of death
42A134	pregnant woman taking a fright, so-called maternal impression
71H311	when Saul sees the army of the Philistines, he is afraid
92L542	Pan terrifying people, so-called panic fear

ICONCLASS has been available in computer editions since 1989 and is now available as a browser on the *ICONCLASS* website and on CD-ROM. While it is a powerful tool for indexing a wide range of visual depictions, it is also a complex tool requiring training and expertise to use. As Baca notes, "this type of indexing must be done consistently, systematically, and by individuals who are trained in cataloging, educated in art history, and have the analytical skills to unravel visual mysteries and propose possible solutions" (Baca n.d.). She also notes that, while being a fan herself, she finds its interface "off-putting" and speculates that more people might be willing to use it if this were changed.

There are other problems with *ICONCLASS*. While it is particularly suited to certain kinds of iconographical problems, it does not provide an equal level of detail for other subjects (Grund 1993). The *AAT* was developed partially to address a lack of architectural terminology in *ICONCLASS*, and a tenth division was added to *ICONCLASS* in 1996 for abstract, nonrepresentational art.

There are problems with its hierarchical structure and with its semantics as well. While the hierarchy permits powerful searching, it combines everything in the world into a single hierarchy, and while arranged in a series of levels, the hierarchical structure is not always obvious. As Bechhofer (1998) explains, in this "single-axial approach" each term has only one immediate parent; in many situations, it would be useful to be able to use so-called multiaxial classifications, where each term can have many parents and can thus be considered in a variety of different ways. As an example, a horse may be considered as either a beast of burden, or an animal used for sport. Providing these differing views of terms is an important facility for expressive querying.

While these problems appear in other hierarchically arranged thesauri, the high degree of precoordination and specificity within *ICONCLASS* in particular makes it difficult to understand and apply. It does attempt to overcome these problems by providing a detailed keyword cross-index to help find where a particular notation might be.

Another problem described by Bechhofer is that of unclear semantics. In this case, there is no clear model of what kinds of terms may appear as narrower terms or what their relationship to a higher-level term may be. For instance, under the Door hierarchy are found a number of things:

41A32	door	[an object]
41A322	closing the door	[an action]
41A323	monumental door	[a kind of door]
41A324	metalwork of a door	[things found on doors]
41A3241	door-knocker	[things found on doors]
41A325	threshold	[a role played by a door]
41A327	doorkeeper (inanimate)	[an object found next to a door]

The variety of relationships found here indicates that the structure is organizational rather than syndetic, and navigating through these hierarchies becomes confusing. Additionally, while the classification structure provides powerful searching, it can also result in false drops, lessening confidence in the system. As another reviewer notes, "the imposition of an arbitrary set of categories seems ill advised, as does the carving up of images into little icon-bites. Too broad and too narrow at once, *ICONCLASS* requires quite a bit of iconographic maneuvering to stuff those images into the available conceptual cells . . . With *ICONCLASS*, the words and numbers come packed with extensive and highly idiosyncratic acts of interpretation . . . the disparity between the various types of signifieds was jarring, as was the eccentricity or microscopy of some of the *ICONCLASS* notations" (Roos 1999).

In spite of these problems, *ICONCLASS* is currently being used in a wide variety of settings to catalog diverse types of images such as posters and multimedia objects, as well as more traditional art images (Gordon 1996). Gordon describes its application in the Witt Computer Index at the Courtauld Institute, and illustrates its application in retrieving items from complex queries. She estimates that staff have applied close to half a million *ICONCLASS* notations to 110,000 works of art. However, she also notes the need to add extensions to the work, as many generalized aspects of modern life (parking meters, skydiving) are missing.

Commercial Systems

The commercial market for images is growing rapidly and is viewed as a lucrative endeavor by a number of companies. Commercial image vendors are particularly concerned with addressing a spectrum of needs, and commercial indexing systems, unlike others, have been at the forefront of providing access to semantic and affective aspects of images.

Bjarnestam (1998) describes the system developed by Tony Stone Images (a part of Getty Communications) to index their collection of contemporary stock photographs.[22] While traditional image indexing has avoided the subjective aspects of images, these are more important for commercial stock photo agencies, as their images are often used in advertising to convey abstract meanings. Bjarnestam notes that these abstractions cannot be inferred from the visible or compositional aspects of images, but must be inferred and manually added. At the time of the article (1998) their thesaurus comprised over 10,500 keywords, divided into nine semantic hierarchical groups: geography, natural, man made, human emotions, image, concepts and topics, people, activity, and description. Index terms describing the content are assigned to the whole image, the main objects depicted, attributes associated with the objects, and their setting. Furthermore, activity terms are often used to link objects (e.g., girl "holding" bucket). "Roof terms" for common topical searches such as "endangered animals" allow searching across hierarchies. The hierarchical structure is used to handle ambiguity in terms (approximately one-fifth of the terms are ambiguous), and a semantic network structure stores approximately 40,000 synonyms and plurals. Manual indexing includes adding a text caption and fielded thesaurus terms and takes about seven minutes per image. Retrieval software allows users to submit and refine queries on simple or advanced levels, searching across all fields or searching specific fields.

The Hulton Archive was formed after Getty Images acquired two of the leading historical stock houses, the Hulton Deutsch (London) and Archive Photos (New York, a division of the Image Bank).[23] With over 40 million images, it is now one of the largest collections of photography and illustrative material in the world, with 230,000 images available digitally. Searching the collection is facilitated either by free-text searching or by selecting from assigned keyword categories: Subject, Mood, Object, People, Action, Setting, and Location, as well as special topics groups such as Fashion and Clothing, War and Conflict, Picture Attribute, or Personality or Date searches. When a category is chosen, a list of category-specific keywords is displayed for the user to choose from; multiple terms can be chosen which will be joined with a Boolean AND.

Another example is Corbis, a commercial collection consisting of over 25 million images, of which 1.4 million are available on-line. Their customers range from large, mainstream publishers to individuals (Stein 1999). Bellas (1999) describes their goal as providing access to images for their customers through indexing four different types of information: factual; depicted; contextual; and conceptual. Corbis uses a controlled vocabulary in which the majority of terms are from everyday language, with a smaller proportion of specialized terms, as well as a separate name authority list. As Corbis grows and acquires new collections, terms from these collections must be mapped into the existing vocabulary. The vocabulary is quite large (approximately 25,000 terms) and growing.

As these vocabularies were developed for a general audience and treat a wide variety of attributes, they would be of interest as a supplementary vocabulary for other more specialized thesauri already in use. However, commercial vendors such as Corbis regard their vocabularies as proprietary, competitive tools and do not make them publicly available for use. An additional problem is a lack of controlled user testing or published evaluation of these systems.

Authority Files

Authority work is the process of determining what variant names exist for an entity, and libraries use authority files to control variant forms of personal, organizational, and geographic names by providing entry terms, preferred and variant terms, and links to other types of information. The major ones related to visual materials are produced primarily to serve the needs of organizations concerned with art and material culture. The J. Paul Getty Trust, through the Getty Vocabulary Program, has developed two supplemental vocabularies to the *AAT*, the *Union List of Artist Names* (*ULAN*), and the *Getty Thesaurus of Geographic Names* (*TGN*).[24] Harrison points out that, strictly speaking, the *ULAN* is a name access control file rather than a name authority file (Harrison 1996). These vocabularies are compiled resources that grow through contributions from various Getty projects and external institutions.

Harpring (1999) provides an overview of the use of the *AAT*, the *ULAN*, and the *TGN* to provide access to a variety of visual materials. The *ULAN* contains around 220,000 names and other information about artists anywhere in the world from antiquity to the present. It includes both individuals and "corporate bodies" (i.e., a group of people working together) involved in the design or creation of art and architecture. Each artist record links to names, locations (for birth, death, and activity), relationships (such as student-teacher relationships), important dates, notes, and sources for the data. It lists variant forms for the artist name, and one is flagged as the preferred name, or "descriptor." The *TGN* emphasizes geographic locations important for art and architecture and contains around one million geographic names and other information about these locations. The *TGN* coverage is global and includes both the modern political world and historical places, and physical features and administrative entities, such as cities and nations.

While authority work is traditionally a labor-intensive intellectual endeavor, current work in digital libraries focuses on automating the process through clustering techniques (French and others 1997).

Image-Enhanced Thesauri

Several research projects have experimented with a thesaurus enhanced with images. The idea behind such a thesaurus is as an aid to searchers when they may not know the term for the item they are looking for (and which may be a common term in a specialized setting). Such a tool also allows testing the limits of a purely visual search mechanism.

The earliest reported experimental work on what is called a "visual thesaurus" was conducted by Rorvig, Turner, and Moncada (1988) at the Project ICON Image Scaling Laboratory at the University of Texas at Austin. Seloff (1990) continued this work and produced a demonstration system (the NASA Visual Thesaurus) with a graphical interface which was used as a frontend for database searching. This visual thesaurus (see also "Searches") functioned much like a traditional text-based thesaurus in that it provided the user with related, broader ,and narrower terms along with corresponding digitized images. Users could search on either images or terms; the search mechanism is a text-oriented retrieval system that constructs data sets based on statistically derived weighted values.

Another early experimental visual thesaurus, ImageQuery, located images in one or more collections at the UC Berkeley campus (Besser and Snow 1990). Three windows presented search operators, a thesaurus of index terms, and the surrogate images. ImageQuery provided users with both text-searching methods and image-browsing mechanisms. The quality of searching was dependent on the quality of the original indexing for each collection and the linking between the various controlled vocabularies for different indexed collections. Specific subject knowledge, including vocabulary and organizational principles, were required for optimal use of the system. Indexing was minimal for some collections, and without some means for establishing and enforcing minimum standards of indexing, ImageQuery could not function as a true visual thesaurus.

Several early articles discuss the theoretical and practical implications of such visual thesauri (Hogan, Jörgensen, and Jörgensen 1991; Jörgensen, Jörgensen, and Hogan 1993). The use of images themselves as indexes into information is currently being implemented in such applications as the Vesalius Anatomy Browser, which provides an interface for navigating 3D anatomical images in which these images are linked to a hierarchical representation of conceptual information (Wacholder and others 2000).

Problems with Text-Based Indexing

Hourihane (1989) summarized the wide diversity of existing text-based classification systems for images, especially for fine arts images. Classification systems for images and objects may employ subject headings (*LC Thesaurus for Graphic Materials*; *Index of Christian Art*)[25] or a thesaurus structure (*Art and Architecture Thesaurus*); may use several levels of classification; and may be hierarchical (*A Subject Index for the Visual Arts*) (Glass 1969) or nonhierarchical (*Yale Center for British Art*)[26] within levels. They may use natural language, numerical notation, codes, or a combination of all three. Natural language-based systems may use either a controlled vocabulary or free-text indexing using detailed descriptions. Some systems focus on a specific area while others are designed to be applicable in more generalized collections of images (*TI*).

The above discussion of the numerous extant text-based classification systems reveals the difficulties encountered in the indexing of pictures, as many attributes are needed to provide full access. There is an underlying tension which exists in classification of images or images of objects: the need to preserve the uniqueness of the object or image, especially as represented by written records of an art historical nature, while providing access to the object through some type of constrained vocabulary within an information retrieval system. Decisions as to what to index are complex, knowledge about image searching is incomplete, guidelines are few, and many valuable access points can be lost in the indexing process.

Decisions as to depth of indexing are a consistent problem encountered across indexers and collections. Elings describes the conflict:

> Subject indexing, depending on how it is applied, can offer the user broad or specific access to these collections. Broad subject indexing helps to unify collections by their content and can aid researchers at a higher level of information retrieval. Specific indexing can be time consuming for the cataloger but rewarding to the researcher. Too much specificity, however, can become an issue of indexing vs. analysis. In the end, the cataloger's task is to make the information broadly available and to provide some reasonable level of access. It is still up to the researcher to interpret the content and analyze the collection at a very specific level (Elings 2000, 13).

Nevertheless, the determination of "reasonable level of access" can be challenging, especially in the context of digital collections available to a wide user base. A dissenting opinion is offered by Fry, who proposes using many associative, subjective, descriptive terms from many institutions to provide innumerable points of access and suggests that "our myriad perceptions and practices, if accepted rather than homogenized, could lead to an exceptionally rich, organic, and intuitive approach to the cyber searching of images," particularly if these descriptions are linked to a uniform title (Fry 1998, 52).

Another of the most difficult problems encountered in image indexing is the need for interaction and linkage between what are typically considered several different domains. As is being noted more and more frequently in the literature, users are frequently looking for visual material that is not "of" a particular object or scene but which expresses concepts (liberty), emotions (sadness), atmosphere (mysterious), changes in state (either physical or conceptual), symbolic action, or other abstract notions. Therefore, there is the need to link both visual percepts and abstract concepts to either visual or textual items.

There is also the need to take into account the "context" of the image, the conditions under which it was created and perhaps grouped with other images. Ohrn speaks of what can be lost when cataloging of images takes place without regard to context (Ohrn 1975, 16–20). He argues that procedures (which included standard access points such as country, community, ethnic group, content, source, and subject) used to catalog a number of his personal slides for the African Studies Slide Archive greatly reduced the usefulness of his slides. He believes that some of the assumptions that underlie the cataloging process are in error: the objectivity of the slides, the importance of primary subject matter, and the independence of the slides from one another. By eliminating data on the circumstances under which the slides were taken, including such information as the photographer's intentions, abilities, technical limitations and social constraints, further evaluation and interpretation are impossible, and the collection becomes an "infinite catalog of random observation"(Ohrn 1975). Ohrn argues that in addition to those terms commonly chosen as descriptive terms for slides, additional verbal and connotative information about the making or viewing of the slides should be included, as well as annotations by the photographer that will allow evaluation of such aspects as point of view. Stam (1996) agrees and argues that these types of collection-level descriptions describing where material comes from in both the physical and intellectual senses are even more important in the networked environment.

Others have suggested similar contexts within which to classify visual materials. Roddy (1991) suggests the framework of cultural geography, which can provide access to objects typical of a particular area. Krause (1988) argues for additional indexing of the "soft" aspects of pictures (feelings and meanings which are "often very clear to the user or indexer"), and gives examples of cultural meaning such as "decline of the movies as a mass entertainment medium," "Victorian paternalism," and "inner-city decay."

One particular problem with existing tools is the strong cultural bias found in them. Stumm describes the unease among Australian image catalogers about the impact of globalization and perceived loss of identity because of domination by overseas tools (particularly American ones), and being forced to adopt overseas standards because it is not cost-effective to maintain their Australian identity (Stumm 1999). This has prompted the creation of country-specific thesauri, such as the *Australian Pictorial Thesaurus*,[27] which contains country-specific terms such as "wharfie," "footpaths," "cattle stations," and "bushwalking." Other thesauri deal with this problem by adopting a multilingual approach (Bjarnestam 1998).

Uneven selection of terminology can also be a source of bias. For instance, a thesaurus can be seen as being too elitist, as was the case with the thesaurus used by archivists working at the Finnish newspaper *Aamulehti* (Markkula and Sormunen 1998). Archivists reported that the thesaurus includes the term "art exhibitions" but not terms for agricultural exhibitions or fashion shows or even common animals such as snakes. It was also criticized for being more suited to indexing the context than the content of photos. This is also the case with the thesauri analyzed above.

Based on the inconsistencies experienced in using controlled vocabularies in the VISION project, Baca (2000) recommends certain steps as necessary to ensure their consistent and effective use: 1) training in the proper use of the tools; 2) a user manual with examples; 3) ongoing updating of the vocabulary; and 4) use of the tools at both the indexing and retrieval stages. However, a more complex classification system (or use of multiple systems) requires more training for catalogers and more time to apply the rules of the system; these in turn translate into greater expense. Indexing times for still images quoted in the literature range from about seven minutes per image for stock photographs at Getty Images, using their in-house system, to more than forty minutes per image for a slide collection at Rensselaer Polytechnic, using the *AAT*; manual indexing times for video are likely to be even longer (Eakins and Graham 1999).

Given the multiplicity of approaches and the complexity in application, providing adequate text-based indexing for images seems to be an insurmountable task given the time constraints normally bounding such activities. Some authors suggest limiting the types of textual indexing done for images based on current knowledge of user needs within specific collections, but this assumes an adequate level of knowledge about the user and the user's needs, a knowledge which most information retrieval researchers would agree is currently lacking (Shatford 1986; Turner 1993). Furthermore, with networked access to digital collections, the user community broadens considerably. Shatford and others call for more user studies to aid in determining the most useful parameters for indexing. Until these studies are done, it seems unwise to limit in an a priori manner the possible retrieval needs of users and the search keys available to them.

Data Content Standards: The Application of Descriptive Terms

There are two important parts to any system of determining the descriptive terms to be used in indexing visual materials. The first is a list of codes or index terms that is sufficient for describing the full range of attributes present in the visual item. However, just as important is a set of heuristics guiding the application of the coding or indexing system to a specific image. When there are many attributes to be considered, it is important to have a framework that can guide the analysis and provide a foundation for choices such as which attributes should have priority in indexing and to what depth this analysis should take place.

While there are many vocabularies addressing a variety of attributes, there may be little explicit information to guide the user in applying terms from these systems, beyond some general guidelines. This has both positive and negative consequences. The application of an indexing system or controlled vocabulary can be modified by local practice, allowing flexibility and customization of a particular system to an institution's needs and user community. However, without sufficient training or guidance, the lack of rules or guidelines for term assignment can result in indexing omissions, incorrect terminology, and both inter- and intra-indexer inconsistency.

Indexing Consistency

Guidelines and rules such as these are especially necessary in the realm of visual indexing because "the subjective analysis inherent in the process of translating visual information into words depends on a number of factors, not the least of which are the experience, knowledge, and tools the translator brings to the task" (McRae and White 1998, 4). Text-based indexing of visual materials requires discernment and labeling of physical and/or interpretative attributes and perhaps even relationships among several images. Indexers assign subject terms to represent visual content and/or "meaning" based on their own understanding of an image's attributes and within the constraints of the particular classification or indexing system they are using. While the use of standards and thesauri is likely to improve consistency in indexing, studies have shown that these do not guarantee either an understanding of or a consistent application of terms within systems. An additional difficulty in term choice is the fact that there is often no one–to–one correspondence among different classification systems.

Among studies of interindexer consistency conducted within the realm of visual materials, Markey (1984) reported that, among three non-subject specialist indexers using *un*controlled vocabulary, interindexer consistency averaged 7% overall. There were variations from a low of 1% for terminology matches for expressional qualities to a high of 27% for concept matches for objects. Others have reported frequencies of from 30% to 60% percent for the most popular term among participants from a variety of backgrounds asked to index or describe images (Pettersson 1988; Turner 1994). Turner and Weiland found little difference in consistency among subject and nonsubject specialists (Weiland 1997). Weiland and Jörgensen both found that a relatively high percentage of participants named the single most frequent term (Jörgensen 1995b). Jörgensen found that term matches could go as high as 90% for color terms; in contrast to the other research she also found good consistency for some abstract terms describing the story of an image, especially using concept rather than term matching.

Inconsistent application of terminology is a persistent database management problem regardless of discipline. Several articles reporting empirical studies of error in classification of artifacts point up some specific problems, such as personal bias (Fish 1978). Another study found that systematic error is introduced into the classification of material culture objects in three ways:

1) Variation in the explicitness with which attributes are described and definitions are applied;
2) Differences among different analysts' perceptions; and
3) Changes in an analyst's perceptions over time (Beck and Jones 1989).

These factors are undoubtedly at work in image indexing as well. Other factors influencing indexing include external workplace factors (workload, workflow) and personal situational factors.

As Soergel (1994) points out, however, indexing consistency is not necessarily important in itself. It has been used as an indicator of indexing correctness but this can be problematic, as indexers can be consistently incorrect. Indexing correctness means the absence of errors, including both errors of omission and commission (assigning an incorrect descriptor). Therefore, indexing guidelines can assist in correct selection and application of terms.

General Guidelines

Early users of subject headings lists had few guidelines to rely on, and local context and the individual indexer's opinions were the primary determining factor in term choice. Creativity was sometimes encouraged; Hill suggests that assigning subject headings "should be seen as a challenge to the imagination" and that an "imaginative application of subject headings will help stimulate teachers and students who use the file to an imaginative approach to the curriculum" (Hill 1975, 52–53). Needless to say, such approaches did little to encourage indexing correctness or consistency.

In the context of devising indexing schemes, Layne suggests that indexing should accomplish two goals: first, providing access to the images through specific attributes, and secondly, providing access to useful groupings of images (Layne 1994). She proposes three questions to consider in relation to attributes to be indexed: which attributes need to be indexed, which can simply be noted in conjunction with the image, and which may be left to the searcher to perceive. These questions need to be considered in relation to the type of collection and its users.

The *Guidelines for Subject Analysis of Audiovisual Materials* (American Library Association 1997) suggest including nontopical as well as topical headings, such as genre (e.g., WESTERN FILMS), form (e.g., COMMERCIALS), and technique (e.g., ANIMATION). These guidelines point up the secondary status of many visual collections as they argue for uniform and consistent subject treatment for all materials in a library's collection.

Several of the major image-indexing tools provide guidelines. For instance, the introduction to the *TGM I* discusses some of the multiple aspects of pictures which catalogers should consider when trying to decide which subjects to index:

- Historical significance of the subject matter

- Novel aspects of the subject matter
- Whether the subject is better represented elsewhere
- Relationship of material to other collections
- The need to highlight significant relationships through consistent description and indexing from one collection to the next
- A particular point of view or message necessitating indexing of context
- Image content which is unique primary evidence of a particular time and place (Parker 1987, xiv–xv).

In addition, indexing should indicate both the specific ("of") and generic ("about") levels of access. These guidelines reveal the particular emphasis of the *TGM I* on historical and collection-level access. The examples of precoordination in the *TGM I* also demonstrate that, in spite of notes to guide term usage, the application of these terms still may require a great deal of interpretation and/or external, cultural knowledge or information on the part of the indexer.

The *TI* provides similar guidelines and notes that if the description is conducted methodically the risks of omission diminish. The *TI* proposes its own logical order of description, first addressing the material disposition of the scenes, then chronological progression, then meanings, in order of decreasing importance. A series of questions to guide the analysis is presented, addressing the following aspects of the image:

- The principal meaning of the image
- What the image is expressing
- The people represented, their characteristics, and their names
- Elements contributing to the expression of the principal meaning
- Important relations such as signifier and signified
- The location—the need for a geographic identifier and description
- Need for reference to a historical context
- Description of elements concerned with secondary meaning (Garnier 1984, 17–29).

These suggestions primarily emphasize access to image meaning and expression, concerns most relevant for the art historical community, as well as specific image elements which support these concerns. Example descriptions provided in the *TI* demonstrate the preponderance of terms describing meanings, symbols, and abstract concepts. For instance, the guidelines for indexing an image with a frontal view of the head of a cow and a man's face side by side suggests, in addition to the physical description, adding the terms "timidity," "baseness," and "laziness" (Garnier 1984, 74). We see once again that these two sets of indexing guidelines were derived introspectively and pragmatically and are situated within the point of view of a particular user group or type of collection.

As these guidelines demonstrate, although systems aim to base their indexing on primary subject matter or visual content, choosing appropriate indexing terms still requires extensive cultural, historical, or pragmatic knowledge. Thus, the application of a set of descriptors or index terms also depends upon guidelines for their use, whether these guidelines are part of the system itself or are derived from local practice.

Specific Guidelines

The *Anglo-American Cataloging Rules II* (*AACR2*) (American Library Association 1998) is the most widely used specific guidelines for formulating access points (such as authors, titles, subjects, related works, and so forth) in bibliographic records. *AACR2* is used in conjuction with the MARC record. However, because it was not developed with the particular needs of visual materials in mind, a host of problems have occurred with its use for these collections. For instance, within libraries and archives that adopted the *AACR2* rules for describing visual materials, access has been by main entry or "author" of a work. The result of this is that for many collections containing historical photographs or slides, frequently the only access point is the name of the photographer, while for art reproductions, access is by name of artist. In either case there may be no access to the subject matter of the picture.

Shatford (1984) discusses the difficulties that can arise in descriptive cataloging as exemplified by *AACR2*.[28] In reproduced or "represented" works, the artist becomes responsible for the reproduction, and the description gives the date of the reproduction, not the original. This is extremely confusing for users, whose purposes usually do not require them to distinguish between a "picture" of a painting and the original title.

Elizabeth O'Keefe (1999) described work using *AACR2* at the Pierpont Morgan Library. In many cases "authorship" may be "probable" rather than certain; therefore author statements such as "designed by" or "attributed to" need to be allowed. Unnamed works of art are problematic; such works may "acquire" titles over time and these may change. "Publication" does not capture the nuances of how art works are "created," or "executed." Descriptive terms in the art world include names of groups or schools of artists; as these convey useful information, headings which explain these relationships would be beneficial. Object type is also fundamental information which deserves more direct entry, comparable to other formats, than simply in note position. A task force was formed in 1997 to deal with the issue of content vs. carrier, among other problems within *AACR2*. A revision of *AACR2* (*AACR2*R, 1998) was proposed, in particular to accommodate new media and new information carriers, and is now in use[29]

Another set of guidelines is the International Standard Bibliographic Description (ISBD) family of tools published by the International Federation of Library Associations and Institutions (IFLA). The *International Standard Bibliographic Description for Non-Book Materials* was recommended for photographs (International Federation of Library Associations and Institutions 1977). Areas covered include standard ones such as title, statement of responsibility, and general material designation. Subject access was through the addition of notes. There are guidelines for cataloging photographs according to the ISBD areas in *AACR2r*.

The *AAT* also includes a user's guide, which provides detailed instructions for indexing and searching with the *AAT*. Many examples are provided, with over 150 pages of cataloging records, including many MARC records. These demonstrate incorporating *AAT* terms for cataloging a wide variety of materials, such as film, maps, paintings, personal papers, electronic resources, and many other types.

An example of an institution-specific system is the one devised for keyword indexing of art images at the Art and Architecture Library, Yale University (Torre 1996). This system was created specifically to divide large groups of items under an artist. The classification is based on genres, themes, and objects frequently sought by patrons, such as "Madonna and child," or "deity." It uses both free text and controlled vocabulary. Each major classification has a set of questions relating to the subject range. The indexing includes type of artwork and subject, who is in the picture and their position or association, symbols and generic attributes (e.g., "halo"), literary theme, setting, objects reflective of the culture, view, and so forth. Specific questions guide the analysis at each step, and question patterns vary depending upon the type of work (for instance, abstract art is analyzed depending upon whether there is an emphasis on color or form). This type of description permits detailed indexing of visual content that is useful in retrieval.

McRae's (2000) description of the shared cataloging effort in the VISION database, which used nine recommended vocabularies and the Visual Resources Association core categories, reinforces the need for some sort of descriptive guidelines for indexing. She notes that successful retrieval is certainly a goal, whether or not shared cataloging is, and emphasizes that record consistency cannot be accomplished by relying solely upon a uniform set of data elements (such as those used in this project).

Data Structure Standards: Metadata Initiatives

As described earlier, data structure tools or metadata frameworks organize descriptors characterizing image attributes. A number of recent metadata standardization efforts have been stimulated by the need to share object and collection information in a networked environment. These efforts hold promise in improving methods for storing art object information and image information in general and in increasing interoperability among systems using these methods. The benefits of using a shared metadata structure, in addition to information exchange, are the sharing of cataloging effort across multiple institutions and the adoption of standardized sources for controlled vocabulary, increasing description consistency. Additionally, some of these metadata initiatives are experimenting with new structures and approaches (e.g., CIMI, Van Eyck, and others). However, as Clarke notes in reference to the use of MARC formats to communicate records either to users or among systems, the database structure used can affect the data, either directly or indirectly. (Clarke 1998) Thus, the depth and type of description and the choice of descriptors depend also on whether these can be accommodated within a particular metadata structure.

There are many metadata schemes currently in existence or being proposed. A review of a number of these standards notes that in order to make this multiplicity more manageable, a common practice is to focus on a particular view of the available information, categorized for instance by function or by subject (Gill, Grout, and Smith 1997). The Getty Information Institute's Object ID project, which focuses on data attributes needed by cultural bodies, law enforcement agencies, and insurance companies to retrieve stolen artifacts, illustrates the functional approach.[30] The Van Eyck project typifies initiatives taking the subject-based approach. The authors note that this approach is not without its pitfalls, as the definition of an object ("archaeological" as opposed to "fine art") is not dependent upon the inherent nature of the object but is more related to a human viewpoint. Therefore, multiple "subject views" of the same object are possible and desirable.

The following discussion highlights a few of the major metadata standards initiatives relevant to visual item description.[31]

MARC Format

A desire for standard access, especially in a networked environment, has led to the use of the existing MARC format (see Figure 3.1 for an example of its use) to describe visual materials. However, as it was developed for a manual filing system and emphasized physical form over intellectual content, it limits the types of descriptions that can be provided. This prompted the development and adoption of the MARC VIM (visual materials) format during the 1980s, one of the earlier metadata structures for visual materials information.

However, in 1983, a proposal for an integrated format was put forth, because of a number of problems incurred with having multiple formats. For instance, if an item was both a multimedia item and a serial, the cataloger was forced to choose between two competing formats, resulting in the omission of information. This change was approved by the American Library Association's Committee on Representation in Machine-Readable Form of Bibliographic Information (MARBI) during its meetings in January and July 1988. The USMARC bibliographic formats are now considered a single integrated format.[32]

```
100  1* $a Lange, Dorothea, $e photographer.
245  10 $a Migrant mother $h [picture] / $c [photographed by]
        Dorothea Lang.
260  ** $c 1936.
300  ** $a 1 photograph : $b b&w ; $c 10 x 7 cm.
500  ** $a Text on verso.
520  ** $a Migrant worker in California, holding her two chil-
        dren.
655  7* $a Migrant laborers $z United States $z California $y
        1930-1940. $2 gmgpc
655  *7 $a Group portraits. $2 gmgpc
```

Figure 3.1. Example of MARC record with relevant visual fields.

While the MARC format has since been expanded to permit inclusion of indexing or thesaurus terms from sources such as the *AAT* (designated by the use of a source code placed in $2 of 6XX fields), many in the museum and art communities maintain that it is still not an adequate representational tool for images. There are several problems associated with the MARC format; a primary one is the difficulty, noted earlier, in distinguishing between an item or object depicted in the surrogate and the surrogate itself (e.g., slide or photograph). When cataloging using *AACR2*, the author of a visual work would become the photographer of the item, not the creator of the original item. This confusing situation is compounded by the lack of disambiguation between the two in the MARC format and results in many catalogers ignoring the "item in hand" in favor of describing the item depicted. This creates a situation where important information may be lost.

An additional problem encountered in visual-item cataloging is the need to link records to indicate various types of relationships among different items in a collection. For instance, different parts of a larger work may have been created by different artists, and multiple components can make up an object (particularly a problem in architecture). Two fields added to the MARC format to accommodate this were 773 (host item entry) and 774 (constituent item entry), which provide links between child and parent bibliographic records. Another accommodation for visual materials was the addition of the 720 tag, a repeatable name field for "creator," for nonstandard records, alleviating the problem of limiting "main entry" to one point of access. Field 856 allows linking of bibliographic records and digital image files.

McRae and White (1998) provide an introduction to the use of MARC in cataloging image and object collections. They found a number of fields relevant to visual materials that are lacking in MARC: Owner's Name and Number, Nationality/Culture, Inscriptions, Conservation, Object/Work Type, Current Site, and Original Site. This situation creates heavy use of the various notes fields. McRae and White review a number of projects using MARC to catalog collections of art and cultural objects and surrogate image collections (slides and microfiche).

Additionally, the MARC flat-file format, while long a standard for the display of bibliographical information, is criticized as lacking in the necessary power to permit retrieval in a relational-database format (Bearman 1990). In contrast, an object-oriented approach would permit linking to external authority files for information relevant to specific fields and would alleviate the need to enter duplicate information for each item.

Recently, the Program for Cooperative Cataloging (PCC) has completed work on "core" bibliographic records for audiovisual materials in terms of required USMARC fields. These records are identifiable by a special code that appears in the USMARC 042 field.[33]

The Categories for the Description of Works of Art

The *Categories for the Description of Works of Art* (*CDWA*) was created by the Art Information Task Force (AITF), funded by the J. Paul Getty Trust and a National Endowment for the Humanities (NEH) grant to the College Art Association (CAA).[34] It is currently a product of the Getty Standards Program, whose mission is to promote the use of data standards and controlled vocabularies for information about art, architecture, and material culture. The needs of academic researchers and scholars guided the creation of its categories, and the need to "uniquely and unambiguously" identify particular art or museum objects or cultural artifacts guided the identification of core categories, which, however, can be modified according to local need and practice. The original version was not intended as a data exchange format but was intended to guide decisions about what information should be included in art information systems. It includes 27 broad categories and 150 subcategories. A core set, designed to enhance accessibility across databases, includes Object/Work, Classification, Titles or Names, Creation, Subject Matter, and Current Location.

In addition to a logical framework into which existing art object information can be mapped, the current version (2.0) provides some modularity through a conceptual framework which distinguishes between information intrinsic to the work and information (related persons, places, and concepts) extrinsic to the work. Extrinsic information is stored in separate authorities which can then be reused. The *CDWA* also distinguishes between information for display (full descriptive texts) and information for retrieval, which they suggest should be carefully chosen from controlled vocabularies and authorities. Thus, the current version is envisioned as guiding art historians, museum personnel, visual resource professionals, and librarians and information managers in making decisions about database content and exchange of information with other institutions or systems.

Core Categories for Visual Resources

Developed by the Visual Resources Association Data Standards Committee, the *VRA Core, (Version 3.0)* is an adaptation of the *CDWA*, expanded to cover architecture and site–specific structures.[35] It provides metadata categories for the description of "works of visual culture as well as the images that document them" (Visual Resources Assocation 2000). The Core is designed to facilitate sharing of information about visual works and is not intended as a complete set of elements; therefore, it can be extended by adding fields according to local needs. The *CDWA* and the *VRA Core* are not rigid systems but may be considered more as templates for developing cataloging records.[36] The previous version provided two element sets: *Work* and *Visual Document*; the current version has combined these two into a single set (the term *Visual Document* has been replaced by *Image*), with the addition of a *Record Type* element to distinguish between the two. The Data Standards Committee recommends the use of controlled vocabularies, such as those created by the Getty and the *TGM*, but cautions that no single vocabulary can provide sufficient terminology for all the elements in the Core. They also recognize that local needs will dictate the use of additional tools.

The Core Categories as listed include:[37]

Record Type	Creator	Culture
Type	Date	Subject
Title	Location	Relation
Measurements	ID	Description
Material	Number	Source
Technique	Style/Period	Rights

Each category includes a definition, data values, qualifiers, and mappings to other metadata schemes. Current work of the committee includes mapping of the Core to other metadata standards, and compilation of a compendium of examples.

Dublin Core

The least-complex metadata structure discussed here is the Dublin Core (DC), which has been extended to accommodate visual materials. The original Dublin Core thirteen-element set and its later versions are intended to facilitate discovery of resources in a networked environment (specifically, the Internet and the World Wide Web). The Dublin Core has been developed through a series of workshops sponsored by Online Computer Library Center, Inc. (OCLC) and such cosponsors as the National Center for Supercomputing Applications (NCSA), and the Coalition for Networked information (CNI). The third workshop focused on description of visual resources of a particular kind, discrete images that can be identified as bounded or fixed (in the sense that the resource looks the same to all users).[38] One conclusion of the workshop was that images and text are quite similar in their "discovery" requirements. Thus, development of this metadata scheme has proceeded with the goal of formulating one structure for both images and text.

The DC version 1.1 consists of a fifteen-element core foundation, which is defined according to a set of ten ISO/IEC (International Organization for Standardization/International Electrotechnical Commission) attributes from a standard for the description of data elements (name, ID, version, language, and so on) (Weibel and Koch 2000). The DC elements are:[39]

Title	Contributor	Source
Creator	Date	Language
Subject and Keywords	Resource Type	Relation
Description	Format	Coverage
Publisher	Resource Identifier	Rights Management

The Dublin Core has added a set of qualifiers to support additional functionalities beyond simple discovery and to meet the needs of diverse domains. There are currently two broad classes of qualifiers: Element Refinements, which narrow the meaning of an element to a more restricted scope; and Encoding Schemes (controlled vocabularies, formal notations, and so forth), which aid in the interpretation of an element value. These are not viewed as a finite set and additional qualifiers for local or domain use may be developed. Many organizations such as the Art Museum Image Consortium (AMICO)[40] and CIMI (see "Data Communication Tools") have used the Dublin Core to describe collections.

Continuing work to make the Dublin Core extensible to meet the needs of specific communities has begun to highlight some of the difficulties involved in maintaining interoperability among institutions with collections of diverse items (Dekkers and Weibel 2002). One group that is dealing with this problem is the World Wide Web Consortium (W3C),[41] in its Resource Description Framework (RDF), a framework for metadata that provides interoperability between applications that exchange machine-understandable information on the Web (see "Data Communication Tools," below).

Markup Languages

Markup languages, which describe the *content* of an item (as opposed to its formatting), offer structured descriptions which can be used for searching. Markup languages include Standard Generalized Markup Language (SGML), HyperText Markup Language (HTML), Extensible Markup Language (XML), and Extensible HyperText Markup Language (XHTML).[42] Document Type Definitions (DTDs) for these can be created which specify a pre-defined set of tags characterizing different types of information. For instance, one of CIMI's (see "Data Communication Tools") first projects (Cultural Heritage Information Online, or CHIO) explored the use of SGML to define item content such as *bibliography* (a complete bibliographic item, such as a series, book, or journal, or a citation from within a bibliographic item), *concept* (an abstract concept, for example one presented in the interpretation of the subject matter of a work of art), and *context* (political, social, economic, or religious events or movements associated with a work of art at its creation and over time) (Light 1996).

Another example is Encoded Archival Description (EAD), an XML DTD specifically for archival finding aids (inventories or lists of collection content). Designed to accommodate a wide variety of finding aids, EAD provides multiple levels of hierarchy and allows item-level description following other standards, such as CDWA or the VRA Core. Detailed description can thus be provided using controlled terms. This approach has been implemented in the Online Archive of California; however, there is no standard way of applying the tagging markup *across* the different finding aids, which represent different collections (Elings 2000).[43]

International Initiatives

The Visual Arts Network for the Exchange of Cultural Knowledge ("Van Eyck") began as a research project subsidized by the European Commission as part of the Libraries Program (Van der Starre 1996); the first phase ended in 1997. Initial work on this project surveyed more than twenty systems worldwide to define the minimum fields needed to retrieve information about art images (Hourihane 1996). Fifty-five fields are grouped in three categories to create a core record: Artist, Object, and Image. As duplicates occur across these (for instance, Artist ID), the implementation is as a relational database, using products from Oracle and Verity. Rather than detailed indexing, the system is aimed at giving the user an overview of data available within the system. The core record's utility is limited in that it focuses on traditional works of art (paintings, prints, and drawings). It does not include architecture, installations, performances, multimedia. or electronic art.

Another aim of the project, which continued in Van Eyck II, was to create a workstation where different relevant databases containing art-historical information could be searched seamlessly.[44] One interesting aspect of this system is that it includes a specific field in the object record for "Morelli fields," visual matching software within the Van Eyck system which allows the user to search on the visual characteristics (matrices of pixels matched on configuration, tonality, and color) of an image as well as its text record. Van Eyck II was operated by four partners—the Netherlands Institute for Art History (RKD) (The Hague, Netherlands), the Bright Side of Life Computer Consultancy, the Witt Library, and IDC Publishers.

A new metadata standard, developed by the Moving Pictures Experts Group (MPEG),[45] is including detailed tools for the content description of both still and moving images and multimedia through textual tools (free-text and controlled vocabulary) and other types of representations. This standard, known as MPEG-7, was launched in 2002. The standard is composed of descriptors, description schemes, and a description definition language (Martinez 2001).[46] The MPEG-7 descriptors are designed for describing the following types of information: low-level audiovisual features such as color, texture, motion, audio energy, and so forth; higher-level semantic features such as objects, events and abstract concepts; content management processes; information about the storage media, and so on. It is expected that most descriptors corresponding to low-level features will be extracted automatically, whereas human intervention will be required for producing the high-level descriptors. The descriptors are gathered into description schemes that provide a standard set of data types and description structures needed for generating XML descriptions of audiovisual content. Description Schemes (DSs) are created using the MPEG-7 Description Definition Language (DDL), a language similar to XML schema, but which supports additional features such as polymorphism, data value inheritance based on spatiotemporal inclusion interval, and extended spatiotemporal and audiovisual data types. Therefore, this standard will allow the combination of both textual and content-based indexing tools. A recent report on the project notes:

> Whatever its merits and drawbacks, it seems certain that MPEG-7 will dominate the development of the next generation of image retrieval systems. It has the support of an impressive range of academic and industrial backers, including systems designers such as IBM and Virage, and large-scale video users such as the BBC and INA, the French national film and TV archive. This will virtually guarantee its widespread adoption over the next few years, and few developers of image management software will be able to ignore it (Eakins and Graham 1999).

Data Communication Tools

The existence of multiple formats for image descriptions and the proliferation of metadata schemas has created the need for tools to understand and manage them, as well as the creation of tools which facilitate the exchange of information with one another. For instance, Lanzi characterizes the MARC format and EAD as data communication standards.[47] One new tool created in response to this situation is the crosswalk, a mapping of two or more metadata schemas' elements to each other or across a common reference scheme.[48] While metadata systems differ in both content and structure, Cromwell-Kessler (1998) explains that the primary obstacle to integration is the structure, as data elements can function at different levels and be designated in widely varying ways. While mappings are often performed based upon the metadata elements themselves, other work has mapped metadata elements according to function (discovery, use, authentication, and administration) and proposes the use of a class-oriented functional metadata schema (Greenberg 2001).

Mappings of MARC to the VRA Core for sixteen institutions are presented in *ArtMARC Sourcebook* (McRae and White 1998). The mapping proved to be very difficult for a number of reasons: data elements not clearly defined by institutions, a lack of correspondence of CDWA data elements and MARC tags or subfields, heavy use of the note fields, and problems determining exactly what *was* the item being cataloged. Another crosswalk mapping is provided at the Getty website and covers the CDWA VRA 2.0 Core, VRA 3.0 Core, USMARC, Dublin Core, CIMI (see below), and EAD, among others.[49]

Other tools include data dictionaries and data element registries. Many types of museums and other organizations have created data dictionaries, alphabetical listings of data elements found within metadata schemes and their definitions.[50] These are either drafted by one or more museums or supported by national and international organizations. Another tool is a national data element registry, which gathers together data elements and their definitions produced by many different organizations. This is seen as a major need by organizations involved in creating digital image collections (Davis 1996).

One organization active in this area is the Computer Interchange of Museum Information (CIMI) consortium of cultural heritage institutions and organizations.[51] Their work focuses on encouraging open, standards-based approaches to creating and sharing digital information and applying standards to museum information in member demonstration projects. Several recent projects include Project MIDIIS (Museum Initiative for Digital Information Interchange Standards), development of an XML DTD which builds on the established museum standard, SPECTRUM,[52] and the Metadata Harvesting Project, which combines the metadata approach with Web search engines by incorporating a metadata "harvester" (similar to having a website crawled and indexed).

A major initiative towards data exchange is the development of the Resource Description Framework (RDF), a general-purpose language for representing and exchanging information without loss of meaning on the World Wide Web (Bray and Brickley 2000). Therefore, existing metadata structures such as the Dublin Core can be expressed within the RDF framework. According to the latest working draft, it is particularly intended for representing metadata such as title, author, and modification date of a Web page, as well as access and rights management information such as copyright, availability, or the description of a Web user's preferences for information delivery.[53] One current project is aimed at collections of photographs and implements RDF with three separate metadata components: the Dublin Core; a Technical schema, which captures technical data about the photograph and the camera (type of camera, film, software used for digitizing, and so forth); and a Content schema, which uses a small controlled vocabulary to categorize the subject (portrait, landscape, architecture, animals, and so forth) (Lafon and Bos 2000).

Advanced Tools

As noted in the preceding discussions, a number of scholars stress the need to preserve multiple diverse interpretations of visual content. Gill and others note that "in the field of cultural information the 'right answer' is often either elusive or manifold" (Gill, Grout, and Smith 1997, n.p.). It can be argued that this is true not only of cultural information but of fine arts, graphics, or indeed of any visual representation, and more sophisticated methods of representing complex information are being explored in response to this.

Semantic Networks

In a manner similar to a thesaurus, a semantic network structures information as a network of related concepts.[54] Within a semantic network, it is possible to assign several relationships between terms with differing weights to provide a clear notion of the semantic strength between terms. Many of the limitations surrounding hierarchical and faceted thesauri may be eliminated by the use of a network structure. Concepts are represented as nodes, and arcs between nodes represent different types of relationships, including not only broader or narrower (generic) relationships but also whole–part relationships and a large number of semantic relationships. These semantic relationships in a thesaurus are generally gathered together under the related-term relationship; in a semantic network these types of relationships can be made much more explicit, to include such relationships as cause and effect or object and process. Semantic networks could provide the missing link between visual elements and their associated meanings. An example of this type of relationship is the use of "masks" to identify visual elements such as color and volume (see Pommert and others, 2000, for a recent example). WordNet (see Chapter Four) is one of the most well-known and is widely used in a variety of search engines and other projects.

Ontologies

Another tool is an ontology; these are being developed largely in the artificial intelligence (AI) and knowledge management (KM) communities. The term has a long history in philosophical discussions, where it refers to the nature of existence. The short definition is usually given as "a specification of a conceptualization." As Gruber explains, an ontology is a description of the concepts and relationships that can exist for an agent or a community of agents (Gruber n.d.). They can represent complex relationships between objects, and include the ability to specify rules and axioms which are missing from semantic networks. An ontology can exist in the abstract, as a conceptual and logical mental construct, or can be instantiated as an explicit and formalized terminological or semantic structure that captures and expresses an abstract logical design.[55] Within the field of AI, the utility of an ontology is in enabling knowledge sharing and reuse. Ontologies are developed to describe knowledge in a specific area within systems for data mining and knowledge management. Metadata structures are also referred to as ontologies; however, a clear understanding of whether the term is being used to describe a conceptual structure or a formalized structure which enables other functionalities is necessary.

A recent project utilizing an ontological framework is the ABC Ontology, developed within the Harmony International Digital Library project. As Lagoze and Hunter (2001) explain, its purpose is to provide a common conceptual model which will facilitate interoperability between metadata ontologies from different domains. The latest version was developed in collaboration with the CIMI consortium, and CIMI museums and libraries provided metadata descriptions of complex objects. Using this model, the researchers have built a system (comprised of a metadata repository of RDF descriptions and a search interface which is capable of handling more sophisticated queries than less-expressive, object-centric metadata models. However, the researchers caution that these systems, while highly expressive, are expensive to construct, and suggest that decisions to implement systems such as these should be based on careful analysis of desired functionality and economic realities. They note that in many cases, it may be more expedient to simply supply high-volume, simply-constructed metadata, such as simple Dublin Core.

Other work in data modeling involves migration from relational to object-oriented formats (see Chapter Four). For instance, the International Committee for Documentation (CIDOC)[56] has published their object-oriented conceptual reference model (CRM), which attempts to create a formal framework in which to express the implicit and explicit semantic concepts of cultural heritage information.[57] This model is a domain ontology which describes concepts relevant to museum documentation, in particular those areas needed to support the interchange of museum information.

Organizational Factors

As can be seen from the above discussion, within organizations and institutions concerned with visual materials, cataloging of images and objects is frequently seen not so much as a means to enhance end-user access but rather to further other intrainstitutional goals and curatorial concerns such as scholarly research, conservation, and creating exhibitions. A report on authority control choices in art information systems identified the purpose of the system as being the most important factor and noted that "the intrinsic merit of the list—its internal logic or beauty of conception—is not a primary determinant" of choice of system (Stam 1986, 63). The purpose of the system often results from a combination of other political, financial, and administrative factors.

The primacy of local needs has often contributed to a lack of cooperation among participating institutions. In contrast, some other countries such as France have been able to take a unified approach to organizing access to visual information (Hourihane 1989). When available, state support does however influence some of the decisions made in system design and implementation. For instance, a database recording artistic properties owned by a state may require recording of information in the national language, regardless of the nationality of the artist. In the Canadian Heritage Information Network funded by the national government, bilingual access to all aspects of the system is paramount. Other projects involved with culturally sensitive materials, such as those of Native American tribes, may end up needing to restrict access to outside users.

One of the main problems in providing access to images noted in the literature has been the lack of a tradition of shared cataloging among those in charge of image collections. Just as there has been no universally accepted method for cataloging or indexing images, there has been no widely accepted institutionalized method for the sharing of that information as there is for textual materials, either in the form of a bibliographic utility such as OCLC or RLIN (Research Libraries Information Network) or in the form of a standard data interchange format such as the MARC record.[58]

If an image collection is part of a library, library standards may be chosen for cataloging and indexing. In the library community, where a large number of image records may already be classified using another system such as the *LCSH* or the *LCTGM*, there is reluctance to accept new methods for cataloging as the organization then faces the problem of maintaining dual-access systems or undergoing expensive retrospective conversion of existing records.

Administrative concern in the museum community has focused primarily on information associated with the images rather than access to the images themselves. Local files store, among other types of information, creator biographical data, sources of terminology, and the history of a particular object. These data files may contain information (such as that concerning local or obscure artists) which may be difficult or virtually impossible to find using conventional sources, yet these files could support cataloging functions and provide more user access if they could be available to other institutions. This information, however, becomes a larger administrative concern in relation to its validity, as these files are not, in any strict sense, authority files. One approach to this problem (currently used by *AAT*) is that of sourcing all data within a record. The problem carries over to the authoritativeness of indexing records as well. As there may be little agreement among experts as to the correct application of a particular term to a particular image, the method of operation has been to "omit rather than commit," thus limiting indexing to all but a few terms of undisputable correctness.

Cataloging of images using some sort of group or collective approach, which recognizes that there may be multiple images, reproductions, or views of well-known subjects, such as St. Mark's of Venice or the Mona Lisa, has been suggested as a possible solution to solving some of the more labor-intensive problems of providing image access. This has been applied at the local level, and has been tried in several test collections (e.g., the VISION project and AMICO; see below), but there are no administrative mechanisms in place to facilitate this approach on the larger scale typical of text cataloging (Keefe 1990).

Recently, digitization projects such as those funded by government agencies such as the Institute for Museum and Library Services (IMLS) and state governments have burgeoned. Organizations such as the J. Paul Getty Trust, the

Research Libraries Group, and the Museum Computer Network have all funded digitization projects. Typically, however, more money than anticipated is needed to digitize these collections, and unevenness of funding (especially in the humanities) can be an obstacle to steady progress in this area. Technical problems, such as the amount of disk storage space needed for image information, translate directly into financial and perhaps intellectual constraints on system development. Systematic or detailed indexing in these systems is often almost an afterthought, with little conscious attention paid to the broader user community now capable of accessing a collection.

The irony of the current situation is that technological advances (and funding for technology) have created a situation in which more images than imaginable are now available digitally, yet finding them easily remains as elusive as ever.

Discussion

One of the striking points that emerges in analyzing the data content and data structure tools is the limitations imposed on the description of visual content of the image, both by guidelines and the actual containers into which such descriptions should fit. Most of the data structure tools only provide one field for describing the subject information, which would hold everything from description of visual content, to specific iconography (symbolic elements), to broad themes and subjects. This information may be expressed as keywords, free-text descriptions, or controlled vocabulary. In some cases it is not clear how to address both specific and generic levels of information. As can be seen from Table 3.7, because so much information could potentially fit in one of these fields, this information will in fact be quite diverse and unstructured. The CDWA provides the most detailed structure in its three broad categories.

As there are a large number of image attributes to be considered in visual indexing, this lack of structure may not only impact retrieval but also lead to inconsistent or incomplete indexing. It may also affect the creation of index languages for visual materials, by limited the types of terms that are considered necessary. We shall return to these topics in more detail in the concluding chapters.

A Note on Moving Images

Moving images share many of the same problems as still images. Cataloging recommendations are usually adapted according to the needs of individual archives, which have established their own cataloging procedures, and this results in a similar lack of standardized descriptive practice and inhibits shared cataloging. A major organization concerned with moving images is the Association of Moving Image Archivists (AMIA).[59] The Cataloging and Documentation Committee is a forum for discussion of cataloging issues in moving-image collections. The committee facilitates the exchange of information through programs and publications, promotes the use of existing national standards, advises standards-making bodies on cataloging standards and issues, and creates new cataloging standards. One project revised the 1984 edition of *Archival Moving Image Materials: a Cataloging Manual* (*AMIM*) (White-Hensen 2000), which focuses on feature films and omits guidance for other moving-image works such as television, newsreels, and other creative works. *AMIM* also suffers from uneven coverage among areas. Another recent project is the *AMIA Compendium of Moving Image Cataloging Practice* (forthcoming), which presents solutions to moving-image cataloging problems from twenty-seven institutions. More detailed information is provided at the AMIA website.

Table 3.7. Fields containing descriptive information in different metadata schemas

Scheme	Field
Dublin Core	Subject
MARC	520 Summary
MARC	650 Subject-topical
EAD	<scopecontent><abstract>
EAD	<notestmt><subject>
EAD	<controlaccess><subject>
CDWA	Subject Matter: Description
CDWA	Subject Matter: Identification (Iconography)
CDWA	Subject Matter: Interpretation (Meaning/Theme)
VRA Core	Subject

Theoretical Basis for Image Classification

As the previous discussion has demonstrated, many of the more recent classification systems for images are designed with the needs of art historians in mind. In order to understand the structure of these systems it is necessary to understand the theoretical foundations underlying some of these systems. The concept of levels of meaning is an important one, and is expressed in many of these classification systems in one way or another.

Levels of Meaning

Erwin Panofsky's discussion of the question of meaning in art forms the basis for much of the theoretical work that has been done on the classification of art images (Panofsky 1955; Panofsky 1962). After visual perception or "apprehension of significant form," Panofsky describes three successive levels of understanding and interpretation:

1) Preiconographical description
2) Iconographical analysis
3) Iconological interpretation

The viewer reaches the first level, *preiconographical description*, when "pure visible forms are linked to their corresponding objects, events, or expressional qualities" (Panofsky 1955, 25). Meanings at this level are primary or natural and need only knowledge acquired from practical, everyday experience to interpret. Thus, a round, red object may be recognized as an apple or a ball. When the observer assigns meaning to image components (such as ascribing "temptation" to the apple), the second level of *iconographical analysis* is reached. An understanding of such meanings can be gained through knowledge and understanding of literary sources as well as through practical experience. Panofsky states that "it differs from the primary in that it is *intelligible* instead of being *sensible*" (Panofsky 1955, 27).

The third level, *iconological interpretation*, is more difficult to grasp and requires the art historian to rely on intuition and to synthesize multiple threads into possibly multiple interpretations. This third level is extremely difficult to apply in any kind of classification system because of the ambiguity of meaning. In considering this level for indexing purposes, Turner (1993) believes that the only possible way to provide access to these types of interpretations is to list them. Shatford (1986) concurs that these interpretations can provide valuable access to information and suggests recognizing the existence of subjective interpretive judgments and providing multiple avenues for retrieval.

Markey explains that one of the advantages of indexing iconographically is that iconographical descriptors succinctly carry additional information about possible content (Markey 1986, 3–5). For instance, a subject heading of "Agony in the Garden" implies a praying Christ, an outdoor scene, and at least three sleeping disciples. In this case, identification of level-one primary subject matter would require that many more entities be listed. With the iconographical descriptor, such content can be inferred without being explicitly named. *ICONCLASS*, discussed above, is an example of an iconographical indexing system.

Hourihane (1989) reviews classification systems and analyzes whether they contain terms which express these primary, secondary, and tertiary levels of meaning in a picture, and whether these levels are explicitly expressed or simply found in the system as a guideline for classifiers. Several of the image classification systems discussed rely on the second, or iconographical level of interpretation. Additionally, many of the collections using iconographical classification systems support scholarly research, and the users of these collections have the training and knowledge that allows them to use these classification systems.

Turner (1993) also discusses the appropriateness of indexing at the first or second levels within specific types of collections or pictures. He proposes that indexing at the first level by simply naming recognizable and significant objects and events in a picture is suitable for collections used for identification purposes or for known-item searching (e.g., picture collections in public libraries and collections of stock film and video footage). Indexing at the second level is more appropriate for completed film and video products, and for still picture collections which are principally used for some kind of psychological analysis. He also states that a guiding principle for these indexing decisions is whether better user access is provided.

Markey describes several problems with iconographical analysis in classification, such as loss of information and increased subjectivity in application of classificatory terms (Markey 1986, 7–8). Problems often occur with iconographical indexing systems when a novice tries to search for an image within them; a novice would not necessarily know that a picture of "Mary" and an angel is often portraying "The Annunciation" and would be unable to choose this as a search term. Certainly, even the identification of "Mary" involves a specific level of cultural and/or literary awareness. Some types of retrieval are not possible at all, as classes of information are lost as well as gained within these iconographical descriptions. Additionally, as one moves from lower to higher levels, interpretation becomes increasingly subjective. Even the first level becomes subjective when trying to describe the expressional as opposed to the purely factual. Enser (1993) noted that a first attempt at preiconic or iconic categorization of queries (after Panofsky) was not useful in the Hulton Deutsch Collection.

Therefore, while iconographical classification systems seem to imply the ability to provide multiple access points for art images, their ability to do so can be quite limited, requiring searchers to possess a specific and extensive knowledge of symbolic, literary, and cultural conventions, interpretations, and meanings. While traditional iconographical systems may be useful for the art historical community, they are less so for a more diverse community of searchers, because the levels of access addressed are frequently quite narrow.

"Of" and "About"

Shatford, concerned with the lack of a theoretical basis for construction of subject-oriented organizational schemes for pictures, extended Panofsky's theory of meaning in art with language and classification theory to provide an expanded basis for image classification (Shatford 1986, 44). She extends the "Of" (factual) and "About" (expressional) of the first level to the iconographic level. This level differs from the first in that the difference is not between objective and subjective, but between objective and mythical, abstract, or symbolic meaning. Therefore, while the first level is complicated by differing subjective interpretations of "objective" information, the second level is made more complex by varying interpretations of symbols.

Shatford proposes that a single image will have many meanings, from the specific object that the image represents (the Golden Gate Bridge) to generic or abstract words ("bridge" or "architecture"). She then extends the concept of "Generic Of" and "Specific Of," as well as the concept of "About," (derived from Panofsky's first and second levels) to a rather complex faceted classification system answering a series of questions such as Who, What, When, and Where. She proposes that, as a minimum, an image should be indexed at the first level with both "Generic Of" (skyscraper, office building) and "Specific Of" (Guaranty Building).

The purpose of this system is to prevent possible useful subjects from being overlooked by those who are classifying these pictures. She cautions that any system for classification must be used within the context of the nature of a specific collection, and that until further research is done on types of user requests, the indexer should concentrate on the main subject of a picture within the framework of a special versus a general collection. However, even determining the "main subject" of a picture can be complex, and depends upon the classifier's point of view.

Primary subject matter

While Shatford and other authors attempt to address indexing in the context of multiple levels of meaning, other indexing systems developed within the last few decades emphasize a return to primary subject matter as a key access point. Hourihane noted (in 1989) that it was only within the last twenty years that there had been major attempts to provide access to images through indexing the subject content. Markey (1986) also advocated describing visual images according to their primary subject matter, as many specialized picture collections contain items of general interest and this type of cataloging can provide broader access to these collections. There are several advantages to this approach, a major one being that users are not biased by the interpretation provided. Other advantages are that only one level of interpretation is required, certain types of information are not lost, highly trained and skilled indexers are not needed, and searching would be easier. She proposed creation of an access tool, a thematic catalog which functions as a translation tool between existing iconographical descriptions and the elements of primary subject matter that compose them.

Keister (1994) described a similar approach at the National Library of Medicine (NLM), visual element cataloging (in addition to topical cataloging), to meet the need for specific types of visual elements by picture professionals, the health community, and the museum and academic community. In order to provide broad enough access to primary subject matter, the NLM catalogers use four controlled vocabularies (NLM's *Medical Subject Headings*, the *Library of Congress Subject Headings*, the *LC Thesaurus for Graphic Materials*, and the *Art & Architecture Thesaurus*). Keister noted, however, that this type of indexing meets the needs of no more than 80 percent of the users and only employs words in the record necessary to describe the picture adequately.

Even with an emphasis on primary subject matter as indexable material, those concerned with cataloging images supply terms to describe inherent and often subjectively interpreted properties or attributes. For instance, Markey noted that indexers asked to identify primary subject matter sometimes included other elements as well (Markey 1986).

Image Users, Queries, and Searches

Several studies have focused on the users of image collections, their queries, the types of searches they conduct, and their searching behaviors. Users, queries, and searches are considered here in relation to the specific types of attributes each can necessitate in the retrieval process.

Users

Several studies describe the users of various types of collections. At the National Library of Medicine, the Prints and Photographs Collection is used by picture and publication professionals (50%) and health professionals (33%), with the remainder divided among the museum and academic community and the general public (Keister 1994). The images are used in books, television documentaries, movies, educational projects, or for reference. The Hulton Deutsch Collection, a general-purpose picture archive (now the Hulton Getty Collection) receives requests from book publishers, advertising and design companies, magazine publishers, newspaper publishers, television and audiovisual companies, and "other" (3%) (Enser 1993). Gordon (1996) reports on users of the Witt Computer Index in the Witt Library at the Courtauld Institute of Art. Individual inquiries account for the majority (58%) and represent a varied audience composed of academics, students, film and theater designers, authors, and the general public. Institutional users (42%) include libraries, museums, universities, special interest groups, quasi-governmental agencies, publishers, the police, and broadcast companies. International users account for about 21% of users.

Armitage and Enser (1997) conducted a later study of users of seven picture libraries, including two moving-image archives; users, not surprisingly, vary according to the nature of the collection. While general historical collections and photographic collections have a broad user base, including the general public, other collections cater to the needs of the subject specialist (natural history), and professional (town planners and engineers) and academic (medicine, art history) users.

A panel on visual reference queries at ARLIS reported anecdotal evidence of library use for visual requests by artists and design students (Tobias 1997). Artists rarely used the library for visual materials, while design students used it when completing an assignment. The most difficult task for art students was finding images; image indexes, describing visual content of photographs (a rat in a cage) or addressing one publication, such as *Life* magazine, could assist greatly. End-of-year photo magazine roundups were noted as being useful.

Two other studies focused specifically on journalists as users of newspaper photo archives. Ørnager (1995) studied thirteen newspaper image archives holding documentary and press photos and interviewed twenty-five archivists, as well as twenty-six journalists using the archives. Markkula and Sormunen (2000) studied requests in a digital photo archive environment. The work was conducted at *Aamulehti*, the second largest newspaper in Finland, containing at the time over 83,000 photos. Users included, in addition to journalists, layout designers and other editorial staff. These users were characterized as often having many ideas in mind, and making "acceptable selections," rather than searching for the "best" picture. Speed was critical for documentary photos of current news events, whereas feature articles were less date-dependent and photos for these could be thematic. Journalists reported trouble finding photos of named geographical locations.

In contrast to these groups, art historians need access to a different set of image attributes, as they employ a variety of analytical approaches such as connoisseurship, formal and stylistic analysis of images, and iconography in their work with images. Several works discuss the types of information that art historians need to conduct their research (Markey 1981; Panofsky 1962; Stam and Giral 1988).

A joint research endeavor between the J. Paul Getty Trust's Art History Information Program (AHIP) and the Institute for Research in Information and Scholarship (IRIS) at Brown University used both interviews and a case-study approach to seek an understanding of how art historians seek images and image information (Bakewell 1988). This study demonstrated how image access is problematic for art historians. One important need of this group is access to "visual traditions" by means of a variety of indices. Several commented on the dream of having imagebases from which to search and download: "One could imagine having a thing where [if, for example] you want to see all the Rouaults in public collections in France, you just tap into it, and you get a sheet of color Xeroxes" (Bakewell 1988, 52). In describing access problems one scholar notes that even crude reproductions of the images would be better than none at all, and could serve to identify which images or works are located in specific collections, particularly in regard to nonattributed works.

For this group, the idea of being able to reorganize text and images is also important, and the "spatial rapport" of visual and textual information serves as a memory and locational aid. As Bakewell notes, "an ideal organizational system would seem to be one that interfiled and coordinated a scholar's collections of verbal and visual materials" and comments that "Dreams of computerized scholarly databases of both verbal and visual resources . . . indexed by all categories, including subject, were rife" (Bakewell 1988, 49–55).

The report concludes that information needs of scholars are dynamic, and the breadth, amount, and quality of information sought as well as the manner in which the literature is browsed varies according to the stage of research. Thus, access to different types of resources as well as different types of searching strategies is appropriate for serving the needs of this group of researchers. With the huge proliferation of image databases and picture files and the expanding use of such resources, this conclusion may also be applicable to the much larger general group of people who will be employing images for a variety of reasons.

Queries

Several studies focus on types of queries to image collections. The staff at the National Library of Medicine reconstructed query logs from staff notes and correspondence and identified not only terms but concepts important to the search request (Keister 1994). A large number of searches are topical, meaning that the content of the picture is less important than the context or circumstances which the image conveys.

Keister notes that types of requests vary among the different image user groups. Picture professionals (still-picture researchers and TV, film, or media personnel) think visually and use art and/or graphics jargon, e.g., "an action shot of George Papanicolau, has to be horizontal and color." Health professionals ask for images in a manner more in keeping with the NLM's orientation: "Do you have pictures of cholera?" The museum or academic community, on the other hand, often has precise citations to images it desires: "'The Cow-Pock, or the Wonderful Effects of the New Inoculation,' by James Gillray, please" (Keister 1994, 9–10).

While some requests are for specific items, "image construct queries" in which images are constructed with words compose one-third to one-half of users' queries. Important to these image constructs are abstract concepts as well as specific objects. Keister cites several examples: "warm picture of a nurse, mother, and baby"; "pictures that would give a sense of the marijuana controversy"; and "polio patients between 1890 and 1914." While these descriptions contain topical elements, the concept behind them is described as a "visual construct." Keister notes that in these queries "patrons usually attempt to construct images with words, and these words define images that the user either remembers or invents to meet a particular immediate communication need." Picture requests also contain many words describing concrete image elements (Keister 1994, 13).

To handle these types of queries, Keister suggests visual-element cataloging supplemented by a visual surrogate, as she considers the aesthetic and emotional needs of the user as being highly subjective and not appropriate for the cataloger to consider. This is a rather interesting conclusion, given that the description of assistance provided to users of the collection appears to rely quite heavily on the familiarity of the staff with the images, and includes individual knowledge about more abstract and interpretive qualities of the images as well as topical access.

The study by Enser (1993) analyzed 2,722 individual requests contained in 1,000 request forms submitted to the Hulton Deutsch Collection Limited, the largest picture archive in Europe. Requests were recorded by assistants and may have undergone some process of mediation; therefore they may not necessarily represent the language of the requester. Thus one observation, that users represented their requests at a greater level of specificity than users of online catalogs, may not be accurate as the specificity may have been added in the intermediary process.

Most requests fell into a unique–nonunique, refined–unrefined two by two matrix. The majority of requests submitted (69%) fell into the "unique" category, which refers to a specific instance of a general category ("George III" as opposed to "kings"). Both unique and nonunique requests were subject to refinement by date (34%), location, action, event, or technical specification (the specification of image orientation or type of image). Enser concludes that general classification systems (such as the Dewey Decimal Classification system) are extremely sparse indexing languages for the mediation of such specific visual information retrieval requests. He suggests that if the Hulton collection is characteristic of non-domain-specific image banks, then a significant proportion of requests could be satisfied by automatic matching operations on picture captions. While nonunique subjects ("purgatory") would need a more detailed indexing system, he concludes that subject indexing of commercial photographic material, because of its expense, is of low utility and that reliance upon experienced intermediaries will continue to be the norm.

A study of 187 user queries in two North Carolina historical photographic collections gave somewhat different results (Collins 1997). Patrons were seeking images primarily for publication or exhibition purposes; they wrote their requests on forms in their own words. Eighty-six percent of these queries included subject terms, with the majority (57%) including generic terms for persons, places, geographical features, objects, activities, and concepts) and 42% including specific or unique terms, largely for persons and organizations. Few queries were for creator or specific physical form. Genre accounted for 10% of terms (landscape, street scene, portrait) and visual terms were also seldom used (7%). Forty-three percent of the queries were refined by date, and 27% by place. As the overwhelming majority of users sought images by subject, this appears to be the critical need in this type of collection. Collins also notes that these results accord well with an earlier study of historians' text searches. This suggests that the research needs of a discipline span formats.

The later study by Armitage and Enser (1997) analyzed 1,749 picture requests from seven libraries. Results supported the earlier work, showing that most requests were for unique items such as named objects and places; however, results varied depending upon the type of collection. The researchers further characterized the requests according to Shatford's 1984 refinement of Panofsky's levels of meaning. Thus, requests were characterized as belonging to the Who–What–When–Where categories, further refined by whether the request is on a specific (unique), generic (type of), or abstract (symbol or abstraction) level. The authors note that this type of facet analysis can handle the difficult situation where an item seems to straddle more than one hierarchical level, and they suggest embedding such a faceted framework within the user interface, as well as using it for image content analysis.

All the studies focusing on newspaper archives found similar results, with specific needs (named persons or objects) dominating the requests. For instance, Ørnager (1995) found that approximately 50% of the requests were concerned with named persons, with the rest covering themes such as sports, politics, geography, and so on. Only 20% were considered complex enough to merit an in-depth interview. Ørnager theorizes that object searches suggest that these users had already come up with a visual concept representing the theme of the article.

One caveat in utilizing these studies for insights into image attributes needed by end-users is that the majority of these searches were interpreted by an intermediary. Therefore, they may represent what Taylor terms a "compromised" need, having been filtered against the contents of the collection and the capabilities of the search system, human or otherwise (Taylor 1968). Additionally, it is a well-known phenomenon that users often express an information need in terms of how they think the system can handle it, rather than as what they really need.

In order to accommodate these factors, Markkula and Sormunen (1998) directly observed eight journalists in their work and interviewed them as they went through the process of conceptualizing a task and searching for images (twenty tasks for a total of twenty-eight searches). They also analyzed 108 requests submitted to archivists. Typical requests were single-word or single-phrase queries; these were again of the "unique" type: named persons, geographical places or buildings. While their needs may have been for general topics, journalists assumed asking for a specific item was the best and easiest search strategy. Results are similar to the other studies in that most searches were for a specific named object or person. Some interesting differences arise between the end user searching and the requests submitted to archivists, though. Twenty percent of the requests archivists received were for types of objects (animals, vehicles, people); these were perceived as being difficult for the end user to retrieve. Conversely, almost a fifth of the end-user searches were for themes, as these were perceived as being too difficult to explain to someone else (and, as the authors note, may be more typical in an iterative type of search. In interviews, journalists emphasized the need for photos dealing with geographical places, types of objects, and themes. More than half of the requests were refined by criteria such as color (versus black and white), shooting distance, time or season, size or number of objects, or activity or item of clothing. In assessing relevance, after topicality and technical features, criteria relating to impression or atmosphere to be conveyed were important (such as thought-provoking, dramatic, surprising, funny).

Often, journalists preferred "nontypical" (unposed) photos. Expressive and aesthetic criteria, like color and composition, played the most important role in the final selection phase. The ultimate criteria depended on other photos selected for a page. A journalist's goal in laying out a page was to make it attractive, balanced, and dynamic, using photos of different types (orientation, single versus groups, and so forth) and with different visual features. Thus, a number of factors entered into the selection process, but these were often considered in a broader context than just the qualities of the individual item.

As for art historians' queries, these frequently concern the search for a particular visual facet of an image, and access to these is strongly desired: "If one could theoretically push a button and get information about all the occurrences of blue cloaks in eighteenth-century German painting [for example] and then use that as a basis to work, that would be the general best thing—the ability to cross-index information (Bakewell 1988, 51)." Another scholar recounted a visual search with an assistant looking for pictures of John the Baptist: "In museums [she] would yell [from another room] "There's a lantern here!" and I would go running . . . and sure enough, there was a John the Baptist with a lantern I'd never seen before. Practically every day I'd come across unknown examples of some of these things" (Bakewell 1988, 148).

Gordon's (1996) analysis of the requests to the Witt Computer Index shows that over 80% involve some element of subject access. Requests are broken down into subject matter by a specific artist, generic subject matter, and specific subject matter, which (similar to Enser's study) was the largest category of requests. Analysis of queries by undergraduate students in art history at the University of Pittsburgh also showed that a wide majority were of the unique, nonrefined category (Chen 2001).

Evaluating requests in an electronic environment such as the Web is more difficult because of issues of user identity and distinguishing among multiple searches which may represent the same or different information needs. Additionally, many of these data records are gathered by commercial search services and are considered proprietary. Thus, to date, there are few studies of user requests in the Web environment. Goodrum and Spink (2001) report data from one study examining user image requests to the Excite search engine. Queries are analyzed by examining the chronological series of actions during a transaction (determined by an anonymous user code assigned by the Excite server). At this time, there was no specific image-search facility, so image queries had to be identified by those containing common image file extensions or terms such as "picture" or "photo." This resulted in 10,000 users with 33,149 requests. Users averaged 3.36 queries per session, and 3.74 terms per query; there was a high rate of search modification (59.6%). Most terms appear infrequently; for the top 100 terms, the top term occurs in less than 9% of the queries. Not surprisingly, sexual or adult content terms (when narrowly defined) accounted for almost a quarter of the top 100 terms, although most terms do appear to be related to such material.

Rather than evaluating requests, other research evaluates users' search failures. An analysis of search failures in the Birkbeck system, a prototype system depending on entity–attribute–relationship modeling, demonstrated that failures occurred mostly because of indexing omissions, incorrect formulation of an information need, and indecisive relevance assessment of the user (Hibler, Leung, and Mannock 1992). In cases where indexer omission occurred, the two most frequent categories were omission of what appeared to be a relatively minor detail (necktie) and failure to index frequently occurring objects (walls, roof). Formulation of information need and relevance are interrelated. As an example, a search on the word "eating" failed to retrieve images of children looking at a birthday cake or standing in a lunch line, both judged to be relevant. The high specificity of the indexing language increased precision but decreased recall, so that searches conducted on general terms ("hats," "landscapes") were less successful.

While there is a need for more user studies, four basic types of image queries emerge from the studies reported so far:

1. Requests for a specific item (the picture of Rouen Cathedral painted by Monet) or a specific piece of information (who painted . . . ?)
2. Requests for a specific instance of a general category (Rouen Cathedral)
3. Requests for a general topical or subject category of images (cathedrals)
4. Requests for images communicating a particular abstract concept or affective response (pictures of cathedrals that show their role and influence in the daily life of an ordinary person of the Middle Ages)

Furthermore, these requests can be modified by a number of other technical, visual, or abstract criteria, such as painting, time of day, symbolic aspect, and so forth. One thing that is notable, and of relevance to the image processing community (see Chapter Four) is that there are very few cases in which a search is composed purely of low-level visual features such as color, texture, or shape. These studies suggest that in addition to topical and object access, users need some access to abstract concepts as well as various aspects of human life such as actions and events. However, because these image facets seem to be situated more within the individual user's own interpretations, these studies generally conclude that this type of access is either inappropriate for catalogers to address or too time-consuming, and therefore too expensive, to accomplish.

Searching Behavior

Knowledge of the types of image searches performed in a variety of contexts could inform design of both indexing and computerized retrieval systems. Information describing searching and the image attributes relevant for the process is needed for determining adequate representational structures for images.

Rorvig (1987) conducted some early work on human image searching with the NASA Visual Thesaurus. This research was based on the broad hypothesis that images can be somewhat robustly substituted for text and that access to images will reduce ambiguity in both term assignment and searching. The NASA Visual Thesaurus functions much like a traditional text-based thesaurus in that it provides the user with related, broader, and narrower terms, but also provides corresponding digitized images. Experimental results indicate that most users, while initially enamored with the ability to search using surrogate images, do not always take advantage of the image-based retrieval functions. Over time, as users become more expert, they revert to the text-based retrieval functions. This suggests that there is more to designing image-based search interfaces than simply substituting visual surrogates for verbal expressions. A deeper understanding of the function of a visual component and the types of searches for which it may be useful is needed.

There have been a number of studies focusing on visual search techniques and retrieval in multimedia systems, but a consistent problem with these studies has been the confounding factor introduced by the system itself (Dunlop 1991). These studies have generally failed to provide information either describing the visual search process or delineating which image attributes are noted in searching.

Several studies describe searching strategies in pictorial databases. Batley (1988) used library staff, university students, and schoolchildren as subjects and identified four visual information search strategies: seeking, focused exploring, open exploring, and wandering, which parallel observations on text information search strategies (Bates 1989). Batley proposes that in a visual information search, given a flexible retrieval environment, users will adopt familiar search strategies and will engage in a range of search activities from the nonexploratory to the unstructured exploratory, in much the same way as in a traditional library environment.

The journalists observed by Markkula and Sormunen (2000) often conducted many search sessions in which different ideas, viewpoints, or strategies were tested. Different search topics produced different kinds of searching behaviors: general search topics led to multiple queries and heavy browsing, while specific needs led more frequently to one or two queries and less browsing. Searching proceeded on a trial and error basis, and browsing was essential. Candidate photos were printed, while final selection often occurred later and was sometimes made by another person. Journalists did not use the advanced search form or the database field structure or thesaurus, which were considered too complex. Ørnager (1995) grouped her searchers according to whether they had broad or specific inquiries, the story "teller" who is open to suggestions, the story "giver" who hands the search over, and the "fill the space" inquirer.

Hastings (1994) conducted an exploratory investigation of the search behavior of eight art historians (with a specialty in Caribbean art) in both a manual and computerized environment. Subjects performed a sorting task and were instructed to organize the images in ways that would be most useful to art historians in general and in ways that would be most useful to them in their own individual research. She found that searches became more complex in the computerized environment, and identified three types of search styles: browse-searcher, subject-searcher, and text-searcher. Browse-searchers created their own categories for the images and used more complex images. Browse-searchers categorized the images by personal appeal, form, composition, style, contrast, color, country of origin, school of painting, and name of artist. Subject-searchers imposed a preconceived classification scheme on the images and used textual information to aid in identification of objects and activities. Text-searchers worked primarily from textual information. Their queries were for identification of such attributes as artist, date, dimensions, place, or title, and their visits to the images were brief.

A later study by the same author investigated search behavior in the Web environment (Hastings 1999). System capabilities necessitated by browsing thumbnails in this environment are the ability to zoom in (in order to analyze brush strokes, for example), enlarge, and group images for visual comparison. Users also expressed the wish to be able to add their own descriptors or index terms in the search process, so that they could then use these terms to create categories for browsing and sorting. Users can thus bring dimensions of their own knowledge to the process; this knowledge could be useful to others as well.

Another study evaluated users' search behaviors in the Art Image Browser project at the University of Michigan's School of Information (Frost and others 2000). Both generalists and specialists were assigned tasks, such as finding an image of a general type of object or a painting by a specific artist. Not surprisingly, specialists preferred direct searching to browsing, and generalists preferred the browsing mode. Failure analysis showed that users had difficulty operationalizing a task into search terms, while the browsing system did not subdivide the image sets into manageable groups. Both groups saw value in a hybrid approach, using both search methods.

Much more research is needed on searching strategies and behaviors in using image storage and retrieval systems. Roddy, speaking of the issue of anticipating a searcher's needs, states: "One of the great failures of image access at present is its inability to provide reliable information on what might be called a typical session," a comment as true today as it was over a decade ago (Roddy 1991, 48).

Current Indexing Practice

Current indexing practice has been evaluated in several recent surveys and inventories. Hourihane (1999), in an updated inventory, reviews subject access in almost fifty collections and specialized thesauri. Subject matter in collections is often treated in a three-tiered manner, with the first level referring to the overall theme, the second level referring to generic objects, and the third level referring to specific details, such as proper names. Of the organizations surveyed, the overwhelming majority use an in-house vocabulary (thirty-two), sometimes combined with free-text or other controlled vocabularies. Free text was used in six, *ICONCLASS* in five, with others such as Dewey Decimal or the *AAT* used by only a few.[60] When controlled vocabularies are used they may be supplemented by free-text. Interestingly, Hourihane reports that natural-language descriptions tend to be easier to generate and more useful in retrieval, in spite of their disadvantages such as lack of consistency and extra length.

Another project surveyed the cataloging and indexing practices of fifty-eight institutional members of the Art Libraries Society (ARLIS) (Graham 1999). The majority (60%) were affiliated with institutions of higher education, with the rest being public, museum, art gallery, archive, and private/commercial libraries. The survey results indicated that the majority of these libraries use in-house rules both for the physical and content description of their image collections. Only a few libraries were using specialized thesauri for visual material; libraries used general controlled vocabularies such as the Dewey and Universal Decimal Classifications and the *Library of Congress Subject Headings* (for videos). Over half of the respondents stated that they were not satisfied with the content indexing of their collections, because of problems in depth and consistency of indexing, and the need for more subject terms and better cross-referencing. Aspects of the indexing process related to these, such as which aspect of an image to index, were also problematic. The report concludes that existing tools for the cataloging and indexing of images are not very satisfactory and that there is general unhappiness amongst both practitioners and users with the current indexing practices for images.

McRae (2000) also found heavy use of local lists for subject indexing in the VISION project, which used the *AAT*, *LCTGM*, *ICONCLASS*, and a number of other sources for terminology. Only 30% of subject terms came from the *AAT* and 5% from *ICONCLASS*, while 40% come from local lists. She notes the ability of the AAT to provide descriptive terms for subject matter may be limited to certain work types and objects, and that for works with narrative content, such as paintings, local lists are preferred. It is unclear from this study whether this is a result of lack of familiarity with specialized thesauri.

Indexing practices in newspaper archives have been investigated by several researchers. Ørnager (1995) interviewed and observed archivists in thirteen Danish newspaper archives. Not all archives had an indexing policy, and lack of indexing consistency was observed to be a problem. Most archives used an in-house indexing language derived from their newspaper's editorial policy. Archivists often utilized captions or other associated texts for indexing and provided detailed indexing of a photo only if they thought it was necessary for finding it later. The archivists indexed themes, and while only half indexed moods or feelings expressed in a photo, most thought this was important.

Markkula and Sormunen's (2000) study also reviewed the indexing practices of *Aamulehti* archivists, who provided access to published and selected unpublished photos in the newspaper archive. The indexing policy consisted of brief, general rules agreed upon in a few meetings, and the basic principle was objective concentration on the concrete content of the photo. Archivists first identified and described concrete objects (named persons, buildings, and places) by selecting keywords from captions and descriptive texts associated with the photos, and by examining the photo. Next they indexed context information, and the final step was classification with a thesaurus term. The indexing interface of the NewsLink system provides a framework for indexing; thirty-nine fields are grouped so that fields containing the same type of information appear together. Several subject fields allow free-text description; some controlled vocabulary (chosen from a news-oriented thesaurus) is used for abstract themes, such as economy. However, observation showed that the archivists did not fully exploit the field structure, instead using "free-text" description fields and not repeating terms elsewhere. The total indexing time per image averaged only a couple of minutes per photograph. Translation and transliteration of English words and proper nouns into Finnish was often problematic.

Markkula and Sormunen provide some detailed analysis of the attributes indexed, noting that all attributes in Layne's (1994) framework were used at least some of the time. Reflecting the composition of the collection, specific objects, places, and events were most frequently indexed, then linear time and the theme of the photo. Generic terms referring to types of objects, places, or events were used less, although archivists did sometimes add common nouns and synonyms for concrete objects. Attributes of objects were occasionally indexed. Archivists had difficulty deciding if the "Of" and "About" levels were represented in a photo. For instance, terms referring to a geographical location may represent the place depicted (Of level) or the place symbolized (About level); archivists solved this by entering place names in the "free description" field. Types of places were seldom indexed. The About level was indexed when easily identified. Archivists indicated that they indexed themes whenever possible, choosing terms from the thesaurus or entering keywords in the free-text field. Themes frequently referred to the domain of the news event (e.g., "finance" for a photo of a government official associated with the budget). While the basic indexing principle was to be objective, the line between concrete/objective and abstract/subjective presented difficulties in the actual indexing. While archivists stated that browsing rather than indexing should accommodate searching for interpretive attributes (atmosphere, moods, or symbolic meanings), nevertheless these were described when obviously depicted.

The generality of the indexing guidelines produced inconsistent output, both in keywords chosen and style of indexing. The thesaurus and the record field structure were also used inconsistently. In terms of granularity, familiar topics and descriptive captions resulted in more-detailed indexing. Overall, while specific search needs were well accommodated, searching for generic object types and themes was most problematic, necessitating browsing as an essential search strategy.

Schroeder (1998) describes the indexing practice at the General Motors Media Archives (GMMA), which houses over 3 million images and large numbers of moving images. These images represent historical and evolutionary aspects of transportation, urban growth, and popular culture, among other subjects. The large quantity combined with cultural and historical context motivated a layered approach to indexing. The Object layer defines the components of the image, including background and action or event. The Style layer defines the purpose for which the image was made: documentary, sales and advertising, or engineering testing. The Implication layer tells the story of the image, i.e., why the image is important, in the context of adding value within the institution. Schroeder's indexing company, Archive Impact, also uses this approach. In most cases, no controlled vocabulary is used.[61]

Few empirical studies have looked in detail at the outcomes of indexing practice. Yandle (1998) analyzed the indexing provided in finding aids for collections of photographs in the Manuscripts Department at the University of North Carolina. She found that 77.3% of the index terms were subject terms, but found that 63% of these were specific subject terms (54% of these were personal names), and only 13.7% were generic terms. Time terms accounted for 13.3% and place terms (city names) for 5.9%. Format, visual, and genre terms account for a small percentage. Collin's (1997) follow-up study is one of the few that attempt to evaluate outcomes of indexing practice. Her analysis of requests for photographs in similar collections to the ones that Yandle studied showed that most requests were for generic rather than specific subjects, and very few were for specific names. This suggests that indexing practice is not aligned with the nature of user requests to these photographic archives; Yandle recommends adding more generic subject access.

Summary

As this chapter demonstrates, there are a number of approaches to organizing image collections and providing access to images in them. A variety of competing requirements and demands shapes system design on a local level, and the presence of digital collections on the Web has stimulated much effort in developing data structures that assist in data exchange among institutions. These factors have resulted in a constellation of considerations surrounding decisions about implementing systems of access. Among these are:

Collection-based considerations. These involve decisions such as whether to index the contents of a collection or simply provide a pointer to the entire collection. When cataloging is at the collection level, then providing links among related collections must be considered. Additionally, provide meaningful links among specific items within collections may also be desirable.

User-based considerations. User-centered indexing (as opposed to document-centered indexing) is considered basic to meeting users' information needs (Fidel 1994). Indexing can be oriented to the users of a specific collection (as has been done with the development of domain-specific thesauri such as the *AAT*). Indexing can also be oriented towards the needs of specific types of users, as has been done for stock photography collections with the addition of attributes of interest to graphic designers and other publication professionals, such as terms relating to image orientation or composition (Romer 1993). However, determining the user group becomes more difficult in the digital environment, and images, with their various interpretations, can serve multiple requirements.

Vocabulary-based considerations. The decision as to which vocabulary to use (if any) should relate to user considerations; the above discussion reveals there are often other factors (organizational, consortial) at work in this decision as well. Choices include controlled vocabulary tools such as a thesaurus or subject headings, the use of free-text description in the form of keywords, or the use of associated texts such as captions, surrounding text, or literary works of critical analysis and interpretation. Each of these choices requires further decisions as to what kinds of structures should carry the information or what kinds of tools are needed to process it. There is little empirical work testing the utility or the outcomes of these various vocabulary choices in relation to user needs. There is also a widespread acknowledgment of the need for a more generalized indexing language, to complement the domain- and collection-specific ones in existence.

Indexing considerations. There are a number of decisions to be made concerning the access points provided for individual items. These relate to the scope of the indexing, whether indexing is limited to descriptors which can be determined automatically such as visual appearance (color, texture, shape; see Chapter Four), is limited to visual content such as the objects in an image, or will include higher-level semantic and interpretive aspects of images (symbolic meanings, "of" and "about," generic and specific). An additional, emerging consideration is whether to provide links among these multiple levels. These decisions obviously impact on the vocabulary considerations and should be contemplated in light of user and collection considerations as well.

Context considerations. These relate to information which is external to the image, such as the circumstances of production and the history of the item. As the discussion above shows, these can affect the understanding and interpretation of the item. Other factors (especially in the case of an image of an art or museum object) would be technique, medium, and other facets related to the production of the original item.

As this summary reveals, these decisions are not mutually exclusive. They are complex decisions which would be facilitated by some framework within which to consider them. This framework, however, should also have a user-centered focus, which has been lacking in many initiatives. Theoretical frameworks, such as Shatford's reinterpretation of Panofsky, move towards this, yet these have not been adequately tested in empirical work with indexers (or users) either (although Armitage and Enser's explication of it suggests that the more abstract levels are not that intuitive to apply, as well as does some of the work discussed in Chapter Five). As frameworks grow more complex, more time is required to use them, and there is more room for error.

The section on users' queries and searches suggests several general types of searches:

1) A *unique* (specific item) search, in which matching of the item is exact
2) A *prototypical* search, a search for a representative instance of a person, place, item, or event
3) An *abstract* search, for an item conveying a particular feeling or concept

Enser (1993) notes that, in the case of searches for "unique" or specific items, the process of searching is often one of "satisficing" rather than one of exhaustive search. Queries in other systems reveal a number of "prototypical" and "affective" searches, such as "neighborhood drug stores" and "a warm picture" (Keister 1994, 21)

The attributes associated with these types of searches range from being highly specified (an image of a specific person or thing) to being less specified ("children eating" could refer to any number of events depicted, from picnics to birthday parties to school cafeteria lines) to being highly unspecified (a "sad" picture could have any number of different types of attributes which would make it "sad," from the specific subject matter portrayed to the color or style).

These studies indicate that, just as in text searching, there are different types and levels of queries, users, and searching behaviors in visual retrieval that need to be accommodated. The broad types of searches discussed above represent the two ends of a continuum between a focused, specific type of searching and a broad, browsing type of searching. Buckland (1979) suggests that browsing is informal searching which is low on document specificity but may be on any level of information specificity. Thus, browsing is an information seeking activity that is transferable across a range of information needs. While many information retrieval system designers have tried to accommodate several types of searches by providing flexible system manipulation, the question remains as to whether this need could also be addressed through new or expanded approaches to indexing or newer forms of knowledge representation.

The fact remains that, in order to develop useful and usable image retrieval systems, there is still a need for more empirical research investigating users' image descriptions, image requests, and searching behaviors. An understanding of image attributes and how they relate to specific types of queries would contribute greatly to image retrieval system design and could be a very useful part of a future research agenda. The next chapter describes some basic research focusing on image attributes.

Notes

1. While an earlier definition of metadata was "data about data," the line between data and metadata is not distinct; one application's data can be another application's metadata. Therefore the more precise definition of metadata as "structured data" is now broadly used to refer to these types of data.

2. This is a reprint of an article originally published in 1911.

3. Philadelphia, Pa., Sunday, March 8, 1998. Summary available at www.arlisna.org/Jtcatpro.txt (accessed on April 18, 2003).

4. *A Slide Classification System for the Organization and Automatic Indexing of Interdisciplinary Collections of Slides and Pictures*, more commonly referred to as the Santa Cruz system, Simons and Tansey (1970). Available at http://slides-www.ucsc.edu/index.html (accessed on April 18, 2003).

5. Museum and cultural-heritage objects share many of these same problems; this discussion focuses on art object information but many of the points here are applicable to these museum and cultural heritage objects as well.

6. See www.artic.edu/ (accessed on April 18, 2003).

7. See www.metmuseum.org/ (accessed on April 18, 2003).

8. See iberia.vassar.edu/~slides/classification.html (accessed on April 18, 2003).

9. See www.nga.gov/library/slidesearch.htm (accessed on April 18, 2003).

10. See ica.princeton.edu (accessed on April 18, 2003).

11. Information about the *TGM I* can be found at lcweb.loc.gov/rr/print/tgm1/ (accessed on April 18, 2003).

12. *TGM II*, available at lcweb.loc.gov/rr/print/tgm2/ (accessed on April 18, 2003).

13. The *TGM I* distinguishes between topical terms and genre or physical characteristic terms as researchers may wish to see an item which is either a "self-portrait" (*type* of image) or in which "self-portrait" is the *subject*. This distinction is an important one for a theoretical approach to indexing, as discussed in the text.

14. While the names in this table are in some cases the same as individual attributes in the current research, they should not be interpreted as one-to-one comparisons, as the methods of analysis were somewhat different.

15. The research which produced the descriptor types (attributes) used for this analysis is discussed more fully in Chapter Five. Objects are frequently named in describing tasks and the "story" of an image is typically described in sorting tasks. For a brief outline of the image attributes and classes of attributes used in this analysis, please refer to Chapter Five, Appendices A and B.

16. Note that this does not correspond to the attribute *Group* in the current research. *Group* would include terms from such areas as Organizations, Business/Industry, Government, Health, and others in the previous analysis.

17. Available for searching at www.ericfacility.net/extra/pub/thessearch.cfm (ac-

cessed on April 18, 2003) through the ERIC Processing & Reference Facility, Computer Sciences Corporation, 4483-A Forbes Boulevard, Lanham, MD, 20706.

18. Description of the *AAT* can be found at www.getty.edu/research/tools/vocabulary/aat/about.html (accessed on April 18, 2003).

19. See www.getty.edu/research/tools/vocabulary/aat/faq.html#scope (accessed on April 18, 2003).

20. See www.getty.edu/research/institute/vocabulary/introvocabs/ (accessed on April 18, 2003).

21. Information about ICONCLASS can be found at www.ICONCLASS.nl/ (accessed on April 18, 2003).

22. See www.tonystone.com (accessed on April 18, 2003).

23. See www.hultongetty.com/ (accessed on April 18, 2003).

24. See www.getty.edu/research/tools/vocabulary (accessed on April 18, 2003).

25. For more information, see www.princeton.edu/~ica/indexca.html (accessed on April 18, 2003).

26. For more information, see www.yale.edu/ycba/ (accessed on April 18, 2003).

27. Available at www.picturethesaurus.gov.au/ (accessed on April 18, 2003).

28. See Shatford (1984) for a full discussion of original, related, and represented works and the necessity for better methods of representing these.

29. See, for instance, Fritz, Deborah A. *Cataloging with AACR2R and USMARC for Books, Computer Files, Serials, Sound Recordings, and Videorecordings*. Chicago, Ill.: American Library Association, 1998.

30. See www.object-id.com/index.html (accessed on April 18, 2003).

31. It should be noted that the MARC format and EAD are also considered data communication standards.

32. For more information, see http://nlc-bnc.ca/9/1/p1-204-e.html (accessed on April 18, 2003).

33. The PCC is an international cooperative effort aiming to increase access to library collections and to facilitate cost-effective cataloging by providing minimum mutually accepted standards for a core record. The PCC homepage can be accessed at: lcweb.loc.gov/catdir/pcc/pcc.html (accessed on April 18, 2003).

34. See www.getty.edu/research/institute/standards/cdwa/index.html (accessed on April 18, 2003).

35. For more information, see www.vraweb.org/ (accessed on April 18, 2003).

36. For a discussion, see Lanzi, Elisa, and Roy McKeown, "Square Pegs and Round Holes: Standards for Visual Resources Collections." *Visual Resources Association Bulletin* 23, no. 4 (1996): 93–103.

37. The Core can be accessed at www.vraweb.org/vracore3.htm (accessed on April 18, 2003).

38. CNI/OCLC Image Metadata Workshop, September 24–25, 1996, Dublin, Ohio

39. As listed at www.dublincore.org (accessed on April 18, 2003).

40. See www.amico.org/ (accessed on April 18, 2003).

41. See www.w3.org (accessed on April 18, 2003).

42. See www.w3.org for more information (accessed on April 18, 2003).

43. See www.oac.cdlib.org/dynaweb/ead/calher/ (accessed on April 18, 2003).

44. The project has now been terminated. See 194.134.65.21/ (accessed on April 18, 2003).

45. The MPEG-7 WG11 is a working group of ISO/IEC: International Standards Organization/International Electrotechnical Commission. The MPEG group creates standards for the bit-efficient representation of audiovisual content (MPEG-1, -2, and -4).

46. For more detailed information, see mpeg.telecomitalialab.com/ (accessed on April 18, 2003).

47. For a useful discussion of these, see Lanzi and McKeown (1996).

48. See Woodley (2000). Available from www.getty.edu/research/institute/standards/intrometadata/ (accessed on April 18, 2003).

49. See www.getty.edu/research/institute/standards/intrometadata/3_crosswalks/index.html (accessed on April 18, 2003)

50. See, for instance, the AMICO data dictionary: www.amico.org/AMICOlibrary/dataDictionary.html (accessed on April 18, 2003).

51. See www.cimi.org/ (accessed on April 18, 2003).

52. SPECTRUM, a UK Museum Documentation Standard, interprets documentation relating to all functions of a museum, not just cataloging However, it is non-prescriptive in specifying the structure of information. It is widely implemented in both manual and automated systems. See www.mda.org.uk/spectrum.htm (accessed on April 18, 2003).

53. See www.w3.org/TR/rdf-primer/ (accessed on April 18, 2003). For an example of how a photograph can be represented, see www.w3.org/TR/photo-rdf/ (accessed on April 18, 2003). The general technical report section of the World Wide Web Consortium (www.w3.org/TR/) has a large number of documents explaining RDF, its relation to XML, and a number of other specifications, protocols, and so forth (accessed on April 18, 2003).

54. For more information, see Sowa (1991).

55. For a number of interesting papers, see the "Ontology and Conceptual Modeling" website at the Institute for Systems Science and Biomedical Engineering of the Italian National Research Council (CNR): www.ladseb.pd.cnr.it/infor/ontology/ontology.html (accessed on April 18, 2003).

56. CIDOC is a constituent committee of the International Council of Museums (ICOM). See www.cidoc.icom.org/ (accessed on April 18, 2003).

57. For further information, see cidoc.ics.forth.gr/what_is_crm.html (accessed on April 18, 2003).

58. One exception to this is the VISION project, in which thirty institutions contributed records to a shared database; see McRae (2000).

59. See www.amianet.org.

60. The *AAT* was specifically excluded from the analysis as, according to the author, it is an object classification system and not a subject classification system. *ICONCLASS* was also excluded, for reasons not stated, but an appendix notes that it is the most widely used system in existence and lists projects using it, sometimes in combination with other systems.

61. For indexing examples using this approach, see www.archiveimpact.com/ (accessed on April 18, 2003).

Chapter 4

Machine Processing of Images

There are a burgeoning number of applications that involve digital storage and retrieval of images, such as CAD systems, robotics, medical imaging, remote sensing, geographic and geological data processing, archaeological data systems, and art, slide, photography, and graphics imagebases. Rapid and relevant retrieval from large data stores such as these are challenging current limits of expertise. Digital image systems need appropriate storage and retrieval mechanisms and interfaces as well as end-user tools for image understanding, analysis, and manipulation. Other systems issues include such factors as database architecture, memory management, and compression/decompression.

The realization that computers can play an important part in image handling occurred early in areas such as defense, criminology, and medicine. Researchers in these areas realized that images must be treated as a central source of information rather than as an appendix to other database information. However, early systems designers did not consider the unique needs of visual information management, resulting in, at best, less-than-optimal systems (Jain 1993, 198–199). The creation, storage, transmission, searching, and retrieval of electronic image information has been and continues to be an area of intense research.

Can current technologies offer methods which will address the hope expressed by some for direct image-to-image retrieval or visual matching methods? Although many significant advances have been made in the last five years, the answer remains, at best, a much-qualified "yes." Images can now indeed be matched based upon several visual parameters, and the primary emphasis in content-based retrieval remains on technical implementation issues, as is evident in the current literature of electronic imaging. There are now several commercial image-retrieval systems available utilizing a variety of image features, indexing structures, and query methods (Flickner and others 1995; Humphrey, Jain, and Shu 1996). As Squire (1998) notes, however, the emergence of commercial systems does not indicate that the technology is mature, only that the demand for it is very strong.

Researchers are also discovering that "visual similarity" is a multifaceted problem. This chapter reviews the general methods currently employed in digital image processing and retrieval systems. Standard techniques are discussed with examples of system implementations. Woven through this review is discussion of the evolution of thinking in the content-based research community and an overview of new approaches that are emerging. Relevant literatures from which research is described include those of image and signal processing, machine vision, content-based retrieval, access methods (indexing structures), artificial intelligence and knowledge representation, and database methods.

As noted in the introduction, the review deals primarily with still images and not with video or moving images. As video consists of many single images, many of the techniques discussed in this chapter have applicability in the video domain, and video processing builds upon this foundation. A fundamental and obvious difference between still images and video is the additional temporal information that must be processed for video understanding and querying. However, this author (and others) would argue that, in some senses, automatic extraction of feature and semantic information is *more* difficult for a single image than for a video segment (Smeulders and others 2000). This is not intended to diminish the complexity of processing and indexing that information or the skill needed to develop these techniques. Indeed, processing more information introduces greater levels of complexity. However, with video the information is likely to be *explicit*, whereas a single image contains more implicit information, requiring more inferential methods and reasoning processes. Additionally, more information is available within a video format. For instance, more information about objects is available when multiple frames exist. As an example, two time-sequenced images of the same object can be closely aligned to digitally subtract and visualize differences. Additional clues are provided by object motion, as points corresponding to one object move together. Other clues are provided by the presence of accompanying textual or audio information. Video has a linear timeline, as important to the narrative structure of video as it is in text, whereas in still pictures, the author's narrative expression of intention exists in such aspects as frame selection, illumination, and composition, and is subject to interpretation. With video, more context and narrative is provided (the "before" and "after" information), whereas with still images that is likely up to the imagination. An excellent overview of video and multimedia representation can be found in Al-Khatib and others (1999).

Image Digitization

Images must be converted from an analog to a digital format to enable powerful and flexible machine and network functionalities such as feature extraction, computation, manipulation, and transmission. Electronic images can be defined as "sets of data . . . produced by recording variations in the intensity of a signal either reflected from the surfaces of objects or partly absorbed when passing through them" (Pavlidis 1988, 121). The term "pixel" refers to a single measurement within a picture produced by this method.

Images can be either converted by scanning in a raster format (composed of a sequence of bits which are associated with a gray- or color-level) or they can be created with a general purpose graphical editor, which produces images in a vector format. Vector graphics store images as mathematical formulas of shapes such as lines and circles, and permit operations such as scaling or rotation to take place. Vector graphics are thus suitable to object-oriented programming. Off-the-shelf statistical and machine learning packages typically expect a set of vectors as input. Raster images must be preprocessed to be transformed into a vector format before they can be manipulated.

As one researcher explains, "biological vision is primarily sensitive to changes in light intensities rather than to the absolute light intensities themselves . . . extraction of basic attributes of light fields, i.e., characteristic features of an image, is the central issue in biological vision" (Raff 1993, 162–163). This has also turned out to be one of the major problems for image digitization. When an image is digitized, distributions of light intensities are encoded in pixel values through a quantization process which assigns a binary value to an analog signal. Light amplitude can be described by several methods, and the information loss in this conversion process can be considerable.

There has been little specific research aimed towards determining exactly what levels of image quality are desirable for different tasks and users. Ester (1990) conducted a study to determine what levels of resolution and dynamic range are desirable for one particular class of images and users, art historians. His results showed distinct breaking points where people were no longer able to tell a "higher-quality" from "lower-quality" image. It is obvious that certain applications, such as those in medicine, require a high level of image quality. More research is required to determine appropriate user groups and contexts for ranges of image quality.

There are a number of major issues associated with image digitization, among them general image quality, resolution and display issues, technologies for image capture, and uses of imaging technology for conservation and preservation.[1] Research has shown that some of these issues go beyond technical parameters and are context- and use-dependent (Beard 1991; Besser 1991). While image quality is critical, it is context-dependent in that it is related to the collection and to the uses that are made of images, and whether the images are used for recognition or for study and analysis. Images may have different contrast, hue, and resolution requirements, and they may also exist in time and space and be related to one another by content, time, modality, or spatial relationship (e.g., images of adjacent portions of an object). In addition to technical implementation challenges, all these factors can come into play in image retrieval.

Image Retrieval

In order to understand why particular techniques are used for retrieval, it is necessary to understand how researchers in machine processing and computer vision have defined the querying process, as this determines the attributes searched for, the methods used, and the types of output returned. Query classes include low-level or primitive features which can be extracted automatically or semiautomatically, such as color, texture, shape, volume, spatial relationships, motion, and text (Gudivada and Raghaven 1995a). While the list of features is from their article, the grouping below is this author's. Specification of geometric and spatial relationships among entities is frequently useful, and is essential in computer vision applications. Spatial queries are common in geographic, medical, and CAD/CAM applications. Query types are discussed further in "Querying Techniques," below. Machine processing of image attributes for retrieval purposes is referred to as "content-based image retrieval"(CBIR or CBR).

CBR Methods

CBR has been an active field of research for well over a decade. In the vocabulary of CBR, an image is represented by a "signature," which is composed of features derived from its pixel values. Therefore, an attribute such as color is derived by the output of some operation upon data and is referred to as a "feature."[2] Retrieval operates by defined rules for comparing features. From the perspective of CBR, image statistics produced by CBR methods should be sufficient for helping users find desired images. Users of these systems "naively expect to search for a specific object or person," but in reality can only search for images with a similar distribution of image properties (such as color or texture) (Sclaroff and others 2001, 261).

Features may be either "global" or "local." A global feature is "coarse-grained," that is, it represents the image in its entirety, such as the overall color distribution. A local feature is a finer-grained representation achieved through segmentation of the image into smaller regions. Such features include color, texture, and shape. Both global and local features offer advantages in processing and querying (Al-Khatib and others 1999). Global features offer advantages in terms of low computational complexity of feature extraction and pattern matching algorithms and can be used when queries deal with single entities. Local features can be used to identify objects within an image and to extract detailed information. A feature (or combination of features) is selected based on various image and system performance criteria, such as its capacity to distinguish among different images, the maximum number of images such a feature could retrieve in a query, and the amount of computation required to derive, store, and compare the features (Mandal, Idris, and Panchanathan 1999).

While a wide range of features and query types is defined as being in the realm of CBR, in practice most research has focused on low-level features which can be extracted automatically, although some current research is combining manual and automatic methods. Image features such as color and texture are derived directly from the pixels in an image (the pixel domain). These low-level features are commonly represented as histograms, and an image composed of one or several such features is represented by fixed-length feature vectors with multiple real values. Such vectors tend to be highly dimensional (the so-called dimensionality curse), and this necessitates further processing to increase efficiency. In determining optimal matching and querying techniques, there is a constant trade-off between speed of processing and the number of image features used (and hence precision in retrieval).

CBR has its early roots in machine vision and image understanding, in which one of the goals is object recognition and the automatic classification of objects.[3] The analysis process for machine vision tries to determine the composition of complex objects in terms of simpler objects. Complex objects are defined using composition rules that require the presence or absence of other objects and rules that impose cardinal and positional constraints among the objects composing the complex object. Thus, machine processing of images proceeds by segmenting an image into processable units and performing some kind of analysis of these units in order to end up with a description in terms of specific features. Object recognition and image understanding involve moving from lower to higher levels of abstraction and require increasing levels of inference and reasoning. The output of these processes can consist of either labeled graphic output or textual description. Such image processing of necessity involves a loss of information; the challenge is to be able to specify more adequately exactly *what* information is lost or filtered out.

We should note here that the area of image processing and understanding is considered to be highly underconstrained. As with human interpretation of images, in which one image can give rise to many subjective interpretations, so too can one data point or data representation arise from many different image attributes. In other words, a given data representation does not necessarily plot back to one unique image. Constraints, such as domain or lighting conditions, are added to make these problems more tractable, but then systems correspondingly become domain- or scene- or application-specific.[4]

There are some useful distinctions between CBR and its roots in machine vision and image processing, According to Eakins and Graham (1999), while CBR draws many of its methods from these fields (and is regarded by some as a subset of these), it differs from these fields principally through its emphasis on the retrieval of images with desired characteristics from a collection of significant size, rather than matching on a few salient characteristics. CBR also differs from classical information retrieval in that image databases are essentially unstructured, since digitized images consist purely of arrays of pixel intensities, with no inherent meaning. The extraction of useful information from the raw data (such as recognizing the presence of particular shapes or textures) is a dynamic process which must be completed before any kind of reasoning about the image contents is possible. Santini and Jain (1997) contend that image databases thus differ fundamentally from text databases, where the raw material (words stored as ASCII character strings), even if unstructured otherwise, has already been logically structured by the author. Others note that CBR relies on several fundamentals: the underlying data model, a priori knowledge of the area of interest, and the scheme for representing the queries (Yoshitaka and Ichikawa 1999). All these obviously have an impact upon what can be retrieved.

While CBR is now a maturing field employing a variety of techniques and exploring other disciplines for relevant heuristics, it retains many of the earlier approaches and techniques (often combined in multiple ways). The following discussion provides a broad overview of image processing in support of retrieval, composed of basic preprocessing, segmentation, and computation of features.[5] A number of reviews offering more detail on many of the techniques and research projects are available (Aigrain, Zhang, and Petkovic 1996; Gudivada and Raghaven 1995b; Marsicoi, Cinque, and Levialdi 1997; Narasimhalu 1995).

Similarity Measures

Psychological models of similarity are discussed in Chapter Two. A primary problem for similarity measures in CBR is the level at which a similarity judgment is made. Perceptual similarity is only one of several components which can affect judgments of similarity. Human similarity judgments have been evaluated through sorting experiments, with the goal of learning which features are most likely to contribute to these judgments (Jörgensen 1995a; Rogowitz and Frese and others 1998). This research demonstrated that similarity judgments are made on a wide variety of aspects of images (purpose, emotional content, meaning, or theme), in addition to perceptual features. Research focusing on the task of illustrating a news story evaluated similarity judgments in a two-stage selection process: selection from thumbnails and from the full image (Markkula and Sormunen 2000). For the small thumbnail images, the number of persons, shooting distance, and colors were the prominent criteria, while for full images, gestures and facial expressions were important determinants in creating the desired atmosphere and feeling in the photo. Other factors included the action taking place, the background, and other objects in the image. Composition (which includes such factors as photo direction, shooting angle and direction of movement) was also important, particularly in relation to specific layout criteria.

Other researchers have compared human and machine grouping of images (Squire and Pun 1998). This research demonstrated not only large individual differences in how users sort images into groups (agreement was approximately 35% higher than expected by chance) but an even wider gap between the human sorts and the machine assessments of similarity.

Similarity within machine vision and image processing traditionally has been operationalized as the distance between vectors or points in a multidimensional space. *Distance measures* are similarity functions that compute and return a value measuring the distance (corresponding to the similarity) between two objects according to some predefined criteria. Distance measures are defined for particular feature sets. The assumption underlying use of these measures to assess image similarity is that machine and human assessments of similarity are sufficiently alike for these measures to be somewhat robust. While most systems rely on these distance measures, in reality very little testing of these assumptions has taken place.

The most basic similarity functions are distance measures such as city block, Euclidean distance, and weighted Euclidean distance. The Euclidian distance is the square root of the sum of the squared differences between the two objects' respective coordinates. An additional problem is the need for non-Euclidean similarity measures, as Euclidian measures do not effectively simulate human perception of some visual content (Rui, Huang, and Chang 1999). Other methods, such as relevance feedback, are being explored to address the multiple levels upon which similarity judgments can be made. Other approaches include the use of fuzzy logic to extend psychological models of similarity, especially in relation to the problem of interference between features, in which relevance of a feature is affected by its relationship to other features (Santini and Jain 1999).

Discussions of similarity measures within CBR refer to *ground truth*, a phrase used to refer to similarity judgments among images. Typically, an image is assigned a "ground-truth relevance score," which measures its similarity to the desired image. Assignment of ground truth relevance scores is, however, problematic. Human judgments are time-consuming to obtain, as each image in a collection must be assessed for its relevance to the query. This makes these judgments both expensive and subject to the problems of human inconsistency and subjectivity. Nevertheless, as these systems are ultimately for the use of humans, similarity scores which mirror human responses to images are desirable.

Low-Level Features

Researchers in machine processing have made significant advances working with several of the more tractable (in terms of being computationally accessible) attributes of images, such as color and texture. These approaches, which operate on the pixels in the image directly, are briefly summarized below. While these are discussed individually, in practice most current systems use a combination of these techniques to provide data for analysis (as it is likely human vision does).

We should note here that, regardless of the feature evaluated or specific approach chosen, noise present in images interferes with image processing and interpretation. Noise may be due to irregularities in the original scene or may be introduced during imaging and sampling. Limited resolution and low contrast also present difficulties for machine processing. In contrast to biological vision systems, in which "the high efficiency of assimilation of complex visual information is related to a powerful mechanism of selective omission of information," and in which selection of relevant from irrelevant information proceeds without conscious thought, it is extremely difficult to model these processes in machine processing (Raff 1993, 161). There are two approaches to dealing with noise in an image: it can be removed through filtering techniques or its effects can be made explicit by associating uncertainty attribute values using probabalistic means or fuzzy logic (Jagadish and O'Gorman 1989, 33–36). Thus a system can associate a degree of certainty with each evaluated feature or recognized object.

Color

We are all familiar with the idea that color is reflected or transmitted light or light from a direct source. Less familiar perhaps (although frequently observed in theatrical stage lighting) is the idea that a perceived color (a color stimulus) results from both the object reflecting or transmitting the light, and the light source which provides the reflected light. A stimulus has what is called a spectral power distribution, which is the product of the spectral power distribution of the light source and the spectral reflectance of the object. The concept of the color stimulus is the foundation for all methods of representing color images in a numerical form. As Giorgianni and Madden (1997) explain, every individual point in a scene or image has a spectral power distribution, and any image can be treated as a collection of individual color stimuli, which can be detected and measured.

Color is considered important as both a visual and semantic retrieval tool. Common objects that are similar often have the same or similar colors. In addition, overall color composition can indicate such semantic factors as whether an image depicts an indoor or outdoor scene (which, in contrast to artificial lighting, may contain a lot of blues and greens).

Global color histograms, which count how much of each color occurs in an image, are widely used for object identification and for characterizing and retrieving similar images. A color histogram is a representation of the distribution of colors in the image. It is obtained by discretizing the colors within the image and counting the number of pixels of each color. The number of colors is finite, as they are transformed into a common discrete color cluster (or bin), meaning that certain colors are considered equivalent. Color histograms are computed within a color space defined by some color axes (commonly three axes of red, green, and blue [RGB]).[6] Such a three-channel histogram may then be transformed into a single variable histogram for convenience.

Researchers in machine vision pioneered early work in color indexing (Funt and Finlayson 1995; Swain and Ballard 1991). Swain's early FINDIT system matched a query image against a database image by use of two-dimensional hue-saturation color histograms (Swain 1993). The results indicated that color histogram intersection is fairly insensitive to changes in image resolution, histogram size, depth, and viewpoint; thus some degree of perspective distortion does not affect retrieval.

Color histograms are also invariant to changes such as translation and rotation about an axis perpendicular to the image, and change slowly as angle of view, scale, and occlusion change. High match values can be obtained, because although shading and camera noise can reduce point-by-point matching for an object, regions will still match well. One example of a refinement to early work provided invariance against changes in illumination by reducing the three-dimensional color histogram into a two-dimensional chromaticity histogram.

Color histograms for different objects can differ considerably, however. To be able to identify objects based on color histograms, the similarity of the color histogram of an image must be measured against the color histograms in the database, and only about 200 different colors are necessary to distinguish a large number of objects. A three-dimensional object can be well represented with a small number of histograms corresponding to a set of canonical views. However, color histograms do not necessarily produce unique object or scene identifiers, as a color histogram can in fact map back to many different objects or scenes. The most common similarity metrics employed for evaluating color similarity are histogram intersection and weighted distance between color histograms (Mandal, Idris, and Panchanathan 1999).

As Yang and Kuo (1999) explain, the number of color clusters indicates the richness of color in a picture and can be used to broadly characterize an image. For instance, images with simple color content have a small number of clusters; these have homogeneous backgrounds or simple objects (note that texture does not affect this). An intermediate number indicates slightly more complex background and/or objects, while many clusters denote complicated backgrounds or objects. Histograms have their limits, especially when applied to very large databases. A 64-bin histogram has discriminating power up to 25,000 images; when a joint histogram is used, the discrimination increases tenfold with high recall (Smeulders and others 2000).

There are a number of techniques that are employed to reduce the complexity of the matching process, such as reducing the number of colors quantized.[7] For instance, the Chabot system increased runtime by using as few as twenty colors for predominant color analysis; this still allowed "glimpses" of minor colors (Ogle 1995). Other techniques include the use of dominant features, different resolutions to produce a lower-dimensional histogram, and spatial location of the colors (color layout). Most CBR systems today use color histograms or variations of these techniques, and often add user control of the proportion of colors desired. This gives the user the functionality of searching for a type of image by specifying color composition. For instance, by searching for an image that is 40% green, 30% blue, and 30% other colors, the searcher could aim for an outdoor scene.

Some examples of advances in color indexing include the use of cumulative color histograms (intersection with some element of spatial matching), spatial constraints (an image is divided into five partially overlapped, fuzzy regions, with each region indexed by its three moments[8] of the color distribution), region-based color querying, and color correlogram (which distills the spatial correlation of colors and describes their global distribution by placing the colors of the pair along the first and second dimension and the spatial distance along the third) (Greenspan and others 1997; Huang and others 1998; Stricker and Dimai 1996; Stricker and Orengo 1995). Other techniques include color histogram refinement, image clustering (clusters with similar colors occurring in about the same location), and image signature methods (which divide an image into rectangular cells of equal size which are represented by one or more colors that exceed a predefined threshold) (Shanbehzadeh, Moghadam, and Mahmoudi 2000).

Texture

Although texture is an intuitive and ubiquitous attribute of visual objects (and of tactile sensory processes as well), no truly satisfactory description of texture has been established, in spite of a large amount of research (Raff 1993). Nevertheless, mathematical models of texture are being incorporated into image retrieval systems. Depending upon the domain (such as target analysis), these models have been quite useful, especially when combined with other low-level features.

Texture has been characterized as an "organized area phenomenon" with two basic components: 1) primitives out of which the texture is composed, and 2) spatial distribution of the primitives (Haralick 1979). Texture is *not* a microscopic property; rather it is a statistical, or syntactic, property of surface features which confers visual homogeneity. The human eye cannot distinguish among separate units below a certain resolution; thus individual components of a region may be perceived as similar because of uniform color, intensity, or, in the case of texture, structural density. Julesz (1981) concluded that, in relation to texture, only first order statistics (the information contained within the pixel) have perceptual significance. In machine processing, the basic texture element is called a texel. A texel is generally composed of several pixels which can be periodic, quasi-periodic, or random in nature.

In research asking subjects to classify textures, researchers identified coarseness, directionality, regularity, contrast, line-likeness, and roughness as the perceptual properties underlying the classification decisions (Tamura, Mori, and Yamawaki 1978). Another characterization of texture, which is both intuitive and agrees well with human descriptions of texture, is the set of Wold features: periodicity, directionality, and randomness (Liu and Picard 1996; Rao and Lohse 1993). These visually meaningful texture representations lend themselves well to more-intuitive CBR systems for end users.

Texture has been described using second-order spatial histograms, which add a relational component by measuring the joint occurrence of pixel pairs from a distance and angle with the horizontal axis. However, it is not always true that textures with identical second-order statistics are indistinguishable. Research in which subjects discriminated changes in these statistics using different natural and synthetic stimulus images suggests there was some variety in the magnitudes of the thresholds for the natural stimulus images (Tadmor and Tolhurst 1994). In fact, the second-order statistics of different natural images were more diverse than previously suggested.

Fractal models were used to facilitate segmentation by texture, but are less used today. Raff explains that "fractals are sets of numbers that have the properties of self-similarity and randomness over many size scales at the same time. These sets can be described with an associated fractal dimension which is characteristic of the physical system that it is describing" (Raff 1993, 176). Subjective rankings agree well with fractal dimensions of texture. Other techniques, such as wavelet transforms (see "Compression," below) are currently widely used to represent texture. Texture, in combination with color or other features, is widely used for segmentation of image regions. For further information, Bergen and Landy (1991) provide a detailed overview of texture modeling.

Shape

According to Pavlidis (1988), within an image, information is found where a signal's intensity changes due to 1) change in reflectivity of a surface; 2) change in orientation of a surface; 3) combined changes in the relation of the object and the viewer; 4) direct occlusion of one object by another; 5) indirect occlusion (shadow) of one object by another. These changes can provide information which serves to distinguish shapes or regions from one another. As shape is frequently closely tied to object identity, shape recognition is a primary component in image segmentation and object recognition techniques.

Shape recognition techniques make use of global and local features. Global features (such as area or perimeter) depend on the entire shape and are simple to detect and robust with respect to noise, but are inappropriate for touching or overlapping objects. Local features, such as edges, corners, and areas of change of direction, can deal with occlusion, but are more sensitive to noise. Local and global features do not map directly to computation of edges or regions, however, as features such as area and compactness are used in both edge-based and region-based techniques. Another way of categorizing shape recognition techniques distinguishes between information-preserving (unambiguous, which allow reconstruction of the original image), and non-information-preserving (allowing approximation but not reconstruction) methods.

Humans can recognize a shape or object even when there is distortion due to perspective, shadow, or other factors, but this is obviously a much more difficult problem for machine methods. Shape descriptors therefore also need to be insensitive to changes in scale, rotation of the object, and translation, to facilitate normalization and matching within a range of variation due to differing viewpoints or occlusion. Simple measures, such as length, area, or radius, are sensitive to changes in perspective or viewpoint, whereas measures such as symmetry or roundness are more robust.

Computationally, object shape is determined by finding boundaries (edge detection), or regions (region growing), or a combination of both. *Edge detection* uses edge-finder algorithms (which detect image intensity changes but ignore interior regions) and is a common first step in image processing. *Region growing* is concerned with finding areas where no changes occur, and makes use of both border and interior information. A number of methods have been proposed to solve the problems of shape retrieval. A few are highlighted here; for a full review see Mehtre, Kankanhalli, and Lee (1997).

Edge-finder algorithms, which detect image intensity changes (and infer one of the five types of changes listed above), are a common first step in image processing. Edge detection is concerned with finding locations in which one or more of the five types of changes listed above occur, and with demonstrating that there is more than one surface. The output of an edge detection algorithm is an edge map, which contains nonzero values at all locations where an edge is detected. An algorithm for producing an edge map must specify both the conditions under which an edge is detected and how the edge will be characterized.

Edge detection depending on gray-level differences is extremely sensitive to noise; noisy images may be more successfully processed incorporating probabilities. Variations in texture and color can also be used to indicate boundaries; however, edge detection is more easily determined in black-and-white scenes than in color images.

Early techniques for edge detection, which simply looked for places of rapid change in an image, involved problems of scale. A "primal sketch" approach draws upon intensity changes and their geometrical distribution and organization (Marr 1982). Multiscaling techniques which generate a sequence of primal sketches have been found to be an improvement, and other approaches use surface geometries. Curve or surface fitting can also be used to detect edges. Corner points are also used.[9] Another approach analyzes distribution of pointwise error for random or systematic variation. Raff gives an overview of edge detection processes and problems, while a detailed source for a number of methods is Nadler and Smith's *Pattern Recognition Engineering* (Nadler and Smith 1992; Raff 1993, 174–196).

Boundaries can be represented by chain codes, which trace the boundary and represent the direction of the next pixel in relation to the current pixel. As these are not insensitive to scaling, an enhancement (called a shape code) which is unique incorporates corners, among other modifications. More recent work focuses on Fourier features (see "Compression," below), which are invariant to the problems of translation, rotation, and scaling.

Region growing attempts to answer the question of which pixels belong to the same region or surface and employs connectivity, making use of the relationship a given pixel has with its neighboring pixels. Attributes such as texture and color are employed to accomplish region growing. Algorithms for accomplishing region growing operate by accretion into larger entities or "split-and-merge" techniques. To compensate for noise or slight irregularities, two-step partitioning is used, with the initial partitioning employing a strict uniformity criterion, and a second phase employing a less-strict criterion to eliminate small irregularities. The order of traversal of the image influences the results, and models of surface geometry and illumination have been incorporated to increase accuracy.

No technique has yet been found which automatically and consistently identifies the high-contrast regions of an image as perceived by humans. Daneels and others (1993) propose a hybrid approach based on active contours, combining the speed of a greedy algorithm with the accuracy of dynamic programming, leading to the concept of user points, and to an incremental approach. Samadani and Han (1993) also describe a technique for interactive, computer-assisted boundary tracking from two-dimensional images. Rui, She, and Huang (1996) describe a method where the user defines where an object of interest is and a segmentation algorithm then groups regions into an object. The process of identifying and outlining objects in arbitrary, unconstrained images currently requires human intervention and guidance, and fast and accurate refinement techniques to complement the human, allowing easy and flexible user control. However, while accurate segmentation is needed for shape features, these researchers note that for overall layout, a coarse segmentation can suffice.

Region-based representations can be classified into those operating in the spatial domain and those operating in the transform domain, with the spatial domain further divided into geometric and structural types. Systems need to employ a combination of edge detection and region growing to overcome the limitations of each method. Mehtre, Kankanhalli, and Lee (1997) compare boundary-based representations such as chain code and Fourier descriptors and region-based representations using various moment descriptions, and demonstrate that combined methods outperform single-method approaches.

Shape Grammars

Shape grammars are formal models for image description, and have been used primarily to generate patterns (Stiny and Gips 1975). Lauzanna and Pocock-Williams (1988) give both an informal and formal definition of a shape grammar. Beginning with an initial shape, a set of replacement rules operate repeatedly on the shape, resulting in a final shape. Shape grammars are a formal grammar, exhibiting "postcorrespondence," enabling them to draw on research in recursive function theory. More specifically, a shape grammar can be characterized by the quadruple *I*, *T*, *NT*, and *R*. *I* indicates an initial or start state. *T* indicates a set of terminals, or the set of items that can appear in a final design. *NT* is the set of nonterminals which appear in the intermediate stage, in the derived sources, or in schematic gestures and global structures. *R* is the set of replacement rules that replace nonterminals with terminals; these rules can be applied repetitively. Shape grammars have been successfully used in the characterization of architectural design for the houses of Frank Lloyd Wright, Hepplewhite chairs, Greek vases, and, in the area of fine art, the paintings of Diebenkorn, Miro, and Kandinsky.

There was considerable interest in shape grammars as a useful tool for the storage and retrieval of collections of art objects, as the development of a shape grammar solves some of the problems of precision and completeness in describing the works of an artist (Kirsch and Kirsch 1988). Experts may be able to recognize a work of art as being that of a particular artist, yet be unable to articulate all the specifics which make up the necessary body of knowledge. Shape grammars are a way of capturing this information in a manner which is computationally accessible. By storing a structured description of a painting in the form of its grammatical derivation, one can search for the painting in terms of a large number of properties that would be hard to anticipate if one were encoding them for storage in some conventional archive.

Additionally, shape grammars could present a significant advantage in terms of storage economy. For instance, the memory needed to specify the grammar for a specific Diebenkorn painting, *Ocean Park No. 111*, is about 68 bits; storing a scanned image of the same painting would require much more memory. Thus complex analysis and retrieval operations could be performed on the objects stored as shape grammars, and then their full images could be displayed. Many however, believed that the area of serious fine art was too complex to allow for mechanization of the process, as shape grammars only describe one narrow attribute area. As applied to paintings, only linear composition has been described using shape grammars; color, texture, and line quality are not addressed. Development and application of shape grammars require domain knowledge as well. Since they were primarily generative, they fell out of use. Recently however, there is a renewed interest in the methodology for sketch recognition, employing learning techniques to reduce the overhead in the process (Alvarado and Davis 2002).

Current Approaches

Recent systems employ a variety of techniques, such as representing the shape as an ordered set of rectangles which are normalized and then described by means of their relative positions and sizes (Jagadish 1991). Gary and Mehrotra (1992) propose an approach which combines a shape representation in terms of both local structural and global features. A shape is represented by a set of structural components which are encoded as points in multidimensional space. A similar or identical component can be found by organizing the data in any multidimensional point-access index structure. Lists are used to hypothesize the objects and define where and in what object various features occur. In the QBIC project (see below), shape was based on global features such as area, circularity, eccentricity, and major axis orientation (Flickner and others 1995). Other systems have focused on local features (points of interest) such as corners and boundary segments (Berretti, Del Bimbo, and Pala 2000).

Shape Similarity

While shape is seen as being a fundamental feature in object recognition, shape retrieval has proven one of the more difficult problems to solve within CBR, as metric distances among feature vectors have not been found to model perceptual similarity between shapes well (Santini and Jain 1999). Mumford (1991) surveys six different methods for assessing shape similarity and notes that it is difficult to account for the various semantic qualities that humans assign to attributes such as shape, as there is no mathematically rigorous definition of specific types of shape similarity. In one of the few research projects conducted into shape similarity, Scassellati and others (1994) evaluated several mathematical shape similarity measures by comparing them to human similarity judgments. While two mathematical measures closely matched human performance on the similarity matching task, no method performed well on all twenty test shapes.

Combined Methods

While the above discussion on color, texture, and shape methods focused on each of three feature-based techniques individually, in reality the division is artificial, as each of these features reveals information about the other. As several researchers have noted, a unified theoretical view on these is needed, as in reality most effective systems use a combination of these features (using a weighted-sum matching metric or other merging methods), and each feature carries information relevant to others (Caelli and Reye 1993; Smeulders and others 2000).

Feature-matching systems employing low-level attributes such as color, texture, and/or shape rely essentially on syntactic feature matching, and do not focus on object recognition, a much more complex problem. One of the earliest systems in which users were able to query features such as shape and color incrementally was VIMSYS; features such as texture and color could be defined and combined, and temporal features such as rotation were included (Gupta, Weymouth, and Jain 1991a; Gupta, Weymouth, and Jain 1991b).

One of the earliest and most well-known feature-matching systems, designed to work in generalized domains, is the QBIC (Query by Image Content) system, developed by the Machine Vision Group at IBM's Almaden Research Center (Flickner and others 1995; Niblack and Flickner 1993).[10] Using manual or semi-automatic identification of objects, areas, or significant edges, the system computes color (average Munsell color values and a 256-element color histogram); texture (coarseness, contrast, and directionality); shape (area, circularity, eccentricity, major-axis direction, a set of features derived from object moments, and a set of tangent angles around the object perimeter); and sketch features (edge map). Similarity functions, such as distance metrics (city block, Euclidean, or weighted Euclidean distance) are computed for each feature set. Queries are either "full-scene" or "object" queries. Other such systems include Virage (Gupta and Jain 1997); Photobook (Pentland, Picard, and Sclaroff 1996); Cypress (Forsyth and others 1999); VisualSeek (Smith and Chang 1997b)[11]; NeTra (Deng and Manjunath 1999); and MARS (Mehrotra and others 1997). Johansson's extensive survey on these and other systems details methods and sources (Johansson 2000).

More recently, there has been an interest in combining low-level feature processing with higher-level semantic classification to partition large databases of images. These methods utilize other techniques which facilitate object recognition and image understanding, within limited object and scene types. These systems are discussed further in "'Semantic' Levels of Retrieval" below.

Features and Human Perceptual Judgments

Another recent trend in CBR has been a heightened understanding of the need to incorporate human perceptual judgments into the process, either by creating system models which attempt to mirror the human perceptual process or, especially, by modeling, measuring, and evaluating the effectiveness of retrieval with respect to human similarity judgments.

Early work by Kurita and Kato (1993) and others attempted to address psychological ambiguity in visual impressions in a system. A subjective similarity measure learned by the system is used as a "personal view model" for each user. Discriminant analysis is used to construct a subjective feature (SF) space that reflects a subjective similarity measure; a "personal index" is thus constructed, based on user classification of samples into nonoverlapping clusters. The assumption is that neighboring images in a SF space will give a similar impression in the user's view. These methods were tested in two systems, one using geometric shapes (TRADEMARK) and one using color paintings (ART MUSEUM). These showed interesting but limited results for the subjective similarity algorithms. In other work on trademarks, a matching technique based on deformable templates is used to refine the process and guarantee that only visually similar shapes are retrieved (Vailaya, Zhong, and Jain 1996). Nevertheless, the authors note that there are still significant differences between the top ten retrieved images and human search and match. The authors note that human retrievals are consistent for two reasons: 1) human subjects can easily decide foreground grayscale, no matter what its variation; and 2) human subjects use conceptual abstraction as well as shape matching. However, humans tend to also miss objects at different orientations.

Recent work provides a review of shape similarity issues and suggests that dual methods are necessary within CBR systems to effectively accommodate perceptual similarity (Berretti, Del Bimbo, and Pala 2000). In the TOKEN system, shapes are partitioned into tokens corresponding with their protrusions and these tokens are modeled according to a set of perceptually salient attributes. Two separate distance functions are used to model token similarity (a metric distance) and shape perceptual similarity (a nonmetric distance, a combination of token distances used to derive a global measure of shape similarity which fits human perception). Testing with 1,637 shapes (sampled at 100 equally spaced points) of objects extracted from twentieth-century paintings shows good results in dealing with problems of occlusion, scaling, and rotation. A caveat, however, is that there appears to be a high degree of similarity of objects depicted within the database.

Other work applies the Gestalt principles of grouping (see Chapter Two) as a method to recognize salient features which detect the presence of man-made structures in grayscale images (Iqbal and Aggarwall 1999). Salient features for buildings include lines in particular orientations, "significant" parallel lines, and lines with specific types of junctions; straight lines not indicative of buildings have more random orientations and junctions. Grouping takes place in a bottom-up fashion and the system places no constraints on viewing angle or depth. The system then uses a Bayesian framework to analyze the features and for classification of a very small database of images.

Researchers have used humans to classify images and have derived and implemented hierarchical semantic categories (outdoor/landscape/sunset) from these sorts (Vailaya, Jain, and Zhang 1998). One problem with these hierarchies is the condition when an image would correctly belong in more than one hierarchy. Another problem typical of this kind of research is that a small number of subjects are frequently used, and the subjects are frequently not a random sample but friends and coworkers.

Learning methods have been proposed as a solution to the difficulties involved in adequately modeling human perceptual and cognitive similarity judgments. Work by Han and Myaeng (1996) testing five features within a neural net implementation and comparing results with human similarity judgments suggests that, in contrast to their system, humans can ignore small details while analyzing an image. The Photobook system uses "FourEyes" (discussed below), an interactive learning agent which selects and combines models based on examples from the user (Minka and Picard 1997).[12] Other work used psychophysical experiments with very small numbers of participants to study PicHunter, a CBR system which employs Bayesian relevance feedback (Cox and others 2000). Factors tested included using the memory of the user's earlier actions, relative versus absolute distance criteria for interpreting user feedback, and use of pictorial and/or semantic cues. However, the limited content of the database (thematic clusters of similar images) leaves the results open to question. Overall results pointed to the fact than humans pay a lot of attention to semantic content when judging image similarity. While one challenge for these systems remains the fact that human perception can combine input from many sources and effectively filter out unnecessary details in ways that systems cannot yet model, another challenge remains in going beyond perceptual to semantic similarity.

Data Reduction

As many of the techniques discussed above produce data-dense representations, further processing is also necessary in machine systems. As Rui and others explain, feature vectors suffer from high dimensionality, normally on the order of 10^2 (Rui, Huang, and Chang 1999). These dimensions need to be reduced, and then multidimensional indexing techniques can be employed. As discussed in Chapter Two, a three-stage data processing model of human visual perception results in data reduction. The challenge for machine processing is to determine what comprises the most useful problem-oriented information and to develop methods of data reduction that retain and emphasize this information.

Statistical Techniques

Principal Component Analysis (PCA) is a multivariate analysis technique used in data reduction and image compression (Hotelling 1933). It is commonly used to reduce the dimensionality of a data set with a large number of interdependent variables. The object of PCA in image processing is to extract the most important features, or principal components, from an ensemble of data so that a replica of any of the data items can be reconstructed from a linear recombination of these features in the appropriate proportions. Most of the information within an image is contained within the first few principal components and relatively few are required for a faithful reconstruction of the image. PCA can be used as a coding mechanism by storing the proportion of the most significant principal components of that image as an element within the code; the greater the number of components used, the more complete the representation of that image.

Compression

In contrast to methods that operate directly on the raw image data (pixels or the "pixel domain"), other methods extract and index features from compressed versions of the image. One advantage of these techniques is that, as less data has to be processed, there are gains in computational efficiency. Transforms operate on spatial domain data (visual feature vectors) to convert these data into another domain (frequency space) by separating the image information according to a set of basic functions. Smeulders and others state that while many compression transforms are known, the quest is for transforms simultaneously suited as retrieval features. They define three requirements for such a transform: 1) the transform has to be applied on a metric space; 2) the components of the transform have to correspond to semantically meaningful characteristics of the image; and 3) the transform should provide a significant computational advantage in indexing (Smeulders and others 2000, 1358).

Mandal, Idris, and Panchanathan (1999) present a detailed review of compressed domain techniques (and example systems), with a focus on deriving feature vectors in the compressed domain. Compression includes transform domain techniques and spatial domain techniques. Examples of transform domain techniques include the Fourier transform, cosine transform, Karhunen–Loeve transform (a distance-preserving transform used by QBIC), subbands, and wavelets. Spatial domain techniques include vector quantization and fractals. A brief explanation of a few of these will clarify their operation and functionality. For detailed information, see the review mentioned above and sources such as *The Image Processing Handbook* (Russ 1998).

The Fourier transform is based upon the fact that most physical devices which receive energy from oscillating waves, including the ear and the eye, respond sinusoidally. The two components of a wave are size/amplitude and frequency/phase; the amplitude spectrum contains shape information and the phase spectrum contains position information. Fourier analysis sums the sines and cosines of a wave to represent other functions, but there is no way to separate these combined components of a transformed image to locate specific objects at specific locations. While image pixel data is not continuous, it is considered a sample of the real analog data. Shape can be represented by Fourier descriptors, which result from transforming boundary or edge information.

The fundamental idea behind wavelets is to analyze according to scale. Wavelet algorithms process data at different scales or resolutions, so that both gross features and small discontinuities are preserved. Wavelets are better suited for approximating data with sharp discontinuities than are Fourier transforms. Some researchers propose indexing techniques based on direct comparison of thresholded wavelet coefficients (Wang and others 1997). Wavelets have been widely used in texture representation. A recent paper evaluates several of the Wavelet transform representations and tests them against human perceptions (Ma and Manjunath 1995).

Fractal geometry is used to describe objects or shapes (fractals) that are self-similar, or scale symmetric. This means that when such objects are magnified, their parts bear an exact resemblance to the whole, and this continues with magnification of parts of parts on to infinity. A rough, jagged quality is maintained at every scale at which a fractal is examined. Fractals cannot be described by Euclidian geometry, but must be described by algorithms. A fractal representation builds on local self-similarities within images. Image blocks are seen as rescaled and intensity-transformed approximate copies of blocks found elsewhere in the image, producing a self-referential description of image data, which, when decoded, shows a typical fractal structure (Saupe, Hamzaoui, and Hartenstein 1996).

There are several widely used standards for compression/decompression. The Joint Photographic Experts Group (JPEG) produced a lossy compression method which became an ISO standard in 1990.[13] The more widely known JPEG JFIF file format (1991) was created for the transport of a single image by the Independent JPEG Group (IJG). The JPEG JFIF file format is widely used on the web.[14]

ISO,[15] working through its Moving Picture Experts Group (MPEG), developed several standards for compression/decompression of video (MPEG-2, MPEG-4).[16] The latest standard, known as MPEG-7, focuses on the content description of multimedia (Martinez 2001). This new standard is emphasizing description of still and moving images on all levels, including semantic information, and has been broadened to include text and other description methods. This is done through the development of description schemes (DS) which form a data model for different types of content information (a standard set of descriptors) and which are related to each other through various linking mechanisms. The standard does not specify the algorithms used to extract the information or the search engine.

Indexing Techniques

One major issue facing researchers is creating efficient noise- and distortion-insensitive index structures (Grosky and Mehrotra 1992). In a very large database, sequential scanning and distance calculation for every single object is time-intensive. Indexing in traditional databases is a well-understood problem and efficient methods have been developed for access to data that enable all records matching a query to be returned without having to search each record in the database. These methods are based on partitioning. As an example of how partitioning methods work, if you want to know which house on a street someone lives in, you can ask them, house by house, if each house is theirs, resulting in many steps. A more efficient method is to divide the houses up by some method, for instance asking if their house is east or west of a certain point, and then to divide the result set into smaller segments in the same manner, resulting in far fewer queries to determine the correct house. These indexing, or data structures, are often referred to as "tree" structures, and the method just mentioned would be a binary tree or *b*-tree.

However, such methods are less applicable in image similarity matching, as feature representations are multidimensional and result in a high-dimensional feature space. For instance, a 256-color histogram requires 256 dimensions to represent it. Comparisons also can involve "cross-talk," in which each component has to be compared not only to the directly equivalent component (blue to blue, for example), but to each other component (to blue-green, green, yellow, and so on). Each *pixel* in an image can also be represented by multiple features. Some systems compute thousands of features for each image. Spatial relations among features may also need to be represented, adding to the complexity. All these methods result in multidimensional vectors. As similarity is generally based upon (Euclidian) distance between points in multidimensional feature space, searching necessitates representations of these clusters of features and methods to index them which can reduce the dimensionality. In order to reduce the dimensionality of the representations, techniques such as filtering and using transforms are also used.

Multidimensional indexing methods can assist in reducing the response time for searching. A basic index structure used is the point access method (PAM) (Berretti, Del Bimbo, and Pala 2000), which clusters a point set into multidimensional regions, with each region being a node in an index tree. Search effectiveness is gained by methods minimizing the overlapping among nodes. In order to work with PAMs, highly dimensional vectors need to be mapped into a low-dimensional distance-preserving space, using appropriate transformations. Smeulders and others (2000) describe several classes of multidimensional indexing structures. *Space*-partitioning methods divide the feature space along predetermined lines, regardless of the size of data clusters. They organize the feature space as a tree; when the number of points in a node (region) exceeds a certain number, it is split. One example is the *k-d* tree, which generalizes a binary tree along *k* dimensions. A node is split along its *k* dimensions, and the data points are split along the median. In *data*-partitioning methods, the space is divided according to the distribution of data objects; a region that represents the neighborhood of a vector is associated with each point in feature space. Several examples are *R**-trees (Beckmann 1990); see Faloutsos (1999) for further detail; *SR*-trees (Katayama and Satoh 1997); and Hilbert *R*-trees (Kamel and Faloutsos 1994). In contrast to PAMs, *distance*-based methods can be thought of as example-based space-partitioning methods. These are concerned only with relative distances between objects rather than their absolute positions, and are suited to query by example when the feature space is metric (*M*-trees). Feature space is divided into concentric rings or spheres around an example point; the divisions can be locally adapting and thus not affected by the distribution of vectors in the feature space. While these techniques work well for low-dimensional spaces, as the number of dimensions (approximately twenty to thirty) increases, their performance degrades; a simple sequential scan has been shown to be effective in dealing with high dimensionality (Weber, Schek, and Blott 1998). There are several reviews of high-dimensional indexing techniques; the reader is referred to these for more in-depth treatment of the subject (Faloutsos 1997; Gaede and Gunther 1998; Ng and Sedighian 1996; White and Jain 1996).

As noted earlier, other methods are necessary to support non-Euclidian and nonmetric similarity measures, which may more closely mirror human similarity judgments. Two such techniques are neural networks and clustering (discussed under "Other Techniques," below).

Queries in a Digitized Environment

There are a variety of search methods employed in CBR; these include direct specifying of features (such as the color composition of an image), sketching, browsing, query by example (in which a query image is submitted for matching), and keyword searching, either with natural language or some sort of structured query language. Queries may also be fuzzy, involving objects within a specified range of size or location. Queries are most frequently represented by feature vectors, and matching consists of calculating the similarity between the feature vectors from the query and images in the database.

A query can specify a whole image match on some feature or combination of features (images containing red), or a subpattern match for a feature occurring at a specific location or area (red round shape in middle), or the presence or absence of a specific feature or object (apple) in a particular location. Degree of match may be exact or within specified parameters (find objects similar to an apple). A "nearest neighbor" match specifies the number of matches that are most similar while "all pairs" specifies all matches that are within a certain distance.

Higher-level, or logical features, denote the deeper semantics of the image. They are abstract representations of images at various levels of detail, and may be synthesized from primitive features or assigned manually. These include objective and subjective attributes and domain concepts. A search for both types of attributes may be either by exact match, fuzzy match, or some sort of interactive process, such as relevance feedback.

Faloutsos (1999) defines the requirements for an ideal querying method: 1) fast; 2) correct (that is, it should return all matching objects without missing any; incorrect matches are permissible as these can be discarded at a later step); 3) small space overhead; and 4) dynamic, allowing for easy insertion, deletion, and updating of objects. These qualities refer to machine performance, and as Smeulders and others (2000, 1365) note, "in practice, the user is not always capable of selecting the features most fit to reach the goal," and the selection of query types is often based upon the methods used to extract features rather than an understanding of user needs in visual retrieval.

Object Recognition and Image Understanding

In contrast to lower levels of processing which involve increasing levels of data reduction, higher levels of processing involve processes of modeling and increasing levels of data abstraction. Therefore, object recognition and image understanding within image database querying and retrieval draw upon additional methods from machine vision and artificial intelligence for modeling and reasoning about image content.[17]

Systems are frequently characterized as consisting of three levels. Low-level processes describe edges, textures, and regions. Intermediate-level processes translate 2-D into 3-D information and are concerned with surface and volume descriptions. Higher-level processes describe objects and scenes. Thus the products of a bottom-up process (image processing) are combined with top-down processes to produce a more holistic description of a scene (image understanding).

Understanding and description of objects or scenes in a machine environment can proceed by many routes. These processes are reasoning-intensive, may involve traversal of multiple representational layers, and may be nonsequential. Thus machine understanding of images, just as human understanding of images, involves not only object recognition but an understanding of the relationships among the objects depicted. It is a multilevel process, since the relationships themselves can function as constraints upon object recognition.

Tsotsos describes in more detail the levels of transformations that are necessary for a system capable of full image understanding:

1. Extraction of meaningful 2-D groupings of pixels
2. Inference of 3-D surfaces or volumes
3. Grouping of information into unique physical entities
4. Transformation of "image-centered" representations into "world-centered" representations (one where object identity is no longer dependent on its specific location in the image)
5. Labeling of entities according to system goals and world models
6. Inference of relationships among entities (which may also assist labeling)
7. Construction of a consistent internal description (Tsotsos 1992, 389–90).

Object Recognition

Object recognition is a central concern in machine vision, and techniques such as shape, texture, and color recognition provide basic information upon which a higher-level process of reasoning about specific image content can operate.[18] Object recognition is discussed in detail in the pattern recognition literature and has been fairly successful in fields such as manufacturing and quality control which operate in restricted domains. Currently, however, only images containing a limited and well-defined set of basic objects can be classified automatically, with the user identifying the basic objects of interest, and "manual examination of output is generally unavoidable" (Al-Khatib and others 1999, 67). Domain-specific systems are reported in areas such as medicine, and only a semiautomatic classification can be done on complex images (Hou and others 1992). While most image retrieval systems are not capable of performing full object recognition, techniques to separate out regions of potential interest can facilitate higher levels of searching. These methods can also provide a basis for research linking lower-level features to semantic interpretation of objects and higher-level image understanding.

After processing of color, texture, and shape, segmentation techniques are used to partition and group data. Object significance may be approximated by the size of an object (region) and its location (nearness to center, background, or foreground), and can be used to indicate the importance of a feature

(Aslandogan and others 1995). This level of processing does not try to identify objects, but operates in a trade-off situation between having more and less information: partitioning results in features with less information, while no partitioning results in having more information. The particular application and domain suggest which route the trade-off should take.

Segmentation Techniques

The process of determining uniformity or separating an image into regions of similar attributes is called segmentation. This process does not try to recognize the segments created, and is accomplished in computer systems in a bottom-up process by recognition of shape, texture, and color attributes, using techniques such as those discussed above. Most research has concentrated on one of these aspects.

A recent review of content-based retrieval techniques defines four types of segmentation (Smeulders and others 2000). In *strong segmentation* the image is divided into regions corresponding to objects; this is very close to impossible in broad domains, and has been accomplished by manual segmentation of the objects in some systems. This technique has been more successfully applied in narrow domains such as trademarks, textiles, and outlines of specific objects, although viewpoint remains important. *Weak segmentation* groups data into homogeneous regions, such that a region is within an object but may not necessarily account for the whole object. Weak segmentation is widely used. A third type of segmentation is referred to as *sign location*, which is used when an object has a nearly fixed shape such as a stop sign. The fourth type, noted as being the weakest, is *simple partitioning*, where an image may be divided into tiles, or divided along some principle of semantic interest, such as center and surrounding areas or horizon.

Feature Analysis

Feature analysis, the next step, operates on the products of segmentation. Features are derived pictorial attributes formed through mathematical functions and other operations. Various pattern recognition techniques are used on these products to extract and recognize features, which can then be used to compute entities or objects. Salient features are those which are most conspicuous and capture essential information concisely.[19]

Swett, Giger, and Doi give the following account of feature analysis (1993, 277–278); also see Raff (1993) for a more detailed exposition. Once images have been segmented into regions or features, common characteristics such as size, contrast, and shape can be calculated. The size of a feature is calculated simply by counting the number of pixels within it. Contrast is measured by determining the difference between the gray levels in the features and those in the surrounding area, and does not depend on absolute light intensities. Local gray-level thresholding techniques can be used to extract features of high contrast. Brightness patterns can also be described by discrete Fourier transforms. Contrast manipulation is performed by histogram equalization. Shape descriptors are used to determine such measures of shape as angularity and circularity. Adequate sampling of signals is necessary.

There is a need for a precise definition of image feature parameters, but Raff notes that there is no mathematical theory of image enhancement because we are unable to objectively describe the perception–cognition relationships (Raff 1993, 164). His suggestion is to approach feature analysis by focusing on basic concepts such as image contrast and detail, which lead to meaningful descriptions of pictorial scenes.

Grouping

Features are next grouped into objects (as yet still unrecognized) by the above methods. Spatial and temporal knowledge also contribute to this process. Spatial relationships such as location and form provide grouping information. Structural relationships among features may be stored as graphs, hierarchies, or other ordered sets. Temporal relationships (as constraints) can be used to provide the context in which spatial relationships are interpreted. With spatial and temporal features we also see the similarities to the Gestalt principles, with grouping functions based on smoothness and continuity of form, spatial proximity, symmetry, similarity of motion, continuity or smoothness of motion, and path of least action.

There are a number of problems that generally hinder object recognition, such as background noise, varying angles of view and object occlusion, and variations in image resolution and lighting conditions. Tsotsos points out that spatial and spatiotemporal events exhibit a natural "scale," and given that a particular operator cannot be optimal for all scales, representation at multiple levels is made more complex (Tsotsos 1992, 391–392). In image analysis generally there are problems of transitions and scaling (the granularity problem), such as those involved in the analysis of a sequence of images of a tree taken at successively closer distances. The leafy part of the tree initially appears as a random field; eventually individual leaves must be identified as surfaces. This type of problem poses great challenges for image analysis. Probabalistic criteria, criteria evolution (in iterative processing), and regularization are all usefully applied in image processing.

Image Understanding

The products of segmentation and feature analysis can then be combined with domain- and task-dependent knowledge to obtain a higher-level semantic description of the image and its components. Semantics is often based on spatial relationships among objects. Representation may take place on several levels, and involve transformations among the levels. Caelli refers to this as "binding what is seen with what is known" (Caelli 2000, 305).

Computationally, there are two basic approaches to higher levels of recognition: the scene recovery or view-based approach (which has been based primarily on shape), and model-based approaches. While a detailed discussion of object recognition and image understanding processes and problems is beyond this chapter's purpose, a brief overview of major approaches follows.

The Scene Recovery Approach

In scene analysis or scene recovery, shape is the factor of prime importance; Scene recovery is based on David Marr's framework for the basis of vision as an information processing system which produces (from images of the external world) a full representation of the world that "is useful to the viewer and is not cluttered with irrelevant information" (Marr 1982, 31). Marr suggests that hierarchical processing takes place, in which object representations are built up by incorporating increasingly specific features and that the flow of information is one-way in the hierarchy. Shape and other object properties (which are invariant under different conditions) are stored with a label in an internal representation (which does not include a direct replica of the retinal image). The early extraction of such information as texture, shading, or contours functions as a constraint which is used to ultimately determine a representation or symbolic description of shape. It is postulated that visual recognition proceeds by matching these internal representations to incoming retinal stimuli. This visual model forms the basis for several computational approaches.

Caelli and Bischof review several other shape-based approaches (Caelli and Bischof 1997, 315–321). *Template matching*, in which a direct replica of a shape is stored, is the simplest. Templates may be either fixed or deformable,[20] and matching proceeds by comparison. This approach suffers from a number of obvious problems, such as those introduced by occlusion, shadows, distortions, or other objects. Multiple templates are sometimes used to compensate for these problems, but template matching works well only for objects in isolation, limiting its usefulness. In the *feature model*, "mini-templates" or feature detectors may be used to represent features. The object representation is a set of feature occurrences or weights for different features, and recognition is again a matter of finding the best match. However, relative locations of features are not accounted for, and choice of features can be an issue. Another method uses spatial *Fourier analysis*, in which the image is represented as the sum of spatial frequency components. Since the transform represents aggregated information and invariances hold only for entire scenes (or isolated objects), disambiguation of individual components prevents recognition of familiar objects, and objects cannot be recognized at particular locations. *Structural* models were created to address this problem and to enable spatial reasoning. These use a data structure which includes the parts, their features, and their spatial relationships. While this can be used to assemble parts into objects, a mechanism is still needed to recognize the parts. These authors are critical of computer models which break up objects into component parts, noting that recognition of the parts is not necessarily an easier problem to solve, and that the decision as to what constitutes a "part" is culturally relative and arbitrary, and does not allow for the production of new "labels" for objects, a process which in the real world occurs dynamically.

The Active Vision Approach

As Jolion notes, there are a number of limits to the scene or visual-recovery approach, perhaps the most serious of which are 1) the need to simplify, which limits the complexity of the final result, and 2) the emphasis on the representation and not upon the processes by which representations are transformed (Jolion 1994, 56–57). The concept of active vision has been proposed as a solution to the ill-posedness problems of scene recovery (Aloimonos, Weiss, and Bandopadhay 1988; Ballard and Brown 1992; Jolion 1994; Wilkes and Tsotsos 1992). Active vision, a goal-oriented paradigm which is based on an understanding of the cognitive tasks involved in image understanding, assumes an observer with a known motion which provides needed constraints on the interpretation of the image. Jolion (1994) notes however that the active observer is not a very strong constraint; a true active observer paradigm implies action as well as perception and leads to methodologies that consider goal, efficiency, and real-time constraints. Thus active vision assumes some control over the image viewing process. He proposes a generalized Gestalt approach to image understanding in which information about both the observer and information about the scene are used, with the addition of a focus on processes as well as forms. He argues that this approach would produce a system that preserves complexity, maintains constraints, and operates adaptively. He concludes, "the power of a vision system is not a particular architecture but its complexity" (Jolion 1994, 69).

Thus, in contrast to a scene recovery approach, complexity is a principal source of richness and must be built into systems modeling. A recent system employing an active vision approach uses a hierarchical scene model with feature-indexed machine learning (Caelli 2000). In this system, attributes are indexed by features, not positions, and learning involves generalizing over labeled feature and feature-relation attribute spaces. The process is interactive, feature extraction is controlled by the current knowledge base, and domain knowledge is used to constrain rule generation and to update knowledge. Recognition comes about through graph-matching strategies.

While there are many systems that could be discussed, one implementation will be outlined here as an example of both techniques and rationale underlying systems for object recognition within a model-based approach. Forsyth and others (1999) describe their approach to object recognition as proceeding from local to global and from generic to specific assumptions about classification. They construct a sequence of successively abstracted descriptors at an increasingly high level through a hierarchy of grouping processes. The assumption at the lower levels is that the coherence of these image descriptors is correlated with the associated scene entities that are part of the same surface. The next stage invokes more class-specific global assumptions in relation to image regions. An example of this is a group that has "skin color," bilateral symmetry, and near-parallel sides; such a group is likely to be a limb and suggests searching for another such group nearby. As recognition proceeds, object class becomes increasingly constrained, but if it fails at some level, information about the object class is still provided. This type of model base consists of information that is oriented to vision.

Retrieval of Higher-Level Features

As can be seen from much of the above discussion, CBR addresses a limited range of image features, and user testing has demonstrated that users do not find such low-level features particularly intuitive to search or relevant to their queries (Chang and others 1997). A more recent focus emphasizes bridging what has come to be called the "semantic gap," the gap between the low-level features addressed by CBR techniques and the associated meanings of these features at the recognition (object) level and more abstract and affective levels within human cognition. The definition of "semantic" can vary across domains and researchers, however, and can include object/event recognition and description, spatial semantics or the relative location of objects within an image, or higher level abstract concepts such as meanings attached to images or emotions depicted or elicited by viewing the image. While retrieval at the more abstract levels is, at present, nearly impossible without human interpretation and annotation, using automated techniques to partition large image collections by semantic concept or category is an area of active research and has enjoyed some successes.

"Semantic" Levels of Retrieval

One approach to capturing the semantics of images is that of "simple semantics," in which researchers do not attempt to solve the more difficult problems of computer vision, but rather try to have the computer correlate features with generally understood "visual concepts" which can translate to higher-level categories.[21] These visual concepts have included categories such as textured–nontextured, indoor–outdoor, objectionable–benign (defined by appearance of "skin"), and graph–photograph. They can enhance retrieval by narrowing down the searching range in a database and permitting semantically adaptive searching methods. Methods such as those for distinguishing between photographs and graphics can take advantage of automatic techniques to detect color transitions, noise, edge quality, color saturation, distribution, and number, and shape and size, all of which differ between the two image types (Athitsos, Swain, and Frankel 1997). Another type of categorization which can be performed is distinguishing between portraits and non-portraits (human and non-human).

Lew (2001) defines visual concepts as anything to which a label can be applied or which can be recognized visually, and they range from concrete objects to abstract concepts.[22] He describes the process as one of asking the computer to understand the human notion of an object or concept through associated features, and terms the process visual learning. In the case of computers, the visual learning of concepts can be defined as 1) feature tuning; 2) feature selection; or 3) feature extraction and/or construction. All of these methods have the goal of optimizing the discriminatory power of the features in reference to the ground truth (similarity between images).

Feature tuning, or parameter estimation, refers to determining the parameters within which use of a feature is optimized. *Feature selection* involves choosing (from an initial set of candidate features) one or more features which best optimize the discriminatory power. *Feature construction* creates new features from a base set of features and integration rules. Of these three, feature selection is becoming a mature approach. Given the large number of features that are often produced by the analysis methods of CBR, the optimum features may vary across different types of images. A more recent approach involves interactive selection of features and models in relation to visual concepts.

One of the earlier systems employing these methods was FourEyes, which uses semi-automatic within-image segmentation and across-image labeling, driven by concurrently active color models, texture models, or manually-provided groupings (Minka and Picard 1997). The system can apply similar semantic labels to areas with similar characteristics and uses user feedback to improve its performance. The SIMPLIcity system represents an image by a set of regions, roughly corresponding to objects, which are characterized by color, texture, shape, and location (Wang and others 1999). Based on segmented regions, the system classifies images into categories that are intended to distinguish semantically meaningful differences.

Other work proposes a dynamic approach, in which visual features and classifiers are selected automatically when building "visual object detectors" (Jaimes and Chang 2000). This technique works within *Recurrent Visual Semantics*, the repetitive appearance of elements, such as objects, scenes, or shots, that are visually similar and have a common level of meaning within a specific context, such as news or sports (Jaimes and others 2000). This method has been used to detect skies and handshakes. While additional computation is required, the method produces more general results.

The concept of a semantic visual template is used in several projects (Vailaya, Jain, and Zhang 1998; Zhuang, Liu, and Pan 2000). A semantic visual template is a small set of templates that are perceptually characteristic of the semantic concept (Chang, Chen, and Sundaram 1998). A semantic template is composed of a set of examples or icons, and this approach works best for concepts with strong visual cues. Semantic visual templates can be built from queries, where a user selects a range of features to express a query, which is given a semantic label (such as "sunset") and stored in a query database for later use. Semantic concepts thus become linked to a range of primitive image features (red, orange, center, horizon) associated with that concept. An advantage of the semantic template approach is that it requires no previously labeled ground-truth or indexing terms. However, as Lew notes, "In practice, there have been a wide variety of promising content-based search systems which could detect limited classes of visual concepts with low misdetection rates. It remains to be seen which methods can be generalized to a large number of interesting visual concepts" (Lew 2001, 160).

Other work, derived from research in semiotics, is extending CBR techniques through the addition of lexical and learning techniques to incorporate higher-level semantic concepts and methods; one example, discussed further below, is MediaNet (Benitez, Smith, and Chang 2000). Relationships among semantic concepts, primitive features, and images or regions of images within the system are built using both automatic (learning) and manual (annotation) techniques. This modeling has also been applied in the narrower domain of fashion (Cavazza, Green, and Palmer 1998).

The MAVIS 2 project is exploring the use of a multimedia thesaurus and intelligent agents to support navigation by visual content and by semantic relationships between concepts in multimedia information systems (Dobie and others 1999). MAVIS 2 utilizes both the media content and semantic concepts to develop paths from media based features to semantic concepts or to generate pseudo-thesaurus groupings by feature clustering when no semantic relations are available. MAVIS 2 makes its semiotic foundation explicit: "In the semiotic model advanced here, the user is explicitly reflecting to the search engine their assessment of the role of the object and interpretant (signified) in relation to other signs. This is a radical advance acknowledging the role of hermeneutic acts in the user's retrieval task, since most other systems ostensibly retrieve based on assumed objective geometric measures of sign similarity and a simple correspondence to object and interpretant" (Joyce and others 2000, 123–124).

Other researchers carry this idea further and propose the idea of *emergent semantics*, in which the meaning of the image is "revealed" to the database by interpreting the user's sequence of queries, rather than a product of image decomposition (Santini, Gupta, and Jain 2001). In this model, the meaning of an image is *contextual* (dependent upon the conditions of querying and the user), *differential* (image meaning is manifested by association with images that share its meaning and differentiation from those that don't), and *grounded in action* (the database can establish the meaning of an image based on user queries). This model also suggests that the interface should support guided exploration rather than simple querying, and has been implemented in a prototype system, El Niño. The database also needs to support arbitrary or almost arbitrary similarity measures and (similarly to some of the systems above) must be able to automatically determine them from the user interface.

Affective Levels

In the computer science community there is a growing interest in and awareness of what is being termed "affective computing." Researchers in the Affective Computing Research Group at the MIT Media Lab define affective computing as "computing that relates to, arises from, or deliberately influences emotions."[23] They continue, "Our research focuses on creating personal computational systems endowed with the ability to sense, recognize and understand human emotions, as well as systems that support the user's emotional nature, abilities, and needs. . . .We also hope to substantially contribute to research on basic human emotions, allowing us to better understand how humans deal with emotions, both within themselves and in interactions with others." A growing interest in this area of research is also reflected in presentations at the Conference on Human Vision and Electronic Imaging. A ten-year overview of the conference notes that Japanese and European colleagues have explored such areas as the subjective aspects of digital imaging systems and affective attributes of images such as their naturalness, colorfulness, and appeal, and states that "there is an increasingly important role for art, aesthetics, and emotion in the design and use of electronic imaging systems" (Rogowitz, Pappas, and Allebach 1998).[24]

While there is increasing interest in subjective and affective aspects of image description, incorporating such aspects into CBR systems is much more difficult. Of the low-level features addressed by CBR systems, color is the only one that is widely considered to have expressive qualities as well. Therefore, access to affective qualities of images has been investigated in relation to color and color quality.

Early research along these lines was conducted by Japanese researchers (Kurita and Kato 1993). These researchers base their experimental work on the assumptions that the dominant impression generated by paintings is coloring and that there is a reasonable correlation among the coloring of a painting, a user's visual impression, and the user's subjective description in words.[25] They use 200 full-color paintings in an art database and canonical correlation analysis to construct a unified feature (UF) space based on color (using distribution and autocorrelation of RGB-intensity values) and a personal index, or "view," through user choice of adjectives. A predetermined set of thirty adjectives make up an adjective vector (with binary values), and words are used as queries to return neighboring images in the UF space.[26] This link between text data and image data is referred to as a "multimedia join," but the subjective descriptions and coloring features cannot be directly compared, as they are in different domains. Few experimental results are reported. Several problems can be noted: user "views" may change over time or even within the course of a session, views may be influenced by a particular task at hand, and different views may be appropriate to different contexts. Because of these, the authors suggest that the system learn a user's preferences.

More recent work with color semantics draws upon early theories by Itten (see Chapter Three) of the usage and semantic associations of color in art and their application by Runge in a chromatic sphere (Corridoni, Del Bimbo, and Pala 1999). This work used Itten's codification of expressive chromatic usage as an access key to a color imagebase by providing methods for segmentation of color images, creating a descriptive method for intra- and inter-region properties (such as luminance, saturation, and warmth), and defining rules for a color description language. As such, the system requires somewhat abstract specification of color qualities by the user. System tests of matching qualities such as luminance contrast with regional specification and color harmonies demonstrate good matches, but there is no comparison with other color-based querying techniques.

Other Techniques

Incorporating Text

Studies have shown that users prefer to search by higher-level concepts (Chang and others 1997). Currently these can only be humanly-assigned and are best represented by text. The CBR community is becoming aware of this: "It is becoming clear in the image retrieval community that content-based Image Retrieval is not a replacement of, but rather a complementary component to, the text-based Image Retrieval. Only the integration of the two can result in satisfactory retrieval performance" (Rui, Huang, and Chang 1999, 56). This awareness has stimulated research into the addition of other text-based techniques to image retrieval systems.

Therefore, in addition to feature-based retrieval, researchers are also investigating processing of text associated with images. The additional information provided by text can help specify or narrow the domain to which the image content pertains, assist in object identification, or add additional semantic information about the image. The emphasis is mainly on the automatic generation of usable indexing from associated text, and techniques used in processing this text include natural language processing, as well as resources such as machine-readable dictionaries or thesauri and ontologies. A variety of types of associated text are used, from Webpage text to captions of photographs and closed-captioning of video. Another approach is text generation from other modalities such as audio. Text is also being explored in its more traditional uses, as additional index points for the image content.

Several researchers have explored methods for exploiting linguistic context in image interpretation, supplementing feature-based approaches. Srihari (1995) used natural language processing of associated text to develop PICTION. This system identifies human faces in newspaper photographs based on the information obtained from the associated caption. Text is used as a set of constraints to identify the spatial relationships among people in the image and associate them with the appropriate text. These methods are combined with techniques developed for automatic face recognition such as face location and gender discrimination. However, limitations of such systems include the difficulty of extracting reliable information from complex captions and the robustness of face location and characterization tools. Other prototype work (Show&Tell) uses spoken language input combined with region specification (through mouse pointing) to describe image regions (Srihari 1999). The language input is then processed by a natural language understanding component which generates visual constraints on the image.

Leung and others (2001) also propose the use of spoken annotation within a framework of semantic data modeling, composed of discrete facts. An elementary fact states the presence of a particular item (flower) within an image, while modified facts (red flower) augment these with descriptive properties. Binary and ternary facts link elementary or modified facts (girl eats red apple on table). A natural language parser then processes these clauses to create index terms. However, indexing cost remains high, and the researchers propose the use of data mining or inferencing techniques to elaborate the existing indexes.

A technique used in text processing is Latent Semantic Analysis (LSA), also known as Latent Semantic Indexing.[27] Latent Semantic Analysis works by using statistical techniques to associate words to the "semantic" context of a given document (Deerwester and others 1990). LSA works on the assumption that there is an underlying or "latent" structure in the patterns of word usage across "documents" (contexts in which words occur, which can be texts, paragraphs, or sentences). Using statistical techniques to analyze associations among words and documents, the goal of LSA is to project words in similar documents to an underlying semantic structure. This approach can thus avoid problems associated with classical keyword vector methods such as synonymy, word sense, lexical matching, and term omission. A term-by-image matrix is created; local and global weights can be applied to prevent bias by increasing or decreasing the importance of a term within and among documents. The matrix is then factored using singular value decomposition (SVD, a technique related to factor analysis) into a set of linearly independent vectors within *k*-space (with *k* most significant dimensions being chosen). These vectors are of smaller dimension, but when multiplied together produce an approximation of the original matrix. It is the reduction of dimensionality that allows the latent semantics to emerge.

Recent work employing LSA uses both visual statistics (color histogram and orientation histogram) and text statistics to precompute feature vectors (Sclaroff and others 1999).[28] In the context of Web pages, words appearing with specific HTML tags are assigned higher weights, based upon the assumption that specific tags (title, header) and words appearing near an image will contain more content-bearing information. Relevance feedback is then used to adjust weights on a combination of distances between subvectors. While the use of text features only produced good results for returning relevant images on the first result page, the best results were achieved when both textual and visual information were used with relevance feedback. Because of the dimensionality reduction necessitated by LSA, it sometimes lacks the specificity provided by using keyword vectors.

Other work uses LSA to automatically associate metadata available for some media objects (museum objects such as glassware, furniture, and paintings) with concept class descriptions drawn from the Dewey Decimal Classification (Tansley and others 2000). The two-phase process first connects the images for which there is sufficient associated metadata to the appropriate concepts by using LSA to give a measure of correspondence. Secondly, CBR methods using low-level features are used to classify the remaining images, by using the image–concept associations created in the first stage as a ground truth. While good results were obtained with objects, paintings proved to be more difficult.

The use of statistical term methods combined with heuristics concerning other text structures within captions was explored by Paek and others (1999). Some parameters which had a major effect on accuracy were using only the first sentence of the caption (as opposed to the entire caption or the entire text document), and using only words from open syntactic classes (nouns, verbs, adjectives, and adverbs), plus prepositions. They also employed machine learning techniques to create classes of words which discriminate between two competing classes of images (i.e. indoor–outdoor). Other systems are also employing limited sets of terms combined with learning techniques (Town and Sinclair 2001). Region descriptors are computed and then fed into neural network classifiers that are trained to label regions with class membership probabilities for sets of semantically meaningful visual categories such as grass, sky, and skin. A searcher can then use natural language terms in a query to retrieve similar images. These techniques, combined with content-based techniques such as feature extraction and region analysis and clustering, produce good results with news photographs in a limited domain (terrorist activities). Research experimenting with a combination of textual and image features produced increased accuracy in distinguishing between photographs and synthetic (human-produced) images, but did not improve portrait–nonportrait distinctions (Gevers, Aldershoff, and Smeulders 2000).

Other work has experimented with a variety of automated and manual techniques to utilize other associated text in the classification of images on the Web. The WebSEEk system uses text derived from image addresses and HTML tags (Smith and Chang 1997a).[29] The system uses a manually constructed subject taxonomy and a key-term dictionary created by semiautomatic methods. Text associated with an image is processed to create a "term histogram," a concordance of terms associated with the image. Dictionary terms are then manually selected from the terms; the dictionary terms are restricted to terms which do not have multiple or ambiguous meanings. These terms are then manually mapped to broad classes (2,128) in the subject taxonomy, e.g., soccer to sports and aircraft to transportation. While their tests showed around 95% precision for classification of images into these broad classes, problems occur when terms are used out of context or refer to subject matter not depicted in the image. Other systems use basic linguistic analysis or other models to determine relevant text to be extracted from Web pages and used for indexing (Rowe and Frew 1997; Shen, Ooi, and Tan 2000).

In addition to text appearing on a Web page with an image, text on other Web pages linked to the images was exploited by Harmandas, Sanderson, and Dunlop (1997). This technique was tested using a collection composed of seven unrelated Web art gallery sites (2,583 images). The best retrieval was obtained by weighting the caption highest and the text on linked Web pages next; other captions on the page were also effective. Interestingly, the least effective was the surrounding text on the original page. Query types that worked well using this technique were queries for images containing certain objects, for types of images (street scene, still life), and specific item queries; queries for more abstract or emotive qualities did not work.

Much smaller sets of terms are used for annotation in other systems; these terms may be displayed to the user, as in the Chabot system (Ogle 1995) or may be hidden. Generally, the terms are derived from the images actually in the database being tested, and therefore exhibit limited conceptual structure. The PicHunter system employed hidden annotation with a small set of semantic attributes (134) in searching for a target image using relevance feedback techniques (Cox and others 1997).

In addition to subject classifications or taxonomies, there is considerable interest in using ontologies for processing associated texts. An ontology is a vocabulary with precise specifications of the conceptual relationships among its terms; these relationships can enable the representation of domain-specific knowledge.[30] In terms of processing, the main purpose of an ontology is to enable communication between heterogeneous applications in a manner that is independent of implementation technologies, information architectures, and application domains.

For instance, WordNet, an electronic lexical system, has been used by several researchers to process text associated with images.[31] WordNet uses synsets, groups of nouns that are synonyms representing a word sense or meaning; a noun can have several word senses and therefore several synsets. Each word sense has other word sets related through specific types of relationships, such as hypernyms/hyponyms (IS_A relation), holonyms (MEMBER_OF relation), and meronyms (PART_OF relation).

Researchers have tested WordNet in a variety of applications. For instance, Aslandogan found that selective use of WordNet to expand both queries and text associated with images produced improvements in recall in a small (250) test set of images (Aslandogan and others 1997). They achieved the best results using a combination of synonyms, hypernyms, and holonyms and using synonyms in all senses of the word. Using all senses and all relationship types degraded the performance. Other researchers used WordNet in constructing a hierarchical generative statistical model trained jointly on image segment features and associated words (Kobus, Moses, and Bloom 1994). Testing on a large diverse data set (10,000 images from the Fine Arts Museum of San Francisco) showed mixed results. Work on manually disambiguated image captions used a WordNet-derived knowledge base to precompute word–word similarities; the authors suggest that future implementation could use fuzzy sets of words in which weights on word senses are incorporated (Smeaton and Quigley 1996).

Another use of WordNet is to automatically construct semantic templates that can map low-level features to high-level concepts (Zhuang, Liu, and Pan 2000). Related to this, there is also research using WordNet to construct a multimedia thesaurus in which conceptual relationships are combined with perceptual features (visual or audio) to provide multimodal examples of an "object." For instance, MediaNet researchers construct a knowledge base using WordNet semantic relationships derived from text annotations of the images and extracted color and texture descriptors (Benitez, Smith, and Chang 2000). Testing of this system produced only marginally improved retrieval effectiveness and the researchers conclude that more experiments are needed.

WordNet has also been used as a tool to select candidate images for ground-truth sets in large databases. For instance, one project uses WordNet to process image-associated text from Web pages, with the goal of producing a manageable set for manual ground-truthing (Shen, Ooi, and Tan 2000).

Knowledge Representation Methods

The field of artificial intelligence has drawn from a number of cognitive models to further develop knowledge representation techniques; these have served as a basis for various computational approaches to object recognition and image understanding. The ability to perform spatial and temporal reasoning is a goal of AI systems and of systems capable of intermediate- and high-level image understanding. A number of systems have been developed that incorporate knowledge representation methods such as semantic networks, prototypes, frames, and scripts. The reader is referred to Crevier and Lepage (1997) for a survey of knowledge-based systems and methods.

A *semantic network* is a graph-based knowledge representation in which nodes represent objects or events and arcs between nodes represent relationships among nodes. Objects and relationships can thus be represented in an entity–relationship model. Semantic networks are efficient in that each concept or object only has to be represented once, with pointers used as cross-references to indicate an object is involved in a relationship. Semantic networks could offer advantages in visual information retrieval. In image understanding, nodes can represent scene elements such as sky, road, car, and so on, and the arcs represent spatial (above, left, right, or under) or other relationships.

Similarity measures between graph representations of logical structures have been used for engineering-plant diagrams (Wakimoto and others 1993). Rabitti and Savino and others working on satellite photos use attributed relational graphs (ARGs) to denote classified regions and spatial relationships between adjacent regions (Kitamoto, Zhou, and Takagi 1993; Rabitti and Savino 1992). Attributes of nodes/branches help to express context, such as the numerical shape features of regions. Other work in a medical context uses ARGs to capture interobject constraints (Petrakis and Faloutsos 1997). Recent work uses the semantic network formalism to represent knowledge for image interpretation and camera actions that are needed in explorative vision (Niemann and others 1996; Paulus and others 1999). Semantic networks have been integrated with neural networks in object recognition (Heidemann and others 1996). Semantic networks are discussed in detail in Sagerer and Niemann (1997).

Two important facets of object representation used in a machine environment are *prototypes* and *concept organization* (Tsotsos 1992, 391). Prototypes (see Chapter Two) provide a generalized definition of the components, attributes, and relationships against which objects must be matched to confirm that the object is an instantiation of the prototype and can be used for fuzzy types of matching (Zadeh 1982). Prototypes are complex and require many levels of representation, from those that describe features and spatial, temporal, or functional relationships to those that assert recognition constraints based on a domain or task.

Concept organization commonly employs three kinds of abstraction: 1) feature aggregation; 2) concept specialization; and 3) instantiation. Feature aggregation, or "PART-OF" relationships, organize concepts into more abstract or more primitive ones, depending on the direction of traversal. The leaves of such a hierarchy are discrete concepts and may represent image features, although they can also represent logical concepts. Concept specialization uses inclusion hierarchies or "IS-A" relationships, which imply specialization or generalization and inheritance of properties from parent to child concepts. Instantiation or the "INSTANCE-OF" relationship is the prototype/token relation. These three relationships are not separate, but rather are used in conjunction with one another, and work well in object-oriented modeling.[32]

Frames or "schemata" are object-oriented representations that draw upon the idea of prototypical events or objects, and they provide a way of representing and manipulating complex objects (Minsky 1975). Frames are composed of slots that carry attribute information; information in these slots can be inherited from a generic frame or these slots can also specify a specific instance or type of instance. Inference can be done by attaching procedures to the attributes of an object; the procedures may be triggered depending on how the attribute is accessed. Constraints may be associated with relationships among the slots. Semantic networks are sometimes used to organize frames. Scripts are used to add temporal or sequence information or goals. As an example, Chabot uses a frame-based knowledge representation and stores attributes in a relational data model (Ogle 1995). Work by Brink, Marcus, and Subrahmanian (1995) also uses this approach.

Description Logics is a class of knowledge representation languages used in frame-based systems, semantic networks, and other object-oriented representations.[33] Concepts, roles, and individuals are the basic building blocks. Concepts gather the relevant common properties among a collection of individuals into a description, forming a class. Roles describe the properties of individuals belonging to a particular class. Several research projects in image and multimedia information retrieval have utilized this approach (Bechhofer and Goble 1999; Meghini, Sebastiani, and Straccia 1998).

Other techniques include constraints-based methods and mathematical logic. Constraints are relationships between two or more objects which must be expressed using formal methods. One example is PICTION (see discussion in "Incorprating Text," above) (Srihari 1995). Mathematical logic can be used to represent high-level spatial semantics. In another approach, "iconic indexing" is used to represent both objects and their properties (Chang 1987; Grosky, Neo, and Mehrotra 1989). Image processing and pattern recognition techniques are applied to segment an image and a symbolic representation of the picture is obtained. This symbolic representation is then converted to a 2-D string representation which is stored as an iconic index for the picture in the pictorial database. This representation supports spatial reasoning and querying. This approach of retrieval by spatial constraint has been used in a medical context (Hou and others 1992).

Machine Learning and Neural Networks

Machine learning techniques have been widely applied to the problems of image processing and retrieval. They have been used primarily for lower-level feature analysis, but are beginning to be used in efforts to associate lower-level features with higher-level concepts (Cox and others 2000; Minka and Picard 1997). Rorvig (1986), working with Project ICON, proposed the "two-domain theory," which links the human and machine domains. The first domain is the machine's capacity to extract primitive information features and cluster images according to these features, and the second domain is the capacity of human beings to order complex sets of stimuli into perceptual distances relative to an ideal point. By mapping the mental ordering of the proximity of representative images onto the collection of digitized images, a machine could be taught to infer the desired image set. This model is now being used in machine learning to facilitate the learning of user preferences and labels for images.

Nilsson (1996) offers a description of the conditions under which machine learning is advantageous. His list also elegantly describes many of the problems inherent in image retrieval, such as:

- Tasks that can only be well-defined by example, rather than description (e.g., query by example)
- Relationships and correlations hidden amongst large amounts of data
- Applications in which the characteristics of the working environment cannot be predicted completely a priori
- The existence of too much information or knowledge to be captured explicitly by human coding
- Changing environments and context, changing knowledge and understanding, changing vocabulary

Neural networks have been proposed as an answer to many of the difficulties listed above. They address several failures of rule-based systems, such as handling the complexity inherent in even small-problem processing and the inability to perform real-time learning. Artificial neural networks (ANNs, also known as connectionist architectures or parallel distributed processing) are systems of data structures and programs modeled on theories of how the human brain works and on adaptive biological learning. Nigrin (1993) defines a neural network as a layered system in which a large number of highly interconnected processors ("neurons") operate in parallel on local information asynchronously; each processor has its own small sphere of "knowledge" and access to data in its local memory. The processors are linked together with weighted connections ("synapses"). Neural networks fulfill the rule known as "Occam's razor," which states that the simplest hypothesis which works is preferable.[34]

Typically, a neural network is initially "trained" or fed large amounts of data and rules about data relationships (for example, "A person's grandfather is older than that person's father"); this training creates adjustments to the weighted connections between neurons ("learning").[35] Training can be either supervised (correct results are known and are provided during training) or unsupervised (clustering). A program can then tell the network how to behave in response to an external stimulus or the neural network can initiate activity on its own.

Neural networks are sometimes described in terms of knowledge layers, with more complex networks having deeper layers. In feedforward systems, learned relationships about data can "feed forward" to higher layers of knowledge. Techniques used in making determinations in neural networks include gradient-based training, fuzzy logic, genetic algorithms, and Bayesian methods. Much work today incorporates machine learning methods, in particular for automatic classification of images.

While neural networks first appeared in the 1950s, the algorithms did not become robust enough until the 1980s for more general applications, such as character recognition. Rickman and Stonham (1993) used a neural network–based coding scheme to retrieve images from a database according to the degree of similarity with a target image. The coding scheme represents each image with respect to a set of feature archetypes learned by the neural network during a training phase. They use a neural network learning law that performs an efficient implementation of Principal Component Analysis and maximizes the amount of information conveyed by the code. While PCA is computationally expensive, it has been shown that an approximation of PCA can be implemented very efficiently using a neural network topology if the size of the input domain is large and the number of principal components is small. This research used a database of machine printed fonts as test material.

Neural networks can learn temporal concepts and have been widely used in signal processing and time-series analysis. They have enjoyed great success in pattern recognition and are used in areas such as processing medical imagery, among others (Chiou and Hwang 1995). One example of a commercial application is the Excalibur Image Datablade module, codeveloped by Informix and Excalibur Technologies. The Datablade uses Adaptive Pattern Recognition Processing (APRP) to enable image-based searching of visual data by color, shape, texture, brightness, color structure, and aspect ratio (Dowe 1993). Based on neural network methods it acts as a self-organizing system that automatically indexes the binary patterns in digital information, creating a pattern-based memory that is optimized for the native context of the data. Such systems are thus capable of combining large amounts of binary data and associated processing techniques with standard relational database techniques such as inverted files for efficiency in searching.

Rui, Huang, and Chang (1999) suggest that neural networks and clustering techniques can support both Euclidian and non-Euclidian similarity measures. Zhang and Zhong (1995) propose a hierarchical indexing scheme which uses a Self-Organizing Map (SOM) to cluster images into groups of visually similar images based on color and texture features. The indexing scheme focuses on eliminating unlikely candidates rather than pinpointing the targets directly. Other work using SOMs includes PicSOM (Laaksonen, Koskela, and Oja 1999). City and landscape images are classified using a weighted nearest neighbor classifier with edge direction-based features having the most discriminative power (Vailaya, Jain, and Zhang 1998). Squire (1998) uses distance learning networks (a newer class of self-organizing network) which attempt to learn mappings from feature space to perceptual similarity space using a frequency-based similarity measure derived from human similarity judgment data. Similar work using SOMs for concept mining in a database of flags enables concept labeling of objects and provides a visual thesaurus (Deng 2001). However, SOMs have two drawbacks: a lack of incremental learning ability (necessitating retraining with additions to the database) and instability of results.

Similarity clustering of images also seems to offer prospects of success, allowing hierarchical access for retrieval and providing a way of browsing the database (Jin and others 1998; Vellaikal and Kuo 1998). In another approach, low-level features are used in a constrained environment (vacation images) to discriminate between limited conceptual image classes (Vailaya and others 2001). Classification is accomplished by Bayesian methods using an initial training set and incremental learning. This hierarchical classifier groups images into indoor–outdoor classes, and then outdoor images are classified into city or landscape; landscape images are classified as sunset, forest, or mountain.

Other Models

Researchers propose other conceptual models as foundations for image searching. For instance, Jaimes and Chang (1999) draw upon models from cognitive science, information and library science, art, and content-based retrieval and attempt to unify these in a ten-level hierarchical model of image features. The model includes both syntactic (visual/perceptual) and conceptual (semantic) features associated with images. The levels indicate the types of processing which may be necessary to index features in each level (lower levels such as local structure and global composition are handled by existing CBR techniques), and increasing levels of knowledge are required at the higher levels, dealing with generic, specific, and abstract objects and scenes. Testing of this framework demonstrated that it appears to be conceptually robust and can be used to organize visual content for retrieval, guide the indexing process, and classify image descriptions (Jörgensen and others 2001).

Imagebases

Because of the proliferation of image-based applications, over the last decade there has been an upsurge of interest in database management systems for non-textual information. Early research in this area concentrated on pattern recognition and image processing, and retrieval was based on textual information associated with image files. A newly emerging paradigm, one which places equal emphasis upon textual and visual (and multimedia including audio and motion) content and querying, is bringing progress in these areas. Research has been conducted by both the database and computer vision communities in relational databases, multimedia and hypermedia databases, spatial databases, iconic indexing, object-oriented databases, and with combinations of database and AI techniques. A number of systems have been developed which require a complex, application-dependent abstraction of the real world. However, there still needs to be much more research cutting across the database and CBR communities.

Earlier, Grosky and Mehrotra (1992) predicted the emergence of a more general field of study: sensor-based data management, in which other modalities such as voice and touch will be used as well. These same authors provide an overview of image database management (Grosky, Neo, and Mehrotra 1989, 7–8). Five categories of information need to be stored, integrated, and managed in an image database:

- Iconic data: an image store composed of analog and/or digital images
- Image-related data: registration, resolution, and format information
- Extracted feature information: data that results from processing images through various kinds of filters
- Image–world relationships: relationships between image components and real-world entities
- World-related data: textual descriptions of the abstracted world pertinent to the given application (world model)

In addition, they stress the ability to perform query operations on iconic information by content in the following retrieval combinations:

- *Image* data from *textual* data
- *Textual* data from *image* data
- *Image* data from *image* data

- *Textual* data from *textual* data (Grosky and Mehrotra 1992, 246)

The first and the fourth operations are currently much more tractable in a machine environment than the second or third. Key issues in the design of visual information systems are data models, feature-based indexing, memory management, query processing, and interface design. According to Jain, visual databases share the following characteristics:

- Large volumes of complex objects in large systems.
- Read/write operations and real-time processing.
- Feature extraction and automated indexing.
- Multiple scales and levels of data representation and organization, and spatial and temporal organization of data (Jain 1993)

The central purpose of organizing information in a database is to enable the location and retrieval of a subset of data or objects that meet specified criteria. Image database systems need therefore to have retrieval functionalities similar to database management systems. In addition, they should be able to support associative access to images (Rabitti and Savino 1992). Visual database design therefore is concerned not only with representational techniques which can accommodate both standard and multimedia data, but also with processes which integrate the various techniques involved in image analysis and querying, as well as textual data management and an efficient user interface. However, several difficult problems exist. Multimedia data pose problems for traditional database storage methods, as these data are typically unstructured rather than structured (encoded into attributes as provided by a data schema). Classification and comparison of objects is also not as easy in image databases as in traditional databases: the main conceptual problem is the difficulty of exactly defining and interpreting the content of images. There are problems on the retrieval end in the formulation of queries for imagebases, as it is difficult to specify in advance all the necessary search keys. Another difficulty is that experimental work in multimedia systems is so diverse and the number of experimental variables so difficult to control that results become difficult to evaluate.[36] Finally, the large storage requirements pose serious problems.

The following sections review selected image database management techniques, discussing multimedia data, examples of relational and object-oriented approaches to database architecture and database querying methods. For an excellent overview of multimedia databases, see Bertino, Catania, and Ferrari (1999).

General Database Architecture

In data representation, three levels of abstraction are common: the physical database level, the conceptual database level, and the external database level (Tsichritzis and Lochovksy 1978). The physical database is concerned with data storage, the conceptual database is concerned with the application-specific world-model, and the external database is concerned with the way in which users of the system view or interact with the data. Data models represent the subject database (the physical database level) and are independent from the other levels. The two most widely used for image databases are the relational and the object-oriented data models.

Relational Databases

The relational database model is so-called because the relationships among database objects are captured. Each data element is represented only once in the database, and the relational database approach provides data independence, integrity, sharing, and controlled redundancy and security for textual information. Relational databases offer ease in querying and simplicity in updating, inserting, or deleting records. In a standard DBMS, the structure (model) associated with a given set of data is known a priori, whereas in an image system the structure needed to represent the data in a specific digitized image may be unknown or only partially known. This loss in semantic capability means that additional image interpretation may be needed.

Kunii, Weyl, and Tenenbaum (1974) pioneered the relational approach to feature retrieval. The relational database approach has been widely used for image database systems such as geographic information systems (GIS). The relational database approach results in data associated with geographic or spatial units which can be manipulated, producing new information which can then be converted to images for display. Map data and image-feature data share similarities in terms of representation, modeling, and query languages. Relational databases have evolved from early systems in which there was no real-time feature interpretation or user control to ones that incorporate object-oriented principles or semantic extensions of the relational model.

Object-Oriented Databases

In the early to mid-1990s it was thought that the relational database paradigm would be replaced by object-oriented techniques, and proposals concerning management of nontextual information were migrating to the object-oriented approach, which was considered more semantically rich. In an object-oriented system, each object has a set of attributes and a set of operations that allow it to interface with other objects. Object models represent complex data structures; an object is stored with the operations that can act upon it, and a data element can appear in more than one place. An object-oriented database can be structurally object-oriented, in which attribute values are objects rather than data types, or behaviorally object-oriented, with IS-A type relationships.

Jagadish and O'Gorman (1989) provide detail in describing the object-oriented data model in relation to images. Each entity (pixel or semantically meaningful image feature) is called an object, and each object is an instance of a particular type, which defines an object's structure, its applicable functions, and some of its properties. Functions and properties are inherited from an ancestor in a type hierarchy and can be nested to any level. Values for properties can be stated explicitly, inherited, or computed on demand by evaluating a function. Computing these functions is a primary task in image recognition. In an object-oriented system, descriptions at higher levels are concise when compared to those at lower levels, and processing at these levels is called symbolic processing. Data is more robust and noise is eliminated. The object-oriented approach saves storage when lower-level details are not stored (important for archival systems) and permits faster processing. However, these higher levels do not carry all the information of lower-level descriptions, and a system cannot reproduce lower level descriptions from stored higher-level ones.

REMINDS combined a relational database with structural object-oriented aspects (Mehrotra and Grosky 1985). In other early work, Orenstein and Manola (1988) adapted the PROBE object-oriented data model for image applications. They defined a geometry filter at selected regions of interest in an image and then applied higher-level functions over regions instead of over the whole image. This approach is still applicable only at the pixel level, however. Another early system in which users could query features such as shape and color incrementally was VIMSYS, an object-oriented prototype in which image objects have multiple representations that are mutually derivable from each other (Gupta, Weymouth, and Jain 1991a). Features such as texture and color could be defined and combined, and temporal features such as rotation were also included.

The later systems permit users to conduct real-time interactive feature detection, utilizing iconic or graphical interfaces. QBIC and Virage extended standard database management systems for image retrieval (Gupta and Jain 1997; Niblack and others 1993). In 1999, AltaVista integrated Virage's search tools for image and video searching. Chabot is another system extending the relational approach by including object-oriented properties such as definition of classes for objects and inheritance of attributes (Ogle 1995). Recent implementations of object-oriented models include the work of Cha and Chung (1998), who use three classes to describe an image object: the visual feature class, the semantic feature class, and the keyword class. Al-Khatib and others (1999) think that object-oriented technology can provide a powerful model for multimedia composition and organizational modeling, but note that (from the database management point of view) very few research results have been reported in the literature.

Relational (and object-oriented) databases share several problems in relation to the complexities of multimedia data:

1) the inability to manage spatiotemporal relations
2) the inability to recognize the content of the multimedia data and thereby the semantics of the multimedia content, and
3) the inability to utilize query by example (Yoshitaka and Ichikawa 1999).

In addition, object-oriented models are often implemented in a nonstandard manner. Therefore, these techniques have been extended by more recent research into combined object-relational and hypersemantic (objects, relations, and rules) models. Object-relational models incorporate the ability of object-oriented systems to represent complex data types, while retaining the advantages of relational databases in storage and query processing. Hypersemantic models enable the representation of constraints and rules, such as "Object A has to be played before object B" (Thuraisingham 2001, 28). Other work proposes a hybrid approach in which a prototype-based language is used as an alternative to the standard class-based languages of object-oriented programming (Lahlou 1997). According to this approach, adapting the object-oriented paradigm to semantic image modeling is difficult because images cannot be easily modeled solely through hierarchical structures or abstraction into well-structured classes, especially as these classes may be difficult to predict. The prototype approach does not use the notion of class, but rather creates objects as needed or by cloning from other objects. This, however, makes retrieval difficult. The hybrid model ties objects to classes, but the object only abstracts a minimal structure from the class and the model can implement individual structures as well.

Commercial Database Systems

Object-Relational Systems

Current commercial systems are utilizing the object-relational model. Off-the-shelf systems have been extended to handle multimedia data by including data types that are not interpreted by the system. For example, unstructured binary large objects are stored as BLOBs. However, one drawback to these systems is a lack of standardization in data types and limited permissible operations. More power is provided when the object type can be defined within the database system. Examples of user-defined types with object-oriented functionalities (which are again proprietary) include datablades (such as Informix/Excalibur's Visual RetrievalWare) and data cartridges (Oracle), which can handle text, spatial data, images, audio, and video.

Web-Based Image Search Engines

Another factor adding to the complexity of developing image databases is their evolution within the networked Web environment. When the Web is used to populate the image database (e.g., WebSEEk) this leads to dynamically changing content of such databases, and static index structures often result in false hits with the degradation of links over time (Smith and Chang 1997b). As Weber and others explain, centrally stored image data does not scale well in searching, and data providers lose their autonomy (Weber and others 1999). Variation in bandwidth also leads to unpredictable response times. On the other hand, Web-based search engines have proven to be fairly scalable, and data providers can maintain their autonomy. When metadata resides in a central database, mechanisms are necessary to ensure consistency between the metadata and the images and their associated components such as features and indexes. With diversity of database providers, providing a common access method for users becomes an issue. One approach to this problem is the development of a Multimedia Retrieval Markup Language (MRML), an XML-based communication protocol.[37] This protocol standardizes access and content-based querying by separating the query interface from the actual query engine.

Prototype Web-based image search engines employ a variety of methods, including content-based techniques and/or standard textual querying.[38] Among Internet-accessible image search engines, several initially implemented content-based and query by example methods. Many, such as AltaVista, have subsequently dropped these in favor of text searching, in which text associated with the images is often used to provide image indexing. Yahoo's Image Surfer[39] organizes images manually into categories; the original site employed Excalibur's Visual RetrievalWare to search within the categories.[40] The Google site (www.google.com) includes an image search, which analyzes image captions and associated text on Web pages, as well as "other factors."

Querying Techniques

Images, unlike alphanumeric strings, need multidimensional indexing or access methods. Typical methods within image databases have included textual querying by (subjective) description (QBD) and query by example (QBE). Querying by visual example (QVE) typically involves shape similarity or feature retrieval and/or sketch retrieval. Another method is to use multiple example images in the query (queries by multiple example or QBME) (Ramakrishna and Nepal 2000). These authors also provide a review of query processing methods. Another type of querying uses visual query languages (VQLs), which use visual representations (most typically icons) to depict the domain of interest and the queries (icons combined according to a spatial syntax) within a visual query system (VQS) (Chang and Jungert 2001). These systems are based upon the assumption that the user interface should be as visual as possible.

There are many types of visual queries, and these may involve objects, attributes, and relationships. Possible types of queries include exact match, similarity retrieval, or either of these with specified transformations such as scaling, translation, rotation, or other transformations, or a combination of two or more of these. Exact-match queries can take the form of matching by spatial location, by specifying composition (such as 50% grass and 50% sky), or by a keyword representing a concept or a class. Similarity retrieval uses an example image as a query and can also be spatial (by example or sketch), compositional, or by group of images. Queries can also be classified as either full-scene (global) or object- or region-based (local).

Queries can also be categorized by the type of method used to satisfy the query. For instance, a recent review defines three broad types of search: 1) target search (exact match), which draws on methods of pattern matching and object recognition; 2) category search (retrieval by class of images), which builds from object recognition and statistical pattern recognition methods; and 3) search by association, where the goal is unspecified; feature sets and similarity functions are employed, but the search is iterative and interactive (Smeulders and others 2000, 1373).

Querying techniques have evolved from standard database techniques to newer feature-based ones being implemented in hypermedia and multimedia systems. Different types of query languages may be needed to support a variety of user needs.[41] For instance, query languages in geographic information systems may be related to planning or locating particular features, while those in general-purpose image systems may relate to subject or visual content, theme, specific features, standard descriptive or textual fields, or any number of other elements. Others note that spatial–temporal multimedia databases (and even virtual reality data sources) will require flexible query languages that can deal with multiple data sources (Chang and Jungert 2001). Query responses may be in terms of statistics, text, or thumbnail or full images.

Santini and Jain (1997) point out similarities and differences between image and text databases. A major difference between retrieval systems for these two modalities is that the goal of traditional text retrieval systems is to partition a database into two sets—relevant items and nonrelevant items (the relevant set may later be ranked, however)—whereas CBR systems sort the database in order of similarity to the query. However, image searching also shares similarities with text searching in that users may not be able to exactly specify their needs or may desire to find items "like this one." Techniques such as ranking, utility estimation, and relevance feedback are being explored in a visual context. Search ambiguity and imprecision has necessitated facilitation of browsing techniques as well. Operations such as these are computationally expensive, and even more so in what may be a transform-intensive image retrieval system. In addition, some types of postprocessing may be desired, such as analysis, manipulation, transformation, or visualization. However, as Jain has noted, the utility of a representation is highly dependent on the nature of the queries: "the search for efficient representations is not absolute, but rather dependent on the nature of queries expected" (Jain 1993, 209).

Query-by-Example

Sketch-Based Retrieval

Sketch-based retrieval allows a user to input a rough sketch as a query; similarities between the query sketch and stored images are automatically evaluated based upon local and global features. Hasegawa, Okada, and Toriwaki (1989) report a sketch-retrieval system in a medical context. Another early sketch-based retrieval system used sketch input and graphic feature (GF) analysis to derive similar matches for searching trademarks (Kato 1992). In this system, based on earlier cognitive studies of how graphic symbols are perceived, vectors represent three graphic features: the spatial distribution of the gray level, the spatial frequency (which measures the complexity of graphic symbols), and spatial structure, as shown by local correlation measure and local contrast measure. A later system allowed the user to draw a rough sketch to retrieve similar images in a small database of paintings (Hirata and Kato 1993). One of the more widely used systems using sketch-based retrieval was the QBIC system. Shape similarity has also been addressed as a deformation problem (Pentland, Picard, and Sclaroff 1996). Later work has focused on improving efficiency through improved indexing structures for shape retrieval (Berretti, Del Bimbo, and Pala 2000).

Similarity Retrieval

An iconic or graphical query is a query composed of input images and conditions on these images. The goal is to retrieve images whose contents satisfy the conditions specified in such a query. In order to process graphical or iconic commands, the query image must be captured and then undergo the same types of representation and interpretation processes as the stored images before matching can take place. Mappings must be flexible enough to refer to attributes at different levels of detail, analysis (such as an unprocessed feature and a derived feature), and representation, and must accommodate a range of uncertainty. Similarity retrieval can be either global or local, focusing on a particular region in an image. This querying scheme is referred to as partial search.

Two systems using a region-based approach are the NeTra system (Ma and Manjanuth 1997) and the Blobworld system (Carson and others 1999).[42] These systems require a user to select a region and also the type of feature for that region to be matched. One problem with defining similarity in this way is that the user's concept of similarity is likely to occur on a higher level than that defined by a specific region and feature. Another problem is that the item of interest for searching may not have been defined as a region by the system. Recognizing that both the image data and the query may need to be defined in fuzzy, rather than exact, terms, Fagin and others have investigated fuzzy querying methods for multimedia (Fagin 1998; Fagin and Wimmers 1997). Researchers have also developed a fuzzy object query language (FOQL) to support querying of fuzzy data (Nepal, Ramakrishna, and Thom 1999).

Relevance Feedback

As already noted in several system descriptions, relevance feedback is used as a technique for finding the best matches to a query. Relevance feedback is seen as a method for bridging the semantic gap, as a user does not need to clearly specify the query. A search using relevance feedback is an iterative process, with the user selecting retrieved items that most closely match the query. The system automatically weights terms or descriptors associated with the relevant documents and repeats the search. Generally, only the top ten to twenty ranked documents need to be reviewed. According to Baeza-Yates and Ribeiro-Neto (1999), relevance feedback offers the following advantages: 1) the user does not need to be concerned with query reformulation because the user only has to provide relevance judgments on the items found; 2) the searching task is broken down into a sequence of small steps; and 3) it offers a controlled process which emphasizes relevant features and de-emphasizes nonrelevant ones.

Relevance feedback can be considered a form of supervised learning. Thus, the goal of relevance feedback in an image retrieval system is to learn correspondences between the images selected by the user, which represent higher-level concepts, and the low-level features obtained by the system from the images. It is generally difficult for a user to specify relationships (in the form of weights) between the low-level features represented in these systems and higher-level description of images at a more conceptual level. Relevance feedback can be used to expand queries in a vector retrieval model or reweight query terms in a probabalistic model. As relevance feedback progresses, more and more data is available to the system. As Koskela and others note, the art of relevance feedback is finding the ways that use this information most efficiently (Koskela, Laaksonen, and Oja 2001, 2).

A number of systems are using relevance feedback techniques on lower-level features. The MARS system formally proposes a relevance feedback architecture and uses relevance feedback at several levels (Mehrotra and others 1997). PicHunter uses a Bayesian relevance feedback framework and uses the complete history of the query to compute the probabilities of each image in the database being the relevant image (Cox and others, 2000). However, a large number of iterations are required even in a small database, making this approach impractical for larger databases. The iFind system incorporates both low-level features and semantic features identified by keywords in its relevance feedback process (Lu and others 2000). Keywords are taken from tagged fields of Web pages and are also added to an image when a user identifies that image as being relevant to a particular keyword query. The keywords have weighted links to images and form a dynamic semantic network, as weights are adjusted as more users query the system. For an overview and discussion of relevance feedback within CBR, see Rui and Huang (2001).

Query Languages

Querying of pictorial relational or semantically enhanced database systems is done by several methods, including traditional text or feature index keys and database query languages such as structured query language (SQL), or extending these to a pictorial or spatial query language (PSQL, Spatial SQL). Query language formalisms range from linguistically based to logical and algebraic ones. SQL merges these in relational databases, and more recent forms incorporate object-oriented capabilities (one example is MOQL, multimedia object query language, Li and others 1997). Many issues still remain unresolved, such as how the parts of a query are combined and how to support refinement of query expression. Matching operations need to be done under different constraints, and similarity of objects must be defined. Jain (1993) calls for integration of the various query-processing capabilities found in such diverse systems as geographic information systems, DBMS, information retrieval systems, and knowledge-based systems, and drawing upon the strengths of each is a goal. Such integration is now being carried out in data fusion research.

Various query languages have been developed to extend the functionalities of standard database query languages. PICQUERY is a query language which works with PICDMS to allow a user to request similarity retrieval or operations such as edge detection or segmentation (Joseph and Cardenas 1988). Images are divided into individual grid elements of a small area for which all attributes (such as boundaries) are recorded. Other work used pictures to describe restrictions involving spatial relationships among objects in the database; the PICSL language primarily used pictures drawn by the user to specify constraints, or unacceptable database states (Pizano, Klinger, and Cardenas 1989). Another query language, PSQL is a spatial data management–based extension of SQL, in which applications-dependent commands are embedded (Roussopoulos, Faloutsos, and Sellis 1988). Hibler, Leung, and Mannock (1992) use an entity–attribute–relationship (EAR) model in a relational database for both a picture description language and a querying language. The picture query language is converted into an SQL representation to query the database. Users familiar with entity-relationship modeling concepts achieved good results, but for users unfamiliar with these concepts, retrieval was less successful (Aslandogan and others 1995). Oakley, Davis, and Shann (1993) defined an application-specific set of primitive visual features which can be extracted from images using low-level image processing. They describe a query language incorporating geometric constructs to enable a user to specify groups of features of interest in an image. While not difficult to construct, application-specific languages are time-consuming to develop and their usefulness is limited. Current research focuses on more generalized features and extensions of standard query languages such as SQL. An example would be ΣQL (Li and others 1997), which allows a user to specify spatial–temporal queries for both multimedia data sources and multimedia databases.

Other researchers propose visualization techniques for both queries and their results, in the form of a concept map (Chen and Chang 2001). The concept map is a two-dimensional graphical representation of both text and feature-based query components that would allow a user to see the influence of a query component in relation to the other components and to modify the search accordingly. In their visualization paradigm users are also able to see graphical displays of feature and distance space.

System Evaluation

The overview presented here demonstrates the breadth and depth of the research projects concerned with CBR methods. The diversity of projects not only makes grasping the multiple approaches difficult, but also (more importantly) increases greatly the difficulty in comparing the approaches and their results. As the discussion has revealed, systems testing a particular technique use different test sets of images and rely on a variety of algorithms (for processing, indexing, compression, and so forth) combined in different ways. At present, there is no consistent way to evaluate the output of content-based processing or of different combinations of these techniques for image indexing, representation, and retrieval.[43] While the literature of CBR is vast, the lack of consistent methods and tools for evaluating and comparing systems contributes to duplication of effort and a slowing of progress in this important research area. As a result, there is an increasing recognition among the CBR community that reliable methods for the evaluation of image indexing and retrieval methods need to be established (Jörgensen 2001; Muller and others 2001). An additional and similarly urgent need is the incorporation of "real" users in usability testing.

Evaluation Components

Problems for evaluation exist in several areas: evaluation methods and measures of system functionality, testbeds, queries, and ground-truthing (e.g., "relevance" of an image to a query). While none of these areas is trivial to address, it is essential to begin making progress towards comparability of experimental results.

In terms of evaluation, there needs to be a recognition that two types of evaluation are required: *performance* evaluation, which evaluates indexing structures, interactions with the operating system, delays in communication channels, and overhead of software layers in terms of efficiency of response time and storage space; and the more complex issue of *retrieval performance* evaluation, which addresses how precise an answer set is in relation to a query. In addition, retrieval performance should be broadened to take into account different modes of searching and user goals as well, so that other user behaviors (besides a specific item or goal-oriented search) such as exploration and browsing can also be accommodated. Evaluation metrics have been the subject of lengthy discussion in several recent papers; the reader is referred to these for in-depth information (Santini 2000; Santini and Jain 1999; Smith 2001). Evaluation metrics need to be chosen in relation to the type of performance being evaluated, the feature levels addressed, and the query types.

Currently, many image *testbeds* continue to be a sample of convenience (i.e., what is readily available), or limited to a specific domain within the context of the needs of specific research projects and funding requests. For instance, many researchers use the Corel Photo CDs, collections of images produced for commercial interests. As such, these images represent much more of an idealized world of images (perfect color, lighting, composition, and so forth) than those typically found in the "everyday" world. These images come conveniently organized by general topic. These topic words are used for ground-truth labeling in some system evaluations, but the keywords assigned to these images are extremely limited, and constrain the notions of similarity to a single object or subject. Additionally, images within a topic group may all be very much alike, while images in other topic areas may be quite different, leading to greater within-group similarity and across-group dissimilarity than may be found in "real-world" images. System tests using these images may therefore produce positive but unrealistic performance outcomes.

The number of images used in a testbed also varies dramatically, from extremely small (250) to large numbers of images harvested from the Web (>300,000). For many projects, the most frequently mentioned size in the literature has been around 2,000 images; scalability is an obvious problem with such small testsets. When researchers are asked how many images should be in such a testbed, the numbers range from 100,000 to one million (Jörgensen and Srihari 1999). Researchers also express a willingness to contribute images to such a testbed, however. Images should not only be of a variety of subjects, but also represent different capture conditions (varying angle, lighting, resolution). Howe proposes a series of algorithmically altered images to serve this purpose within a testbed (Howe 2000). Images would be manipulated to represent different conditions such as variations in lighting, camera gain, contrast, and color balance (challenges to color-based processing); another alteration would be the "jumbling" of image segments to test object identification.

It should be noted that large numbers of images are available from several existing collections, notably collections from various digital library projects, such as the UC Berkeley Environmental Digital Library and the UC Santa Barbara Alexandria Digital Library. These and other images have been made available through the D-Lib Forum as the D-Lib Test Suite.[44] Other large image sets are available through other government agencies such as NASA and the Library of Congress. These images are accompanied by varying amounts of text, but the format of the text metadata varies from institution to institution, making merging of text descriptions across these image sets and use of the text for annotation difficult. The MPEG-7 initiative provided a test set of images and video for those working on the standard, but these are expensive and not widely available, and suffer from the same sorts of general problems described above, especially the limited subject matter portrayed. A small cooperative project at the University of Washington is attempting to provide annotated images for a testbed.[45] The annotations consist of a few keywords describing the main objects in the image (e.g., for the group of images *green lake*: clear sky, trees, bushes, grass, water, people, ducks, trail), and the collection of images is under a thousand images at this point.

However, the ready availability of these collections poses problems as well as seemingly easy solutions to amassing restriction-free images for testbeds. A major problem yet to be addressed is the influence of the content of a large collection upon the types of queries possible and the outcomes of testing within what ultimately becomes a domain defined not by principle, but as noted above by convenience. Projects need careful planning as to the image domains to be included, *as a first step*; these existing collections of images can then be mined in accordance with these plans. The domains of a testbed should ideally also address the needs of two communities: the research community performing system evaluations, and the real-world users of images. Thus, the content should be grounded in the reality of image communities who make heavy use of images in their jobs, as well as providing suitable testing material for a variety of techniques. This will ensure both reliability and validity of testing results.

Test *queries* and their relevant matches are another thorny problem for system evaluation. The simplest type of query is the use of a query image, where the system task is to find the best matches for the image. When testbeds are small, obviously the image has to be chosen carefully so that a match or matches can in fact be made in the imagebase, and the solution to the query may very well end up defining the problem query. Another problem is the notion of similarity (measures of similarity have been discussed earlier), which can exist on a number of levels, from visual features such as color or texture to the presence of specific objects, to higher-level abstract concepts or even the relevant usage of an image. Most notions of similarity in system testing have dealt only with the lower levels of feature matching or a single object, and frequently with only a single relevant feature. A system optimized for one or several features may not perform well when these particular features are not relevant to a different collection of images. While it may certainly be appropriate to develop feature processing for limited applications, when testing remains within a limited domain defined by a single testbed and constrained queries, claims as to high levels of system performance are often not appropriately bounded.

A possible solution is to develop queries within the context of the level of retrieval being addressed (feature, structure, object, and semantic levels). Within these levels, queries should also progress from the *performance* to the *retrieval performance* levels. At the retrieval performance level, queries should be developed spanning a range of types (single word to more complex phrase) and within the context of knowledge about how real humans query image retrieval systems (humans generally prefer to query at higher semantic levels). The use of queries developed for CBR evaluation could be shared with other communities as well, for instance to test human-created indexing tools such as thesauri, or metadata structures, and so forth. A consistent methodology for developing the queries is necessary to remove the ad hoc nature from which such queries (and their resultant retrieval) often suffer.

The development of *ground-truth relevance scores* has also been problematic, primarily because of the amount of time involved for humans to evaluate similarity among images in a large image collection. Several papers have proposed using a pooling of results from lower-level CBR processing similar to methods used in the Text REtrieval Conferences (TREC) (Jörgensen and Srihari 1999; Muller and others 2001; Smith 2001). This is a potentially useful technique for limiting the set of relevant images, using either a specific number of top-ranking images as a final set or as an input set for further human similarity judgments. However, pooling based on lower-level features currently addresses the feature and structure levels, with very limited access to higher levels of object identification or semantics. Using this output as an input set for human similarity judgments further guarantees the accuracy of the image similarity but only *within the same levels*.

In what some may consider a best-case scenario, text already accompanies images, in which case descriptors are available and ambiguity may be reduced. Techniques for text and caption processing exist, and text is being processed in combination with CBR techniques. Using a combination of methods to batch process images which are then further evaluated for similarity across various levels is one possible approach. However, it must also be noted that these captions or associated text are also developed within particular contexts, and may thus also have only limited or domain-specific information. Other researchers have proposed the use of structured text annotation (preserving subject-object relationships) of a collection as a simulation of the user's needs (Muller and others 2001). Beyond the immediate needs of ground-truthing, text indexing combined with CBR feature descriptors can pave the way for an understanding of how low-level features begin to map to higher-level objects and semantics in an image.

Retrieval performance evaluation also relates to the issue of appropriate measures for performance evaluation. Precision and recall are well-known measures from text retrieval and have been applied in image retrieval evaluation as well, but these measures imply that there is one or a limited set of correct answers to a query.[46] When dealing with higher-level semantics of images, there appear to be multiple levels upon which similarity can be based, making precision and recall less applicable for evaluating image retrieval results. Tansley reviews other measures of retrieval performance and notes that such issues as predictability or the number of logical decisions required to satisfy an information requirement may also be usefully included in evaluation (Tansley 2000, 43). Other authors note that a major problem in evaluating performance is the failure to consider chance agreement, frequently leading to inflated measures of system performance (Squire and Pun 1998).

User Testing and Usability

Obviously, retrieval performance evaluation needs to incorporate much more end-user testing; there have been few user studies of image retrieval systems to inform system design. Little attention is paid to the users of these systems: what questions they ask of systems, how they ask these questions, what tasks they need to perform, or how they interact with image retrieval systems. The lack of this kind of testing is partially the result of the difficulties involved such as time to conduct such experiments or lack of suitable (nonexpert) participants, as well as a lack of a framework for evaluation.

Early researchers noted the need for user testing. Swain (1993) suggested taking advantage of interactions with users to find out what types of variation are expected in a database and to rely on users to discriminate between similar-looking objects. Jain (1993) noted the need to do research to characterize and recover qualitative descriptions of attributes in images. He also suggested that the methodology for research and development in this area needs to move out from the laboratory and into real-life contexts and noted the need to encourage in situ style studies. Hibler and others comment: "Our belief is that the most fruitful advances will be made as much through a more informed understanding of human processes of search and retrieval in collections of images as through increasing sophistication in hardware and software" (Hibler, Leung, and Mannock 1992, 92).

In work evaluating the PicHunter system, the authors note that they believe that "this is the first time a baseline measurement has been performed for similar-target-search algorithms, yet it is clear that use of such baselines is essential for comparing performances of CBR systems. In particular, our experiments demonstrate that even random search may appear to perform surprisingly well when users are given the ill-defined task of judging when images are similar rather than identical to a query" (Papathomas and others 1998, 601). Others suggest that user testing needs to be conducted by expert users within the context of particular tasks in order to be effective (Sormunen, Markkula, and Järvelin 1999). An additional problem, as pointed out by Tansley (2000), is that user trials inherently evaluate the interface to a system; therefore the underlying techniques employed cannot be evaluated in isolation.

An evaluation of the user interface of two systems (ImageFinder and IMatch) against ten heuristic principles of usability noted both systems placed a cognitive load on the user. The authors note that, in terms of existing prototype systems, "a heavy and unnecessary burden of responsibility is brought to bear on the user with regards to understanding the systems' functionality. It is highly possible that this burden will have a severe negative effect on a user's perception of the system's retrieval effectiveness. The two systems subjected to the heuristic evaluation suggest that there is considerable scope for improvement" (Venters and Cooper 2000, 31–32).

Evaluation Efforts

There have been some evaluation efforts, which have been of two kinds. One type of evaluation is a comparison of features offered by different systems. For instance, the MIRA (Multimedia Information Retrieval Applications) working group[47] (part of ESPRIT, the European Union Information Technologies Program) concentrated on the evaluation on multimedia information retrieval systems, in particular interactive systems.[48] Another study tested three systems (ImageFinder, IMatch, and QBIC) to determine whether the matching features accomplished the tasks that they had been designed for (global color distribution) (Venters and Cooper 2000, 30). The authors suggest that in a number of instances the results were questionable and unpredictable, with not only widely varying degrees of precision and recall but retrieval results that are "extremely dubious."

A second type of initiative currently underway attempts to quantitatively analyze the performance of systems. One example is the TREC Video Retrieval Track, the investigation of content-based retrieval from digital video.[49] There are also voluntary efforts aimed towards establishing benchmarking systems, most notably the "Benchathlon," part of the Internet Imaging II conference (Gunther and Beretta 2000).[50] However, establishing continuing leadership and a sustained level of effort in volunteer projects is extremely difficult without some level of funding. The field of image retrieval has reached a point of maturity that now calls for a new initiative to establish consistent means of evaluating results, especially within contexts more closely related to real users and real queries.

Conclusion

As we have seen, there is a large body of literature concerning data models, pattern and feature recognition, database architectures, and machine learning and image understanding through applications of artificial intelligence. Clearly, the emphasis in the computer science literature has been largely on what is computationally possible, and not on discovering whether essential generic visual primitives can in fact facilitate image retrieval in "real-world" applications. Some have noted that a common problem among image databases is a lack of integration and a shared, coherent conceptual framework (Jain 1993; Pavlidis 1988). Research remains fragmented, and synthesis among the various approaches will be necessary if effective image retrieval is to become a computational reality.

Many different processing and representational mechanisms are available; the question becomes which one or what combination should be used. Representations and techniques that are efficient in one context may be inefficient in others (see, for example, the discussion of the task- and data-dependent performance of different texture models in Minka and Picard (1997). The space–time trade-off that is to be performed is also a consideration. Some authors contend that differences in methodologies sometimes have more to do with politics than with the processes involved (Pavladis 1992). Others criticize the popularity of such techniques as being "more due to their generality and mathematical tractability than their suitability in computer vision" and argue that researchers use favorite tools learned in graduate school rather than first analyzing the problems to be solved, and then developing appropriate tools (Jain and Binford 1991).

Early researchers noted several problems, which remain today. There is an inevitable mismatch between idealized models and bottom-up data (Brolio and others 1989). The ideal data representation scheme—one that matches the abilities of the computer, the structure of visual data, and the information management needs of the user—remains elusive. Others ask whether it will be necessary to maintain two representations of data, one for human comprehension and the other for machine processing (Kasturi and others 1989). Both model-driven and data-driven approaches are used in object recognition, but efficient searching remains difficult to achieve.

These early researchers concluded that problems in image processing require both long-term programs and researchers with broad educational backgrounds, and could profit by the incorporation of context. Recent initiatives focusing on the semantics of images and drawing upon other fields such as semiotics for theory are a move in the right direction. However, many research endeavors still suffer from limited theoretical models and a lack of cross-disciplinary interaction and feedback, or a hasty application of models without an understanding of user and domain needs and tasks, and user-system interactions.

A 1993 National Science Foundation (NSF) Workshop on Visual Information Management Systems (VIMS) included the following recommendations for system capabilities related to feature-based indexing and retrieval:

- Database systems which include the capability of defining and installing content- and semantic-based operators
- Efficient indexing methods for a high number of image dimensions, but preserving efficient retrieval
- The ability to handle fuzzy queries and imprecise content or semantic representations
- New indexing capabilities (such as temporal), or informed partial indexing
- Development of a general theory of similarity and also of distance which will allow matching of objects using similarity based on several features
- Research in expressing pictorial attributes used by humans to develop easily expressible, intuitive, quantitative query terms (Jain 1993, 206–207)

While much progress has been made in some of these areas, nevertheless these goals remain as relevant to the field (and as elusive) as they were almost a decade ago. Other aspects not mentioned here and not yet touched on to any great extent include interactive manipulation of and visualization techniques for results. In order to address these issues, a necessary next step in advancing CBR involves not only establishing tools and methods for both objective and user-oriented evaluation of such systems, but a widening of the primary community involved in such efforts and of the perspective taken. A recent article by Benitez and Smith suggests this approach and states: "We believe that the next-generation of multimedia information systems will be marked by the full introduction of intelligence into the systems," and they define intelligence as "the capabilities of the systems to build and maintain situational or world models, utilize dynamic knowledge representations, exploit context, and leverage advanced reasoning and learning capabilities." They continue, "We argue that that these elements are essential to producing effective systems for retrieving audio-visual content at semantic levels matching those of human perception and cognition" (Benitez and Smith 2001, 141).

These new frontiers bolster the need not only for new *interdisciplinary* research initiatives but also for thorough familiarity of researchers with all relevant work, regardless of its temporal and geographical origins, and the incorporation of this work into a common, sensible, and easily understood framework that will facilitate these new research directions. Smeulders and others (2000), in their extensive review, comment that in some research articles it was not clear what problem the authors were trying to solve or whether the suggested method would work better than any other alternative. They propose a classification of usage types, aims, and purposes, with hard criteria for distinguishing among domain types, and note the importance of domain knowledge and the man–machine interface.

The Literature

A few personal observations and a note about the general nature of the literatures related to machine processing of images may be appropriate at this point. Adjectives such as "vast" are often applied to the various literatures reviewed above related to image processing, but even this designation is an understatement. A number of review articles have been published, but each can cover only a tiny fraction of the reported research. Keeping up with this literature is a major undertaking for researchers. This can perhaps partially explain some of the tendencies noted here. Researchers in these areas (as is typical of most scholarly research) tend to work within their own invisible colleges, and cite their colleagues from these. Literature reviews are often lacking an international perspective, and literature searching (at least as represented by the bibliographic citations of many articles) often seems rather incomplete.

The tradition in computer science publishing is to disseminate research results quickly, in conference proceedings and workshops, followed by a later journal article. This is necessitated by the need to disseminate interesting results rapidly and improve the research through discussion with colleagues. However, this also results in multiple publications of essentially the same work, and is one of the factors contributing to the huge publication repository. Those interested in seeking the latest (and perhaps unproven) research should consult conference proceedings such as those of SPIE (The International Society for Optical Engineering) that are voluminous.[51] Another valuable Web-based research resource is the citation database at the NEC (Nippon Electronic Company) Research Institute site.[52]

Notes

1. The literature related to digitization issues and techniques is enormous, and a full discussion of these issues is beyond the scope of this chapter. One useful resource on digitization issues is *Guides to Quality in Visual Resource Imaging* from the Digital Libraries Federation, available at www.rlg.org/visguides/ (accessed on April 18, 2003)

2. In reality, terminology is not always used in its strictest sense, and "feature" and "attribute" may be used interchangeably in the literature.

3. A useful introductory text is *Machine Vision* (Jain, Kasturi, and Schunck 1995).

4. Coherent description of the contents of different classes or domains (such as fingerprints, medical images, or weather maps) is an additional challenge.

5. The reader should note that the CBR literature is huge; one recent review described the number of papers published since 1997 as breathtaking (Smeulders and others 2000).

6. While a discussion of color space is too lengthy for consideration here, the reader should note that there are a number of color spaces in use, and choice of color space is an important consideration. Swain and Ballard (1991) found improvements (from a retrieval standpoint) with opponent color axes, which isolate the brightness information on the third axis. Other approaches use Munsell or CIE L*a*b*, which was designed so that the Euclidian distance between two color representations models human perception of color differences.

7. For a review, see Mandal, Idris, and Panchanathan (1999).

8. Moments refer to statistical characteristics of data; most information is concentrated in the first moment (mean), and the second and third central moments (variance and skewness).

9. This draws upon early work in psychology demonstrating that more information is contained in curved line segments that in straight line segments; missing information can be filled in when only corners or short curved lines are present (Attneave, 1954).

10. Demos of the system are available at the State Hermitage Museum digital collection website: www.hermitagemuseum.org/ (accessed on April 18, 2003).

11. A demo is available at www.ctr.columbia.edu/visualseek (accessed on April 18, 2003).

12. More information and a system demo on face recognition is available at www-white.media.mit.edu/vismod/demos/facerec/ (accessed on April 18, 2003).

13. See www.jpeg.org/ (accessed on April 18, 2003).

14. See www.w3.org/Graphics/JPEG/ (accessed on April 18, 2003).

15. See www.iso.org/iso/en/ISOOnline.frontpage (accessed on April 18, 2003).

16. See mpeg.telecomitalialab.com/ (accessed on April 18, 2003).

17. However, Smeulders and others (2000) note that image retrieval does not necessarily entail solving the general image understanding problem.

18. Face recognition, an area of high interest, uses different methods than object recognition because of the high degree of structure present. Face recognition involves

processes for face detection, feature extraction, and face recognition. A discussion of these methods is beyond the scope of this chapter; for an introduction see *Face Recognition: A Literature Survey* (Zhao, Chellappa, Rosenfeld, and Phillips 2000).

19. Saliency has been defined as the "points which survive longest when gradually blurring the image in scale space" (Lindeberg and Eklundh 1992).

20. For a discussion of template matching and other object recognition methods see Al-Khatib and others (1999).

21. Petkovich, cited in Lew (2001).

22. Note that this loose definition follows that of Medin and Barsalou (1987).

23. Affective Computing group, MIT Media Lab: http://affect.media.mit.edu/AC_about.html (accessed on April 18, 2003).

24. This is referred to as the field of kansei engineering, related to human interfaces.

25. Based on the work of Chijiwa, *Chromatics* (1983).

26. Adjectives include "authentic," "natural," "chic," "romantic," "cool," "sober," "sporty," and others.

27. Latent Semantic Analysis is basically principal component analysis of text.

28. A demo is available at www.cs.bu.edu/groups/ivc/ImageRover/ (accessed on April 18, 2003).

29. A demo is available at www.ctr.columbia.edu/webseek/ (accessed on April 18, 2003).

30. For further information, see Fellbaum, Christiane D., ed. *WordNet: An Electronic Lexical Database*. Cambridge, Mass.: MIT Press, 1998.

31. See www.cogsci.princeton.edu/~wn/ (accessed on April 18, 2003).

32. For an example, see Yoshitaka and others (1994).

33. See the more detailed explanations available at the Description Logics homepage (dl.kr.org/) and the definition at www.cs.man.ac.uk/ ~franconi/dl/ (both accessed on April 18, 2003).

34. An excellent introduction to neural nets can be found at a monthly posting to the Usenet newsgroup comp.ai.neural-nets, whose purpose is to provide basic information for individuals who are new to the field of neural networks, available at ftp://ftp.sas.com/pub/neural/FAQ.html (accessed on April 18, 2003).

35. Parts of this description are taken from whatis.techtarget.com (accessed on April 18, 2003).

36. See, for instance, Dunlop (1991).

37. See mrml.net/ (accessed on April 18, 2003).

38. For instance, WebSeer (Frankel, Swain, and Athitsos 1996); AMORE (Hirata and others 1998), system demo available at www.ccrl.com/amore (accessed on April 18, 2003); ImageRover (Sclaroff and others 1999); PicToSeek (Gevers and Smeulders 2000), demo available at zomax.wins. uva.nl:5345/ret_user/ (accessed on April 18, 2003).

39. See gallery.yahoo.com/ (accessed on April 18, 2003).

40. One highly rated (by users of the BIG Search Engine Index, www.search-engine-index.co.uk/Images_Search/ (accessed on April 18, 2003) image search engine, Diggit!,

was for sale (as of October 2001) as a result of the technology investment slowdown.

41. For a review, see Li, Ozsu, and Szafron (1995).

42. Demos available at maya.ece.ucsb.edu/Netra/netra2.html (NeTra) and dlp.CS.Berkeley.EDU/photos/blobworld/ (Blobworld) (both accessed on April 18, 2003).

43. A step in the right direction has been taken by Berretti, Del Bimbo, and Pala (2000). The TOKEN system performance is compared to QBIC and QVE systems and the elastic matching approach, and three indexing methods are compared with respect to I/O and CPU requirements.

44. See www.dlib.org/test-suite (accessed on April 18, 2003).

45. See www.cs.washington.edu/research/imagedatabase/groundtruth/ (accessed on April 18, 2003).

46. For further discussion, see also Smeulders and others (2000).

47. See www.dcs.gla.ac.uk/mira/ (accessed on April 18, 2003).

48. A comparison of nine systems is available at compass.itc.it/compareIt.html (accessed on April 18, 2003); system features such as number of visual descriptors and type of query are presented.

49. See www-nlpir.nist.gov/projects/trecvid/ (accessed on April 18, 2003).

50. See also www.benchathlon.net (accessed on April 18, 2003).

51. The website at www.spie.org (accessed on April 18, 2003) allows searching on all of its publications.

52. See citeseer.nj.nec.com/cs (accessed on April 18, 2003).

Chapter 5

Image Attributes: The Research Framework

As noted earlier, the research review herein presented first began as a prelude to the author's dissertation research ("Image Attributes: An Investigation"), whose goal was to discover what image features or attributes image indexing can most usefully focus upon. The results of that exploratory research, as well as results from other researchers, can now be related to the context of the chapter discussions in the current work.

Image Attributes: An Investigation

The goal of this research was to establish a baseline description of typical image attributes as revealed in several types of tasks: describing, sorting, and searching. The research used exploratory, qualitative, and analytical methods to investigate typically noticed image attributes. The dynamic driving the choice of these research methods was the same one that underlies the motivation for the current work: the need for comprehensive, holistic evaluative techniques capable of bringing together a diverse number of literatures, methodologies, and perspectives in order to understand more fully human needs and behaviors in image interaction and access.

The methodology, limitations, and research results from the dissertation have been presented in much more detail in other publications (Jörgensen 1995a; Jörgensen 1995b; Jörgensen 1998). A brief summary is presented here, and related research is presented below. This research accepted two assumptions based in the literatures of aesthetics and semiotics: 1) that viewing an image is to some extent an interpretive act (Solso 1994), and 2) that the interpretation of both images and texts is to some extent socially mediated (Barthes 1977). Rosch (1978) notes that formation of categories occurs in a particular culture at a particular point in time. Keil proposes that individuals may be constrained by a communicative principle, in which the need to communicate an idiosyncratic representation of the world forces adoption of category structures that are more analytical, and therefore more stable, or consistent across individuals (Keil 1987, 193). It is thus the interaction between the individual perceptions of images and the socially constructed contexts for categorizing and communicating about these perceptions that is fertile ground for investigation and for seeking evidence concerning image attributes. Therefore, while the nature of the task, the individual, and the image may impose varying constraints on image description, the social and cultural background which an individual brings to the viewing of and communicating about an image can provide a basis from which to derive descriptive models of image attributes. While this social/cultural bias is often considered in a negative light, making it explicit (such as has been done with the Australian Pictorial Thesaurus, see Chapter Three) could also both simplify system design and data interchange through metadata.

A limitation to be noted here is that the tasks, although designed to mimic naturalistic and realistic tasks, were nevertheless assigned by the author in a controlled environment. However, as the goal was to establish a range of attributes through exploratory research, these methods were adequate. These methods have since been repeated in similar tasks with a wider variety of images, including images from art (including abstract art), science, graphic design, photography, and charts and diagrams, and results remain consistent with the original research.

Describing Tasks

There were two major types of tasks, a set of describing tasks and a sorting task. For the describing tasks, participants in a classroom setting were asked to write individual descriptions of projected color images. The images were randomly chosen from *The Society of Illustrators Twenty-Fifth Annual of American Illustrators* (Weithas 1984). Groups of participants received different instructions setting three different contexts for the image-describing tasks, description, search, and memory. For the descriptive Viewing Task, participants were instructed to produce a simple spontaneous description, writing down words or phrases that "pop into their heads" until they could think of no more, or the time for the task ended (see Table 5.1 for examples of responses). The descriptive Search Task context was finding the image in a collection, i.e., retrieval. The participants were told to imagine that these were images that they wished to find within some type of image storage and retrieval system, of any type that they preferred, from a more traditional picture library to a sophisticated computerized image database. The participants were told to visualize their ideal "intermediary," to whom they would be describing the image. In the descriptive Memory Task, thirty-one participants from the descriptive Viewing task were later asked to write descriptions of the images from memory. This task took place five weeks after the first, and participants were not told in advance that they should try to remember the images. Participants for the tasks were entering graduate students in the M.L.S. program at the School of Information and Library Studies at the University at Buffalo, State University of New York. These students are typical of new M.L.S. students in that they had diverse backgrounds and undergraduate (and other graduate) degrees, as well as diverse demographics and English language abilities.

Table 5.1. Two sample records from descriptive Viewing Task

Participant "A"	Participant "B"
stars	maybe a whale jumping
fuzzy white	not a photo—more stylized
reddish at bottom	attractive blue
whale	white dots—random— that
burst of water at bottom	look like water splashed
white off [sic] flipper	a camera lens
white fine [sic] near head	action—attractive overall
black border	sliver of moon
motion	I would not want to look at it
crescent moon	for long— it's not
swirl of red at top	interesting enuf [sic]

The data analysis for the describing tasks consisted of content analysis (using grounded theory in which categories emerge from the data rather than being predefined). This analysis produced forty-seven *attribute* categories, of which forty were applicable to the question of image description for retrieval purposes.[1] The total number of responses and terms for each task are shown in Table 5.2.

For the set of describing tasks, the most typically reported attributes across all tasks (Table 5.3) are *Object, People, Social Status, Color, Body Part, Location-Specific* (spatial location of item in picture), and *Activity.* Appendix A of this chapter lists attributes and their definitions, and Appendix C shows attribute occurrence across the three tasks. If we look at the top half of attribute occurrences, there are several interesting trends to note. *Emotion* and *Abstract* occur in the top half of the Viewing Task attributes but drop below the midpoint for the Search Task. This suggests that when participants formulated their search statements, they may have modified them in accordance with their expectations of what kind of input a retrieval system would expect. *Category* (genre, such as "Western," "Sci-Fi") rises above the midpoint, but *Theme* (subject of picture, typical of the broad classification often attached to images) ranks below the midpoint in the Viewing Task and drops even lower in the Search Task. This supports the idea of the "story" or narrative of the image as being an important access point.[2]

Table 5.2. Statistics for the descriptive Viewing, Search, and Memory Tasks

	Viewing	Search	Memory	Total
Number of participants	48	58	31	137
Number of descriptions	288	348	116	752
Total terms	4,728	8,998	740	14,446
Average terms per record	16.5	25.9	6.4	
Range of terms per record	2 to 60	5 to 88	0 to 52	

Table 5.3. Most frequently occurring attributes averaged across the describing tasks

Attribute	Percentage
Object	18.5%
People	10.1%
Social Status	7.9%
Color	7.8%
Body Part	6.4%
Location-Specific	6.1%
Activity	5.3%

The attributes were grouped into broad categories (henceforth, "Classes"), which contained variable numbers of attributes. Attribute Classes also mirrored the distribution of the individual attributes (Table 5.4), with the OBJECTS Class the most typically described, followed by PEOPLE, COLOR, STORY, and SPATIAL LOCATION. STORY includes attributes such as *Activity* and *Setting*. In addition, two broad types of Classes emerged, those of "Perceptual" attributes, related to the physical content of the image (nineteen attributes), and "Interpretive" attributes, which are stimulated perceptually but require additional internal interpretive and intellectual processes in order to name the attribute (twenty-four attributes).[3] Perceptual Classes include OBJECTS, PEOPLE,

COLOR, SPATIAL LOCATION, and VISUAL ELEMENTS

Interpretive Classes include STORY, ART HISTORICAL INFORMATION, PEOPLE RELATED (those relating to such things as relationships among people and social status), EXTERNAL RELATION, ABSTRACT, and DESCRIPTION. VIEWER RESPONSE included personal reactions to the items and is not discussed here.

Table 5.4. Distribution of Classes by average percentage across three describing tasks

CLASS	Viewing	Search	Memory	Average
OBJECTS	34.3%	27.4%	26.2%	29.3%
PEOPLE	8.7%	10.3%	11.1%	10.0%
COLOR	9.2%	9.7%	9.0%	9.3%
STORY	7.4%	10.8%	9.4%	9.2%
SPATIAL LOCATION	8.3%	10.7%	7.7%	8.9%
DESCRIPTION	6.0%	9.0%	8.8%	8.0%
VISUAL ELEMENTS	7.2%	5.4%	9.2%	7.2%
ART HISTORICAL INFO.	3.8%	5.7%	7.6%	5.7%
PEOPLE RELATED	5.2%	3.9%	2.6%	3.9%
EXTERNAL RELATION	3.3%	3.8%	4.0%	3.7%
VIEWER RESPONSE	3.7%	1.9%	3.1%	2.9%
ABSTRACT	3.0%	1.5%	1.3%	2.0%

When analyzed by Class, what is striking is the general overall similarity among the tasks of the most frequently occurring Classes. Four Perceptual Classes suggest themselves as potential members of a baseline framework for choosing useful indexing terms to describe images in a linear fashion such as in Keister's "image construct." OBJECTS far outstrips all other Classes in terms of sheer counts, and participants consistently named the object content of pictures. PEOPLE, COLOR, and SPATIAL LOCATION all are typically and consistently described. Within these Classes, the most frequently noted specific attributes are *Object*, *Body Part*, *Clothing*, *People*, *Color*, *Location-General,* and *Location-Specific* (both location attributes refer to general and specific spatial location of objects or visual elements within the picture).

In addition, other aspects of an image besides a broad subject need to be addressed. The occurrence of attributes in the STORY Class (which, intriguingly, is higher for the Search Task than for the Viewing Task) suggests that in addition to subject categorization, specific human activities are of interest (*Activity*), as well as other "story" elements such as *Social Status*. For instance, for an image of a whale jumping out of the water, one participant describes the image as "whale *performing* by jumping out of the water." The choice of the word "performing" reveals an additional layer of meaning attached to the image which is not captured by a simple listing of image contents. The image "stories" are drawn from a number of image elements. Attributes which formed part of the story of an image were those which described the "Who, What, When, and Where" aspects of the image representation. Specific attributes included activities, events, settings, and time aspects (historical time period as well as seasons, time of day, and duration of activity) of the story. The following examples demonstrate these as well as affective aspects such as emotions and relationships among people:

this man seems to be paying close attention to what he sees
the woman appears to be overly concerned with appearance—she appears to be putting on lipstick and looking at some kind of colorful material
[she is] worn out from too many years of stress

While not as frequently occurring, attributes representing emotions, abstract ideas, themes, and atmosphere also appeared in the descriptions:

apparent <u>female control</u> of beast
picture gives a <u>feeling of triumphance</u> [sic]
the kid is <u>having a great time</u>
<u>angry looking</u>—<u>ready to fight</u>
<u>sinister, violence, threatening</u>
seems to have a <u>religious connotation</u>

Taken all together, attributes representing story elements (including terms describing such things as social status or occupation), emotions and relationships, themes, and abstract ideas such as the "atmosphere" of an image accounted for about 15% of the attributes named in the image-describing tasks. Therefore, these attributes represented a small but significant part of spontaneous image descriptions.

The data from the Memory Task produced far fewer terms than the original Viewing Task. In terms of the Memory Task, the major factor in memory for a specific image seems to have been the original presentation order of the images in the Viewing Task, as Table 5.5 shows. Memory for the first and last images viewed was high (based on the number of terms written down for each image); for the second and next to last images, memory was lower; and less than half of the participants remembered the two images viewed in the middle of the sequence. The original images in the Viewing Task were projected to the class in a random order. The author, however, informed the participants in advance that they would be viewing a total of six images. Therefore, there seems to have been an effect of presentation order, in that the participants' attention may have been higher with the first images, lagged somewhat after the novelty of the task wore off, and then reached a new height when participants were aware that the task was almost finished. This memory data is consistent with other data concerning attention span when people process information being presented in classrooms. Other than presentation order, there does not seem to have been any specific attribute-related memory degradation, as all attributes experienced an overall decrease.

Therefore, overall memory for image attributes *as measured by the ability of participants to write descriptions of the images* is very low. This is not to say that participants could not perform extremely well on a forced recognition test of these images, for as discussed in Chapter Two, recognition memory for images appears to be very high, while recall is more problematic to evaluate. However, the Memory Task does demonstrate participants' inability to articulate image descriptions verbally (under the conditions of this task) that were as complete as those from the previous Search Task. This task does not provide data about *how* the image information is stored, and may be only a test of the memory of the *written* descriptions of the images. One participant commented to the author after the task that she remembered phrases which she had used to describe the images, not the actual images. However, the results are interesting given that, for a *known-item* search, current image indexing and retrieval systems often rely heavily on a textual description of an image by the image searcher.

Table 5.5. Image presentation order and number of images remembered

Order of presentation	1	2	3	4	5	6
Participants recalling image	28	16	14	14	19	25

The above analysis for the describing tasks focuses on the description, analysis, and distribution of attributes and Classes of attributes within textual descriptions of images by nonspecialists. This data is a rich source of information about the specific types of image attributes typically communicated in a set of describing tasks. This overall knowledge about distribution of attributes and Classes for a describing task can guide creation of heuristics for the indexing of pictorial images.

Term Variability

Even though general Classes and specific types of attributes seem to exhibit some consistency in this and other research discussed below, an important component to applying these results in any kind of indexing or retrieval system design is the extent of actual term variability within the Classes and attribute types.

Several studies have found great variability in the terms which people use to describe common objects or illustrations of objects (Collantes 1995; Furnas and others 1987; Kwasnik 1989). These researchers used several different techniques to assess term variability, including measures used in studies of indexing consistency and the repeat rate. One of the first steps in data analysis in the author's dissertation research (Jörgensen 1995b) was to assess the extent of term variability in the data. The author was reluctant to eliminate a priori a number of terms in the image descriptions which are frequently considered stop words (such as prepositions, which indicate relationships among terms). A measure which can compensate for frequently occurring words, the "repeat rate," satisfies this requirement and was the measure chosen for analysis of term variability (Herdan 1960, 297–299). The repeat rate (Σp_i^2) is equivalent to the standard probability calculation of sampling with replacement. By using this as a characteristic, the p_i of high-frequency words will, according to Herdan, "settle down to sensibly constant values." Thus the repeat rate compensates for extreme values of high-frequency words.

As might be expected from previous research results, the overall repeat rate amongst all terms in the corpus was quite low (.0070, meaning that given that two terms occur in the descriptions, there is a 0.7% chance of those two words being the same word). However, when terms are listed by specific attribute type, there is less variability among terms. For instance, a simple listing of color terms (*Color*) for a specific picture shows that, given that a particular color is mentioned, there is a high level of consistency in the terms chosen (Table 5.6). The overall repeat rate for *Color* for this specific image is .4676, while the repeat rate for *Color* for the main figure is .9445.

In order to facilitate a methodical analysis, the author sorted the raw data terms alphabetically within attributes (as in Table 5.6), and then calculated the repeat rate both within specific attributes and for specific occurrences of terms having the same perceptual stimulus. The rationale for taking this approach lies in the fact that, when a physical stimulus triggers a response, the nature of the stimulus (in this case, the specific image or image component), must also be taken into account. In a typical response, it is reasonable to expect that the physical presence of the color red is likely to evoke "red" *Color* terms ("red," "reddish," "brownish-red") and not "green" *Color* terms.

Comparing the general variability of terms in the describing tasks as measured by the repeat rate of individual terms across the whole corpus per task, as well as terms within specific attributes and Classes, demonstrates some interesting trends (Table 5.7). Classes which seemed likely to exhibit more consistency, the Perceptual Classes (OBJECTS, PEOPLE, COLOR, SPATIAL LOCATION, and VISUAL ELEMENTS), were used in this analysis.[4] The overall individual term variability is high (as indicated by the low repeat rate), yet there is a decrease in variability for the Search and Memory Tasks compared to the Viewing Task. Thus the terms for the Search and Memory Tasks appear to be more constrained than the terms for the Viewing Task. The terms in the Search Task were part of carefully constructed search statements; therefore it is reasonable that there would be less variability in these terms. The Memory Task demonstrated a very limited range of recall of the images and it is perhaps also reasonable that there would be less variation in these terms, as only major components would be recalled. In contrast, the Viewing Task had fewer constraints (either task-related or participant- related) on the nature of the descriptions; therefore it is logical that there would be the greatest amount of term variability for this task.

Table 5.6. Sample of data sorted by participant, term, and attribute for Viewing Task

Participant	Term	Attribute
#102	"hand"	Body Part
#111	"hand"	Body Part
#114	"hand"	Body Part
#114	"hand"	Body Part
#117	"hand"	Body Part
#117	"hand"	Body Part
#125	"hand"	Body Part
#144	"hand"	Body Part
#148	"hand"	Body Part
#105	"knee"	Body Part
#114	"knee"	Body Part
#106	"adventure"	Category
#132	"adventure"	Category
#140	"adventure"	Category
#145	"adventure"	Category
#120	"fantasy"	Category
#114	"clothing"	Clothing
#137	"fedora"	Clothing
#148	"fedora"	Clothing
#103	"hat"	Clothing
#109	"hat"	Clothing
#111	"hat"	Clothing

Analyzing the repeat rate within attributes and Classes by task shows a similar increase among all tasks in the participants' consistency in term usage. The increase in term consistency within attributes and Classes is to be expected, as the "perceptually stimulated" attributes were the ones the author selected for analysis. Thus it would appear that limiting analysis to specific attributes and Classes removes some of the variability associated with simple term analysis. These results also have implications for selection of suitable indexing terms.

Table 5.7. Repeat rate for three describing tasks by individual term, by attribute, and by Class

Describing Tasks	By Term	By Attribute	By Class
Viewing	.0065	.3347	.3319
Search	.0163	.2955	.3180
Memory	.0175	.2892	.3257

The next step in analysis involved computing the repeat rate for a sample of conceptually related words within an attribute. This step is necessary for two reasons, the first of which is the determination of the extent to which synonymy is significant in lowering the repeat rate for a specific image attribute. Secondly, given that some attributes naturally exhibit a wide range of possibilities (such as *Object*, which may include any of a large number of objects depicted within an image), it was desirable to determine whether the range of possibilities within specific attributes a priori precludes any kind of consistency for terms used.

For instance, in the attribute *Setting*, there are a number of terms and phrases referring to the specific setting of one picture: "space," "outer space," "in space," "universe," "cosmos." The repeat rate for this attribute (*Setting*) is .4711, but when these words are grouped conceptually as synonyms, the repeat rate rises to greater than .8000.[5]

The repeat rate was thus used to measure term variability among attributes, as well as within attributes for specific perceptually stimulated groups of terms. The description of those attributes which exhibit more or less term variability provides not only interesting data for researchers studying image description but may assist indexers and system designers in determining which attributes may be most efficiently addressed in image access systems. However, the large number of attributes[6] still made it difficult to discern any meaningful trends in the rankings. The author then used the rankings to evaluate repeat rate by Classes of attributes rather than by individual attribute. When attributes are grouped into their higher-level Classes, three Classes have all their constituent attributes ranked above the median repeat rate (Table 5.8). This would imply that these classes exhibit a higher degree of uniformity in relation to actual term variability. These Classes were PEOPLE (which is a class of one attribute), COLOR (two attributes), and interestingly, ABSTRACT CONCEPTS (five attributes). STORY had four of five attributes (80%) falling above the median. Those Classes with half of their attributes falling above the median were SPATIAL LOCATION (with a total of two attributes) and ART HISTORICAL INFORMATION (eight attributes). VISUAL ELEMENTS (eight attributes) and OBJECTS (four attributes) had 25% above, and DESCRIPTION (two attributes) and PEOPLE RELATED (three attributes) had zero above the median. It is possible that a higher average repeat rate within Classes would be related to the total number of attributes within a Class. That is, the more different attributes within a Class, the lower the repeat rate would be. However, from these figures it appears that there is no systematic relationship between a "higher" repeat rate (defined as a repeat rate above the median) and the number of attributes per Class.

Table 5.8. Descriptive Viewing Task: Total number of attributes in Class, and number and percentage of attributes above median by Class

Class	# Attributes in Class	# above Median	% above Median
PEOPLE	1	1	100%
COLOR	2	2	100%
ABSTRACT CONCEPTS	5	5	100%
STORY	5	4	80%
SPATIAL LOCATION	2	1	50%
ART HISTORICAL INFO.	8	4	50%
VISUAL ELEMENTS	8	2	25%
OBJECTS	4	1	25%
DESCRIPTION	2	0	0%
PEOPLE RELATED	3	0	0%

Therefore, it would appear that the description of PEOPLE, COLOR, ABSTRACT CONCEPTS (which includes subject), and STORY elements (setting, time) exhibits more consistency in the terms chosen than Classes such as OBJECTS, which can include a large variety of elements in a picture, and DESCRIPTION (adjectival) terms. This suggests that these Classes of attributes (or types of information) are appropriate candidates for assignment of indexing terms. The reader is referred to (Jörgensen 1995b) for more detail on the analysis of the repeat rate.

Term variability was assessed using a second method as well, by term level, to determine if in fact participants tended to use "basic-level" terms to describe objects as described in Chapter Two (Rosch and others 1976). The author evaluated the term levels using Rosch's guidelines and those of Smith, Balzano, and Walker (1978), wherein basic-level objects are ones that are most inclusive in their numbers of common attributes. Superordinate-level objects have fewer common attributes, and slightly more common attributes occur for subordinate-level objects. As an example, for the object "gun" in one image, ten participants used the basic-level term "gun," while five used the more specific, subordinate term "rifle," and one used the superordinate term "weapons."

As most research on basic-level objects has focused on concrete objects, counts were performed first for three attributes of the Perceptual Class OBJECTS (*Object*, *Clothing*, and *Body Part*), and for the attributes *People* and *Color*. Across the Viewing and Search Tasks, results were very consistent, with an average of 76% of terms being described at the basic level, and approximately equal numbers described at the superordinate and subordinate levels (Table 5.9). For the Memory Task, there were fewer terms listed at the basic level (73.5%) than for the other tasks, and slightly more at the superordinate level (14.6%, an increase in 3% over the other two describing tasks). The increase in superordinate terms seems reasonable, as it seems likely that memory of specific items could revert to a more general category of item. Memory on the subordinate level remains similar, although the actual percentage is the highest of all three tasks. These results overall agree well with earlier findings which indicate that objects are first recognized and named almost exclusively at the basic level.

Table 5.9. Percentage of terms in each level for describing tasks

Term Level	Viewing (*N*=1,745)	Search (*N*=1,385)	Memory (*N*=31)	Average
Basic level	76.6%	77.9%	73.5%	76.0%
Superordinate	11.8%	11.7%	14.6%	12.7%
Subordinate	11.6%	10.5%	11.7%	11.3%

These results are thus consistent with the theory that the basic level of description of objects is most typical and suggests that this theory may be applicable to objects depicted within complex images as well as to images of single objects.

The author also explored a subset of the "Interpretive" Classes for the distribution of basic-level, superordinate, and subordinate terms. The author had noted the presence of superordinate-level terms for the interpretive attributes as well as the perceptual attributes during the development of the coding scheme. Other researchers have found evidence for a basic level in events (Morris and Murphy 1990; Rifkin 1985) and for a basic level for categories of scenes (Tversky and Hemenway 1983). Iyer suggests category structure for such abstract terms as "knowledge," "emotion," "virtue," and "sensation" (Iyer 1995). For instance, an example for emotion would be: emotion—love—romantic love.

The author chose two Classes for analysis based upon their somewhat contrasting types of attributes: ABSTRACT (*Abstract*, *Atmosphere*, *Symbolic Aspect*, *State*, and *Theme*) and ART HISTORICAL INFORMATION (*Artist*, *Format*, *Media*, *Representation*, *Style*, *Technique*, *Time Reference*, and *Type*). The determination of subordinate terms was slightly less obvious with these more conceptual attributes than with the ART HISTORICAL attributes or for the perceptual OBJECTS and COLOR terms. For example, for the attribute

Format, an example of a superordinate—basic-level—subordinate hierarchy would be: publication—magazine—*National Geographic*. It is less obvious what the subordinate term for an ABSTRACT attribute hierarchy such as *Atmosphere* would be: atmosphere—threatening—?? Most participants modified abstract terms on the basic level to a greater level of specificity by using descriptive modifiers such as "very": atmosphere—threatening—very threatening.

The distribution of superordinate, basic-level, and subordinate terms is, in fact, quite similar to that of the perceptual attributes, suggesting that these terms also carry category structure. While this has been studied extensively for objects, more research is needed to establish the occurrence of category structure in concepts. Nevertheless, if most terms are found at the basic level in a hierarchy, this implies that these terms carry the most salient information about that object (or concept). This has implications for indexing and retrieval, in that it may be useful for indexers to focus on including more of these types of terms in indexes.[7]

Sorting Task

The Sorting Task provided an additional method for elicitation of attributes. Multiple sorting tasks can reveal people's own concepts through their own constructs, uninhibited by prespecified concepts (Canter, Brown, and Groat 1985). Bornstein defines categorization as "treating a set of indiscriminable or discriminable stimuli as equivalent in some way (for example, by giving all of them the same name)," and notes that this is the many-to-one characteristic of categorization (Bornstein 1987, 287). Kwasnik (1989) demonstrated that "natural," individually-generated classifications are situated within a specific, person-oriented context, which, in addition to intrinsic features, often incorporates task or other nonobject attributes. Therefore, this task was designed to elicit additional attributes in a different context than describing images, attributes which may play a part in notions of similarity among images.

Eighteen participants from all levels of an academic setting and in a variety of disciplines at Syracuse University performed the Sorting Task. They sorted seventy-seven color and black-and-white images (also chosen randomly from the *Illustrators Twenty-Fifth Annual)* into groups, such that if they wished to find an image at a later time, this would be the group in which they would look. The eighteen participants created a total of 292 different image groups, ranging from 6 to 29 groups and with an average of about 16 groups per participant. Data gathering during the Sorting Task consisted of videotaping and verbal protocols, which were also analyzed using content analysis. The participants' commentary and the participants' sorted groups were analyzed, with respect to both the groups created and the attributes associated with the groups.

Analysis consisted of coding both attributes represented in the sorting transcripts and attributes represented in the names of the sorted groups of images. The distribution of Classes and attributes for the group names followed somewhat closely the distribution of the Classes over all image descriptions in the Sorting Task. This task, in addition to generating several new attributes related to the purpose of the image, produced a quite different distribution of attributes (Table 5.10). The largest attribute Class[8] represented in this set of data was the Class ART HISTORICAL INFORMATION, followed by VIEWER RESPONSE, ABSTRACT, OBJECT, EXTERNAL RELATION, PEOPLE, and STORY.

Table 5.10. Attribute Classes by percentage for Sorting Task

CLASS	Average	CLASS	Average
ART HISTORICAL INFO.	23.8%	STORY	8.5%
VIEWER RESPONSE	14.1%	PEOPLE RELATED	4.0%
ABSTRACT	13.8%	VISUAL ELEMENTS	3.8%
OBJECTS	8.7%	DESCRIPTION	2.7%
EXTERNAL RELATION	8.7%	COLOR	2.6%
PEOPLE	8.6%	SPATIAL LOCATION	0.8%

In discussing the Sorting Task, the first item of note is the high occurrence of ART HISTORICAL INFORMATION attributes. A closer analysis revealed that this was because, in their verbal descriptions, the participants used the terms "painting," or "picture" repeatedly in their verbal descriptions; this repetition did not occur in the written descriptions. Therefore, this peak is less important than the initial numbers would suggest. The next two most frequently mentioned classes of attributes were VIEWER RESPONSE, which included personal reactions and accounted for 14.1% of the total, and ABSTRACT, which accounted for 13.8%. PEOPLE (8.6%) and PEOPLE RELATED attributes (4.0%) represent 12.6% of the total. The STORY Class represented about 8.5% of the total. OBJECTS and EXTERNAL RELATION both measure 8.7%.

There are several interesting aspects to this set of data when compared to data from the describing tasks (Table 5.11). The first is the much lower occurrence of the OBJECTS Class when compared to the describing tasks, in which it was the most frequently occurring class (accounting for well over 25% in most cases and for over 30% in one of the describing tasks). The second is the higher occurrence of ABSTRACT attributes, which describe such things as abstract concepts, themes, and symbolic interpretations. The third is that the Sorting Task also showed a strong effect for the presence of humans or human activity. When a human figure appeared in an image, no matter how small or seemingly insignificant (dwarfed by the landscape or drawn in with only "blotches" or "squiggles"), one-third of the participants still named attributes (across several

Classes) related to the presence of humans and their activity in that setting. These results are also consistent with ecological views concerning the evolution of vision discussed in Chapter Two. The fourth is the low frequency of the perceptual attribute Classes of COLOR, SPATIAL LOCATION, and VISUAL ELEMENTS. These categories each account for less than 5% of the attribute class distribution. Therefore, for the Sorting Task participants appear to rely more heavily on what are termed "interpretive" attributes rather than perceptual attributes, at least in terms of what they choose to communicate about these images in their process of sorting and placing the images in groups.

Table 5.11. Comparison of Class frequency by percentage for the describing tasks and the Sorting Task

CLASS	Describing	Sorting
OBJECTS	29.3%	8.7%
PEOPLE	10.0%	8.6%
COLOR	9.3%	2.6%
STORY	9.2%	8.5%
SPATIAL LOCATION	8.9%	0.8%
DESCRIPTION	8.0%	2.7%
VISUAL ELEMENTS	7.2%	3.8%
ART HISTORICAL INFO.	5.7%	23.8%
PEOPLE RELATED	3.9%	4.0%
EXTERNAL RELATION	3.7%	8.7%
ABSTRACT	2.0%	13.8%
VIEWER RESPONSE	2.9%	14.1%

One point to note in comparing the describing tasks and the Sorting Task is that the classes of STORY, PEOPLE RELATED, and PEOPLE are unique in that they are typically described at about the same frequency level across both types of tasks. PEOPLE RELATED, an Interpretive Class, appears to be closely related to STORY in its consistency of appearance across the describing tasks and the Sorting Task. The *Emotion* and *Social Status* attributed to the persons in an image also contribute to the idea of the "story" of the image. Thus PEOPLE RELATED may more logically belong as a set of attributes to the STORY Class rather than being a separate Class. The stability of these Classes across both types of tasks implies that this dimension of images is likely to be relevant across a variety of tasks and suggests a larger role for these attributes in indexing than has been sanctioned by existing vocabulary tools and guidelines.

One question that arises is the effect that the different sets of images used in the two tasks may have upon the results of the distribution of attributes and Classes. In order to evaluate this, the author compared the distribution of attributes for the six images used in the describing tasks with the distribution of attributes for those same six images within the larger set of images used for the Sorting Task. Even though the images remain the same, the distributions of attributes and Classes are quite different between the two tasks. The distribution of Classes for the subset of the six images within the Sorting Task matches those for the Sorting Task as a whole, and not the describing task distributions (Table 5.12).

Table 5.12. Class distributions, by percentage, for the same six images for the Sorting Task and the describing tasks (averaged across three describing tasks)

Class	Sorting Task	Describing tasks	% Difference
OBJECTS	8.7%	29.3%	+20.6%
ART HISTORICAL INFO.	23.7%	5.7%	-18.0%
ABSTRACT	13.8%	2.0%	-11.8%
VIEWER RESPONSE	14.1%	2.9%	-11.2%
SPATIAL LOCATION	0.8%	8.9%	+8.1%
COLOR	2.6%	9.3%	+6.7%
DESCRIPTION	2.7%	8.0%	+5.1%
EXTERNAL RELATION	8.7%	3.7%	-5.0%
VISUAL ELEMENTS	3.8%	7.2%	+3.4%
PEOPLE	8.6%	10.0%	+1.4%
STORY	8.5%	9.2%	+0.7%
PEOPLE RELATED	4.0%	3.9%	-0.1%

The highest occurrence of attributes for the Sorting Task as a whole is within ART HISTORICAL INFORMATION, and there is also a large difference in the OBJECTS Class. Attributes in the ABSTRACT Class rise, while VISUAL ELEMENTS, COLOR, SPATIAL LOCATION, and DESCRIPTION are all much lower. PEOPLE RELATED and STORY remain similar across the tasks. Thus, the results for the six-image subset within the Sorting Task are much more similar overall to the Sorting Task than to the describing tasks. This indicates that the data for the same six images vary according to the task; therefore, it appears that the nature of the image has less influence upon which types of attributes are reported by participants than does the task. This is an area for further testing.

Other Images

An obvious question arises with the describing tasks as to whether the particular type or content and subject matter of image, as well as the type of task, significantly affects the distribution of the attributes and Classes. This is discussed above and evaluated in considerable detail in Jörgensen (1995b). The following discussion covers two other types of images that have been evaluated: fine arts images and scientific diagrams.

Fine Arts Images

In order to evaluate the effects of a particular type of image, a pretest set of describing data using fine arts images as the stimuli was recoded according to the full coding scheme developed in the course of the dissertation research. Relevant data pertaining to the fine arts images in the pretest is presented here.

The methodology for the pretest was substantially the same as for the dissertation research, with the exception that the participants included some undergraduate volunteers as well. The pretest images were fine arts images ranging from stylized to Impressionist to realistic. As these were fine arts images, they were somewhat familiar to most participants (as a "type," if not necessarily the specific image) and in some cases the level of familiarity was high enough that participants correctly named specific artists. It therefore seemed reasonable to expect a distribution more similar to that reported for the Sorting Task as reported above, with an increase in ART HISTORICAL INFORMATION and less emphasis on OBJECTS. There was, in fact, a slight increase in ART HISTORICAL INFORMATION, but overall the distribution remained quite similar to the describing task images, with a large peak at OBJECTS (27.4%), followed by PEOPLE, COLOR, and SPATIAL LOCATION (Table 5.13).

Some slight differences are evident: the Perceptual Classes DESCRIPTION, OBJECTS, and VISUAL ELEMENTS decrease in the fine arts data, while PEOPLE (Perceptual), and STORY, ABSTRACT, and PEOPLE RELATED (Interpretive) attributes increase. It is reasonable to assess these changes in light of the actual subject matter of the images. The fine arts images were primarily of people engaging in activities, while the describing tasks' images included several that were more abstract in terms of subject matter and yet generally more realistically portrayed.

Other research by the author with a different set of fine arts images investigated the distribution of attributes in images varying in style, ranging from pictorial (realistic) to abstract (Jörgensen 1999b). Six images were presented to participants; only two of these images contained human figures ("Teach" and "Hopper" in the Table 5.14). Other images were representation types that are familiar in the fine arts realm: a still life ("Bounty") and an interior ("Room"), both with strong geometric elements, a stylized landscape ("Jungle"), and a geometric abstract image ("Blocks"). Of note is the fact that, even without the presence of the human figure in four of the images, overall results were not that much lower than were obtained as with the earlier describing tasks and Sorting Task, in which five of the six images had people in them. In particular, even though the image "Room" had no people in it, it still had occurrences of *People* terms, and also PEOPLE RELATED terms. Thus, it appears that participants "read" a human element even into those images in which the human figure is not explicitly displayed.

Table 5.13. Comparison of the describing tasks' images (illustrations) with the pretest images (fine arts)

Classes	Illustrations	Fine Arts	Difference
OBJECTS	29.3%	27.4%	- 1.9%
PEOPLE	10.0%	10.8%	+ 0.8%
COLOR	9.3%	9.0%	- 0.3%
SPATIAL LOCATION	8.9%	9.5%	+ 0.6%
DESCRIPTION	8.0%	5.7%	- 2.3%
VISUAL ELEMENTS	7.2%	5.2%	- 2.0%
ABSTRACT	2.0%	2.6%	+ 0.6%
ART HISTORICAL INFO.	5.8%	6.3%	+ 0.5%
STORY	9.2%	11.1%	+1.9%
PEOPLE RELATED	3.9%	6.8%	+2.9%
EXTERNAL RELATION	3.7%	1.0%	- 2.7%
VIEWER RESPONSE	2.9%	4.9%	+ 2.0%

Especially interesting were the results with the still life ("Bounty," a picture of harvest vegetables and storage containers), which are generally not thought to have a strong "story" element associated with them:

> "bounty," "fruit of the earth," "hard work," "harvest," "abundance," "autumn," "plenitude," "comfort," "preparedness," "sexuality," "religion," "serenity," "accomplishment of purpose"

These results also raise a question as to where in the retrieval process the content-based methods discussed in Chapter Four are most useful. A more detailed look at some of the results from the research discussed above may be useful in these deliberations. In the author's empirical research, the image attributes which most closely align with those addressed by content-based retrieval systems are those in the VISUAL ELEMENTS (texture, shape) and COLOR classes. The SPATIAL LOCATION class, which includes spatial positional information, may also be of interest. Table 5.14 presents data for these and other Classes by individual image, in order of the image's increasing departure from realistic depiction.

Table 5.14 demonstrates some interesting trends as the images move from more realistic to more abstract, and also indicates that the presence of pictorial elements such as objects or people cannot be ignored. VISUAL ELEMENTS and COLOR increase as images become more abstract, while PEOPLE

RELATED attributes such as *Emotion* decrease and there is a complete absence of STORY elements in the purely abstract image composed of blocks of color. As would be expected with fine arts images, ART HISTORICAL INFORMATION attributes occur across all the images, with a peak for the abstract image and the still life. While analysis by individual image speaks dramatically to the impact that an image's content will have upon terms used to describe the image, it also suggests that certain classes of attributes cannot be ruled out a priori. For instance, with these fine arts images, ABSTRACT attributes (*Atmosphere*, *Symbol*, *Theme*) occur across all the images to a greater or lesser degree. Other researchers have suggested that modeling artistic representations, which are often based on abstraction of visual content in images, may be useful for image retrieval (Dalton 1997).

Table 5.14. Frequency of selected Classes for images of decreasing realism

Class	All images	"Teach"	"Bounty"	"Hopper"	"Jungle"	"Room"	"Blocks"
OBJECTS	19.3	4.6	24.5	18.9	32	10.3	7.2
PEOPLE	7.2	10.7	0.0	10.0	2.1	1.0	0.0
ART HIST.	7.3	2.0	13.2	9.1	4.1	8.8	14.9
VIS. ELEM.	7.4	1.0	3.9	6.1	6.6	18.6	32.6
COLOR	7.1	2.5	4.4	9.1	15.6	6.2	12.7
LOCATION	5.3	0.0	0.5	9.4	11.8	0.5	4.4
STORY	14.3	21.3	21.6	16.1	6.7	11.9	0.0
PEOPLE REL.	8.8	37.6	1.5	6.3	1.0	5.7	1.1
ABSTRACT	13.6	12.7	25.0	3.0	3.4	26.8	14.9
DESCRIPT.	4.4	5.6	2.5	6.4	8.0	4.1	2.8

Scientific Diagrams

The exploratory methods of the previous research were also extended to scientific diagrams (Brunskill and Jörgensen 2002). The *Oxford English Dictionary* (Oxford 2001) defines a diagram as "an illustrative figure that, without representing the exact appearance of an object, gives an outline or general scheme of it, so as to exhibit the shape and relations of its various parts . . . or results of any action or processes which characterize it."[9] However, the question remains as to the specific attributes that may set diagrammatic images apart from pictorial images. Diagrammatic representations often possess a strong spatial component, and the manner in which objects are presented spatially in the two-dimensional plane is often as important to understanding the diagram as the objects themselves. The objects, or visual components of the representation, may also often possess an iconic feel, given the economical manner in which vast quantities of information are often presented. Diagrams must also often go to great lengths to make information typically represented by text explicit for visual interpretation and understanding. According to Larkin and Simon (1987), a diagram functions well because it puts information into a form that facilitates computation. This point once again ties into the background knowledge that a particular user brings to the table, but it also highlights the notion of what constitutes a good diagram.

Therefore, in scientific diagrams one would expect that the attributes that participants would typically describe would include perceptual or structural attributes such as those in VISUAL ELEMENTS and COLOR, and attributes related to SPATIAL LOCATION. One would not expect to find STORY attributes or other abstract or affective attributes. However, despite the importance of these factors, one must also consider that the ability to derive information from diagrams is often more a function of the user than the characteristics of the image itself, and this distinction often imparts a bipolar scale through which users are characterized as either naive or expert.

To ascertain the importance of certain image attributes among different genres of images, the following experiment was conducted in a manner similar to that of Jörgensen (1998). In this experiment six scientific diagrams were presented to a group of naive participants for description. One hundred twenty-two University at Buffalo students (half graduate and half undergraduate) participated in this experiment. The graduate-level subjects were taking introductory M.L.S. classes offered through the Department of Library and Information Studies. The undergraduate subjects participated to satisfy an introductory psychology course requirement. Participants viewed projected images of two weather maps, a cart assembly diagram, a stadium seating chart, elephant organ systems, a water treatment facility, and completed either the Viewing or Search Task.

The sessions yielded over 10,958 coded responses to the two describing tasks: 5,886 individual responses to the Viewing Task, and 5,072 responses for the Search Task. In the Viewing Task, subject responses consisted of short one-word answers, or phrases describing certain aspects of the diagrams. Common examples of responses include "dark red," "Buffalo," or "elephant digestive system." Search Task responses included short sentences such as "how a water treatment center works," or "shows weather of warm fronts and cold fronts." Some categories from the original research were expanded to include the distinction between information that is visible in the diagrams and information that is symbolized, or may be derived, from visible relationships among diagram components (such as the response "seating charts" when all that is visible are colored blocks).

One of the questions underlying the current discussion surrounds the degree to which the attribute distribution in the author's earlier work was applicable across other types of images, namely scientific diagrams. Overall, the results of the current study support the primary class distinctions set forth in the previous investigation. The results confirm the importance of OBJECTS as a highly salient Class of attributes for image description. More surprisingly, STORY attributes were important in this research, as well as EXTERNAL RELATION attributes. The importance of STORY and EXTERNAL RELATION reflect the importance of subject efforts to characterize the meaning, or perhaps theme, of each representation. In one sense, the diagrams forced participants to think harder about the exact content, and context, of each diagrammatic image, since the content was not readily apparent. This reinforces the importance of function, rather than the structure, of these diagrams (with the caveat that it is the underlying structure that allows the functional knowledge to be conveyed). The Classes PEOPLE, PEOPLE RELATED, and to a lesser extent, COLOR exhibited lower levels of description. These results are to be expected in light of the fact that people were not present in the images, and the presence of color was minimized, or nonexistent, within a few diagrams.

Implications

There are several ways to assess the implications of this research. We may consider these results in relation to a widely used thesaurus discussed in Chapter Three, the *Library of Congress Thesaurus of Graphic Materials (LCTGM)*. This research demonstrates that the OBJECT Class is important for description. The *LCTGM* does include a high percentage of OBJECTS terms (19.1%), but contains no terms for spatial LOCATION specification, and very few terms relating to VISUAL ELEMENT or ART HISTORICAL INFORMATION (the latter by design). It contains terms relating to abstract concepts and some thematic and "story" elements, but its high degree of precoordination, as noted previously, creates a very narrow application of many of these terms. It serves its stated purpose (of providing historical access to pictorial materials), as do many other domain- or audience-specific thesauri. These thesauri, however, lack utility for more general applicability to a wider variety of pictorial materials, in which a full range of access points for other Classes of attributes may be important.

Another research project evaluated a template for image description to be used by naive image searchers in recording their descriptions of images (Jörgensen 1996b). The attribute Classes derived in the research discussed above were used to model the image description template. The results indicate that users would need training and guidance in order to correctly assign terms to higher-level classes. Thus the template may be of more use to indexers, in guiding decisions about what to index, than as a guide to searchers in formulating structured image search requests.

One interesting result is that when participants were exposed to the full range of attribute Classes in the template, the distribution of attribute Classes changed from that of the unprompted descriptions in the describing tasks, and matched more closely the results from the image Sorting Task. This supports the suggestion that searchers modify their requests according to the mental model of the system they have. Image indexing, by accommodating a wider variety of attributes (including interpretive attributes), could serve unexpressed needs of searchers in image searching.

Work by Other Researchers

There are several other research projects which have investigated the types of terms which users spontaneously ascribe to images. While using similar elicitation methods, each one focuses on a slightly different problem and uses different methods of analysis, making direct comparisons of results impossible. Nevertheless, the research discussed below reinforces many of the implications of the author's dissertation research.

Describing Tasks

Other researchers have used photographs of contemporary objects and scenes in a describing task (O'Connor, O'Connor, and Abbas 1999). This research used a Web-based presentation of a variety of images and asked participants (M.L.S. students from four different sites) to describe any 100 images of their choosing. The analysis was based on eighty-two images for which there were at least ten responses. Subjects were asked to "respond" to an image (Response), assign a subject to it (Subjects), and to write a caption for it (Captions). This work demonstrates results similar to the author's in terms of affective, thematic responses. For instance, an image of a cowboy (with standard subject headings of "Cowboys" and "Horsemen and Horsewomen") elicited the following terms in spontaneous descriptions:

"tension," "ruggedness," "determination," "anger," "tough," "resolute," "strong"

Other less emotive images (cows in a field, a ranch house in Idaho) also elicited similar terms:

"free of burdens," "desolate," "peaceful," "serene," "hot and dusty" (cows)

"peace," "independence," "relaxing," "solitary," "barren and sad" (ranch house) (O'Connor, O'Connor, and Abbas 1999, 686)

These data were analyzed by noting such broad term aspects as introductory phrases, allusions to literature, subjects, narrativity ("little story") and antonymy, associativity, and functionality (general adjectival terms). Additionally, it was noted whether terms relate directly to the image content (although they may still also be narrative). Adjectives describing states or emotions (which often demonstrated antonymy) were also noted. The authors note that the responses they gathered gave rise to "arenas of response" rather than closely defined categories. Analyzing the data presented in the article, it appears that the Response task elicited mainly personal emotional responses to the image, the Subjects task elicited description of the objects in the image (and exhibited the most consistency), and the Captions task stimulated the respondent's creative instincts. The authors note that "the variety of responses speaks again to the enormous burden taken on by a system of a priori assigning of terms or category membership. In a very important sense, this exploration reminds us of the dynamic relationship between documents and users" (O'Connor, O'Connor, and Abbas 1999, 691). Their results especially support the author's STORY Class and the importance of affective descriptions and attributes.

In other work, Turner (1994) investigated the terms assigned to a stock footage videocassette by research participants. Their task was, for each shot, to supply words or phrases which they felt were obvious keys for retrieval at a later date by themselves or others. The most frequently occurring terms for each of the shots on the tape were chosen for analysis. One of the significant findings was that, across all the 181 participants and all forty-four shots, on average almost 60% of the participants named the most frequent term for each shot. Another important finding was that participants overwhelmingly simply named the objects and events they saw in the shots, thus supplying preiconographical ("ofness") terms rather than iconographical ("aboutness") terms.

A follow-up study compared these terms to terms assigned by professional indexers for these shots in the source files (Turner 1995). Turner found a high degree of correspondence between the indexing and/or the written description of the shots, and analysis showed that a match would occur between the searcher's term and the indexing or description on average 79% of the time. Turner notes that this high occurrence of matches may be the result of a built-in subject unity inherent in the choice of shots. Based on the high degree of matching, he suggests extending indexing the "ofness" level to art images as well.

Sorting Tasks

Other researchers have also reported sorting task results. Korf Vidal (1995) used a unique approach by having subjects sort images all depicting the same subject matter (the Brooklyn Bridge) but created in a wide range of media. She proposes that the motive for creating the image produces three different types of images: expressions (creative images), messages (information), and evidence (data). The use of the same visual subject in this research appears to have forced other organizing principles—the potential *use* to which the image could be put or the purpose for which the image was created—to the fore. Some aspects of use also emerged in the group names assigned by participants in the author's

Sorting Task (e.g., "advertisement," "National Geographic"). Rogowitz, Frese, and others (1998) used ninety-seven carefully selected images from the PhotoDisk collection in a sorting task in both a computerized and a manual environment. Their research found that color was an important dimension in visual similarity, as were the dimensions of "human–nonhuman" and "natural–man-made." However, visual examination of the images shows that the selection process could predispose the sorters to produce these categories.

Another sorting study of landscape photographs suggests that participants conceptualize photographs differently depending upon whether they are instructed to sort them by simply looking at the places in the photograph or to sort after thinking about the places, imagining being there and experiencing the places (Scott and Canter 1997). When doing the visual sort, items were sorted according to their content (landforms, water), whereas when sorting by thinking and imagining, they sorted by memories and sense experiences in addition to visual information. Respondents wrote down terms describing their sorted groups. The second sort produced twice as many terms as the first. There is a distinct and significant difference between the two groups of terms as well, with the first group (visual sort) using terms describing visual objects ("moors," "water") and subjects such as agriculture or farming. The second sort produced more conceptual terms ("familiar," "free," "peaceful"). Similar to other research, the authors also found that there are references to human activity in describing the photos ("busy," "relaxing"), although there are very few people in the photographs.

Scientific diagrams have been investigated at some length by Lohse (Lohse and others 1991; Lohse and others 1990). Their first project had subjects evaluate different types of visualizations (maps, tables, graphs, diagrams, networks, and icons) and identified two dimensions that distinguish these: 1) whether a graphic could express continuous or discrete information, and 2) efficiency in conveying information. A second study investigated the effect of graphic arts training on these classifications. Subjects without this training confirmed the previous categories, while subjects with graphic arts training used color, form, shape, and pattern to classify them slightly differently. The third piece of research confirmed the categories and identifies the categorical differences among several types of visualizations, such as spatial or temporal properties, the attractiveness of an image, static–dynamic representations, the amount of information conveyed, and so forth (Lohse and others 1994). Many of these variations result from the varying production techniques and the varied purposes, or audiences, which they serve. The researchers developed a structural (based upon form) classification based upon several of these attributes, adding time charts, network charts, process diagrams, cartograms, and photo-realistic pictures to the original six, and they specify the types of knowledge (temporal, spatial, relationships) conveyed by each type. Photo-realistic images were distinct from the others and were characterized as spatial, attractive, nonnumeric, and as conveying the least amount of information.

In summary, these research projects demonstrate the need to address a wide variety of image attributes, including "interpretive" as well as perceptual attributes, across a wide range of images and tasks. The following section discusses various attempts to further synthesize these data into a framework which could guide both decisions as to how to index images and future research into the image indexing process.

Towards Synthesis

There have been several attempts at synthesizing the various research results reported so far. Chen (2001) conducted research comparing the author's Classes with Enser's four categories of searches (Unique, Nonunique, Unique with refiners, and Nonunique with refiners) and Fidel's Data and Objects Poles. This research found good agreement among these except for Fidel's Poles, which focused on more abstract attributes of types of data in relation to type of information search. Armitage and Enser (1997) combined Shatford's specific, generic, and abstract levels (Shatford 1984) with their categories as well, using a type of facet analysis to slot generic and specific objects and events (such as carnivals, Rio carnivals, Rio carnival 1988) into the scheme. However, problems arose with this approach, especially in relation to geographic locations, suggesting that the notion of refiners should be left as an additional set of attributes to be assigned.

Of interest here is where the author's attributes fall in these organizational schemes. Rather than use Classes, the author grouped the appropriate attributes into the specific–generic–abstract framework adopted by earlier researchers. While some of the author's attributes may seem to be rather finely distinguished (e.g., *Body Part* and *Clothing*), they are listed here because both cognitive and exploratory research suggest they are typically noticed. Other attributes were grouped according to the function that they serve in relation to specific elements within an image or to the whole image (Table 5.15). In this diagram, on the specific and generic levels, "Who" refers to objects or persons, "What" refers to events and activities, "When" is time, and "Where" is setting of the image.

As can be seen here, in Table 5.15 the generic "Who" (which corresponds to the Class OBJECTS) is the only category that contains perceptual attributes.[10] While the analysis did not break down the specific attribute percentages between the generic and specific levels, as noted earlier, the basic-level (generic) attributes for the perceptual classes accounted for about 75% of attributes; therefore the generic level would be approximately 30% for the "Who" group and the specific level would be approximately 10%, as would be expected with a general describing task. The rest are interpretive attributes, requiring more than simple identification and involving various levels of inference and of world knowledge and experience. These attributes relate to the "story" (what, when, where, abstract, etc.) of the image, and when combined account for 16.6% of the total. The attribute *Symbolic Aspect* runs across all categories at the abstract level.

Table 5.15. Attributes grouped by generic, specific, and abstract levels

	Who	What	When	Where
Generic	(39.3%) *Object* *People* *Clothing* *Body Part* *Text*	(7.6%) *Activity* *Event* *Motion*	(0.9%) *Time Aspect* *Time Refer-ence*	(2.1%) *Setting*
Specific	Proper Names	Proper Names	Dates	Proper Names
Abstract	(4.5%) *Emotion* *Social Status* *Relationship* *Description* *State* *(Symbolic Aspect)**	(2.0%) *Abstract* *Atmosphere* *Category* *Theme* *(Symbolic Aspect)**	*Time Reference** *(Symbolic Aspect)**	*Setting** *(Symbolic Aspect)**

* Not enough data

The rest of the attributes shown in table 5.16 apply either to the image in its entirety (Inferred Image Gestalt and Perceptual Image Gestalt), or to the generic and specific levels of the "Who" and, to a lesser extent, the "What" (the recursive perceptual Visual Elements which can modify these other attributes). The Inferred Image Gestalt refers to attributes that again need some knowledge and experience for users to be able to infer them from the visual clues. The Perceptual Image Gestalt refers to attributes which are broad visual percepts stimulated by the occurrence or combination of various VISUAL ELEMENTS. The VISUAL ELEMENTS such as *Color*, *Texture*, and *Shape* are perceptual attributes of physical objects in the world. Again, DESCRIPTION terms, as modifiers, can apply across all these categories. This more detailed breakdown of the attributes according to levels and function may be of use in conceptualizing the types of indexing needed in different environments and by different users.

Table 5.16. Recursive attributes (VISUAL ELEMENTS) and Gestalt attributes

VISUAL ELEMENTS Who/What (Generic/Specific) (17.7%)	Inferred Image Gestalt (Entire Image) (5.4%)	Perceptual Image Gestalt (Entire Image) (4.1%)
Color	*Artist*	*Visual Component*
Texture	*Style*	*Composition*
Shape	*Medium*	*Focal Point*
Location-General	*Type*	*Orientation*
Location-Specific	*Format*	*Perspective*
	Technique	*Number*
	Reference	
	Representation	
(*Description*) (7.8%)	(*Description*)*	(*Description*)*

* Not enough data

There have been very few published studies of the actual indexing process, and almost none of the process of indexing images. Another recent study attempted to formalize a conceptual structure for the indexing of images, and tested this structure in a simulated indexing environment (Jörgensen and others 2001). The conceptual model (the "Pyramid") was developed drawing upon research in cognitive science, library science, and computer science (Jaimes and Chang 2000). The Pyramid (Figure 5.1) contains ten levels: the first four refer to *syntax* and are directly related to *percept*, and the remaining six refer to *semantics* and are related to visual *concept*. The levels of the Pyramid also relate to automated techniques for processing attributes at the first four levels (see Chapter Four).

Of the Syntactic Levels, *Type/Technique* is the most basic and describes the general type of image or the technique used to produce it. *Global Distribution* classifies images based on their overall perceptual content such as color and texture. The *Local Structure* refers to the individual components of the image such as Line, Tone, Color, and Texture. The *Global Composition* level focuses on the spatial layout of basic elements in the image. The Semantic Levels focus on higher levels of understanding of the image components, such as *Generic Objects* and *Scenes* (basic-level items) and *Specific Objects* and *Scenes* (identified and named items). Attributes at the *Abstract Object* level refer to specialized or interpretative knowledge about what the objects represent. Similarly, the *Abstract Scene* level refers to what the image as a whole represents. These indexing levels are the most difficult in the sense that they are subjective and assessments between different users may vary greatly. The shape of the structure reflects the amount of knowledge required to perform indexing; it is apparent that at the lower levels of the Pyramid, more knowledge and information is required to make appropriate determinations of content.

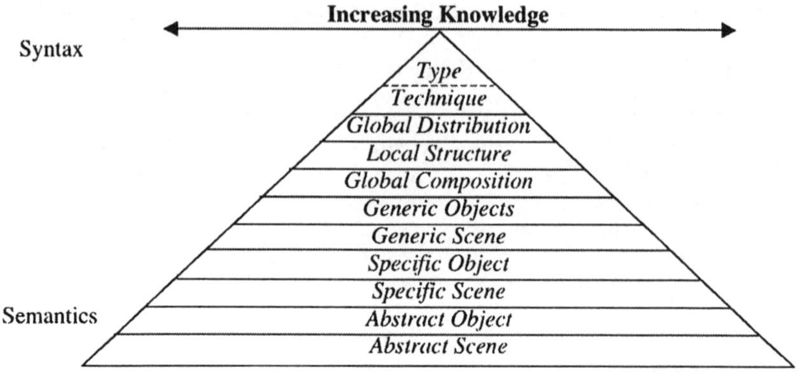

Figure 5.1 The Pyramid

The Pyramid was tested in a variety of contexts, as a classification tool for several sets of descriptors obtained in different ways: 1) for terms generated in describing and searching tasks; 2) for terms resulting from a structured approach to indexing; and 3) for terms varying across the specific, generic, and abstract conceptual levels.[11] Of interest here is the fourth area of investigation: How well can a structure such as the Pyramid guide the process of generating and assigning a full range of indexing attributes to images?

For this task, the indexers were twenty-two students that had received training in the theory and practice of indexing images. The images indexed consisted of a random sample of approximately 550 images taken from the World Wide Web, including some color photographs of current news events. The students produced structured indexing records using an Indexing Template designed to organize the author's image attributes within the Pyramid levels. Given that these attributes are typically and spontaneously described in other tasks, testing how well they were understood by indexers in the Pyramid structure should indicate to some degree its parsimoniousness in facilitating the indexing process. The indexers used a controlled vocabulary which they developed for the project using selected terms from existing thesauri such as the *AAT* and the *TGM I* (see Chapter Three); these terms were selected based on their appropriateness for *visual* description.

Indexers spent an average of ten to twenty minutes indexing each image and produced detailed indexing records. The generic and specific levels of data are handled well by this conceptual structure. However, indexers found the abstract qualities slightly more problematic to distinguish and in some cases these were not felt to be particularly intuitive. The Pyramid defines an *Abstract Object* as a localized entity with abstract meaning (e.g., flag = patriotism); if the abstraction cannot be localized it becomes an *Abstract Scene* (e.g., democracy). The specific attribute types of *Theme*, *Symbol*, and *Emotion* seem to provide a more comfortable "fit" for more abstract terms such as "democracy," "patriotism," and "respect," rather than the concept of the *Abstract Scene*. The lengthier indexing times indicate a potential problem with understanding as well. It may be that at the "abstract" level the object/scene distinction is less useful than a finer-grained analysis, or perhaps than a unitary approach (a *single* "abstract" level). Additionally, the Pyramid does not make a distinction between object and event, which is a natural part of descriptive language; this distinction is usefully made by the attributes. Both of these are open issues in relation to the Pyramid conceptual structure and bear further consideration and testing.

The goal in the research projects discussed above is to determine useful ways of conceptualizing the essential components of visual materials and instantiating those conceptualizations within efficient image indexing and retrieval systems. That users would "like it all" is undoubted; the research is motivated partly in response to the knowledge that, as librarians know all too well, providing it all is much more difficult than asking for it. Indexing decisions must be made within the context of a number of constraints, and with the utility, understandability, and ease of application of a particular system in mind. While none of this research yet seems to point directly to a new theory of image indexing, by contributing to a better understanding of the conceptual nature of the various image components it can point the way to new approaches to image retrieval system design. The final chapter will discuss what some of these future directions may be.

Appendix A. Attributes and Summary Definitions

Note: this list does not contain codes for attributes used for data management purposes or those pertaining to personal reactions to the task or image.

1. *Abstract* (Abst). Abstract terms used to describe the image as a whole ("unique," "strange," "exotic," "interesting") which express concepts not easily depicted or mapped to specific objects within the image. If these types of terms are used to describe objects portrayed in the image, then they are classified as *Description* ("pretty"). If the term refers to an affective response in the viewer ("It makes me feel strange"), it is classified as *Atmosphere*. A subject or topic of a picture is classified as *Theme*.
2. *Activity* (Actv). Any physical action in which a human or animate being participates, either individually or as a group ("sitting," "running"). Includes positional information about the human body ("slouched") or conversational actions ("arguing").
3. *Artist* (Art). Naming of a specific artist ("Picasso," "Hockney").
4. *Atmosphere* (Atms). Refers to general mood or atmosphere portrayed but not necessarily seeming to be personally experienced by humans in the picture ("dreamlike," "funny," "lonely," "warm," "sad").
5. *Body Part* (BoPt). Any part of human or animal anatomy, either specific ("head," "hand," "knee") or more general ("torso"). Includes hairstyle ("beard," "bun").
6. *Category* (Catg). A noun referencing a type or genre of literature in relation to the image ("romance," "adventure," "fairy tale," "myth," "science fiction," and so on). Use of this type of term as an adjective ("a romantic picture") is coded not as *Category* but as *Atmosphere*.
7. *Clothing* (Clot). Specific items of clothing mentioned ("shirt," "dress"). Includes accessories ("tie," "jewelry"). May also include animal "gear" ("harness," "saddle").
8. *Color* (Colr). Mention of a specific color ("red, "blue," "reddish-orange").
9. *Color Value* (ColV). Description of a group of colors related by a similar color value, or other color qualities such as hue, tint. Includes general color modifiers such as "warm" or "dark" or "light."
10. *Composition* (Comp). Mention of method by which perceptual attention is focused on one area, or general compositional or spatial relationships ("warm-colored object comes to foreground").
11. *Description* (Desc). Adjectives referring to objects or people depicted. Includes materials of which objects are composed ("elderly," "wooden").
12. *Emotion* (Emot). Refers to specific affective states or mental activity or states of being experienced or seeming to be experienced by the humans or animals in the picture ("sad," "confused," "concentrating," "afraid").
13. *Event* (Evnt). Group activity, performance, social gathering ("picnic," "cir-

cus," "protest").

14. *Focal Point* (FocP). Area upon which attention is focused ("the man with the straw hat") by the use of another visual element, such as *Composition* (all heads are turned toward) or *Color*. The result itself is coded separately.
15. *Format* (Frmt). Audience aimed at or specific publication type produced for ("children's art," "textbook," "movie," "cartoon," "poster").
16. *Location-General* (LocG). A generalized location within the two-dimensional framework of the image indicated by such terms as "foreground" or "background." Can also refer to a general section of the picture ("sky").
17. *Location-Specific* (LocS). Locations of objects or specific picture elements specified by prepositions ("on," "under," "above," "around") or specific locational words ("left," "right," "center").
18. *Medium* (Medm). Materials in which item is executed ("oils," "pencil").
19. *Motion* (Motn). Motion or perceived motion of inanimate objects or depiction of motion ("swoops," "rushing," "splashes") or mention of sensation of motion as a result of some artistic device. Depiction of human motion is coded *Activity*.
20. *Number* (Numb). Number, quantity, size ("three," "lots," "large").
21. *Object* (Objt). Mention of a specific object or category of objects. Includes living things such as animals or plants ("table," "dog"). Does not include *People*, *Body Part*, or *Clothing*.
22. *Orientation* (Ornt). Direction of visual element ("diagonal," "left to right," "vertical").
23. *People* (Peop). Any mention of a human, either singular or plural, of any age or sex. Refers to specific persons depicted in picture and includes pronoun references ("he," "she," "they," "his," "her").
24. *Perspective* (Pers). Comments on quality or type of perspective. Also includes point of view and scale ("very flat," "no depth," "top-down view").
25. *Reference* (Refn). Reference to external literary or entertainment figure or work by way of comparison ("John-Boy Walton," "Dracula"). Also references to external proper noun objects, institutions, or locations ("Coca-Cola," "Jersey Shore").
26. *Relationship* (Reln). Describes relationship experienced by humans in the picture or which seems to be portrayed ("intimate," "mother and child").
27. *Representation* (Repr). Type of representation, such as photograph, painting, drawing, illustration, and so on.
28. *Setting* (Sett). General external setting of a scene or activity ("restaurant," "outdoors").
29. *Shape* (Shap). Specific shapes mentioned ("round," "triangular," "flat").
30. *Social Status* (SocS). Status of humans specifically commented upon, in addition to or in place of terms coded *People*; includes occupation, race,

nationality ("upper class," "Japanese," "cab driver").

31. *State* (Stat). Condition of picture component or function filled by component ("full," "to support,"). For condition of object used as an adjective, use *Description* ("torn," "rusty"). For human mental or emotional states use *Emotion.*
32. *Style* (Styl). Specific or general type of style mentioned ("Impressionism," "abstract," "naturalistic," "artsy," "cartoony," "loose," and so on). A noun form such as "cartoon" is coded *Format.*
33. *Symbolic Aspect* (SymA). Statement that visual item is symbolic of specific meaning ("man is so precise").
34. *Technique* (Tech). Mention of artistic technique such as brushwork.
35. *Text* (Text). Mention of specific text in picture, such as artist's name or other words present ("Corot," "Phillies").
36. *Texture* (Texr). Mention of textural quality of depicted object or of picture ("shiny," "quilted," "metallic").
37. *Theme* (Them). Subject or topic of picture ("transportation," "exploration"). Also specific discipline of study mentioned ("psychology," "religion").
38. *Time Aspect* (TimA). Duration of activity or reference to time component ("during," "while"). Also time of day, seasons ("sunset," "summer").
39. *Time Reference* (TimR). A reference to an era or time period in which the picture takes place ("early '20s"), or description of picture or style of picture as "old" and so on.
40. *Type* (Type). General type of representation ("portrait," "landscape," "nude").
41. *Visual Component* (VisC). Mention of types of visual components or qualities such as line, lighting, contrast, or other qualities ("stripes," "reflection," "shadow").

Appendix B. Perceptual and Interpretive Attributes by Class

PERCEPTUAL ATTRIBUTES

1. OBJECTS
   - *Object*
   - *Text*
   - *Body Part*
   - *Clothing*
2. PEOPLE
   - *People*
3. COLOR
   - *Color*
   - *Color Value*
4. VISUAL ELEMENTS
   - *Composition*
   - *Focal Point*
   - *Motion*
   - *Orientation*
   - *Perspective*
   - *Shape*
   - *Texture*
   - *Visual Component*
5. SPATIAL LOCATION
   - *Location-General*
   - *Location-Specific*
6. DESCRIPTION
   - *Description*
   - *Number*

INTERPRETIVE ATTRIBUTES

7. PEOPLE RELATED
   - *Relationship*
   - *Social Status*
   - *Emotion*
8. ART HISTORICAL INFORMATION
   - *Artist*
   - *Format*

8. ART HISTORICAL INFORMATION (continued)
   - *Medium*

Representation
Style
Technique
Time Reference
Type

9. ABSTRACT
   Abstract
   Atmosphere
   State
   Symbolic Aspect
   Theme

10. STORY
   Activity
   Category
   Event
   Setting
   Time Aspect

11. EXTERNAL RELATION
   *Comparison**
   *Similarity**
   Reference

REACTIVE ATTRIBUTES

12. VIEWER RESPONSE
   *Personal Reaction**
   *Conjecture**
   *Drawing**
   *Uncertainty**

* Note: these attributes occurred at very small levels and were not included in the current discussion.

Appendix C.1. Ranked Counts and Percentages of Attribute Codes by Task, Sorted by Frequency within Task

Viewing			Search			Memory		
Attribute	no.	%	**Attr**	no.	%	**Attr**	no.	%
Object	754	21.7	*Objt*	492	16.8	*Objt*	172	19.2
People	298	8.6	*Peop*	302	10.3	*Peop*	99	11.1
Social Status	287	8.3	*SocS*	267	9.1	*Colr*	60	6.7
Color	266	7.7	*Colr*	252	8.6	*SocS*	58	6.5
Location-Specific	201	5.8	*Actv*	201	6.8	*Repr*	52	5.8
Clothing	160	4.6	*LocS*	200	6.8	*Numb*	50	5.6
Body Part	147	4.2	*Numb*	153	5.2	*Actv*	50	5.6
Activity	123	3.6	*Clot*	135	4.6	*LocS*	37	4.1
Description	105	3.0	*LocG*	113	3.8	*LocG*	32	3.6
Visual Component	89	2.6	*Repr*	109	3.7	*Motn*	28	3.1
Reference	88	2.5	*Refn*	61	2.1	*Clot*	25	2.8
Location-General	82	2.4	*BoPt*	76	2.6	*Refn*	24	2.7
Number	79	2.3	*Sett*	58	2.0	*Sett*	23	2.6
Emotion	71	2.0	*Motn*	43	1.5	*ColV*	20	2.2
Representation	70	2.0	*VisC*	41	1.4	*VisC*	18	2.0
Setting	61	1.8	*Desc*	37	1.3	*Desc*	18	2.0
Shape	56	1.6	*Styl*	33	1.1	*Comp*	12	1.3
Motion	51	1.5	*ColV*	33	1.1	*Styl*	10	1.1
Color Value	47	1.4	*Catg*	27	0.9	*Shap*	8	0.9
Abstract	36	1.0	*Stat*	24	0.8	*Ornt*	7	0.8
Time Aspect	32	0.9	*TimA*	22	0.7	*Abst*	7	0.8
State	30	0.9	*Ornt*	21	0.7	*BoPt*	7	0.8
Category	29	0.8	*Shap*	20	0.7	*Type*	5	0.6
Style	25	0.7	*Emot*	19	0.6	*Pers*	5	0.6
Composition	17	0.5	*Evnt*	10	0.3	*Catg*	5	0.6
Theme	17	0.5	*Abst*	10	0.3	*TimA*	5	0.6
Atmosphere	15	0.4	*TimR*	9	0.3	*Emot*	5	0.6
Focal Point	13	0.4	*Type*	8	0.3	*FocP*	3	0.3
Perspective	13	0.4	*Pers*	6	0.2	*Atms*	3	0.3
Type	11	0.3	*Them*	6	0.2	*Stat*	2	0.2
Text	8	0.2	*Tech*	3	0.1	*Texr*	1	0.1
Event	7	0.2	*SymA*	3	0.1	*TimR*	1	0.1
Format	7	0.2	*Medm*	3	0.1	*Evnt*	1	0.1
Medium	5	0.1	*Frmt*	3	0.1	*Text*	1	0.1
Symbolic Aspect	5	0.1	*Reln*	2	0.1	*Reln*	0	0.0
Orientation	4	0.1	*Texr*	2	0.1	*Art*	0	0.0
Technique	4	0.1	*Comp*	2	0.1	*Tech*	0	0.0
Time Reference	4	0.1	*Text*	2	0.1	*SymA*	0	0.0
Artist	3	0.1	*FocP*	2	0.1	*Medm*	0	0.0
Texture	1	0.0	*Art*	0	0.0	*Frmt*	0	0.0
Relationship	0	0.0	*Atms*	0	0.0	*Them*	0	0.0

Appendix C.2. Attributes Sorted by Task and Frequency

Viewing	Search	Memory
Object	*Object*	*Object*
People	*People*	*People*
Social Status	*Social Status*	*Color*
Color	*Color*	*Social Status*
Location-Specific	*Activity*	*Representation*
Clothing	*Location-Specific*	*Number*
Body Part	*Number*	*Activity*
Activity	*Clothing*	*Location-Specific*
Description	*Location-General*	*Location-General*
Visual Component	*Representation*	*Motion*
Reference	*Reference*	*Clothing*
Location-General	*Body Part*	*Reference*
Number	*Setting*	*Setting*
Emotion	*Motion*	*Color Value*
Representation	*Visual Component*	*Visual Component*
Setting	*Description*	*Description*
Shape	*Style*	*Composition*
Motion	*Color Value*	*Style*
Color Value	*Category*	*Shape*
Abstract	*State*	*Orientation*
Time Aspect	*Time Aspect*	*Abstract*
State	*Orientation*	*Body Part*
Category	*Shape*	*Type*
Style	*Emotion*	*Perspective*
Composition	*Event*	*Category*
Theme	*Abstract*	*Time Aspect*
Atmosphere	*Time Reference*	*Emotion*
Focal Point	*Type*	*Focal Point*
Perspective	*Perspective*	*Atmosphere*
Type	*Theme*	*State*
Text	*Technique*	*Texture*
Event	*Symbolic Aspect*	*Time Reference*
Format	*Medium*	*Event*
Medium	*Format*	*Text*
Symbolic	*Relationship*	*Relationship*
Orientation	*Texture*	*Artist*
Technique	*Composition*	*Technique*
Time Reference	*Text*	*Symbolic Aspect*
Artist	*Focal Point*	*Medium*
Texture	*Artist*	*Format*
Relationship	*Atmosphere*	*Theme*

Appendix C.3. Attributes by Task and Occurrence

	Viewing		Search		Memory	
Attribute	no.	%	no.	%	no.	%
Abstract	36	1.0	10	0.3	7	0.8
Activity	123	3.6	201	6.8	50	5.6
Artist	3	0.1	0	0.0	0	0.0
Atmosphere	15	0.4	0	0.0	3	0.3
Body Part	147	4.2	76	2.6	7	0.8
Category	29	0.8	27	0.9	5	0.6
Clothing	160	4.6	135	4.6	25	2.8
Color	266	7.7	252	8.6	60	6.7
Color Value	47	1.4	33	1.1	20	2.2
Composition	17	0.5	2	0.1	12	1.3
Description	105	3.0	37	1.3	18	2.0
Emotion	71	2.0	19	0.6	5	0.6
Event	7	0.2	10	0.3	1	0.1
Focal Point	13	0.4	2	0.1	3	0.3
Format	7	0.2	3	0.1	0	0.0
Location-General	82	2.4	113	3.8	32	3.6
Location-Specific	201	5.8	200	6.8	37	4.1
Medium	5	0.1	3	0.1	0	0.0
Motion	51	1.5	43	1.5	28	3.1
Number	79	2.3	153	5.2	50	5.6
Object	754	21.7	492	16.8	172	19.2
Orientation	4	0.1	21	0.7	7	0.8
People	298	8.6	302	10.3	99	11.1
Perspective	13	0.4	6	0.2	5	0.6
Reference	88	2.5	61	2.1	24	2.7
Relationship	0	0.0	2	0.1	0	0.0
Representation	70	2.0	109	3.7	52	5.8
Setting	61	1.8	58	2.0	23	2.6
Shape	56	1.6	20	0.7	8	0.9
Social Status	287	8.3	267	9.1	58	6.5
State	30	0.9	24	0.8	2	0.2
Style	25	0.7	33	1.1	10	1.1
Symbolic Aspect	5	0.1	3	0.1	0	0.0
Technique	4	0.1	3	0.1	0	0.0
Text	8	0.2	2	0.1	1	0.1
Texture	1	0.0	2	0.1	1	0.1
Theme	17	0.5	6	0.2	0	0.0
Time Aspect	32	0.9	22	0.7	5	0.6
Time Reference	4	0.1	9	0.3	1	0.1
Type	11	0.3	8	0.3	5	0.6
Visual Component	89	2.6	41	1.4	18	2.0

Notes

1. There were some data management attributes, such as missing data, and others specific to the memory task. There was also a "reactive" category of four attributes (VIEWER RESPONSE) which included responses such as conjecture or emotional reaction to the image (four total attributes) or a nonverbal response, such as a drawing, or conjecture about an image without a codable conclusion. The determination of specific attribute and category inclusiveness was guided by the content of the data; therefore, some categories could certainly also be further subdivided (*Object*) and others (*Body Part*) may seemingly be inappropriate as a stand-alone class. However, in this analysis, frequency of occurrence was taken as an indication of importance or typicality.

2. It should be noted that a subject heading such as "Pickets" can also carry narrative qualities.

3. This total includes viewer response attributes; as these do not relate to the current issues in the overview, they will not be discussed.

4. However, the discussion below of Classes above the median suggests otherwise. Therefore, these may not be the best Classes for analysis, and this would bear further investigation. However, it could also suggest that focusing on different Classes would also increase the overall repeat rate exhibited.

5. Since the overall repeat rate for individual words within the corpus is .0070, a repeat rate of .4711 falls above the median and could be considered on the high end.

6. For the repeat rate analysis, two Classes were not evaluated, those of VIEWER RESPONSE and of EXTERNAL RELATIONSHIP, as these were not directly related to the range of descriptive attributes for a specific image.

7. See Shatford (1986) and Turner (1995) for a similar suggestion.

8. Individual attribute percentages are not reported, as the numbers were considerably less than with the describing tasks; this data is reported only by categories of attributes.

9. Oxford University Press (2001, March 15). Oxford English Dictionary Online. Available from dictionary.oed.com/entrance.dtl (accessed on March 15, 2001).

10. The reader is reminded that, as explained in Chapters Two and Four, various models of visual processing draw the lines between perception, identification, and understanding at different levels. These processes are not well understood and it is highly likely they are not one-way, but involve information exchange among the levels. Therefore, it should be understood that this diagram is an approximation with some "fuzziness" to the levels.

11. For a full discussion of these areas, see Jaimes and Chang (2000).

Chapter 6

Towards the Future

This research review has provided detailed empirical and theoretical evidence about the perception, representation, and available retrieval methods for a wide variety of image attributes. In addition, it has considered research concerning these attributes within diverse contexts such as users' information needs, searching behaviors, and types of queries. Based on this evidence, it appears that the range, typicality, and consistency of image attributes varies across types of tasks, and that there are a number of attributes that should be addressed within image retrieval systems. However, there are also a number of real-world constraints affecting the development and implementation of these systems. Within libraries, archives, and cultural heritage organizations, these include not just institutional constraints, but also perceptions of authority, audience, and appropriate boundaries for the indexing process itself ("getting it right"). The machine processing community, in contrast, focuses largely on technical implementation ("getting it to work") and has to date paid little attention to users' needs and usability.[1]

While operating from quite different perspectives, these communities of practice and research have nevertheless developed a staggering set of tools to assist in making image attributes accessible. The challenge then becomes one of selection: which attributes should be represented and made searchable, which should have priority within a given context, and what methods should then be chosen for their representation? However, given the fairly rigid disciplinary, professional, and theoretical boundaries within which these communities function, each naturally operates within its own paradigms and gravitates towards its own methods. Thus, these communities tend to treat all image attributes as being amenable to their favored methods (following what is known variously as Baruch's observation or Maslow's maxim: "When all you have a hammer, everything looks like a nail").

Based upon the evidence discussed in previous chapters, it appears that different types of images and different attributes within these images may require different types and combinations of techniques to best represent them. Images are complex entities, stimulating perceptual, interpretive, and affective responses. The unique aspects of individual images require a variety of discriminable attributes to be sufficiently described both for precise retrieval and efficient and satisfactory browsing. However, as the situation now stands, each community concerned with access to images creates systems of representation based upon their understanding of the common needs of their own users and their underlying intellectual traditions. Nevertheless, given the digital networked environment in which many institutions now operate, providers can no longer ignore either the needs of other communities of users or the possibilities of wider utility or new uses for their images.[2]

An overriding theme in this chapter's discussion is the locus of authority for the description of images and other materials, and whom that locus of authority serves. Dervin (1977) was one of the first researchers to raise these issues, and characterized librarians as fitting users into sociodemographic stereotypes and information into rigid classification systems. Users, on the other hand, create different ideas or interpretations from the same external information because of personal, affective, and social inclinations and conditions. The "document" and its caretakers are the authority in the traditional view, whereas, as Neill points out, "the objects and information have value as *tools*, not in or for themselves" [italics added] (Neill 1987, 196). Eliade makes the case for images more strongly:

> It is therefore the image as such, as a whole bundle of meanings, that is true, and not any one of its meanings, not one alone of its many frames of reference. To translate an image into a concrete terminology by restricting it to any one of its frames of reference is to do worse than mutilate it—it is to annihilate, to annul it as an instrument of cognition (Eliade 1991, 15).

This chapter refocuses the discussion on types of image attributes in relation to their selection, indexing, and retrieval. It gathers insights from research and practice to suggest heuristics guiding the selection of specific attributes for indexing. It reviews current methods that facilitate the indexing of these attributes, as well as newer approaches and future directions in accessing images in multivalent ways. Suggestions for research into new types of representations and how future systems could implement these follow. Overall, the goal is to emphasize that there are a variety of techniques which should be considered, rather than a single unitary approach, and to stimulate the recognition that diverse communities of practice can and should usefully contribute to the representation of the image in its not one, but many gestalts. Craftspeople know that there are many types of hammers, and selecting the right tool for planishing, as opposed to roofing, produces products that satisfy their users' needs.

This overview of image retrieval has demonstrated that, to date, there are far more questions than answers about how best to solve the problem of finding images. The chapter concludes with a list of some of the major questions that emerge and that constitute a vital research agenda for the future.

Image Attributes

The research review reveals evidence about the types of attributes typically noted and requested across a variety of tasks and settings. As discussed in the previous chapters, there currently appears to be a very incomplete match between the attributes addressed by major textual image indexing systems and thesauri in use and the attributes described by participants in empirical research. More guidance is needed for institutions and indexers to decide exactly which of a range of attributes it is most desirable and feasible to provide access to, as well as what kinds and levels of access should be provided. Additional evidence presented in the literature review points to some intriguing suggestions for the development and testing of useful heuristics to guide selection of specific attributes or classes of attributes. Most importantly, situating groups of image attributes within specific user and indexer *contexts* may contribute to a useful partitioning of image attributes for indexing. As noted, image attributes encompass perceptual features such as object name, shape, and color, interpretive aspects such as the traditional aesthetic considerations of composition and style, and abstract or affective elements such as meaning and emotional impact. The use of different contexts may guide choices among which groups of attributes are most usefully focused upon within various communities and to what methods these attributes are most amenable.

Perception seems to require as much information as possible. Moates and Schumacher (1980) suggest that this information can be derived in two ways, either directly from the object itself or indirectly from the context. Contextual information facilitates perception of the environment with less direct information, and the more information that is available from one procedure, the less is needed from the other. The literature review in Chapter Two suggests that cognitive constructs such as *informativeness*, *prototypes* and *exemplars*, *figure–ground*, and *schemata* appear to have applications in several areas concerned with image attributes, and could be used as contexts within which decisions relating to the representation of image attributes may be usefully situated.

The following section is a wide-ranging exploration of these constructs and current and potential applications of these in relation to the findings of this and previous research concerning image attributes. The discussion is meant to be suggestive, not conclusive, and draws heavily on material presented in previous chapters, which is not repeated here. The author discusses a variety of image attributes in relation to one or more of these constructs, with the goal of suggesting heuristics that could be further specified, employed, and tested in the indexing of pictorial materials. Unless otherwise noted, research examples are from the author's research (Jörgensen 1995b; Jörgensen 1999a; Jörgensen 1999b).

Objects and Human Figures

As a large body of data and practical experience indicate, objects and human figures are typically requested and frequently described in relation to image content. Currently, the major tools used to address these within LIS and cultural heritage initiatives are textual: thesauri with more generalized application such as the *TGM I* and its parent, the *LCSH*, thesauri for art and museum objects such as the *AAT* and the *British Museum Object Names Thesaurus*,[3] and more specialized, domain-specific tools within such areas as archaeology and costume history. There are additional tools for names, such as the *ULAN*; these are generally used for indexing the creator of an image, but can also be used for people depicted. There is currently no wide-ranging, generalized thesaurus for image indexing, and most organizations select from existing thesauri and supplement heavily with free text. Access through textual descriptors remains an uncertain endeavor, and results in fragmented and inconsistent records for searching.

Similarly, within machine processing the general problem of object identification is far from being solved. Again, domain-specific pattern recognition tools exist for restricted application areas such as medical imaging, manufacturing, and inspection; these tools can identify regions of interest ranging from possible tumors to (in a seemingly esoteric application) olive pits. Text also supplements these types of records. There has been more success in recognizing the presence of humans using automated methods, as flesh tones occupy a unique part of the color spectrum, but little information can be gained beyond the presence or absence of figures (and their possible state of undress). Face recognition techniques can also identify the presence of faces in various orientations, but claims for actual recognition in real-world applications remain to be substantiated. Therefore, in spite of a large amount of work, providing semantic access to objects and the human presence through automated methods is currently very limited.

However, even after choosing textual access and selecting vocabulary tools, the question still remains as to *which* objects and *which* aspects of the human figure are most usefully represented. Some of these decisions can be made within the guidelines of specific institutions and the nature of their collections and users (e.g., the Prints and Photographs Division of the Library of Congress and the use of the *TGM I* for access to collections of historical photographs). Nevertheless, these tools still exclude a large amount of image content that could potentially be addressed. While not everything can be indexed, some of the concepts from cognitive psychology discussed in Chapter Two may be useful in guiding decisions as to how to limit the range of attributes addressed by zeroing in on those with the most utility in retrieval. These concepts are integrated into the discussion below without further elaboration; for more details see Chapter Two.

New Models and Representations

The concept of "figure–ground" may help to determine which are the major figures or objects in the image. As explained in the review of Gestalt processes, figure–ground seems to be a fundamental organizational principle for human visual perception and understanding. Eye-tracking research also reveals a concentration of fixations in the "central portion" of the image (the *figure*) and a number of more apparently random fixations in the rest of the image (the *ground*). Such research also demonstrates that even the extremely short duration of a fixation (a fraction of a second) is still enough time to attend to certain features *wherever* they appear in the image, suggesting that objects that *stand out* in the ground will also be noted. The frequency of spatial location attributes in image descriptions noted in the author's research suggests the use of the figure–ground concept as a template in indexing pictorial content. For instance, the following statements by test participants very clearly describe the background against which the main figure in one particular image stands:

The background is the solor [sic] system part of two planets or moons are shown on the far left and right. Also smaller planets are in the background.

The whale is in the foreground in a jumping position. A night sky and mountains are in the background. Stars are also on the image of the whale.

Traditional approaches to visual composition largely place the important objects in a central area, and human-made images all share purposeful composition, whether they are photographs, paintings, drawings, or computer-generated images. As Batley comments after reviewing the literature on pictorial and visual communication, "looking at a picture is very different from looking at the real world where we can concentrate our vision where we please. . . . The composition of a picture assists in concentrating the viewer's attention on the main point of interest" (Batley 1988, 17). Human-made images are not random views, and therefore purposeful composition is likely to hold true across a variety of types of human-created pictorial images, regardless of the method of their production. As Batley suggests, purposeful composition becomes an innate behavior in image makers; it is in many cases organized according to the figure–ground principle and "will guide the perceiver's vision to the informational centre of the picture."

It is obvious from this that the concept of *figure* can assist in choices of which primary objects and people to provide access to. What is not so obvious is that *ground* must also be attended to. The order of participants' terms generated in the describing tasks was also assessed and showed that while figure is initially attended to, the lengthier the image description the more terms describing the ground appear (Jörgensen 1995b). Thus, access to description of the ground, whether by use of a simple *Color* term ("blue"), several object words ("sky with many stars"), or an abstract concept or schema ("the solar system") would appear to be useful in providing full access to the visual content of the image.

We can also return to the definition of "informativeness" offered by Loftus and Mackworth: "An object in a picture is informative to the extent that the object has a low a priori probability of being in the picture given the rest of the picture" (Loftus and Mackworth 1978, 566). Researchers have found such areas, considered to be of "low predictability," to be also fixated upon. This suggests that a group of objects within an image is likely to activate a schema that places them in some kind of context. If an object is *not* consistent with this context (such as a bowling ball in a kitchen), then it is more likely to capture attentive processing.

Another supporting example from the author's work (Jörgensen 1995b) shows how such anomalies, even when part of the image details, are remarked upon. In a fantasy image, a horselike animal is wearing bracelets on legs that have human feet. Data show that the bracelets and human feet are consistently remarked upon, as well as the detail that there are bracelets on only three of the creature's four legs (almost 50% of participants noted this). Therefore, in addition to what could be considered the major objects and figures, anomalous objects and figures that run counter to expectations should also be noted in indexing. A wide range of anomalies can be considered: unusual size, shape, color, position, location, number, use, or even action or emotion (e.g., a smiling teapot).

There is also a cognitive foundation for indexing on both the specific and generic levels. While research suggests that objects are perceived and described largely on the "basic (generic) level," there is also the recognition that the hierarchy can vary across communities of expertise and according to the task. There is ample evidence from users that representing both the specific and generic levels of objects could be of great utility in searching. Any one image attribute may typically be understood on several different levels, and different tasks require retrieval on these different levels.

Another type of object or figure that could be usefully represented is one that could serve as a "prototype" or "exemplar" of a class of objects, as image searchers are often seeking for "a good picture of . . . " and need access to an image exhibiting the typical qualities of a class of objects or an exceptionally good example of an object. For instance, a graphic artist described needing good object examples for a scene of the interior of a diner, such as ketchup and mustard bottles and vinyl-covered seats.[4]

Research demonstrates that a large number of eye fixations fall upon the human figure, especially the face. This suggests their priority in description. We can extend information about anomalies ("very bushy eyebrows") and prototypes (a "typical businessman") to apply to description of the human figure as well. Attributes related to the human figure, such as *Clothing* and *Body Part*, were frequently described under the two conditions of their being unusual ("very large nose") or their being a prototypical example.

A schema framework or frame-based approach may simplify decisions as to the number of objects to be indexed. For instance, the "kitchen" schema implies a number of possible objects which could fill slots in the representation: pots and pans, bowls (kitchen utensils); a sink, a kitchen towel (furnishings); a toaster, a stove (appliances); food cooking (objects and events); an apron (clothing); perhaps a dog or cat underfoot (objects, themes, and symbols). In the same manner, the "diner" schema carries with it slots for such objects as ketchup and mustard bottles and vinyl seats. Similarly, activities and associated objects also lend themselves to a schema approach. Using schemas to guide decisions about selection of image content for indexing could be a parsimonious approach. If schemas are well designed, inference (on the system or user side) can substitute for exhaustive indexing.

Both schemas and prototypes may also provide a mechanism to address both the generic and specific levels of object indexing. The author's research demonstrates that while about 80% of objects are described at a basic level, the other 20% encompass subordinate and superordinate terms. It does not, however, seem necessarily useful to include all these terms in each individual image description. Rather, for implementation purposes, such terms could be linked automatically through some type of implicit thesaurus structure, which could utilize existing thesauri or newer methods for associating text and images.

For instance, Humphrey applied a frame-based approach in an *AAT* indexing prototype using the knowledge-base design of the Medline indexing system.[5] The *AAT* thesaurus structure was converted into a frame knowledge base with INHERITS-FROM and CHILDREN slots to point to superordinate and subordinate terms, respectively. The prototype demonstrated how such a frame-based approach could assist indexing with a multifaceted tool such as the *AAT* by facilitating searching within the thesaurus and by providing appropriate slots based on the knowledge structure for the indexer to fill in.

Another means for exploring the coupling of text to pictures could be the model of the print "visual dictionary," a tool that has existed for centuries, and is well known in field guides (Corbeil 1986; Dorling Kindersley 2000). As other types of relationships are typically exhibited within visual dictionaries, the term "visual thesaurus" may also be aptly applied to these tools. Categorization is frequently communicated by context; the association of items on a page with one another adds meaning to those items. For example, when stone is depicted with bricks, concrete blocks, and steel (all building materials), stone in this case becomes a "building material." Thus, items in these thesauri can exhibit several relationships beyond a hierarchical genus–species type: similarity relationships based on structure and/or function, and part–whole relationships. Items may be similar because they belong to a particular class as determined by an existing taxonomy or because of a shared context. Color becomes an important identifying characteristic for objects in the natural world. Work in MAVIS 2 is exploring automating the linking of concepts to objects in images through the use of latent semantic indexing to process associated texts (Tansley and others 2000). A larger goal is to build up a multimedia thesaurus that could function in retrieval of images and of objects depicted within images.

Location

Very few textual systems address spatial or locational aspects of images. The *AAT* has a very few general placement terms, while the *TI* leads all others with forty-three attributes for indexing specific location. Many others have none. Within the subfield of machine processing focusing on CBR, research has focused on a variety of methods using color, texture, and shape for determining regions within images. Other methods localize color or texture and support some region-based querying on limited visual objects such as grass or sky, or attempt to determine the global configuration of an image. While many of these techniques work well for particularly well-defined areas, they also tend to return unexpected and anomalous search results.

While there is at present little access to locational information, the author's work revealed that terms referring to location of image elements occur frequently in image descriptions. As described above, the literature review provides data indicating that the central portion of an image is more highly attended to; therefore utilizing the concepts of figure–ground may also be useful in characterizing location of image elements in a broad manner. In terms of image memory, left–right orientation seems to be more problematic, while other more general spatial concepts such as "above," "below," and "on" are better remembered.

In the describing tasks reported in Chapter Five, there were approximately twice as many *Location-Specific* terms as *Location-General* terms in the describing tasks:

> *He's <u>in</u> a tomb or other interior with a statue <u>behind</u> him, pottery <u>on</u> the floor and a burning torch.*

However, as this example demonstrates, location is frequently described by prepositions, and these are difficult to utilize within any kind of existing structured vocabulary system. Access to this information is usually through some kind of keyword search of free-text description or abstracts, but this results in much less precision in searching. These types of relationships should be preserved in an image description, as they indicate spatial–schematic organization. Nevertheless, analyzing these relationships and incorporating these terms in a text-based system is very time-consuming and produces a small return for a large investment.

A number of methods discussed in Chapter Four have applicability for adding a spatial component to the indexing of image elements. There are other methods that could also be explored. For instance, the author has proposed the concept of *spatial iconic indexing*, in which icons are placed in a grid or template (Jörgensen, Jörgensen, and Hogan 1993). In this model, locations are automatically assigned, and retrieval can take place through fuzzy matching. Text indexing could also proceed through a graphical interface using similar methods, with text placed into a grid instead of icons (*spatial keyword indexing*").

Color and Other Visual Elements

Color terms, as noted in Chapter Five, were typically reported in the describing tasks. Color appears to cue attention to certain other attributes or regions and provides additional information about these attributes. Within textual tools, the *AAT* provides a vast (and potentially indiscriminable) number of color terms, while other systems, not being concerned with visual content (or relying on a visual surrogate), supply none. In contrast, the CBR community relies heavily on color and has produced useful tools and methods for its analysis and indexing, allowing access to global and regional color distributions. Color composition is accessible; however, color can as of yet be tied semantically to objects only in limited ways within these systems.

Color functions in several ways, as a pointer, an organizing (or disorganizing) factor, and an emotive factor. Color is also subject to the considerations concerning anomalous content of images. *Color* terms were noted in image descriptions under several different circumstances in the images: 1) when there was one predominant color for the entire image; 2) when either the *figure* or the *ground* was one major color; 3) when there were colors associated with the main figure of the image; or 4) when there was a contrast between lack of color and colored areas of the image.

Color terms were also highly consistent across participants. The individual and environmental variability in human color perception and the human tendency to group colors into a limited number of basic categories suggest questioning the need for detailed indexing of colors or for provision of exact matching of colors by technical means. A limited number of color terms applied under such circumstances as those described above *and* linked to specific contexts, such as background, or anomalous objects (red camel) could be useful to the delineation of image content. Techniques discussed in Chapter Four are applicable to the use of prototypical color groups and some measure of "fuzzy" matching can be utilized.

Other visual elements (*Texture*, *Shape*, *Pattern*) are infrequently mentioned in natural image descriptions. As explained in Chapter Two, their contribution seems to lie more in the "composing" of the image into an understandable whole or gestalt. Eye-tracking experiments suggest that when one of these attributes is particularly striking, it will be attended to. The *AAT* does provide a large number of terms for shape, pattern, and texture, many of which are highly specialized to the fields of visual and decorative arts. These attributes are heavily used within CBR systems, but do not map well, or automatically, to higher semantic levels such as an object's name. Indexable features such shape and color may need to be related to such traditional aesthetic considerations as composition, contrast, and complexity through mechanisms such as the Gestalt principles, and these attributes may also need to be interpreted in light of and associated with such abstract or affective concepts such as meaning or emotion (e.g., a gray sky implies a "gloomy day").

Art Historical information

Much of this information (e.g., *Artist*, *Medium*, *Technique*, *Representation*) is addressed through standard cataloging and indexing practice, and terminology is extensive in the *AAT* and name authority files. There is also evidence that a number of typical art constructs, such as iconography and style, could themselves be usefully represented as schemas (Gombrich 1969). Solso discusses the utility of an art schema and states that even with limited knowledge of styles, it is possible to develop such a schema (Solso 1994). Berlyne suggests that a person can "learn the redundancies and transitional probabilities that characterize particular art forms, styles, and cultural traditions" through increased exposure (Berlyne 1971). The attributes of *Style* ("modern," "photo-realistic," "impressionistic," and *Type* ("landscape," "still life") in the current research are common representations for organizing images and seem to follow a schematic organization. Developing a set of schematic representations for these attributes would be an interesting research area; not only could this assist in indexing and retrieval, but again, this type of approach could facilitate modular reuse of descriptions.

Within CBR, color indexing combined with region-based methods and the use of visual semantic templates could be a promising approach to recognition of types of representations. There has been little work looking at such areas as detection of brush strokes utilizing CBR methods. However, work in interactive artistic rendering (Kaplan, Gooch, and Cohen 2000), which produces painterly renderings by means of a variety of brush strokes, suggests that these techniques could also be used for analysis, indexing, and retrieval.

The "Story" of a Picture

Several research projects demonstrate that many descriptions of image content include a "story" connected with the image; this was especially apparent in the work of O'Connor (O'Connor, O'Connor, and Abbas 1999) and in the author's Sorting Task (*she's getting drunk at a party*; *this guy looks ready for a fight*)(Jörgensen 1995b). Even in the briefer comments associated with the Viewing Task, the structure of the phrase or sentence was frequently composed of an "actor" (*a fairy*) and an "action" (*riding a large red animal*). Thus, just as the participants create a visual construct of image elements using words for objects and locations, they also create a "story construct" with words.

Story elements were represented by a number of different attributes, in addition to objects and events, such as *Setting*, *Time Reference*, *Activity*, *Social Status*, *Emotion*, *Atmosphere*, *Category* ("genre"), and *Theme*. These eight attributes were the ones most frequently used to create story constructs. Current tools such as the *AAT* and the *TGM I* contain quite a few terms relevant to describing story attributes, especially for such aspects as setting, event, and type of activity. The *AAT* contains a large number of terms referring to occupation and social status, and the *TGM I* contains a large number for describing emotions and mental states.

However, while the Who, What, When, and Where ("data") are considered amenable to indexing, the more affective and abstract aspects are generally considered too subjective to be addressed within formal systems. Most image indexers have considered addressing interpretive or abstract elements within an image to be beyond the scope of their job. Therefore, even if one decides to provide access to such attributes through textual indexing, there is currently no easy place to begin, and it is little wonder that these more abstract and emotive terms have not been a strong research focus in electronic image retrieval systems either.

Therefore, for more semantic aspects of stories, the problem in textual indexing is less with a lack of tools than with the disinclination to perform such indexing. Access to these attributes within the LIS and cultural heritage communities, when provided, is frequently relegated to free-text descriptions in notes or abstracts fields with little or no internal structure. Commercial image providers, on the other hand, have been more aggressive in providing access to these attributes through keyword indexing, as their clients (advertisers, publishers) often wish to use an image to evoke an emotional response.

Within the CBR community, there is increasing recognition that these attributes should also be addressed, but little real progress towards scalable systems.

Some systems utilize forms of natural language processing on captions or other related text to add keywords or capture specific story elements, such as proper nouns or dates, all with limited success in relation to consistency. Captions often contain narrative elements as well, but these are more difficult to process, especially in any kind of generalized domain.

New Representations and Models

Research reveals the typicality with which certain story attributes are noted in image descriptions and suggests that these could aid in image access and retrieval. One aspect that may contribute to the reluctance to address story attributes may be the lack of a widely accepted conceptual framework within which to make indexing decisions. As described in Chapter Five, Shatford and others have suggested such a framework or template for guiding indexing decisions, and story attributes such as Who, What, When, and Where, as well as more abstract interpretative levels of these facets, have been mapped to this template. Another type of representation could be schema-based. Thus, the use of a template with specific types of attributes, or a story schema with "slots" for these attributes, are two representations that could guide indexing.

Following Gordon's experimental research, in which terms in the *TGM I* were reorganized into schemas called "expectation packages," schemas for common activities could be constructed to facilitate indexing, and could serve as templates to guide indexing (Gordon 2001). Thus, instead of having a precoordinated phrase, such as the Library of Congress descriptor CHILDREN PLAYING IN SAND, a more generalized template, hinged upon an actor or "agent" and/or an event or activity, could facilitate indexing efficiency and consistency (Table 6.1). Additionally, schemas could lend themselves to reuse, following Small's suggestion that a "modular approach means that specific classification sets can be developed independently and individually over a period of time" (Small 1991, 59).

Table 6.1. Schema for CHILDREN PLAYING IN SAND

Attribute	Example	Type	Type
People	"children"	Perceptual	
Object	"sand"	Perceptual	
Activity	"playing"	Perceptual	Interpretive
Setting	"beach"	Perceptual	Interpretive
Time Reference	"1990s"		Interpretive
Emotion	"happy"		Interpretive
Theme	"vacation"		Interpretive

Note that not all slots necessarily need to be filled, and also that some slots can be inferred from others (e.g., "playing" and "sand" can infer "beach"; "beach" can infer "summer vacation"; "playing" infers "happy"). The slots can be filled in with other objects (ball, dolls), settings (park, kitchen), or emotions or themes (excited, tea party). Interpretive attributes can be filled in objectively when textual information is available. Terms could also be included on the specific and generic levels.

Another area that can be drawn upon for insight into providing access to these more semantic elements of images is that of fiction indexing. Those wishing to find works of fiction face many of the same problems that image searchers face: retrieval points such as author and title frequently reveal little content information. Genre arrangements have proven useful for access to fiction (Baker 1988; Pejtersen 1989), and Small states that access to "genre" scenes such as banqueting would be useful (Small 1991). Genre, as used for indexing fiction, corresponds to the attribute *Category*, whose presence in visual image descriptions suggests that people organize their thoughts about images in a similar manner ("romance," "mystery," science fiction").

Beghtol notes that certain domains, such as fiction, may not be amenable to traditional classification approaches that emphasize mutually exclusive categories and exhaustivity. She describes some of the ways in which fiction varies from nonfiction:

> First, fiction may not be "about" a "subject" in the usual sense; a novel set, for example, in a chemistry laboratory does not deal with chemistry as a "subject." Second, fiction is not restricted to the "possible or the "real"; it can contain anything the imagination can invent and these imaginary things are considered "true" in the fictional world. Third, fiction authors do not eschew ambiguity in the same way authors of non-fiction are assumed to do; the details and outcome of a story may be deliberately unresolved by the author and unresolvable by the reader (Beghtol 1991, 3).

These are all qualities that pictorial materials strongly share with fiction.

Beghtol suggests that rather than using a summarization approach to fiction, it may be more fruitful to extract various kinds of data elements and to classify individual instances of these elements.[6] She notes that characters, events, spaces, and times may be taken as fundamental elements in fiction; the current research review indicates that these same elements are some of the more typically described attributes in pictorial images as well. She notes that fiction and pictorial images also communicate imaginary, nonexistent, or impossible things, making controlled vocabulary difficult to establish. Some of the problems of ambiguity which Beghtol notes could be solved in both fiction and image indexing by use of the specific and generic levels of indexing, as discussed earlier.

Research on narrative conventions also suggests that some fiction elements are universal. There are a number of systems of narrative analysis. In early work, Jones used a narrative analysis for film, especially in relation to characters and motivations (Jones 1942). Ruthrof proposed that narrative is composed of eight elements: 1) time; 2) space; 3) personae (characters); 4) actions, physical and mental; 5) events (nonhuman); 6) tonal aspects (character's world view and method of interacting with the world); 7) atmospheric aspects; and 8) ideological patterns of identification of the world (Ruthrof 1981). Again, the first five correspond to typical story elements, but the last three lead to a different semantic and interpretive level. Beghtol sees less utility in providing access to the latter three, or to other aspects such as "theme," as she characterizes these as "less like sources of 'data' about a fictional world and more like 'information' constructed from a summation of data elements and possibly further cumulated into 'knowledge'" (Beghtol 1994, 128). However, mood, emotion, and theme are elements that can distinguish images that are almost identical in their factual content, such as objects, events, and settings depicted (e.g., the face of a man at a window can be anguished or threatening).

Affective and Abstract Elements

The more interpretive or abstract attributes, such as atmosphere, theme, and meaning as well as emotions or social status ("role") appear to be important in browsing. The author demonstrated that they are consistently described in a Sorting Task (Jörgensen 1995b). Although not used heavily in describing tasks, when they appear they are also somewhat consistently described at the specific term level. As can be seen in indexing systems such as the *TI* and *ICONCLASS*, they also tend to be very important in an art historical or art object context. While a variety of thesauri provide useful terminology, the *TI* has no English translation, and *ICONCLASS* is extremely specialized and complex. There is thus little consistent access provided to these attributes within current indexing practice. Broad subject access is provided by the use of standard thesauri in libraries and archives or keyword lists in areas such as newspaper indexing (which use broad headings such as "accident," "disaster," "invention," and so forth). CBR methods provide little access to subject, although research efforts in automated analysis of video and audio in narrow areas such as sports or news reporting are producing useful data. Some image retrieval systems have used automatic processing to provide a broad subject categorization, often referred to as an "ontology" (Park and others 2000). Other interpretive aspects are generally not dealt with. As with story elements, commercial image retrieval systems have attempted to address emotive and abstract aspects of images through a searchable free-text description, yet again a lack of structure in the record carries with it the problem of inaccuracy of representation and produces large numbers of nonrelevant items in a search (e.g., "fear" retrieves the place Cape Fear, the movie "Fear," and so on).

New Models and Representations

Abstract elements such as *Theme* and *Symbol* appear to be more important in a browsing search. As empirical research suggests the need to provide access to these affective types of attributes, the question now becomes how to best represent them in an IR system. Given that there are already a number of thesauri available, the first step would be to extend textual indexing methods to a broader range of attributes. However, as noted above, the main barrier here is the notion that these elements are "out of scope" for indexing.

There are several approaches that could be adopted to facilitate access to the interpretive attributes of images. One of the earliest research efforts focused on the problems of iconographical terminology. Markey (1986) tested a process for compiling a thematic catalog of primary and secondary subject matter. She used cluster analysis of composite pre-iconographical descriptions[7] to create clusters in context, which were then interpreted for secondary meaning by iconographers. The clusters and their secondary meaning were used to create a keyword-in-context thematic catalog linking primary and secondary subject matter. The primary use of such a catalog was to enable those who are unfamiliar with themes in art to link descriptive words or phrases to such a theme. Following Markey's suggestions and evidence from Bakewell, interpretive attributes may thus be amenable to a schematic approach, particularly within the field of iconographical analysis (Bakewell 1988). While *ICONCLASS* addresses iconography in detail, the precoordinated phrase approach adopted lacks the flexibility that a schema can allow. This is an area in which research could be particularly fruitful.

A sequenced approach to indexing is another method that could result in more access. Basic information can be described initially; schemas or other representations dealing with abstract elements could be added at a later time to provide access to a wider group of users. This introduces another whole issue, touched upon earlier, that of the "authority" of the indexing record ("getting it right"). In a novel approach, the Fine Arts Museum of San Francisco (FAMSA) added free-text terms provided not by catalogers but by docents to their image records, in an unstructured "word soup" field.[8] This provides the ability for visitors to their website to search on mood terms for images and retrieve images that might otherwise be missed (e.g., "desolate" returns a lithograph by George Biddle, *Death on the Plains*). There have been benefits to curators as well, who have been able to implement exhibits based on themes that were previously unsearchable across the entire collection. Thus, in addition to the notion of "free-text" description, we have the notion of what could be termed "free-range" or distributed description, coming from a variety of human sources.

These ideas introduce the concept of distributed indexing, certainly a foundation that the library community has implemented well. Concepts of authority of the record, however, are paramount within bibliographic communities adopting this approach, and extensive tools and training are necessary to insure acceptable standards of performance. However, this approach also limits the knowledge base that can be drawn on in the application of these tools to only those who have received such training, and excludes a large number of subject specialists from contributing to this process. In addition, it puts a tremendous workload on a small group of professionals, thus frequently narrowing the treatment that any one item can receive to a small set of basic descriptors.

The opening up of indexing to a wider audience has been referred to as "democratic indexing," and has been proposed for works of fiction and implemented in a public library project (Albrechtsen 1997; Gaut and Gaut 1999). Others have suggested this approach for images (Jörgensen 1995b; O'Connor 1996). In a project described by Brown and Hidderley, each image is indexed by users and librarians on different levels, ranging from significant objects within the image to its overall interpretation. The users' indexing terms are reconciled into a public view, which becomes a shared vocabulary of terms associated with the images. Users can search the image database using this shared vocabulary and also by using their own private view of terms (Brown and Hidderley 1996).

When description of materials is opened to a wider audience, there is the potential for a large amount of information to be contributed (for instance, as with popular recipe databases available through the Web). There are two obvious concerns with this approach: the authority or knowledge of the person describing the item, and the correctness of the terminology used for description. However, there are ways to approach both these problems. FAMSA addressed these by using a particular group of knowledgeable participants and by keeping this information in a separate field. With the use of such a field it is important to clearly indicate where this information comes from so that users can make decisions as to its trustworthiness and applicability (as in the project reported by Brown and Hidderley). Additionally, terminology can be controlled by automatically running it against various relevant thesauri and keyword lists. This eliminates inappropriate contributions from a language standpoint, but does not deal with conceptually inappropriate terms. Again, the clear distinction of where this information comes from is important here.

There are several other approaches that could be applied, such as the use of natural language processing of the large body of critical and interpretive work associated with artworks. To the author's knowledge, this approach has not been tested. An early program, SYNONAME, was used for identifying possible forms of a single personal name, for use in matching different versions of personal names.[9] Rose and others (2000) use natural language processing (NLP) techniques to extract linguistic relationships between terms from short image captions assigned by the researchers in a small set of images.[10] With a larger collection and longer descriptions, they note the need to find the right balance between accuracy and the computational overheads that this incurs.

Summary

Table 6.2 summarizes the major groups of image attributes reported as frequently described by participants in a number of research projects. It gives examples of the primary approaches adopted by different communities in providing access to these attributes, as well as suggestions for future approaches to representing these attributes. This table demonstrates that different attributes are being addressed by different communities to varying degrees, and that, for more interpretive and semantic attributes, minimal access is currently being provided.

However, a major component still missing from all the representation techniques and models discussed above is the notion of relationship, or interaction, among image elements. While discussed briefly in the context of spatial location, there are many other types of relationships that need to be expressed (in addition to the simple presence of objects), such as who is doing what and with what and with whom. Keyword indexing does not capture these types of relationships, and leads to many retrieval problems, as is demonstrated in the example queries given by Tam and Leung (2001), searching within the Corbis database (where the goal was to find a picture of a woman *on* a bicycle):

woman bicyclist—six images
woman bicycling—thirteen images (two not relevant)
woman on bicycle—797 screens of hits with nine images per screen. Woman is not on bicycle in many images
woman riding bicycle—820 screens, nine images each, most of which contain either a woman or a bicycle, or neither (Tam and Leung 2001, 932)

There are several tools that are used for the purpose of providing a more structured description. For example, within LIS, string indexing methods use a string or set of indexing terms for each entry. The terms within a string are connected by relationships to each other, according to a set of rules for the specific system. Humans generate the strings, which can then be manipulated to produce multiple access points.

PRECIS (Preserved Context Indexing System), developed by Derek Austin at the British Library in the late 1960s for subject indexing of the British National Bibliography, is a string indexing system which defines a set of roles such as agent or instrument of action, key system (thing towards which action is directed), action or effect of action, and location (Austin 1984). It also includes secondary operators for viewpoint (perspective) and intended audience of the document. Thus terms are arranged and connected by relationships found in the original text or context, rather than from a specific classification scheme. Interest has been expressed in PRECIS as a method for indexing images and image captions (Chipman 1986).

Table 6.2. Current methods representation using textual and machine processing and future approaches, by attribute Classes

Class	Types of Representation		
	Textual Methods	**Machine Methods**	**Future Methods**
OBJECTS	*AAT*; *LCTGM* Domain-specific thesauri	Pattern recognition Machine vision Narrow domains	Visual thesauri Schemas Multimedia thesauri
PEOPLE	LC authority file *ULAN*	Face recognition, Caption processing Associated audio, text processing	Face/Body recognition Face generation
LOCATION	None	CBR techniques	Spatial indexing
COLOR	*AAT*	CBR techniques	Fuzzy retrieval
VISUAL ELEMENTS	*AAT*; *TI*	CBR techniques	Refined CBR techniques
ART HISTORICAL INFO.	*AAT*; *LCTGM*	None	CBR Schemas NLP
STORY	*ICONCLASS*; *LCTGM* Free text Captions	Free-text Caption processing	Schemas Multiple thesauri Distributed indexing NLP
PEOPLE RELATED	"Democratic Indexing," Free-text	Color associations (little) Kansei	Schemas Multiple thesauri Distributed indexing NLP
ABSTRACT	Subject–*LCTGM*, *LCSH*, *DDC*, otherwise little	None	Schemas Multiple thesauri Distributed indexing NLP
DESCRIPTION	Free-text	Free-text	Enduser index terms

Within linguistics and computer science, models for these types of relationships are well developed in the entity–relationship model. An entity is a "thing" that can be identified, and a relationship is an association between such items. While such modeling allows complex relationships to be expressed, it is also time-consuming. A small project cataloging images on two CD-ROMs using an entity–attribute–relationship model took six weeks for 435 images, or just under half an hour per image (Hibler, Leung, and Mannock 1992). Tam and Leung have proposed a structured annotation method utilizing the components Agent,

Action, Object, and Recipient, with optional modifying phrases and Setting, and they implement these components as database fields. Each component may be drawn from an existing thesaurus, ontology, or knowledge base. Tam and Leung note that their structure can accommodate the wide variety of attributes in Jörgensen (1995b) and present examples of how their method can improve precision (Tam and Leung 2001). However, the feasibility of this approach has not been tested on a large scale.

Other methods that could be applied include semantic networks and ontologies. One project uses the notion of structured annotation (with a Who–What–When–Where framework) as an ontology combined with a subject-specific ontology and a generalized ontology (WordNet); this approach requires mapping the relationships between the multiple ontologies (Schreiber and others 2001). Tests against a commercial engine[11] demonstrated that in specific category searches almost identical results are obtained, but with generalized searches the ontologies work better. For instance, searching for an image of an ape with its mouth open showing its teeth requires many keywords, whereas utilizing the ontologies such a query can be precisely formulated. Additionally, use of a domain-specific ontology prevents confusion between concepts such as ape and monkey. Limitations include the inability to specify more than one agent, and user difficulties understanding the ontology-specific default knowledge. The authors note that there is still a long way to go to prove that an ontology-based approach is better (in some respects) than keyword searching.

Given the as yet little-understood nature of similarity in a visual environment, current tools that focus on strictly linguistic relationships among terms and on complex real-world ontologies may need to be reinterpreted for the visual environment. Researchers have found that the application of a generalized subject heading list such as the *LCSH* (constructed upon the structure of language) for the indexing of visual materials is not particularly useful; assumptions about the utility of existing tools in a *visual* environment should be carefully considered.

A Research Agenda for the Future

The above discussion suggests a large number of areas for research. Current research is focusing on several broad areas: cognitive aspects of image perception and understanding, image indexing and classification; image searching and image users and uses; and machine methods for image parsing. There are a number of theoretical and practical questions to be addressed within each research area. While much more research in each of these areas is needed, a broader research agenda should also include investigation of the interplay and complementarities among these facets to enable understanding of more fundamental questions underlying these areas of research, such as the nature of visual similarity and the nature of images. The following list of research areas points to some of the higher-level theoretical questions that need to be addressed, as well as some practical considerations.

Image Perception and Understanding

The Nature of Visual Similarity

An overarching and fundamental question concerns the nature of similarity in a visual environment. While there are current efforts to delineate similarity in a precise mathematical manner, data from the various research projects discussed in Chapter Five reveal that similarity in a visual context encompasses many facets. As noted earlier, similarity among images cannot be represented solely by perceptual attributes but must also take into account the more interpretive attributes. Representing these higher-level attributes precisely using traditional mathematical measures while retaining their complexity is a challenge. Attributes on this level may require other means; the challenge then becomes designing systems that are flexible enough to be able to handle multiple types of representations.

It is useful here to consider the different broad types of searches as well, which may each have their own requirements. When one is conducting a known-item or type-of-item search, the retrieval system should gather together items that share similar and sufficient attributes. In a browsing, or more unfocused search, the requirement may be first to separate the set of items worthy of browsing from the much larger set of less relevant items. However, even with a known-item search, the final determination of value may rest again, not upon similarity, but upon the "critical difference." There is thus a duality of need in intelligent retrieval:

> "Similar" and "different" judgments have been described as qualitatively distinct. . . . "Similar" judgments are seen as holistic, facilitated by processes that unify patterns. All potentially relevant features must be exhaustively examined to determine if two patterns are indeed "similar." In contrast, "different" judgments are viewed as analytical, focusing on discriminating features. When a sufficient number of distinguishing features are found, the process of comparison terminates (Cupchik, Winston, and Herz 1992, 38).

The nature of visual similarity is not well understood, and much research remains to be done in this area. Evidence suggests that human similarity judgments encompass perceptual features such as object name, shape, and color, and traditional aesthetic considerations such as composition, contrast, and complexity, as well as abstract or affective elements such as meaning and emotion. An understanding of the nature of visual similarity requires further research into the essential nature of images and the relationships and interactions among image attributes, the interactions that take place between human and image, and a much more thorough understanding of human needs in image retrieval. Further research in all these areas is necessary to form a foundation for developing coherent and functional methods of representation and systems for image retrieval.

While a host of attributes can contribute to notions of visual similarity, there are some fundamental questions that arise, among them:

1) What are the criteria (both visual and cognitive) that determine what is "visually relevant" or "visually similar"?
2) Are there some attributes that are more influential than others, regardless of other factors? The literature review suggests that color may be one such attribute.
3) What part do other less quantifiable attributes, such as affective impact, symbolic meaning, and other abstract notions, play in human similarity judgments? What methods could be used to quantify these?
4) Can visual similarity be adequately represented by existing mathematical models of similarity?
5) What other factors (task, time, etc.) influence the weightings of both tangible and seemingly intangible attributes in human similarity judgments?

The Nature of Images

The discussion reviews a vast amount of work investigating specific image features and creating methods for processing and representing them, and we have at hand a wide range of image components that can be addressed by these methods. Some work has been done to delineate a conceptual framework for understanding and relating these various features, especially in defining syntactic, semantic, and abstract levels of features. While systems tend to separate these levels, for the human these levels are not always mutually exclusive, as "red" can be understood at the syntactic level as a region color, but also at the semantic level as conveying "danger" or "excitement."

As human cognitive processes do not tend to analyze a single feature or attribute of an image, but appear to utilize Gestalt processes in image understanding, further questions concern the nature and structure of the relationships among individual attributes. Several researchers have conceptualized models as hierarchical structures, such as those for object recognition by component shapes or image composition using pyramidal mappings from syntactic to higher levels. The hierarchical nature of many of the classification tools also limits the number and types of relationships that can be expressed in their vocabulary structure. A number of research questions arise here as well:

1) Is a hierarchical model the most appropriate means for representing relationships among attributes?

2) If a hierarchical model is adopted, what is the nature of the mappings from lower levels to higher levels? Is there a linear relationship among these levels, with semantic object recognition facilitated by perception of lower-level components, or do other factors enter in which overpower the linear model? Are there other intervening levels that we are unaware of?
3) If such a hierarchical structure can reliably be demonstrated to exist, can we then create efficient "dictionaries" of visual components that can be used to build, analyze, and index images?
4) Regardless of the nature of the structure of an image, is there a useful relationship between the structure of an image and its function? Can images be divided into useful and discriminable classes on the basis of structure alone, in the manner of current CBR methods?
5) Is there a "discourse structure" for certain types of images as there is for certain types of text? If such a structure exists, is it (or are parts of it) universal? What part do cultural, social, and media influences play in a visual discourse structure, if indeed it exists?
6) What methods (textual, linguistic, symbolic) can be employed to represent the relationships among image components? Are different methods more appropriate and efficient for different levels of attributes, or for different types of images?

Image Indexing and Classification

Regardless of whether image indexing is accomplished by a human or by machine processing, many basic questions remain to be answered. Although sophisticated computer methods for the representation and retrieval of fundamental image attributes such as color and texture already exist, it is not yet clear what the appropriate role for these methods is in relation to user needs. A related question in feature representation (whether by text or by automated methods) is the extent to which a single method can adequately represent a variety of image features and different levels of features. Some major research questions include:

1) Are existing methods sufficiently general to be applicable to a range of features, or do more refined or specific methods need to be developed for each type of attribute? What other types of feature or image representations could be useful, intuitive, efficient?
2) What are the most effective ways (in terms of efficient use of resources) to combine automated techniques with human indexing or classification?
3) What is the appropriate level of specificity of indexing? Are varying levels of specificity needed for different domains and tasks?
4) What factors enable the economic viability of different methods of indexing to be maintained or maximized?

5) To what extent can and/or should we use existing classifications developed for text-based materials? Are these even appropriate, or should new *visually*-oriented classifications be developed?
6) What types of indexing are necessary for different user groups? Is there a basic level of indexing (such as some of the proposed metadata standards) which would maximize retrieval among diverse user groups and across a variety of tasks?
7) What current text-based tools for image indexing (or portions of them) are appropriate for indexing visual materials in a *generalized* environment such as the Web?
8) Can current text-based tools for image indexing be successfully integrated with automated techniques? What kinds of structures are necessary to accomplish this?
9) Is there a role for distributed indexing in visual retrieval? What changes are necessary in concepts such as authority control if this were to take place?

A lingering theoretical and philosophical question for image indexing and classification is the appropriateness of text-based retrieval for materials in other cognitive modalities than text. Classification questions include the range of image attributes that need to be represented and balancing the representation of domain-specific images meeting specialized needs with the need for a generalized, domain-spanning indexing system for images (paralleling a similar problem in natural language processing). The use of a heuristic, such as situating of image attributes within specific *contexts*, may contribute to a useful elaboration of which of a range of image attributes are amenable to indexing, and what methods may be usefully applied. On a practical implementation level, there is the question of how to balance the access needs of users with time and money constraints on the classification process itself.[12]

The notion of image typologies is related to the topics of classification and indexing. Just as textual materials can represent not only data but a wide range of human thought and creativity, so too can images represent a variety of perceptual content, from raw data, organized information, or creative illustration to "art." And just as text may represent more than one type of communication at a time (for instance, poetry can still communicate information), so too can images be both creative and informative. At present, in the wake of the uniformity and lack of context which keyword searching has imposed on vastly dissimilar types of texts, we are only just beginning to understand that different texts and domains may have different search requirements (Albrechtsen 1993), and that we still have a very imperfect model for textual searching.

Thus, in addition to a sound knowledge of the full range of image attributes and an understanding of user search behaviors in a visual environment, the development of image typologies could provide heuristics for indexing particular types of images, as well as guiding image indexing in a more generalized retrieval context. Some very interesting research has been performed in this area already (Lohse 1994). Other work towards developing image typologies was discussed at a recent conference of the American Society for Information Science and Technology.[13] There needs to be more investigation into the utility of both structural and functional image typologies, especially in relation to such areas as automated partitioning of large imagebases.

Searching for and Using Images

There are still few studies of the cognitive processes involved in searching for an image. These studies are difficult, as they involve a great deal of time and produce a great deal of data. Nevertheless, detailed observations of the search process in a variety of contexts are needed for heightened understanding of the cognitive aspects of searching for images. Similarly, more research is needed investigating different user communities and their unique requirements related to the types of images they use.

Another larger question, which has barely been asked in the community of researchers investigating image retrieval, is the function of the *process* of searching for an image. If the goal of the process is to stimulate and enhance creativity rather than to conduct a precise and efficient search, then methods for browsing or perhaps for revealing unexpected connections or human-centered perspectives would in fact be more appropriate. Research scientists tend to forget that, in the humanities, the process is often at least as important as the product, and the process itself can be used to produce new knowledge and understanding.

Some areas for research include the following:

1) What are the cognitive processes involved in searching for visual materials? Do these processes differ significantly from those involved in searching for other types of information?
2) What are the models that can be developed from observations of these processes? Would these models differ significantly from those developed for text searching, or are there overarching similarities between these two modes?[14]
3) What is the role of the Gestalt processes of perception in understanding images? Could these processes be effectively modeled and integrated into systems for image analysis?
4) What are the similarities and differences among different user *communities* in terms of their cognitive and intellectual processes when searching for images?
5) What is the impact of task upon the search process? Can specific attributes or types of attributes be related to specific types of tasks?
6) Several researchers have proposed indexing of attributes to facilitate

searching from particular points of view. Would providing some predefined points of view which target specific attribute sets of interest to particular groups of users be useful, or prove too limiting?

There are a host of broad systems implementation issues related to users' needs in searching. Questions relating to the total system configuration include aspects of human interaction, and they provide yet another research agenda. While some areas are being investigated, many questions remain unanswered. Some examples follow:

1) What are the most effective and intuitive search methods to provide to a user? Should some search methods, such as those of CBR, be "hidden" from the user because they tend to be difficult to understand and use?
2) How much flexibility in searching should be provided to the user? Is there one "optimal" search interface, or will it vary by task and user community?
3) How many different search methods should be made available? Are users able to navigate successfully between different methods, such as a precisely formulated search and "fuzzy" retrieval?
4) What levels of resolution are necessary for different types of searching, such as a browsing search or a focused search?
5) What are the most effective methods for displaying search results?
6) What are the best methods for determining relevancy ranking of retrieved results in a visual environment?
7) What is the utility of relevance feedback in a visual search, and how much is gained with its implementation?
8) Are the standard measures of precision and recall adequate for measuring retrieval results, or do more "humanly intuitive" measures need to be implemented for visual retrieval?

An additional problem area is the ability to share image information among different organizations and across different computing platforms. A host of metadata initiatives are attempting to accommodate this need, both for textual and visual materials. However, there remain a number of unanswered questions pertaining to metadata generally as a search tool as well:

1) Are existing metadata systems adequate for representing visual materials? How can an appropriate balance between simplicity and complexity in metadata systems be achieved?
2) Mappings across different metadata systems are complex and not one-to-one. How will this affect the end user in searching for visual materials?
3) Is metadata efficient when scaled up to vast collections of digital images? Many metadata representations are themselves complex, yet often fail to capture essential aspects of visual materials.

4) Will visual metadata ultimately fall prey to the same problems associated with indexing and classification (e.g., high level of complexity, time-consuming and expensive, unintuitive to end users)?
5) What is the utility of metadata as a method for interoperability in relation to the costs incurred in producing it?[15]

Machine Methods for Image Parsing

Machine methods include technical aspects such as feature processing, indexing structures, and database architecture, and many technical areas for research were covered in detail in Chapter Four. There is a need for additional methods of representing images and for structuring, organizing, manipulating, supplementing, and using these image representations, but also a need for *evaluating* the results from textual and automated processes. Some interesting and fundamental questions emerge for the image processing community across these methods, especially in relation to issues of users' cognitive and task-related needs in visual searching:

1) Are particular CBR methods more suited (i.e., most pertinent and efficient) to specific types of attributes?
2) Which indexing structures are most efficient in relation to specific types of attributes and processing methods?
3) What is the appropriate level of granularity of analysis when looking for pattern regularities or other specifications of similarity across a set of images? Do these vary by specific type of attribute, image, or task?
4) Can a variety of types of processing data (CBR, text indexing) be efficiently integrated within one record structure?
5) How can "real-time" processing be integrated with static records?
6) Which techniques will scale up well to large imagebases? What are the issues involved in scaling up from test collections to realistic collection size?

Related to the last question, the most critical need for the CBR community is the establishment of reliable methods for the evaluation of existing image indexing and retrieval methods (discussed in detail in Chapter Four). At present, there is no way to evaluate the effects of different techniques for image indexing, representation, and retrieval, as systems use different test sets of images and rely on a variety of algorithms combined in different ways. Currently, image testbeds are generally a sample of convenience (i.e., what is readily available), or limited to a specific domain within the context of the needs of specific research projects and funding requests. In addition, there are variations in measures of system functionality. While the literature of CBR is vast, the lack of methods and tools for evaluating and comparing systems contributes to duplication of effort and a slowing of progress in this important research area.

One recent advance by image researchers is the realization that progress depends upon the consideration of image indexing within a larger framework that includes the image, the system, and the user. Answers to the questions outlined above could facilitate practical system implementations which match users' unique and group needs with pertinent attribute-set indexing, and a variety of searching behaviors could also be accommodated within a flexible interface design.

A Wish List for the Future

There are probably as many wish lists for the future of image retrieval as there are researchers in this area. For this author, several broad key issues and needs have emerged through the years, shaped by experience and interactions with researchers across several communities. This short list represents a personal perspective, and is offered here as food for thought and future discussion.

A Testbed for Evaluation

As discussed above, comparative evaluation of methods has been acknowledged as critical for advancements in image retrieval. One factor hampering evaluation is the lack of a suitably diverse and large image testbed. The domains of the testbed content should address the needs of two communities, real-world users of images, and the research community performing system evaluations. Thus, to ensure both reliability and validity of testing results, the content should be grounded in the reality of image communities who make heavy use of images in their jobs, as well as providing suitable testing material for a variety of techniques. An "ideal" testbed would incorporate large numbers of images from diverse broad and narrow domains (particular features and areas of interest are listed for each domain):

1) Natural science images (color; low-level features; variety of objects, such as animals, flowers; multiple viewpoints)
2) Historical photographs (black-and-white or color; structure; variety of viewpoints; semantics; narrative)
3) Art images, pictorial and abstract (color; low-level features; structure; highly semantic)
4) Consumer/Web/advertising photos/graphic images (highly diverse: indoor/outdoor, faces, natural scenes; semantic to highly semantic)
5) Textures (black-and-white; structure–regions)
6) Aerial photographs (black-and-white or color; low-level features; structure; semantic inference and mapping)

A second testbed component, and one of the most difficult faced by researchers in image retrieval, is the establishment of a meaningful set of benchmark queries. The standard query has frequently taken the form of retrieving more images similar to a query image. This is a rather imprecise query, as it does not specify the *level* of similarity upon which retrieval should be based. Developing more meaningful queries runs into the problem of needing to use queries which are appropriate for the particular test set of images, as it is of no use to search for images of an apple when there are none in the test set (a problem which is further exacerbated by the small size of many testbed sets).

Four factors need to be taken into consideration when developing queries:

1) The level of retrieval to be tested (feature, structure, object, or semantic)
2) Performance level (queries should test both performance and retrieval performance levels). At the retrieval performance level, queries should span a range of types (single word to more complex phrase) and be created within the context of knowledge about how real humans query image retrieval systems (humans generally prefer to query at higher semantic levels).
3) Uni- or cross-domain queries
4) User community (queries should be both narrow and broad, to address the retrieval needs within single domains represented in the database and to represent retrieval across the entire database)

A consistent methodology for developing queries is necessary to remove the ad hoc nature from which current testbed queries (and their resultant retrieval) often suffer. Once a database is developed, various communities could be solicited to contribute existing queries or to develop queries for the project.

The development of ground-truth relevance scores is another component of a testbed. These have also been problematic, primarily because of the amount of time involved for humans to evaluate similarity among images in a large image collection. There are several approaches that could both assist in this process and provide more complete descriptions of similarity than the largely global measures in widespread use today. Several papers have proposed using a TREC-like pooling of results from lower-level CBR processing (Jörgensen 2001; Müller and others 2001; Smith 2001). However, pooling based on lower-level features currently addresses the feature and structure levels, with very limited object access and no semantic access. Using this output as an input set for human similarity judgments further guarantees the accuracy of the image similarity but only *within the same levels.*

Given our present techniques, in order to obtain similarity judgments for higher semantic levels referring to objects, events, activities, and other aspects of images, some additional text-based indexing is needed. This, however, generally has been avoided for several reasons. It has been regarded not only as highly problematic (from the standpoints of subjectivity and indexer consistency), but nearly impossible within the context of large numbers of images. In what some may consider a best-case scenario, text already accompanies images, in which case descriptors are available and ambiguity is reduced. Techniques for text and caption processing are being developed, and these techniques could assist in enhanced indexing. However, it must be noted that these captions or associated text are also developed within particular publishing contexts, and may have only limited or domain-specific information.

Thus, thoughtful attention should be paid to the personnel involved in developing such a testbed. For instance, content and metadata managers should have a broad understanding of the issues involved from multiple disciplinary perspectives. Indexing (both human and machine) is an essential component for the project. For a benchmarking project to be successful, an understanding of user communities and user needs in searching is also essential. When one starts studying users, it quickly becomes apparent that they "want it all," but an understanding of specific needs related to varying levels of feature description should open the door to increased efficiencies in providing access and retrieval.

The need for a testbed has been discussed in some detail as the development of its components are directly related to most of the other "wish list" items discussed below.

A Visual Indexing Language

Chapter Three reviewed the various vocabularies available for describing image content. To briefly reiterate, the type of indexing generally applied to an image collection is designed to serve the specific user community responsible for the collection or for whom the collection is created, and is often composed of a specialized language for that community. Thus, the tools created for indexing in these environments are somewhat narrowly conceived. This is demonstrated by study results that show that many organizations concerned with providing access to images express dissatisfaction with these vocabularies and use locally developed systems as supplementary tools (Graham 1999).

A factor increasing the need for additional indexing is the increasingly large number of digitization projects taking place and the new user communities that such projects bring to a collection. With networked access to image collections the user community is becoming much more diversified: an artist may seek inspiration through scientific images such as optical mineralogy specimens. An author or a student wishes to find an illustration communicating a particular feeling to illustrate a story or poem. The examples are as numerous as the number of people searching for images. Thus, a generalized indexing vocabulary covering a wide range of everyday objects, people, and events, as well as their relationships and meanings, would be a useful adjunct to current vocabulary tools to increase the accessibility of these collections. It would be worthwhile to develop such a vocabulary relying heavily on visual materials as source material ("visual warrant," as opposed to literary warrant), as specific visual relationships and a method for describing them need to be included as well (see, for instance, Drucker and McGann's 2001 discussion on metagraphic logic).

A related problem is the issue of expressing relationships among visual items within an image. Entity-relationship modeling has been used in experimental work, and the types of relationships capable of being expressed using this or similar tools seem to be essential, yet research is still needed to determine which are the most important relationships in relation to visual similarity.

The idea of indexing images using text seems to many hopelessly old-fashioned and inefficient in the face of newer automated techniques for processing. However, at this point there has also been very little funded research directed towards applicable "human technologies," so a lack of attention and progress in this area is not unexpected. The author contends that the problems associated with text indexing are tractable if held within a carefully conceived framework. For the foreseeable future, some form of text indexing is necessary to bridge the gap among the various levels comprising image content and among the automated techniques addressing these levels, as well as to address the higher-level semantic content of images. Research funding could indeed advance progress in these human technologies.

An Integrated Indexing Record

From the standpoint of a user searching for an image containing a red apple, it makes no difference how the notion of the color red is determined to exist within a particular image (by text term, histogram, etc.) or whether the notion of apple is represented by the word, a vector, an XML tag, or some other means. The user simply wishes to find an appropriate image. The user also does not appreciate a search which returns, in addition to red apples, red balls, red balloons, and so forth. The searcher simply hopes that the search returns all relevant material. With the wealth of techniques at hand, the development of an integrated record that can accommodate multiple types of data from both human and machine processes would begin to address user needs more completely. However, the user must not be given the additional burden of needing to understand how these different techniques work in order to use them; the behind-the-scenes processing must be transparent.

From the standpoint of furthering research, the creation of systems that can accommodate descriptions derived from both manual and automatic processes is especially critical. There are a number of important research questions that can be addressed only within the context of image records containing multiple sources of information. For instance, as mentioned earlier, there remains a vast gap in our understanding of the relationships between the lower-level perceptual features and higher-level interpretive or semantic features. The creation of a large number of image records containing detailed information about the image on syntactic, semantic, and higher levels could facilitate the search for patterns of relationships, connections, and regularities among the attributes and for mapping these across levels. Regularities could suggest possible heuristics for inference, which could reduce the need for further processing. Integrated descriptions could also help in the determination of which attributes can be most efficiently addressed by machine methods or by human processes.

Many other topics could be researched within such a rich context, such as whether there are regularities that would suggest predictable relationships between image structure and function, or between structure and image type.

Widening Communities of Research and Practice

In order to accomplish these wish-list items, new approaches to research are necessary. The creation and funding of truly interdisciplinary research teams is essential to bring together the wide-ranging types of expertise necessary to solve these problems. There has generally been a myopic tendency among the various communities of researchers, using primarily familiar sources and their own collegial networks to situate their research questions and agendas. In the same way that having one favored tool determines the methods used to solve a problem, having one favored perspective determines the very questions that can be asked. There are a variety of problems to be solved in addition to indexing and retrieval (e.g., storage, manipulation, migration, preservation, etc.), each benefiting from different kinds and levels of expertise.

For the CBR community, a necessary next step for advancement involves not only establishing tools and methods for both objective and user-oriented evaluation of such systems, but a widening of the primary community involved in both evaluation efforts *and* in the initial specification and creation of these systems. Similarly, within the LIS community, practitioners need to be able to communicate the needs of their patrons to researchers effectively, and with the realization that there may be multiple ways to solve the problems of retrieval. Researchers in all areas need to learn to formulate their research questions in a variety of ways and from different perspectives.

In addition to multidisciplinary teams, multinational research teams should be developed. Recently, the National Science Foundation has been encouraging international research efforts; more of this support needs to take place, especially given tools (such as the Web) which now exist to facilitate research. Cognitive psychologists may wish to begin considering more thoroughly the role and impact of such factors as emotion and culture in visual perception and processing. Researchers in CBR may profit from looking at the last decade of classification research to come out of Scandinavia. Classification researchers may also wish to consider *kansei* research in Japan. New approaches to database design and the incorporation of a variety of new techniques within databases are coming out of Europe and Australia.

A complementary effort would include a widening of communities of practice, especially in the area of textual description of images. While questions of authority dominate discussions of most indexing and classification practice (whether explicitly or implicitly), other voices argue for the value of multiple perspectives. For example, many popular feedback tools are emerging in such commercial contexts as book reviews (Amazon.com) or recipe reviews (Epicurious.com), with end users being able to add their own comments to a book description or recipe. As discussed earlier, some image databases have experimented with input from other groups besides catalogers (e.g., www.thinker.org). There is great potential for rich image descriptions by allowing input from a variety of users, both expert and nonexpert, as long as users understand the nature of the description and where the descriptions are coming from. In addition to description of image content, these methods could allow access to other aspects of images, such as function, story, and affect, which are usually considered out of scope.

Usable, Flexible Interfaces

How would the "ideal" image retrieval system work, from the end user's point of view? There have been some descriptions by art historians of features they would like (Bakewell 1988), but there have been few user studies and almost no others asking for descriptions of ideal systems by end users. However, it is often not useful to ask users what they want, as they frequently have no idea of what the possibilities are. Even when a researcher is familiar with a broad range of techniques, it is difficult to imagine the possibilities outside of the design boundaries of current information retrieval systems. With these caveats, the author offers a description of some capabilities that an ideal image indexing and retrieval system would include. The discussion brings forward a whole host of interface and usability issues which have not been covered in detail in this review; needless to say, these constitute another entire research agenda in their own right. It would be useful to explore some of these interface methods, even if the tools which are necessary to support these interactions are not yet available or efficient, as information about users' preferred modes of interaction may suggest which indexing and retrieval methods should be focused upon.

The most obvious modification to current systems is the addition of a suite of search tools for the end user, including the ability to search by text and by various automated methods in a seamless environment. The existence of an integrated record as described above and efficient search tools and indexing structures within an appropriate database structure is assumed for this discussion. Thus, these methods differ from current implementations, which allow several types of searching but limit the fields or records searched according to the type of input. The choice of search method (automated or text) would not limit the fields searched, but would return all items containing "red" regardless of how or where it is represented within the image record or within the database.

For text searching, the interface would include the standard methods of typing in a text term or choosing from a list of controlled vocabulary. If desired, the user should be able to initially narrow a search using several parameters, such as color or black-and-white, or image format, or image collection. In addition to searching for image records containing a particular feature, the user would be able to "localize" text terms spatially by dragging and placing them on a blank image. Indexing records would include coordinates or other spatial locators for text terms, allowing an efficient spatial image description using only text. Indexing could be accomplished using the same direct manipulation techniques, choosing a word from a list and dragging it onto a template.

Visual search tools would also be provided as a complement to text searching. In addition to some of the tools already in use, such as specifying overall color composition, basic shapes, textures, and colors could be pulled from a palette and placed on a template or "easel," allowing a user to build a visual search query. Palettes could be designed for specific domains (such as costume, medicine, natural history). Tools such as these can compensate for a user's lack of familiarity with a particular vocabulary associated with a specific domain. Searchers could also use direct manipulation methods, being able to segment and rearrange components from one or more images on an easel or within a single image, and using this reconstituted image as input (a variation on the "get more like this" query method). Users should also have available the basic drawing tools (line tool, color, etc.) to construct an image query. Again, these methods could be used as tools for image indexing as well.

Queries should also be able to be formulated using the "get more like this" scenario, but it could be advantageous to be able to formulate a query using several images. The utility and limitations of relevance feedback methods needs to be explored in more depth, however, before these techniques are adopted.

These methods would work well for known-item or well-formulated queries, or for exploring the range of content that may be contained within a system. Additional browsing capabilities, under the control of the user, could take advantage of expanded indexing records, with other factors, such as potential uses of images, emotional reactions, or "stories" that images convey being accessible for searching and browsing. These descriptions can be contributed by multiple parties. Tools would also need to be available which would allow users to find more images created by the same person or organization, or more images from the same repository. Searches should be able to be expanded to provide additional contexts surrounding the production of an image (historical, social, cultural, biographical), drawing upon additional textual sources as resources of information.

Methods of interaction could include the familiar and comfortable (for many) keyboard, a drawing palette or other direct drawing tools, the use of a touch-sensitive screen, or the use of a scanner for input. One can even imagine a virtual reality scenario with the searcher using a data glove to pluck elements from images and reassemble them into a query on a floating "easel," or assembling three-dimensional queries.

The components of this wish list themselves represent a vast research agenda. While in many cases the user interaction methods are usually tacked on towards the end of the design process, it may be useful to refocus and start with the endpoint, the user's desired methods of interaction. By doing this, researchers could elicit valuable parameters for designing and constructing the rest of an image retrieval system.

Conclusion

While image indexing and retrieval may seem a narrow area of interest within information retrieval research, it is an area worthy of more attention than it has received, as the issues associated with access to a range of image facets have implications for the indexing and retrieval of all of stored knowledge, in whatever modality. As Neill notes:

> The history of the development of intellectual access to the store of knowledge is a history of the tension between the fluid uniqueness of the individual inquirer and the essential stability and concreteness of the store of knowledge itself. One of the most important problems facing the next generation of librarians will be the relative "fluidity" of information stored electronically. . . . There is, of course, the promise . . . that the fluidity of the computer will be a more appropriate store of knowledge for the searching process of the unique and fluid inquirer (Neill 1987, 208).

The promise will be fulfilled when the various research communities and communities of practice begin to work together to address some of the issues and challenges discussed in this book. In spite of the difficult nature of some of these problems, the research arena is a fascinating and stimulating one. A few researchers are dipping their toes in the waters of interdisciplinary inquiry; the author hopes that this book will stimulate new conversations and new lines of investigation, and inspire more researchers to take a collaborative plunge into the interdisciplinary ocean of image retrieval research.

Notes

1. The user, is, of course, simply concerned with "getting it."

2. There are obvious concerns expressed about this wider access to images as well. For instance, see Besser's (1997) discussion on issues such as the possible erosion of the authority of the museum and its curators, and issues related to authorship, authenticity, and the commodification of images. On the positive side, Besser notes a potential democratizing effect and the shift from viewing to interacting.

3. See www.mda.org.uk/bmobj/Objintro.htm.

4. Tom Gullo, conversation with author, New York City, New York, December 29, 1994.

5. Susanne Humphrey, telephone conversation with author, November 15, 1993.

6. For an in-depth discussion, see Beghtol (1994).

7. Preiconographical or primary subject matter included objects (things and people), expressional qualities (effects, feeling states, sensations, and psychological nuances), and events (actions and goings-on).

8. Bob Futernick, conversation with author, Boston, Mass., November 20, 2001. See www.thinker.org/ (accessed on April 18, 2003).

9. Copyright J. Paul Getty Trust. See ftp://clr.nmsu.edu/CLR/tools/ling-analysis/synoname/ (accessed on April 18, 2003).

10. See also Chapter Four for other work in this area.

11. The search engine in use at gettyone.com at the time.

12. Because of its time-consuming nature, one problem often cited with text-based classification is the expense involved. However, one can note with some irony the vast amounts of money that are spent researching and developing automated methods. While a number of interesting prototype systems exist, there is as yet no efficient, usable system in sight. There is no telling what advances could be made in classification research and automated support for the classification process if similar levels of research support were available to this community.

13. Panel presentations on "Theory and Practice in the Indexing and Retrieval of Images and other Visuo-Spatial Data." American Society for Information Science Annual Conference, 1998.

14. While the differences in searching for text and images are widely assumed, because of the physiological differences in perceptual processes, there is little empirical evidence demonstrating that such a difference actually exists. This issue is related to the discussions within cognitive psychology as to whether there are different representations in memory for visual and verbal input ("dual-coding theory").

15. These are unanswered questions for metadata production regardless of whether it is for textual, visual, or other types of material.

Bibliography

Aigrain, P., Hong-Jiang Zhang, and D. Petkovic. "Content-Based Representation and Retrieval of Visual Media: A State of the Art Review." *Multimedia Tools and Applications* 3 (1996): 179–202.

Aks, Deborah J., and Julien C. Sprott. "Quantifying Aesthetic Preference for Chaotic Patterns." *Empirical Studies of the Arts* 14, no. 1 (1996): 1–16.

Albrechtsen, Hanne. "Subject Analysis and Indexing: From Automated Indexing to Domain Analysis." *The Indexer* 18, no. 4 (1993): 219–224.

Albrechtsen, Hanne. "The Order of Catalogues: Towards Democratic Classification and Indexing in Public Libraries." A paper delivered at the 63rd IFLA (International Federation of Library Associations and Institutions) General Conference, August 31–September 5, 1997.

Al-Khatib, Wasfi, Y. Francis Day, Arif Ghafoor, and P. Bruce Berra. "Semantic Modeling and Knowledge Representation in Multimedia Databases." *IEEE Transactions on Knowledge and Data Engineering* 11, no. 1 (1999): 64–80.

Allen, Bryce L. "Cognitive Research in Information Science: Implications for Design." In *Annual Review of Information Science and Technology*, ed. Martha E. Williams, Vol. 26, 3–37. Medford, N.J.: Learned Information, 1991.

Aloimonos, Y., I. Weiss, and A. Bandopadhay. "Active Vision." *International Journal of Computer Vision* 2, no. 1 (1988): 333–356.

Alvarado, Christine, and Randall Davis. "A Framework for Multi-Domain Sketch Recognition." A paper delivered at the AAAI Spring Symposium on Sketch Understanding, Stanford University, Palo Alto, California, March 25–27, 2002.

American Library Association. Joint Steering Committee for Revision of AACR. *Anglo-American Cataloging Rules, Second Edition (AACR2).* Vol. 2. 2nd ed. Chicago, Ill.: 1998.

Anderson, John R. *Cognitive Psychology and Its Implications*. 3rd ed. New York: W. H. Freeman and Company, 1990.

Ando, Michiyo. "Adults' and Children's Recognition of Items Added to or Deleted from Scenes: Salience, Complexity, and Unnaturalness." *Perceptual and Motor Skills* 90, no. 3, pt. 2 (2000): 1113–1121.

Anstis, Stuart, and V. S. Ramachandran. "2-D or Not 2-D: That Is the Question." In *The Artful Eye*, ed. R. Gregory, J. Harris, P. Heard, and D. Rose, 249–267. New York: Oxford University Press, 1995.

Antes, James R. "The Time Course of Picture Viewing." *Journal of Experimental Psychology* 103 (1974): 62–70.

Antes, James R., and J. G. Penland. "Picture Context Effects on Eye Movement Patterns." In *Eye Movements: Cognition and Visual Perception*, ed. D. F. Fisher, R. A. Monty, and J. W. Senders, 157–170. Hillsdale, N.J.: Lawrence Erlbaum Associates, 1981.

Armitage, Linda H., and Peter G. B. Enser. "Analysis of User Need in Image Archives." *Journal of Information Science* 23, no. 4 (1997): 287–299.

Arnheim, Rudolf. *Toward a Psychology of Art.* Los Angeles: University of California Press, 1966.

Arnheim, Rudolf. *Art and Visual Perception: A Psychology of the Creative Eye*. Berkeley, Calif.: University of California Press, 1974.

Arnheim, Rudolf. "Dynamics and Invariants." In *Perceiving Artworks*, ed. John Fisher, 166–184. Philadelphia: Temple University Press, 1980.

Arthur, April G., and Hedy White. "Children's Assignment of Gender to Animal Characters in Pictures." *Journal of Genetic Psychology* 157, no. 3 (1996): 297–301.

Aslandogan, Y. Alp, Chuck Thier, Clement T. Yu, C. Liu, and K. Nair. "Design, Implementation, and Evaluation of SCORE." A paper delivered at the IEEE–ICDE 95, March 1995.

Aslandogan, Y. Alp, Chuck Thier, Clement T. Yu, Jon Zou, and Naphtali Rishe. "Using Semantic Contents and WordNet™ in Image Retrieval." A paper delivered at the ACM SIGIR 97, Philadelphia, Pa., 1997.

Association for Library Collections and Technical Services. *Guidelines for Subject Analysis of Audiovisual Materials*. Chicago, Ill.: American Library Association, 1997.

Athitsos, V., M. Swain, and C. Frankel. "Distinguishing Photographs and Graphics on the World Wide Web." A paper delivered at the Workshop in Content-Based Access to Image and Video Libraries, San Juan, Puerto Rico, 1997.

Attneave, F. "Some Informational Aspects of Visual Perception." *Psychological Review* 61 (1954): 81–88.

Aumont, Jacques. *The Image*. Translated by Claire Pajackowska. London: British Film Institute, 1997.

Austin, Derek. *PRECIS: A Manual of Concept Analysis and Subject Indexing*. London: The British Library Bibliographic Services Division, 1984.

Avital, Tsion, and Gerald C. Cupchik. "Perceiving Hierarchical Structures in Nonrepresentational Paintings." *Empirical Studies of the Arts* 16, no. 1 (1998): 59–70.

Baca, Murtha. "Evaluating the Use of Controlled Vocabularies on the VISION Project." *Visual Resources Association Bulletin* 27, no. 1 (2000): 44–48.

Baca, Murtha. "Review of 'Dutch Printer's Devices 15th–17th Century.'" In *eSpectra*: Museum Computer Network, n.d.

Baddeley, A. D. *Working Memory*: New York: Oxford University Press, 1986.

Baeza-Yates, Ricardo, and Berthier Ribeiro-Neto. *Modern Information Retrieval*. New York: ACM Press, 1999.

Baker, Sharon L. "Will Fiction Classification Schemes Increase Use?" *RQ* 27, Spring (1988): 366–376.

Bakewell, Elizabeth. *Object, Image, Inquiry: The Art Historian at Work*, ed. Marilyn Schmitt. Santa Monica, Calif.: Art History Information Program (AHIP), 1988.

Ballard, D. H., and C. M. Brown. "Principles of Animate Vision." *Computer Vision, Graphics, and Image Processing (CVGIP): Image Understanding* 56, no. 1 (1992): 3–21.

Ballesteros, Soledad, ed. *Cognitive Approaches to Human Perception*. Hillsdale, N.J.: Lawrence Erlbaum Associates, 1994.

Barry, Ann Marie. *Visual Intelligence: Perception, Image, and Manipulation in Visual Communication*. Albany: State University of New York Press, 1997.

Barthes, Roland. *Image, Music, Text*. New York: Hill and Wang, 1977.

Bartlett, F. C. *Remembering*. Cambridge, England: Cambridge University Press, 1932.

Bates, Marcia J. "The Design of Browsing and Berrypicking Techniques for the Online Search Interface." *Online Review* 13 (1989): 407–424.

Batley, Susan. "Visual Information Retrieval: Browsing Strategies in Pictorial Databases." Ph.D. thesis, University of Aberdeen, 1988.

Beard, David Volk. "Computer Human Interaction for Image Information Systems." *Journal of the American Society for Information Science (JASIS)* 42, no. 8 (1991): 600–608.

Bearman, David. "Can MARC Accommodate Archives and Museums?" In *Beyond the Book: Extending MARC for Subject Access*, ed. Toni Petersen and Pat Molholt. Boston, Mass.: G. K. Hall & Co., 1990.

Bechhofer, S. *STARCH: Introduction.* University of Manchester, 1998. Accessed February 21, 2001 from potato.cs.man.ac.uk/starch/motivation.htm.

Bechhofer, S., and C. Goble. "Classification Based Navigation and Retrieval for Picture Archives." A paper delivered at the 8th International Federation for Information Processing (IFIP) Conference on Data Semantics (DS-8), Rotorua, New Zealand, January 1999.

Beck, C., and G. T. Jones. "Bias and Archaeological Classification." *American Antiquity* 54 (1989): 244–262.

Beck, J. "Effect of Orientation and of Shape Similarity on Perceptual Grouping." *Perception and Psychophysics* 1 (1966): 300–302.

Beckmann, N. "The *R**-tree: An Efficient and Robust Access Method for Points and Rectangles." *Association for Computing Machinery Special Interest Group on Management of Data (SIGMOD) Record* 19, no. 2 (1990): 322–331.

Beghtol, Clare. "The Classification of Fiction." In *American Society for Information Science SIG/CR News (Special Interest Group/Classification Research News)*, 3–4, 1991.

Beghtol, Clare. *The Classification of Fiction: The Development of a System Based on Theoretical Principles*. Metuchen, N.J.: Scarecrow Press, 1994.

Bellas, Elizabeth. "Subject Access to Visual Images: The Online Horizon from Where We Stand." A paper delivered at the Art Libraries Society of North America 27th Annual Conference, Vancouver, B.C., Canada, March 27, 1999. Available from www.arlisna.org/Conf_1999/subjacc.htm (accessed on April 23, 2003).

Benitez, Ana B., and John R. Smith. "New Frontiers for Intelligent Content-Based Retrieval." A paper delivered at the Storage and Retrieval for Media Databases conferernce, San Jose, Calif., 2001.

Benitez, Ana B., John R. Smith, and Shih-Fu Chang. "MediaNet: A Multimedia Information Network for Knowledge Representation." A paper delivered at the Internet Multimedia Management Systems conference, Boston, Mass, 2000.

Bergen, J. R. "Theories of Visual Texture Perception." In *Vision and Visual Dysfunction*, ed. D. Regan, Vol. 10B, 114–134. New York: Macmillan, 1991.

Bergen, J. R., and M. S. Landy. "Computational Modeling of Visual Texture Segregation." In *Computational Models of Visual Processing*, ed. M. S. Landy and J. A. Movshon, 253–271. Cambridge, Mass.: MIT Press, 1991.

Berlin, B., and P. Kay. *Basic Color Terms*. Berkeley: University of California Press, 1969.

Berlyne, D. E. "The Influence of Complexity and Novelty in Visual Figures on Orienting Responses." *Journal of Experimental Psychology* 55 (1958): 289–296.

Berlyne, D. E. *Aesthetics and Psychobiology*. New York: Appleton-Century-Crofts, 1971.

Berlyne, D. E. "Uniformity in Variety: Extension to Three-Element Visual Patterns and Non-Verbal Measures." *Canadian Journal of Psychology* 26, no. 3 (1972): 277–291.

Berlyne, D. E. *Studies in the New Experimental Aesthetics*. New York: Wiley, 1974.

Berlyne, D. E. "Psychological Aesthetics." In *Handbook of Cross-Cultural Psychology*, ed. H. C. Triandis and W. J. Lonner, Vol. 3, 323–361. Boston, Mass.: Allyn and Bacon, 1980.

Berretti, S., A. Del Bimbo, and P. Pala. "Retrieval by Shape Similarity with Perceptual Distance and Effective Indexing." *IEEE Transactions on Multimedia* 2, no. 4 (2000): 225–239.

Bertino, Elisa, Barbara Catania, and Elena Ferrari. "Multimedia IR: Models and Languages." In *Modern Information Retrieval*, ed. Ricardo Baeza–Yates and Berthier Ribeiro-Neto, 325–343. New York: ACM Press, 1999.

Besser, Howard. "Imaging: Fine Arts." *Journal of the American Society for Information Science (JASIS)* 42, no. 8 (1991): 589–596.

Besser, Howard. "The Changing Role of Photographic Collections with the Advent of Digitization." In *The Wired Museum: Emerging Technology and Changing Paradigms*, ed. Katherine Jones-Garmil, 153–169. Washington, D.C.: American Association of Museums, 1997.

Besser, Howard, and Marily Snow. "Access to Diverse Collections in University Settings: The Berkeley Dilemma." In *Beyond the Book: Extending MARC for Subject Access*, ed. Toni Petersen and Pat Molholt, 203–224. Boston: G. K. Hall, 1990.

Betz, Elizabeth W. *Subject Headings Used in the Library of Congress Prints and Photographs Division*. Washington, D.C.: Prints and Photographs Division, Library of Congress, 1980.

Biederman, Irving. "Perceiving Real-World Scenes." *Science* 177 (1972): 77–80.

Biederman, Irving. "On the Semantics of a Glance at a Scene." In *Perceptual Organization*, ed. M. Kubovy and J. R. Pomerantz. Hillsdale N.J.: Erlbaum Associates, 1981.

Biederman, Irving. "Recognition-by-Components: A Theory of Human Image Understanding." *Psychological Review* 94, no. 2 (1987): 115–147.

Biederman, Irving, and Ginny Ju. "Surface versus Edge-Based Determinants of Visual Recognition." *Cognitive Psychology* 20 (1988): 38–64.

Biederman, Irving, A. L. Glass, and E. W. Stacy. "Searching for Objects in Real-World Scenes." *Journal of Experimental Psychology* 97 (1973): 22–27.

Biederman, Irving, Robert J Mezzanotte, and Jan C. Rabinowitz. "Scene Perception: Detecting and Judging Objects Undergoing Relational Violations." *Cognitive Psychology* 14, no. 2 (1982): 143–177.

Biederman, Irving, E. Beiring, G. Ju, and T. Blickle. *A Comparison of the Perception of Partial vs. Degraded Objects*. Buffalo: State University of New York at Buffalo, 1985. Unpublished manuscript.

Birren, Faber. *Principles of Color*. New York: Van Nostrand Reinhold, 1969.

Bjarnestam, Anna. "Description of an Image Retrieval System." A paper delivered at the The Challenge of Image Retrieval, Newcastle upon Tyne, England, February 5, 1998.

Bjorklund, D. F. *Children's Thinking: Developmental Function and Individual Differences*. Pacific Grove, Calif.: Brooks Cole, 1989.

Black, John A., and Sethuraman Panchanathan. "Using a Model of the Human Visual System to Identify and Enhance Object Contours in Natural Images." A paper delivered at the Image and Video Communications and Processing Conference, San Jose, Calif., 2000.

Blank, Paula, Christine Massey, Howard Gardner, and Ellen Winer. "Perceiving What Paintings Express." In *Cognitive Processes in the Perception of Art*, ed. W. R. Crozier and A. J. Chapman, 19, 127–143. Amsterdam: Elsevier, 1984.

Borges, Marilyn A., Mary A. Stepnowski, and Leland H. Holt. "Recall and Recognition of Words and Pictures by Adults and Children." *Bulletin of the Psychonomic Society* 9, no. 2 (1977): 113–114.

Bornstein, M. H. "Perceptual Categories in Vision and Audition." In *Categorical Perception: The Groundwork of Cognition*, ed. S. Harnad. New York: Cambridge University Press, 1987.

Boucart, Muriel, and Glyn W. Humphreys. "Integration of Physical and Semantic Information in Object Processing." *Perception* 26, no. 9 (1997): 1197–1209.

Boucart, Muriel, Glyn W. Humphreys, and J. Lorenceau. "Automatic Access to Object Identity: Attention to Global Information, Not to Particular Physical Dimensions, Is Important." *Journal of Experimental Psychology: Human Perception and Performance* 18 (1995): 584–601.

Brant, Linda, Philip H. Marshall, and Bret Roark. "On the Development of Prototypes and Preferences." *Empirical Studies of the Arts* 13, no. 2 (1995): 161–170.

Bray, Tim, and Dan Brickley. *What is RDF?* O'Reilly & Associates, 2000. Available from www.xml.com/pub/a/2001/01/24/rdf.html (accessed on April 20, 2003).

Brewer, W. F., and J. C. Treyens. "Role of Schemata in Memory for Places." *Cognitive Psychology* 13, no. 2 (1981): 193–209.

Brink, A., S. Marcus, and V. S. Subrahmanian. "Heterogeneous Multimedia Reasoning." *Computer* 28, no. 9 (1995): 33–39.

Brolio, John, B. A. Draper, J. R. Beveridge, and A. R. Hanson. "ISR: A Database for Symbolic Processing in Computer Vision." *Computer* 22, no. 12 (1989): 22–30.

Brown, P., and G. R. Hidderley. "The Democratic Indexing of Images." *The New Review of Hypermedia and Multimedia* 2 (1996): 107–120.

Bruce, Vicki, and Andy Young. *In the Eye of the Beholder: The Science of Face Perception*. New York: Oxford University Press, 1998.

Bruner, Jerome S. "Going beyond the Information Given." In *Contemporary Approaches to Cognition*, ed. H. Gruber, E. Brunswik, L. Festinge, F. Heider, K. F. Muenzinger, C. E. Osgood, and D. Rapaport, 41–69. Cambridge, Mass.: Harvard University Press, 1957.

Bruner, Jerome S. *Beyond the Information Given: Studies in the Psychology of Knowing*. New York: W. W. Norton & Company, 1973.

Brunskill, Jeff, and Corinne Jörgensen. "Image Attributes: A Study of Scientific Diagrams." A paper delivered at the 65th Annual Meeting of the American Society for Information Science, Philadelphia, Pa., November 2002.

Buckland, M. K. "On Types of Search and the Allocation of Library Resources." *Journal of the American Society for Information Science* 30, no. 1 (1979): 143–147.

Buckner, Randy L., Marcus E. Raichle, Francis M. Miezin, and Steve E. Petersen. "Functional Anatomic Studies of Memory Retrieval for Auditory Words and Visual Pictures." *Journal of Neuroscience* 16, no. 19 (1996): 6219–6235.

Burnham, Denis K., Lynda J. Earnshaw, and Maria C. Quinn. "The Development of the Categorical Identification of Speech." In *Perceptual Development in Early Infancy: Problems and Issues*, ed. Beryl E. McKenzie and Ross H. Day, 237–275. Hillsdale, N.J.: Lawrence Erlbaum Associates, 1987.

Buswell, Guy T. *How People Look at Pictures*. Chicago: University of Chicago Press, 1935.

Cabeza, Roberto, and Takashi Kato. "Features Are Also Important: Contributions of Featural and Configural Processing to Face Recognition." *Psychological Science* 11, no. 5 (2000): 429–433.

Caelli, Terry. *Visual Perception: Theory and Practice*. New York: Pergamon Press, 1981.

Caelli, Terry. "Learning Paradigms for Image Interpretation." *Spatial Vision* 13, no. 2-3 (2000): 305–314.

Caelli, Terry, and Walter F. Bischof, ed. *Machine Learning and Image Interpretation*. Advances in Computer Vision and Machine Intelligence, ed. Martin D. Levine. New York: Plenum Press, 1997.

Caelli, Terry, and David Reye. "On the Classification of Image Regions by Colour, Texture, and Shape." *Pattern Recognition* 26, no. 4 (1993): 461–470.

Calder, Andrew J., Andrew W. Young, David I. Perrett, Nancy L. Etcoff, and D. Rowland. "Categorical Perception of Morphed Facial Expressions." *Visual Cognition* 3, no. 2 (1996): 81–117.

Calder, Andrew J., Duncan Rowland, Andrew W. Young, Ian Nimmo-Smith, Jill Keane, and David I. Perrett. "Caricaturing Facial Expressions." *Cognition* 76, no. 2 (2000): 105–146.

Canter, D., J. Brown, and L. Groat. "A Multiple Sorting Procedure for Studying Conceptual Systems." In *The Research Interview: Uses and Approaches*, ed. M. Brenner, J. Brown, and D. Canter. New York: Academic Press, 1985.

Carnine, D. "New Research on the Brain: Implications for Instruction." *Phi Delta Kappan* 71, no. 5 (1990): 372–377.

Carson, C., M. Thomas, S. Belongie, J. M. Hellerstein, and J. Malik. "Blobworld: A System for Region-Based Image Indexing and Retrieval." A paper delivered at the 3rd International Conference on Visual Information Systems, June 1999.

Cavazza, M., R. J. Green, and I. J. Palmer. "Multimedia Semantic Features and Image Content Description." A paper delivered at the International Conference on Multimedia Modeling, Lausanne, Switzerland, October 12–15, 1998.

Cave, Carolyn Backer, Preston R. Bost, and Ronald E. Cobb. "Effects of Color and Pattern on Implicit and Explicit Picture Memory." *Journal of Experimental Psychology: Learning, Memory, and Cognition* 22, no. 3 (1996): 639–653.

Cawkell, A. E. "Picture Queries and Picture Databases." *Journal of Information Science* 19 (1993): 409–423.

Cha, Guang-Ho, and Chin-Wan Chung. "Object-Oriented Retrieval Mechanism for Semistructured Image Collections." A paper delivered at the ACM conference on Multimedia '98, Bristol, U.K., September 12–16, 1998.

Chan, Lois Mai, Phyllis A. Richmond, and Elaine Svenonius, ed. *Theory of Subject Analysis: A Sourcebook*. Littleton, Colo.: Libraries Unlimited, 1985.

Chang, Shih-Fu, William Chen, and Hari Sundaram. "Semantic Visual Template: Linking Visual Features to Semantics." A paper delivered at the International Conference on

Image Processing (ICIP) '98 Workshop on Content Based Video Search and Retrieval, Chicago, Ill., October 10–12, 1998.

Chang, Shih-Fu, John R. Smith, Mandis Beigi, and Ana Benitez. "Visual Information Retrieval from Large Distributed Online Repositories." *Communications of the ACM* 40, no. 12 (1997): 63–71.

Chang, Shi-Kuo. "Visual Languages: A Tutorial and Survey." *Institute of Electrical and Electronics Engineers (IEEE) Software* (1987): 29–39.

Chang, Shi-Kuo, and Erland Jungert. "Query Languages for Multimedia Search." In *Principles of Visual Information Retrieval*, ed. Michael S. Lew, 199–217. New York: Springer, 2001.

Chen, Hsin-Liang. "An Analysis of Image Queries in the Field of Art History." *Journal of the American Society for Information Science and Technology* 52, no. 3 (2001): 260–273.

Chen, W., and Shih-Fu Chang. "VISMAP: An Interactive Image/Video Retrieval System Using Visualization and Concept Maps." A paper delivered at the International Conference on Image Processing (ICIP '01), Thessaloniki, Greece, October 7–10, 2001.

Chijiwa, H. *Chromatics*. Fukumura Printing Co., 1983.

Chijiwa, H. *Color Harmony*. Rockport, Mass.: Rockport Publishers, 1987.

Childress, Eric. "Traditional and Emerging Library Standards for Intellectual Control of Image Objects: An Overview." *Visual Resources Association Bulletin* 23, no. 4 (1996): 88–92.

Chiou, G. I., and Jeng-Neng Hwang. " A Neural Network-Based Stochastic Active Model (NNS-SNAKE) for Contour Finding of Distinct Features." *IEEE Transactions on Image Processing* 4 (1995): 1407–1416.

Chipman, Alison. "Providing Access to Picture Collections: Applying PRECIS to Slides and Photographs." In *PRECIS: Recent Applications*, ed. Mary Dykstra. Occasional Papers Series No. 39. Halifax, Nova Scotia, Canada: Dalhousie University School of Library and Information Studies, 1986.

Chokron, Sylvie, and Maria De Agostini. "Reading Habits Influence Aesthetic Preference." *Cognitive Brain Research* 10, no. 1–2 (2000): 45–49.

Christal, R. E. "Factor Analytic Study of Visual Memory." *Psychological Monographs* 73, no. 13 (1958): Whole issue No. 466.

Chu, Heting. "Research in Image Indexing and Retrieval as Reflected in the Literature." *Journal of the American Society for Information Science and Technology* 52, no. 12 (2001): 1011–1018.

Clarke, Sherman. "Forward." In *ArtMARC Sourcebook: Cataloging Art, Architecture, and their Visual Images*, ed. Linda McRae and Lynda S. White, v–vi. Chicago: American Library Association, 1998.

Clore, Gerald L, Norbert Schwarz, and Michael Conway. "Affective Causes and Consequences of Social Information Processing." In *Handbook of Social Cognition*, ed. Robert S. Wyer Jr. and Thomas K. Srull. Vol. 1: Basic Processes, 323–417. Hillsdale, N.J.: Lawrence Erlbaum Associates, 1994.

Cohen, Barry H., and Monique Saslona. "The Advantage of Being an Habitual Visualizer." *Journal of Mental Imagery* 14, no. 3–4 (1990): 101–112.

Collantes, Lourdes Y. "Degree of Agreement in Naming Objects and Concepts for Information Retrieval." *Journal of the American Society for Information Science* 46, no. 2 (1995): 116–132.

Collins, Karen. "Providing Subject Access to Images: A Study of User Queries." M. S. thesis, University of North Carolina at Chapel Hill, 1997.

Conesa, Jorge, Cynthia Brunold-Conesa, and Maria Miron. "Incidence of the Half-Left Profile Pose in Single-Subject Portraits." *Perceptual and Motor Skills* 81, no. 3, pt. 1 (1995): 920–922.

Congressional Research Service. Legislative Indexing Vocabulary. Washington, D.C.: Congressional Research Service, n.d. Available from www.loc.gov/ library/libarch-thesauri.html (accessed on April 25, 2003).

Corballis, Michael C. "Neuropsychology of Perceptual Functions." In *Neuropsychology*, ed. Dahlia W. Zaidel, 83–104. San Diego: Academic Press, 1994.

Corbeil, Jean-Claude. *The Facts on File Visual Dictionary*. New York: Facts on File, 1986.

Coren, Stanley, and Joan Stern Girgus. *Seeing Is Deceiving: The Psychology of Visual Illusions*. Hillsdale, N.J.: Lawrence Erlbaum, 1978.

Corridoni, J. M., A. Del Bimbo, and P. Pala. "Image Retrieval by Color Semantics." *Multimedia Systems* 7, no. 3 (1999): 175–183.

Coss, Richard G. "The Ethological Command in Art." *Leonardo* 1 (1968): 273–287.

Coulter, R. G., M. L. Coulter, and J. A. Glover. "Details and Picture Recall." *Bulletin of the Psychonomic Society* 22, no. 4 (1984): 327–329.

Couprie, Leendert. "ICONCLASS, an Iconographical Classification System." *Art Libraries Journal* 8, no. 2 (1983): 32–49.

Cox, Ingemar J., Joumana Ghosn, Matt L. Miller, Thomas V. Papathomas, and Peter N. Yianilos. "Hidden Annotation in Content Based Image Retrieval." A paper delivered at the IEEE Workshop on Content-Based Access of Image and Video Libraries, June 1997.

Cox, Ingemar J., Matt L. Miller, Thomas P. Minka, Thomas V. Papathomas, and Peter N. Yianilos. "The Bayesian Image Retrieval System, PicHunter: Theory, Implementation, and Psychophysical Experiments." *IEEE Transactions on Image Processing* 9, no. 1 (2000): 20–37.

Crevier, D., and R. Lepage. "Knowledge-Based Image Understanding Systems: A Survey." *Computer Vision and Image Understanding* 67, no. 2 (1997): 161–185.

Cromwell-Kessler, W. "Crosswalks, Metadata Mapping, and Interoperability: What Does It All Mean?" In *Introduction to Metadata: Pathways to Digital Information*, ed. M. M. Baca, 19–22. Los Angeles: Getty Information Institute, 1998.

Crozier, W. Ray, and Antony J. Chapman. "The Perception of Art: The Cognitive Approach and Its Context." In *Cognitive Processes in the Perception of Art*, ed. W. Ray Crozier and Antony J. Chapman, 19, 3–26. New York: North-Holland, 1984a.

Crozier, W. Ray, and Antony J. Chapman, ed. *Cognitive Processes in the Perception of Art*. Vol. 19 of Advances in Psychology, edited by G. E. Stelmach and P. A. Vroon. New York: North-Holland, 1984b.

Cupchik, G. C., A. S. Winston, and R. S. Herz. "Judgments of Similarity and Difference Between Paintings." *Visual Arts Research* 18, no. 2 (1992): 36–49.

Cutting, James E., and Manfredo Massironi. "Pictures and Their Special Status in Perceptual and Cognitive Inquiry." In *Perception and Cognition at Century's End*, ed. Julian Hochberg, 137–168. New York: Academic Press, 1998.

Dalton, John. "Image Similarity Models and the Perception of Artistic Representations of Natural Images." A paper delivered at the Human Vision and Electronic Imaging II conference, San Jose, Calif., February 10–13, 1997.

Dane, William J. *The Picture Collection.* 6th ed. Hamden, Conn.: Shoe String Press, 1968.

Daneels, Dirk, David Van Campenhout, Wayne Niblack, William Equitz, Ron Barber, Erwin Bellon, and Freddy Fierens. "Interactive Outlining: An Improved Approach Using Active Contours." A paper delivered at the Storage and Retrieval for Image and Video Databases Conference, San Jose, Calif., February 2–3, 1993.

Danko-McGhee, Katherina. *The Aesthetic Preferences of Young Children.* Vol. 49, Mellen Studies in Education. Lewiston, N.Y.: Edwin Mellen Press, 2000.

Davies, Duncan, Diana Bathurst, and Robin Bathurst. *The Telling Image: The Changing Balance between Pictures and Words in a Technological Age.* Oxford, England: Clarendon Press, 1990.

Davis, Stephen. "The RLG Digital Image Access Project. Panel on Digital Imagery: Photographs and Art." A paper delivered at the American Society for Information Science (ASIS) conference, Baltimore, Md., October 21–24, 1996.

Davis, W. J., M. A. Rahman, L. J. Smith, A. Burns, L. Senecal, D. McArthur, J. A. Halpern, A. Perlmutter, W. Sickels and W. Wagner. "Properties of Human Affect Induced by Static Color Slides (IAPS): Dimensional, Categorical, and Electromyographic Analysis." *Biological Psychology* 41, no. 3 (1995): 229–253.

Deerwester, S., S. T. Dumais, T. K. Landauer, G. W. Furnas, and R. A. Harshman. "Indexing by Latent Semantic Analysis." *Journal of the American Society for Information Science* 41, no. 6 (1990): 391–407.

De Graef, P., D. Christiaens, and G. d'Ydewalle. "Perceptual Effects of Scene Context on Object Identification." *Psychological Research* 52, no. 317–329 (1990).

De Houwer, Jan, and Dirk Hermans. "Differences in the Affective Processing of Words and Pictures." *Cognition and Emotion* 8, no. 1 (1994): 1–20.

Dekkers, Makx, and Stuart L. Weibel. "Dublin Core Metadata Initiative Progress Report and Workplan for 2002." *D–Lib Magazine* 8, no. 2 (2002).

DeLoache, Judy S., David H. Uttal, and Sophia L. Pierroutsakos. "What's Up? The Development of an Orientation Preference for Picture Books." *Journal of Cognition and Development* 1, no. 1 (2000): 81–95.

Deng, D. "Mining Visual Concepts for Image Retrieval: A Case Study." A paper delivered at the Fifth Biannual Conference on Artificial Neural Networks and Expert Systems (ANNES 2001), Dunedin, New Zealand, November 24–27, 2001.

Deng, Y., and B. S. Manjunath. "An Efficient Low-Dimensional Color Indexing Scheme for Region-Based Image Retrieval." A paper delivered at the IEEE International Conference on Acoustics, Speech, and Signal Processing (ICASSP), Phoenix, Arizona, March 15–19, 1999.

Denis, Michel, and Christine Colonelli. "Memorization of Drawings or Nouns According to the Material Utilized at Recognition Time." *Année Psychologique* 76, no. 1 (1976): 39–53.

Deregowski, J. B. *Illusions, Patterns, and Pictures: A Cross-Cultural Perspective.* New York: Academic Press, 1980.

Deregowski, J. B. "Pictorial Perception: Individual and Group Differences within the Human Species." *Cahiers de Psychologie Cognitive* 18, no. 5–6 (1999): 1031–1063.

Dervin, Brenda. "Useful Theory for Librarianship: Communication, Not Information." *Drexel Library Quarterly* 13, no. 3 (1977): 16–32.

Detenber, Benjamin H., and Byron Reeves. "A Bio-Informational Theory of Emotion: Motion and Image Size Effects on Viewers." *Journal of Communication* 46, no. 3 (1996): 66–84.

Dickinson, A., and M. F. Dearing. "Appetitive-Aversive Interactions and Inhibitory Processes." In *Mechanisms of Learning and Motivation*, ed. A. Dickinson and R. A. Boakes, 203–231. Hillsdale, N.J.: Lawrence Erlbaum Associates, 1979.

Dimberg, Ulf, and Barry Karlsson. "Facial Reactions to Different Emotionally Relevant Stimuli." *Scandinavian Journal of Psychology* 38, no. 4 (1997): 297–303.

Dobie, Mark, Robert Tansley, Dan Joyce, Mark Weal, Paul Lewis, and Wendy Hall. "A Flexible Architecture for Content and Concept-Based Multimedia Information Exploration." A paper delivered at CIR-99: The Challenge of Image Retrieval, Newcastle upon Tyne, England, February 25–26, 1999.

Dondis, Donis A. *A Primer of Visual Literacy*. Cambridge, Mass.: MIT Press, 1973.

Dorling Kindersley, Inc. *Ultimate Visual Dictionary*. New York: Dorling Kindersley Publishing, 2000.

Dowe, J. "Content-Based Retrieval in Multimedia Imaging." A paper delivered at the Storage and Retrieval for Image and Video Databases conference, San Jose, Calif., February 2–3, 1993.

Drucker, J. and J. McGann. "Images as Text: Pictographs and Pictographic Logic." Information Design Journal 10, no. 2 (2001): 95–106. Available from jefferson.village.virginia.edu/%7Ejjm2f/pictograph.html (accessed on April 20, 2003).

Dunlop, Mark D. "Multimedia Information Retrieval." Ph.D. thesis, University of Glasgow, 1991.

Durgin, F. H. "Texture Contrast Aftereffects Are Monocular; Texture Density Aftereffects Are Binocular." *Vision Research* 41 (2001): 2619–2630.

Durran, Jennifer. "Art History, Scholarship, and Image Libraries: Realising the Potential of the Digital Age." *Library Automated Systems Information Exchange (LASIE)* 28 (June 1997): 14–27.

Eakins, John P., and Margaret E. Graham. *Content-Based Image Retrieval: A Report to the JISC Technology Applications Programme*. Institute for Image Data Research, University of Northumbria at Newcastle, 1999. Available from www.unn.ac.uk/iidr/report.html (accessed on April 20, 2003).

Edelman, G. M. *Neural Darwinism: The Theory of Neuronal Group Selection*. New York: Basic Books, 1987.

Ekman, P., and W. V. Friesen. *Unmasking the Face: A Guide to Recognizing Emotions from Facial Clues*. Englewood Cliffs, N.J.: Prentice-Hall, 1975.

Eliade, Mircea. *Images and Symbols: Studies in Religious Symbolism*. Translated by Philip Mairet. Princeton, N.J.: Princeton University Press, 1991.

Elings, Mary W. "Pictorial Archives and EAD: Indexing Collections for Online Access." *Art Documentation* 19, no. 2 (2000): 10–14.

Enser, P. G. B. "Query Analysis in a Visual Information Retrieval Context." *Journal of Document and Text Management* 1, no. 1 (1993): 25–52.

Enser, P. G. B. "Visual Image Retrieval: Seeking the Alliance of Concept-Based and Content-Based Paradigms." *Journal of Information Science* 26, no. 4 (2000): 199–210.

Ester, Michael. "Image Quality and Viewer Perception." *Leonardo* (Digital Image–Digital Cinema Supplemental Issue) (1990): 51–63.

Evans, Hilary. *Picture Librarianship.* New York: K. G. Saur, 1980.

Fagin, Ronald. "Fuzzy Queries in Multimedia Database Systems." A paper delivered at the 17th ACM Symposium on Principles of Database Systems (PODS), Seattle, Wash., 1998.

Fagin, Ronald, and E. Wimmers. "Incorporating User Preferences in Multimedia Queries." A paper delivered at the 6th International Conference on Database Theory, Delphi, Greece, 1997.

Faloutsos, Christos. *Searching Multimedia Databases by Content.* Boston, Mass.: Kluwer Academic Publishers, 1997.

Faloutsos, Christos. "Multimedia IR: Indexing and Searching." In *Modern Information Retrieval,* ed. Ricardo Baeza-Yates and Berthier Ribeiro-Neto, 345–365. New York: ACM Press, 1999.

Farley, Frank H., Arie Cohen, and Aurora Sanfeliz. "Aesthetic Dimensions and Picture Memory: A Structural Re-Analysis." *Perceptual and Motor Skills* 48, no. 3, pt. 1 (1979): 729–730.

Fechner, G. T. *Vorschule der Aesthetik (Introduction to Aesthetics).* 2 vols. Leipzig: Von Breitkopf and Härtel, 1876.

Federmeier, Kara D., and Marta Kutas. "Meaning and Modality: Influences of Context, Semantic Memory Organization, and Perceptual Predictability on Picture Processing." *Journal of Experimental Psychology: Learning, Memory, and Cognition* 27, no. 1 (2001): 202–224.

Fehr, Dennis E. "Color/Form Classification Strategies: A Review of Relevant Research." *Visual Arts Research* 15, no. 1 (1989): 86–94.

Fellbaum, Christiane D., ed. *WordNet: An Electronic Lexical Database.* Cambridge, Mass.: MIT Press, 1998.

Fidel, Raya. "User-Centered Indexing." *Journal of the American Society for Information Science* 45, no. 8 (1994): 572–576.

Fidopiastis, Cali, Donald D. Hoffman, William D. Prophet, and Manish Singh. "Constructing Surfaces and Contours in Displays of Color from Motion: The Role of Nearest Neighbors and Maximal Disks." *Perception* 29, no. 5 (2000): 567–580.

Fish, P. R. "Consistency in Archaeological Measurement and Classification: A Pilot Study." *American Antiquity* 43 (1978): 86–89.

Fisher, D. F., R. B. Karsh, F. Breitenbach, and B. D. Barnett. "Eye Movements and Picture Recognition: Contribution or Embellishment." In *Eye Movements and Psychological Functions: International Views,* ed. R. Groner, C. Menz, D. F. Fisher, and R. A. Monty, 193–210. Hillsdale, N.J.: Lawrence Erlbaum Associates, 1983.

Fisher, John. *Perceiving Artworks.* Vol. 3 of Philosophical Monographs. Philadelphia: Temple University Press, 1980.

Flexner, Stuart B. *Random House Unabridged Dictionary.* New York: Random House, 1993.

Flickner, M., H. Sawhney, W. Niblack, J. Ashley, Q. Huang, B. Dom, M. Gorkani, J. Hafner, D. Lee, D. Petkovic, D. Steele, and P. Yanker. "Query by Image and Video Content: The QBIC System." *IEEE Computer* 28, no. 9 (1995): 23–30.

Fodor, Jerry. *The Language of Thought.* Cambridge, Mass.: Harvard University Press, 1975.

Forsyth, David A., Jitendra Malik, Thomas K. Leung, Chris Bregler, Chad Carson, Hayit Greenspan, and Margaret M. Fleck. "Finding Pictures of Objects in Large Collections of Images." *Library Trends* 48, no. 2 (1999): 119–139.

Frankel, C., M. J. Swain, and V. Athitsos. *Webseer: An Image Search Engine for the World Wide Web.* Chicago, Ill.: University of Chicago, 1996. Technical Report, TR-96-14.

Freedman, J., and R. N. Haber. "One Reason Why We Rarely Forget a Face." *Bulletin of the Psychonomic Society* 3 (1974): 107–109.

Freeman, Norman H. "The Emergence of a Framework Theory of Pictorial Reasoning." In *Drawing and Looking: Theoretical Approaches to Pictorial Representation in Children. The Developing Body and Mind*, ed. Christiane Lange-Kuettner and Glyn V. Thomas, 135–146. Hertfordshire, England: Harvester Wheatsheaf, 1995.

Freeman, Norman H., and Michael J. Parsons. "Children's Intuitive Understandings of Pictures." In *Understanding and Teaching the Intuitive Mind: Student and Teacher Learning*, ed. Bruce Torff and Robert J. Sternberg, 73–91. Mahwah, N.J.: Lawrence Erlbaum Associates, 2001.

French, J. C., A. L. Powell, E. Schulman, J. L. Pfaltz. "Automating the Construction of Authority Files in Digital Libraries: A Case Study." A paper presented at the First European Conference on Research and Advanced Technologies for Digital Libraries, Pisa, Italy, September 1–3, 1997.

Friedman, A. "Framing Pictures: The Role of Knowledge in Automatized Encoding and Memory for Gist." *Journal of Experimental Psychology: General* 108, no. 3 (1979): 316–355.

Fritz, Deborah A. *Cataloging with AACR2R and USMARC for Books, Computer Files, Serials, Sound Recordings, and Videorecordings*. Chicago, Ill.: American Library Association, 1998.

Frois, J. P., and Hans J. Eysenck. "The Visual Aesthetic Sensitivity Test Applied to Portuguese Children and Fine Arts Students." *Creativity Research Journal* 8, no. 3 (1995): 277–284.

Frost, C. Olivia. "The University of Michigan School of Information Art Image Browser: Designing and Testing a Model for Image Retrieval." In *Knowledge Organization and Change*, ed. Rebecca Green, 5, 182–188. Frankfurt/Main, Germany: Indeks Verlag, 1996.

Frost, C. Olivia, Bradley Taylor, Anna Noakes, Stephen Markel, Deborah Torres, and Karen M. Drabenstott. "Browse and Search Patterns in a Digital Image Database." *Information Retrieval* 1, no. 4 (2000): 287–313.

Fry, Eileen. "Image Access and Cyber Searching: The Philadelphia Experiment." *Art Documentation* 17, no. 2 (1998): 51–52.

Fry, Eileen. "CORE Foundations for Image Indexing: From Punchcards to the Web." A paper delivered at the Art Libraries Society of North America (ARLIS) 28th Annual Conference, Pittsburg, Pa., March 19, 2000.

Funt, B., and G. Finlayson. "Color Constant Color Indexing." *IEEE Transactions on Pattern Analysis and Machine Intelligence* 17, no. 5 (1995): 522–529.

Furnas, G. W., T. K. Landauer, L. M. Gomez, and S. T. Dumais. "The Vocabulary Problem in Human–System Communication." *Communications of the ACM* 30, no. 11 (1987): 964–971.

Furnham, Adrian, and Margaret Avison. "Personality and Preference for Surreal Paintings." *Personality and Individual Differences* 23, no. 6 (1997): 923–935.

Furnham, Adrian, and John Walker. "Personality and Judgments of Abstract, Pop Art, and Representational Paintings." *European Journal of Personality* 15, no. 1 (2001): 57–72.

Futterweit, Lorelle R., and Harry Beilin. "Recognition Memory for Movement in Photographs: A Developmental Study." *Journal of Experimental Child Psychology* 57, no. 2 (1994): 163–179.

Gaede, V., and O. Gunther. "Multidimensional Access Methods." *Association for Computing Machinery Computing Surveys* 30, no. 2 (1998): 170–231.

Gardner, Howard. "Children's Sensitivity to Painting Styles." *Child Development* 41, no. 3 (1970): 813–821.

Garnier, Francoise. *Thesaurus Iconographique, système descriptif des représentations.* Paris: Le Leopold d'Or, 1984.

Gary, J. E., and R. Mehrotra. "Shape-Similarity-Based Retrieval in Image Database Systems." A paper delivered at the Image Storage and Retrieval Systems conference, San Jose, Calif., February 13–14, 1992.

Gattegno, C. *Toward a Visual Culture: Educating through Television.* New York: Outerbridge and Dienstfrey, 1969.

Gaut, Britt, and Philip Gaut. "Indexing Fiction: The Debate Continues." *The Finnish Library Journal* November 2 (1999).

Gernsbacher, M. A. "Surface Information Loss in Comprehension." *Cognitive Psychology* 17 (1985): 324–363.

Gevers, Theo, Frank Aldershoff, and A. W. M. Smeulders. "Classification of Images on the Internet by Visual and Textual Information." A paper delivered at the Internet Imaging conference, San Jose, Calif., January 2000.

Gevers, Theo, and A. W. M. Smeulders. "Pictoseek: Combining Color and Shape Invariant Features for Image Retrieval." *IEEE Transactions on Image Processing* 9, no. 1 (2000): 102–119.

Gibson, J. J. "The Information Available in Pictures." *Viewpoints* 47, no. 4 (1971): 73–95.

Gibson, J. J. *The Ecological Approach to Visual Perception.* Boston: Houghton Mifflin, 1979.

Gilbert, Karen Diane. *Picture Indexing for Local History Materials.* Monroe, N.Y.: Library Research Associates, 1973.

Gill, Tony, Catherine Grout, and Louise Smith. *VADS Information Standards Review.* Farnham, Surrey, England: Visual Arts Data Service, 1997.

Giorgianni, Edward J., and Thomas E. Madden. *Digital Color Management: Encoding Solutions.* Reading, Mass.: Addison-Wesley, 1997.

Glass, Elizabeth. *A Subject Index for the Visual Arts.* 2 vols. Victoria and Albert Museum, Department of Prints and Drawings and Department of Paintings. London: Her Majesty's Stationery Office, 1969.

Goethe, W. *Theory of Colors.* Cambridge, Mass.: MIT Press, 1976.

Goldman, Alan H. *Aesthetic Value.* Boulder, Colo.: Westview Press, 1995.

Goldmeier, E. "Similarity in Visually Perceived Forms." *Psychological Issues* 8, no. 1 (1972): 1–135.

Goldstein, Alvin G., and June E. Chance. "Visual Recognition Memory for Complex Configurations." *Perception and Psychophysics* 9, no. 2-B (1971): 237–241.

Gombrich, E. H. *Art and Illusion: A Study in the Psychology of Pictorial Representation.* 2nd ed. Princeton, N.J.: Princeton University Press, 1969.

Gombrich, E. H., Julian Hochberg, and Max Black. *Art, Perception, and Reality.* Baltimore, Md.: Johns Hopkins University Press, 1972.

Goodman, Gail S. "Picture Memory: How the Action Schema Affects Retention." *Cognitive Psychology* 12, no. 4 (1980): 473–495.

Goodman, N. *Languages of Art: An Approach to a Theory of Symbols.* Indianapolis, Ind.: Bobbs-Merrill, 1972.

Goodrum, A., and A. Spink. "Image Searching on the Excite Web Search Engine." *Information Processing and Management* 37, no. 2 (2001): 295–312.

Gordon, Andrew S. "Browsing Image Collections with Representations of Commonsense Activities." *Journal of the American Society for Information Science and Technology* 52, no. 11 (2001): 925–929.

Gordon, Catherine. "Patterns of User Queries in an ICONCLASS Database." *Visual Resources* 12 (1996): 177–186.

Goude, Gunnar. "A Multidimensional Scaling Approach to the Perception of Art. II." *Scandanavian Journal of Psychology* 13 (1972): 272–284.

Gould, John D. "Looking at Pictures." In *Eye Movements and Psychological Processes*, ed. Richard A. Monty and John W. Senders, 323–345. Hillsdale, N.J.: Lawrence Erlbaum Associates, 1976.

Gould, John. D., and A. Dill. "Eye Movement Parameters and Pattern Recognition." *Perception and Psychophysics* 6 (1969): 311–320.

Graefe, Thomas M., and Michael J. Watkins. "Picture Rehearsal: An Effect of Selectively Attending to Pictures No Longer in View." *Journal of Experimental Psychology: Human Learning and Memory* 6, no. 2 (1980): 156–162.

Graham, Margaret E. *The Description and Indexing of Images: Report of a Survey of ARLIS Members, 1998/99.* Newcastle, England: University of Northumbria, 1999.

Green, Christopher D. "All That Glitters: A Review of Psychological Research on the Aesthetics of the Golden Section." *Perception* 24, no. 8 (1995): 937–968.

Green, Stanford J. *The Classification of Pictures and Slides.* Denver, Colo.: Little Books, 1984.

Greenberg, Jane. "Intellectual Control of Visual Archives: A Comparison Between the *Art and Architecture Thesaurus* and the *Library of Congress Thesaurus for Graphic Materials.*" *Cataloging and Classification Quarterly* 16, no. 1 (1993): 85–117.

Greenberg, Jane. "A Quantitative Categorical Analysis of Metadata Elements in Image Applicable Metadata Schemas." *Journal of the American Society for Information Science and Technology* 52, no. 11 (2001): 917–924.

Greenspan, H., S. Belongie, C. Carson, and J. Malik. "Recognition of Images in Large Databases Using Color and Texture." A paper delivered at the Computer Vision and Pattern Recognition conference (CVPR '97), San Juan, Puerto Rico, June 17–19, 1997.

Gregory, Richard L. *Eye and Brain.* Princeton, N.J.: Princeton University Press, 1997.

Grosky, William I., and Rajiv Mehrotra. "Image Database Management." In *Advances in Computers*, ed. Marshall C. Yovits, 34, 237–291. New York: Academic Press, 1992.

Grosky, William I., Peter Neo, and Rajiv Mehrotra. "A Pictorial Index Mechanism for Model-Based Matching." A paper delivered at the Transactions of the 5th International Conference on Data Engineering, Los Angeles, Calif., February 6–10, 1989.

Gruber, Tom. "What Is an Ontology?" In *MITECS: The MIT Encyclopedia of the Cognitive Sciences (online abstracts)*: The MIT Press, n.d.

Grund, Angelika. "ICONCLASS: On Subject Analysis of Iconographic Representations of Works of Art." *Knowledge Organization* 20, no. 1 (1993): 20–29.

Gudivada, Venkat N., and Vijay V. Raghaven. "Content-Based Image Retrieval Systems." *IEEE Computer* 28, no. 9 (1995a): 18–22.

Gudivada, Venkat N., and Vijay V. Raghaven. "Special Issue on Content-Based Image Retrieval Systems." *IEEE Computer* 28, no. 9 (1995b): 18–62.

Guest, Steve, and Darren Van Laar. "The Structure of Colour Naming Space." *Vision Research* 40, no. 7 (2000): 723–734.

Gunther, Neil J., and Giordano B. Beretta. "Benchmark for Image Retrieval Using Distributed Systems over the Internet: BIRDS-I." A paper delivered at the Internet Imaging II conference, San Jose, Calif., Jan. 25, 2000.

Gupta, A., and Ramesh C. Jain. "Visual Information Retrieval." *Communications of the ACM* 40, no. 5 (1997): 71–79.

Gupta, A., T. E. Weymouth, and Ramesh C. Jain. "An Extended Object–Oriented Data Model for Large Imagebases." A paper delivered at the 2nd Symposium on the Design and Implementation of Large Spatial Databases, Zurich, Switzerland, August 1991a.

Gupta, A., T. E. Weymouth, and Ramesh C. Jain. "Semantic Queries with Pictures: The VIMSYS Model." A paper delivered at the 17th International Conference on Very Large Databases, Barcelona, Spain, August 1991b.

Hagen, Margaret A. "Generative Theory: A Perceptual Theory of Pictorial Representation." In *The Perception of Pictures*, ed. Edward C. Carterette and Morton P. Friedman, 2, 3–46. New York: Academic Press, 1980.

Haig, A., and A. Whitfield. "Predicting the Aesthetic Performance of Web Sites: What Attracts People?" A paper delivered at the 1st International Symposium on Smart Graphics, Hawthorne, N.Y., March 21–23, 2001.

Hall, James. *Dictionary of Subjects and Symbols in Art*. New York: Harper & Row, 1979.

Hamel, Cheryl J., and David L. Ryan-Jones. "Effect of Visual Detail on Scene Recognition: Some Unexpected Sex Differences." *Perceptual and Motor Skills* 84, no. 2 (1997): 619–626.

Hamm, Alfons O., Mark K. Greenwald, Margaret M. Bradley, and Bruce N. Cuthbert. "The Fear Potentiated Startle Effect: Blink Reflex Modulation as a Result of Classical Aversive Conditioning." *Integrative Physiological and Behavioral Science* 26, no. 2 (1991): 119–126.

Han, Kyung-Ah, and Sung-Hyun Myaeng. "Image Organization and Retrieval with Automatically Constructed Feature Vectors." A paper delivered at SIGIR '96, Zurich, Switzerland, August 18–22, 1996.

Haralick, R. M. "Statistical and Structural Approaches to Texture." *Proceedings of the IEEE* 67 (1979): 786–804.

Harmandas, V., M. Sanderson, and Mark D. Dunlop. "Image Retrieval by Hypertext Links." A paper delivered at SIGIR '97, Philadelphia, Pa., 1997.

Harnad, Stevan. "Psychophysical and Cognitive Aspects of Categorical Perception: A Critical Overview." In *Categorical Perception*, ed. Stevan Harnad, 1–25. New York: Cambridge University Press, 1987a.

Harnad, Stevan, ed. *Categorical Perception.* New York: Cambridge University Press, 1987b.

Harpring, Patricia. "Resistance Is Futile: Inescapable Networked Information Made Accessible Using the Getty Vocabularies." A paper delivered at the ASIS 62nd Annual Meeting of the American Society for Information Science, Washington, D.C., October 31–November 4, 1999.

Harrison, E. R. "Classification Redefined: Research and Implications for Art Education." *Visual Arts Research* 18, no. 1 (1992): 43–49.

Harrison, Harriet W. "Cataloging Visual Images: The View from LC." *Art Documentation* 15, no. 2 (1996): 13–16.

Hasegawa, J., N. Okada, and J. Toriwaki. "Intelligent Retrieval of Chest X-Ray Image Database Using Sketches." *Systems and Computers in Japan* 20, no. 7 (1989): 29–42.

Hastings, Samantha K. "An Exploratory Study of Intellectual Access to Digitized Art Images." Ph.D. thesis, The Florida State University, 1994.

Hastings, Samantha K. "Evaluation of Image Retrieval Systems: Role of User Feedback." *Library Trends* 48, no. 2 (1999): 438–452.

Heaps, C., and S. Handel. "Similarity and Features of Natural Textures." *Journal of Experimental Psychology: Human Perception and Performance* 25, no. 2 (1999): 299–320.

Heidemann, G., F. Kummert, H. Ritter, and G. Sagerer. "A Hybrid Object Recognition Architecture." A paper delivered at the International Conference on Artificial Neural Networks (ICANN '96), Bochum, Germany, July 16–19, 1996.

Hekkert, Paul, and H. M. J. Snelders. "Prototypicality as an Explanatory Concept in Aesthetics: A Reply to Boselie (1991)." *Empirical Studies of the Arts* 13, no. 2 (1995): 149–160.

Hekkert, Paul, and Piet C. W. van Wieringen. "The Impact of Level of Expertise on the Evaluation of Original and Altered Versions of Post-Impressionistic Paintings." *Acta Psychologica* 94, no. 2 (1996): 117–131.

Heller, Wendy. "Cognitive and Emotional Organization of the Brain: Influences on the Creation and Perception of Art." In *Neuropsychology*, ed. Dahlia W. Zaidel, 271–292. New York: Academic Press, 1994.

Hemphill, Michael. "A Note on Adults' Color–Emotion Associations." *Journal of Genetic Psychology* 157, no. 3 (1996): 275–280.

Hendee, William R. "Cognitive Interpretation of Visual Signals." In *The Perception of Visual Information*, ed. W. R. Hendee and Peter N. T. Wells. New York: Springer-Verlag, 1993.

Hendee, William R., and Peter N. T. Wells, ed. *The Perception of Visual Information.* 2nd ed. New York: Springer-Verlag, 1997.

Henderson, John M., and Andrew Hollingworth. "Eye Movements During Scene Viewing: An Overview." In *Eye Guidance in Reading and Scene Perception*, ed. Geoffrey Underwood, 269–293. New York: Elsevier, 1998.

Henderson, John M., Phillip A. Weeks Jr., and Andrew Hollingworth. "The Effects of Semantic Consistency on Eye Movements during Complex Scene Viewing." *Journal of Experimental Psychology: Human Perception and Performance* 25, no. 1 (1999): 210–228.

Herdan, Gustav. *Type–Token Mathematics.* 'S-Gravenhage: Mouton & Co., 1960.

Hibler, J. N. David, Clement H. Leung, and K. L. Mannock. "System for Content-Based Storage and Retrieval in an Image Database." A paper delivered at the Image Storage and Retrieval Systems conference, San Jose, Calif., February 13–14, 1992.

Hill, Donna. *The Picture File: A Manual and a Curriculum-Related Subject Heading List.* Hamden, Conn.: Linnet Books, 1975.

Hirata, Kyoji, and T. Kato. "Rough Sketch-Based Image Information Retrieval." *NEC Research and Development* 34, no. 2 (1993): 263–273.

Hirata, Kyoji, Sougata Mukherjea, Wen-Syan Li, and Yoshinori Hara. "Integrating Image Matching and Classification for Multimedia Retrieval on the Web." A paper delivered at the International Conference on Multimedia Computing and Systems, Austin, Tex., June 28–July 1, 1998.

Hochberg, Julian. "In the Mind's Eye." In *Contemporary Theory and Research in Visual Perception*, ed. R. N. Haber, 309–332. New York: Holt, Rinehart, and Winston, 1968.

Hochberg, Julian. "The Representation of Things and People." In *Art, Perception, and Reality*. Baltimore, Md.: Johns Hopkins University Press, 1972.

Hochberg, Julian. *Perception.* 2nd ed. Englewood Cliffs, N.J.: Prentice–Hall, 1978.

Hochberg, Julian. "Representation of Motion and Space in Video and Cinematic Displays." In *Handbook of Perception and Human Performance*, ed. K. J. Boff, L. Kaufman, and J. P. Thomas, 1, 22:1–22:64. New York: John Wiley and Sons, 1986.

Hochberg, Julian. "Gestalt Theory and Its Legacy." In *Perception and Cognition at Century's End*, ed. Julian Hochberg, 253–306. New York: Academic Press, 1998.

Hochberg, Julian, and E. McAlister. "A Quantitative Approach to Figural 'Goodness.'" *Journal of Experimental Psychology* 46 (1953): 361–364.

Hochberg, Julian, and A. Silverstein. "A Quantitative Index of Stimulus-Similarity; Proximity vs. Differences in Brightness." *American Journal of Psychology* 69 (1956): 456–458.

Hoffman, Donald D. *Visual Intelligence: How We Create What We See.* New York: W. W. Norton & Company, 2000.

Hoffman, Donald D., and W. Richards. "Parts of Recognition." *Cognition* 18 (1985): 65–96.

Hogan, Matthew, Corinne Jörgensen, and Peter Jörgensen. "The Visual Thesaurus in a Hypermedia Environment: A Preliminary Exploration of Conceptual Issues and Applications." A paper delivered at the International Conference on Hypermedia and Interactivity in Museums, Pittsburgh, Pa., October 14–16, 1991.

Hoge, Holger. "The Golden Section Hypothesis: Its Last Funeral." *Empirical Studies of the Arts* 15, no. 2 (1997): 233–255.

Hollingworth, Andrew. "Does Consistent Scene Context Facilitate Object Perception?" *Journal of Experimental Psychology: General* 127, no. 4 (1998): 398–415.

Hollingworth, Andrew, and John M. Henderson. "Object Identification Is Isolated from Scene Semantic Constraint: Evidence from Object Type and Token Discrimination." *Acta Psychologica* 102, no. 2–3 (1999): 319–343.

Homa, Donald, and Cynthia Viera. "Long-Term Memory for Pictures under Conditions of Thematically Related Foils." *Memory and Cognition* 16, no. 5 (1988): 411–421.

Hotelling, H. "Analysis of Complex Statistical Variables into Principal Components." *Journal of Educational Psychology* 24 (1933): 417–441, 498–520.

Hou, T., A. Hsu, P. Liu, and M. Chiu. "Content-Based Indexing Techniques Using Relative Geometry Features." A paper delivered at the Image Storage and Retrieval Systems conference, San Jose, Calif., February 13–14, 1992.

Hourihane, Colum. "A Selective Survey of Systems of Subject Classification." In *Computers and the History of Art*, ed. William Vaughan, Anthony Hamber, and Jean Miles, 117–129. London: Mansell Publishing Limited, 1989.

Hourihane, Colum. "The Van Eyck Project, Information Exchange, and European Art Libraries." *Visual Resources Association Bulletin* 23, no. 2 (1996): 57–60.

Hourihane, Colum. "Subject Classification for Visual Collections." *Visual Resources Association Special Bulletin* 12 (1999): 49 pp.

Howe, N. R. "Using Artificial Queries to Evaluate Image Retrieval." A paper delivered at the IEEE Workshop on Content-Based Access of Image and Video Libraries (CBAIVL-2000), Hilton Head, S.C., June 16, 2000.

Huang, J., S. R. Kumar, M. Mitra, and W. J. Zhu. "Spatial Color Indexing and Applications." A paper delivered at the 8th International Conference on Computer Vision, Bombay, India, January 4–7, 1998.

Hughes, Howard C., George Nozawa, and Frederick Kitterle. "Global Precedence, Spatial Frequency Channels, and the Statistics of Natural Images." *Journal of Cognitive Neuroscience* 8, no. 3 (1996): 197–231.

Humphrey, N. K. "The Illusion of Beauty." *Perception* 2 (1973): 429–439.

Humphrey, R., Ramesh C. Jain, and C. Shu. "Virage Image Search Engine: An Open Framework for Image Management." A paper delivered at the Storage and Retrieval for Image and Video Databases Conference, San Jose, Calif., January 28–February 2, 1996.

Humphreys, Glyn W., and Vicki Bruce. *Visual Cognition: Computational, Experimental, and Neuropsychological Perspectives*. Hillsdale, N.J.: Lawrence Erlbaum Associates, 1989.

Humphreys, Glyn W., and Hermann Mueller. "A Search Asymmetry Reversed by Figure–Ground Assignment." *Psychological Science* 11, no. 3 (2000): 196–201.

Working Group on the International Standard Bibliographic Description for Non-Book Materials. *International Standard Bibliographic Description for Non-Book Materials*. London: International Federations of Library Associations and Institutions International Office for Universal Bibliographic Control, 1977.

Intraub, Helene. "Presentation Rate and the Representation of Briefly Glimpsed Pictures in Memory." *Journal of Experimental Psychology: Human Learning and Memory* 6, no. 1 (1980): 1–12.

Intraub, Helene. "Rapid Conceptual Identification of Sequentially Presented Pictures." *Journal of Experimental Psychology: Human Perception and Performance* 7, no. 3 (1981): 604–610.

Intraub, Helene. "Contextual Factors in Scene Perception." In *The Role of Eye Movements in Perceptual Processes*, ed. E. Chekaluk and K. R. Llewellyn, 45–72, 88. New York: North Holland, 1992.

Intraub, Helene, Carmela V. Gottesman, Edward V. Willey, and Ilan J. Zuk. "Boundary Extension for Briefly Glimpsed Photographs: Do Common Perceptual Processes Result in Unexpected Memory Distortions?" *Journal of Memory and Language* 35, no. 2 (1996): 118–134.

Intraub, Helene, and Michael Richardson. "Wide-Angle Memories of Close-Up Scenes." *Journal of Experimental Psychology: Learning, Memory, and Cognition* 15, no. 2 (1989): 179–187.

Iqbal, Q., and J. K Aggarwall. "Applying Perceptual Grouping to Content-Based Image Retrieval: Building Images." A paper delivered at the Conference on Computer Vision and Pattern Recognition (CVPR '99), Fort Collins, Colo., June 23–25, 1999.

Itten, Johannes. *The Elements of Color.* New York: Van Nostrand Reinhold, 1970.

Itten, Johannes. *The Art of Color: The Subjective Experience and Objective Rationale of Color.* New York: Van Nostrand Reinhold Company, 1973.

Iyer, Hemalata. *Classificatory Structures: Concepts, Relations, and Representation.* Vol. 2, Textbooks for Knowledge Organization. Frankfurt/Main, Germany: Indeks Verlag, 1995.

Izard, Carroll E. "Innate and Universal Facial Expressions: Evidence from Developmental and Cross-Cultural Research." *Psychological Bulletin* 115, no. 2 (1994): 288–299.

Jagadish, H. V. "A Retrieval Technique for Similar Shapes." A paper delivered at the ACM SIGMOD Conference, Denver, Colo., June 1991.

Jagadish, H. V., and Lawrence O'Gorman. "An Object Model for Image Recognition." *Computer* 22 (1989): 33–36.

Jaimes, Alejandro, and Shih-Fu Chang. "Model-Based Classification of Visual Information for Content-Based Retrieval." A paper delivered at the Storage and Retrieval for Image and Video Databases conference, San Jose, Calif., January 1999.

Jaimes, Alejandro, and Shih-Fu Chang. "Automatic Selection of Visual Features and Classifiers." A paper delivered at the Storage and Retrieval for Media Databases conference, San Jose, Calif., January 2000a.

Jaimes, Alejandro, and Shih-Fu Chang. "A Conceptual Framework for Indexing Visual Information at Multiple Levels." A paper delivered at the Internet Imaging conference, San Jose, Calif., January, 2000b.

Jaimes, Alejandro, Ana B. Benitez, Shih-Fu Chang, and Alexander C. Loui. "Discovering Recurrent Visual Semantics in Consumer Photographs." A paper delivered at the IEEE International Conference on Image Processing (ICIP 2000), Vancouver, Canada, September 10–13, 2000.

Jain, Ramesh C. "NSF Workshop on Visual Information Management Systems." A paper delivered at the Storage and Retrieval for Image and Video Databases conference, San Jose, Calif., February 2–3, 1993.

Jain, Ramesh C., and T. O. Binford. "Ignorance, Myopia, and Naivete in Computer Vision Systems." *Computer Vision, Graphics, and Image Processing (CVGIP): Image Understanding* 53, no. 1 (1991): 112–117.

Jain, Ramesh C., Rangachar Kasturi, and Brian G. Schunck. *Machine Vision.* McGraw-Hill Series in Computer Science, ed. C. L. Liu. New York: McGraw-Hill, 1995.

Jaynes, Julian. *The Origin of Consciousness in the Breakdown of the Bicameral Mind.* Boston: Houghton Mifflin, 1976.

Jin, Jesse S., Ruth Kurniawati, Guangyou Xu, and Xuesheng Bai. "Using Browsing to Improve Content-Based Image Retrieval." A paper delivered at the Multimedia Storage and Archiving Systems conference, San Jose, Calif., 1998.

Johansson, Björn. *A Survey on Contents Based Search in Image Databases*, February 2000. Available from www.isy.liu.se/cvl/ScOut/TechRep/PaperInfo/bj2000.html (accessed on April 20, 2003).

Johansson, Gunnar. "Visual Motion Perception." *Scientific American* 232, no. 6 (1976): 75–88.

Johnson, Carla J., Allan Paivio, and James M. Clark. "Cognitive Components of Picture Naming." *Psychological Bulletin* 120, no. 1 (1996): 113–139.

Jolicoeur, P., M. Gluck, and S. Kosslyn. "Pictures and Names: Making the Connection." *Cognitive Psychology* 16 (1984): 243–275.

Jolion, Jean-Michel. "Computer Vision Methodologies." *Computer Vision, Graphics, and Image Processing (CVGIP): Image Understanding* 59, no. 1 (1994): 53–71.

Jolley, Richard P., Zhang Zhi, and Glyn V. Thomas. "How Focus of Interest in Pictures Changes with Age: A Cross-Cultural Comparison." *International Journal of Behavioral Development* 22, no. 1 (1998): 127–149.

Jones, Dorothy B. "Quantitative Analysis of Motion Picture Content." *Public Opinion Quarterly* 6, no. 3 (1942): 411–428.

Jörgensen, Corinne. "Classifying Images: Criteria for Grouping as Revealed in a Sorting Task." A paper delivered at the Proceedings of the 6th ASIS SIG/CR Classification Research Workshop, Chicago, Ill., October 8, 1995a.

Jörgensen, Corinne. "Image Attributes: An Investigation." Ph.D. thesis, Syracuse University, 1995b.

Jörgensen, Corinne. "The Applicability of Existing Classification Systems to Image Attributes: A Selected Review." In *Knowledge Organization and Change*, ed. Rebecca Green, 5, 189–197. Frankfurt/Main, Germany: Indeks Verlag, 1996a.

Jörgensen, Corinne. "Indexing Images: Testing an Image Description Template." A paper delivered at the 59th Annual Meeting of the American Society for Information Science, Baltimore, Md., October 8, 1996b.

Jörgensen, Corinne. "Image Attributes in Describing Tasks: An Investigation." *Information Processing and Management* 34, no. 2/3 (1998): 161–174.

Jörgensen, Corinne. *Image Indexing: An Analysis of Selected Classification Systems in Relation to Image Attributes Named by Naive Users.* : OCLC Library and Information Science Research Grant Program. Research Report, Annual Review of OCLC Research 1999a.

Jörgensen, Corinne. "Retrieving the Unretrievable: Art, Aesthetics, and Emotion in Image Retrieval Systems." A paper delivered at the Human Vision and Electronic Imaging Conference, San Jose Calif., 1999b.

Jörgensen, Corinne. "Towards an Image Testbed for Benchmarking Image Indexing and Retrieval Systems." A paper delivered at the NSF/INRIA Multimedia Content-Based Indexing and Retrieval Workshop 2001 (MMCBIR 2001), Paris, September 24–25 2001.

Jörgensen, Corinne, Alejandro Jaimes, Ana B. Benitez, and Shih-Fu Chang. "A Conceptual Framework and Empirical Research for Classifying Visual Descriptors." *Journal of the American Society for Information Science and Technology (JASIST)* 52, no. 11 (2001): 938–947.

Jörgensen, Corinne, Peter Jörgensen, and Matthew Hogan. "The Visual Thesaurus: A Practical Application." A paper delivered at the 6th International Conference of the Museum Documentation Association, Cambridge, England, September 20–24, 1993.

Jörgensen, Corinne, and Rohini Srihari. "Creating a Web-Based Image Database for Benchmarking Image Retrieval Systems: A Progress Report." A paper delivered at the Human Vision and Electronic Imaging conference, San Jose, Calif., 1999.

Joseph, Jane E., and Dennis R. Proffitt. "Semantic versus Perceptual Influences of Color in Object Recognition." *Journal of Experimental Psychology: Learning, Memory, and Cognition* 22, no. 2 (1996): 407–429.

Joseph, T., and A. F. Cardenas. "PICQUERY: A High Level Language for Pictorial Database Management." *IEEE Transactions on Software Engineering* 14, no. 5 (1988): 630–638.

Joyce, Dan W., Paul H. Lewis, Robert H. Tansley, Mark R. Dobie, and Wendy Hall. "Semiotics and Agents for Integrating and Navigating through Multimedia Representations of Concepts." A paper delivered at the Storage and Retrieval for Media Databases conference, San Jose, Calif., January 2000.

Julesz, B. "Textons, the Elements of Texture Perception and Their Interactions." *Nature* 290 (1981): 91–97.

Kahn, J. L., and D. H. Foster. "Visual Comparison of Rotated and Reflected Random-Dot Patterns as a Function of Their Positional Uncertainty and Separation in the Field." *Quarterly Journal of Experimental Psychology* 33A (1981): 155–166.

Kahneman, D. *Attention and Effort.* Englewood Cliffs, N.J.: Prentice-Hall, 1973.

Kaiser, Julius O. "Systematic Indexing." In *Theory of Subject Analysis*, ed. Lois Mai Chan, Phyllis A. Richmond, and Elaine Svenonius, 52–70. Littleton, Colo.: Libraries Unlimited, 1985 (article originally published 1911).

Kamel, Ibrahim, and Christos Faloutsos. "Hilbert *R*-tree: An Improved *R*-tree Using Fractals." A paper delivered at the Proceedings of the Very Large Data Base Conference, Santiago, Chile, September 1994.

Kaplan, M., B. Gooch, and E. Cohen. "Interactive Artistic Rendering." A paper delivered at the 1st International Symposium on Non Photorealistic Animation and Rendering, NPAR 2000, Annecy, France, June 5–7, 2000.

Kasturi, R., R. Fernandez, M. Amlani, and W. C. Feng. "Map Data Processing in Geographical Information Systems." *Computer* 22, no. 12 (1989): 10–21.

Katayama, N., and S. Satoh. "The *SR*-tree: An Index Structure for High-Dimensional Nearest Neighbor Queries." A paper delivered at the International Conference for the Management of Data, SIGMOD, Tucson, Ariz., May 13–15, 1997.

Kato, Toshikazu. "Database Architecture for Content-Based Image Retrieval." A paper delivered at the Image Storage and Retrieval Systems conference, San Jose, Calif., February 13–14, 1992.

Katsikitis, Mary. "The Classification of Facial Expressions of Emotion: A Multidimensional-Scaling Approach." *Perception* 26, no. 5 (1997): 613–626.

Katz, B. F. "Color Contrast and Color Preference." *Empirical Studies of the Arts* 17, no. 1 (1999): 1–24.

Keefe, Jeanne M. "The Use of the Visual Materials Format for a Slide Library Integrated into an OPAC." In *Beyond the Book: Extending MARC for Subject Access*, ed. Toni Petersen and Pat Molholt. Boston: G. K. Hall & Co., 1990.

Kehrer, Lothar, and Cristina Chapter Meinecke. "Perceptual Organization of Visual Patterns: The Segmentation of Textures." In *Handbook of Perception and Action*, ed. Wolfgang Prinz and Bruce Bridgeman, Vol. 1: Perception, 25–70. San Diego, Calif.: Academic Press, 1996.

Keil, F. C. "Conceptual Development and Category Structure." In *Concepts and Conceptual Development: The Ecological and Intellectual Factors in Categorization*, ed. U. Neisser, 175–200. Cambridge, England: Cambridge University Press, 1987.

Keister, Lucinda H. "User Types and Queries: Impact on Image Access Systems." In *Challenges in Indexing Electronic Text and Images*, ed. Raya Fidel, Trudi Bellardo Hahn, Edie M. Rasmussen, and Philip J. Smith. Medford, N.J.: Learned Information, 1994.

Kessler, B. "Response." *Visual Resources Association Bulletin* 23 no. 2 (1996): 67.

Kinsbourne, Marcel. "Neuropsychology of Attention." In *Neuropsychology*, ed. Dahlia W. Zaidel, 105–123. San Diego: Academic Press, 1994.

Kirsch, Joan L., and Russell A. Kirsch. "The Anatomy of Painting Style: Description with Computer Rules." *Leonardo* 21, no. 4 (1988).

Kitamoto, A., C. Zhou, and M. Takagi. "Similarity Retrieval of NOAA Satellite Imagery by Graph Matching." A paper delivered at the Storage and Retrieval for Image and Video Databases conference, San Jose, Calif., February 2–3, 1993.

Kobus, David A., John D. Moses, and Faye Alvarado Bloom. "Effect of Multimodal Stimulus Presentation on Recall." *Perceptual and Motor Skills* 78, no. 1 (1994): 320–322.

Koffka, K. *Principles of Gestalt Psychology*. New York: Harcourt, 1935.

Konecni, Vladimir J. "The Vase on the Mantelpiece: The Golden Section in Context." *Empirical Studies of the Arts* 15, no. 2 (1997): 177–207.

Korf Vidal, Noni. "Experimental Image Taxonomy: An Inquiry into Spontaneous Image Organization." M.S. thesis, Cornell University, 1995.

Kose, G. "The Psychological Investigation of Art: Theoretical and Methodological Implications." In *Cognitive Processes in the Perception of Art*, ed. W. Ray Crozier and Antony J. Chapman, 19, 27–44. New York: North-Holland, 1984.

Koskela, Markus, Jorma Laaksonen, and Erkki Oja. "Comparison of Techniques for Content-Based Image Retrieval." A paper delivered at the 12th Scandinavian Conference on Image Analysis (SCIA 2001), Bergen, Norway, June 2001.

Kosslyn, Stephen M. "Scanning Visual Images: Some Structural Implications." *Perception and Psychophysics* 14, no. 1 (1973): 90–94.

Krause, Michael G. "Intellectual Problems of Indexing Picture Collections." *Audiovisual Librarian* 14, no. 2 (1988): 73–81.

Kreiger, Gerhard, Ingo Rentschler, Gert Hauske, Kerstin Schill, and Christoph Zetzsche. "Object and Scene Analysis by Saccadic Eye-Movements: An Investigation with Higher-Order Statistics." *Spatial Vision* 13, no. 2–3 (2000): 201–214.

Kristjanson, Arlinda F., and James R. Antes. "Eye Movement Analysis of Artists and Nonartists Viewing Paintings." *Visual Arts Research* 15, no. 2 (1989): 21–30.

Kueppers, Harald. *The Basic Law of Color Theory*. Woodbury, N.Y.: Barron's, 1982.

Kuhl, Julius. "Emotion, Cognition, and Motivation: II. The Functional Significance of Emotions in Perception, Memory, Problem-Solving, and Overt Action." *Sprache und Kognition* 2, no. 4 (1983): 228–253.

Kunii, T. L., S. Weyl, and J. M. Tenenbaum. "A Relational Data Base Schema for Describing Complex Pictures with Color and Texture." A paper delivered at the 2nd International Joint Conference on Pattern Recognition, Lyngby-Copenhagen, Denmark, August 1974.

Kurita, T., and T. Kato. "Learning of Personal Visual Impression for Image Database Systems." A paper delivered at the 2nd International Conference on Document Analysis and Recognition, Tsukuba Science City, Japan, October 20–22, 1993.

Kwasnik, Barbara. "The Influence of Context on Classificatory Behavior." Ph.D., thesis, Rutgers, The State University of New Jersey, 1989.

Laaksonen, Jorma, Markus Koskela, and Erkki Oja. "PicSOM: A Framework for Content-Based Image Database Retrieval Using Self-Organizing Maps." A paper delivered at the 11th Scandinavian Conference on Image Analysis, Kangerlussuaq, Greenland, June 1999.

Lafon, Yves, and Bert Bos. *Describing and Retrieving Photos Using RDF and HTTP*. W3C, September 28, 2000. Available from www.w3.org/TR/photo-rdf (accessed on December 12, 2000).

Lagoze, Carl, and Jane Hunter. "The ABC Ontology and Model." *Journal of Digital Information* 2, no. 2 (2001).

Lahlou, Youssef. "Mixing Classes and Prototypes: An Object Oriented Approach to Semantic Image Indexing." A paper delivered at the 4th DELOS Workshop: Image Indexing and Retrieval, San Miniato, Italy, August 28–30, 1997.

Laiacona, M., E. Capitani, and R. Barbarotto. "Do Living and Nonliving Categories Need Further Fractionation? A Study of Picture Naming in a Pathological Sample." *Brain and Cognition* 43, no. 1–3 (2000): 291–296.

Landy, M. S., and N. Graham. "Visual Perception of Texture." In *The Visual Neurosciences*, ed. L. M. Chalupa and J. S. Werner. Cambridge, Mass.: MIT Press, forthcoming.

Lane, Richard D., Phyllis M. L. Chua, and Raymond J. Dolan. "Common Effects of Emotional Valence, Arousal and Attention on Neural Activation during Visual Processing of Pictures." *Neuropsychologia* 37, no. 9 (1999): 989–997.

Lane, Richard D., Gereon R. Fink, Phyllis M. L. Chau, and Raymond J. Dolan. "Neural Activation During Selective Attention to Subjective Emotional Responses." *Neuroreport: An International Journal for the Rapid Communication of Research in Neuroscience* 8, no. 18 (1997): 3969–3972.

Lang, Peter J., Margaret M. Bradley, and Bruce N. Cuthbert. "Motivated Attention: Affect, Activation, and Action." In *Attention and Orienting: Sensory and Motivational Processes*, ed. Peter J. Lang, Robert F. Simons, and M. T. Balaban, 97–135. Mahwah, N.J.: Lawrence Erlbaum Associates, 1997.

Lanzi, Elisa, and Roy McKeown. "Square Pegs and Round Holes: Standards for Visual Resources Collections." *Visual Resources Association Bulletin* 23, no. 4 (1996): 93–103.

Larkin, J. H., and H. A. Simon. "Why a Diagram Is (Sometimes) Worth Ten Thousand Words." *Cognitive Science* 11 (1987): 65–99.

Lasaga, Maria I. "Gestalts and Their Components: Nature of Information Precedence." In *Object Perception: Structure and Processes*, ed. Bryan E. Shepp and Soledad Ballesteros, 165–202. Hillsdale, N.J.: Lawrence Erlbaum, 1989.

Lassaline, Mary E., Edward J. Wisniewski, and Douglas L. Medin. "Basic Levels in Artificial and Natural Categories: Are All Basic Levels Created Equal?" In *Percepts, Concepts, and Categories: The Representation and Processing of Information*, ed. Barbara Burns, 93. New York: North-Holland, 1992.

Latto, Richard, Douglas Brain, and Brian Kelly. "An Oblique Effect in Aesthetics: Homage to Mondrian (1872–1944)." *Perception* 29, no. 8 (2000): 981–987.

Lauzzana, Raymond Guido, and Lynn Pocock-Williams. "A Rule System for Analysis in the Visual Arts." *Leonardo* 21, no. 4 (1988): 445–452.

Lawson, Rebecca, and Pierre Jolicoeur. "The Effects of Plane Rotation on the Recognition of Brief Masked Pictures of Familiar Objects." *Memory and Cognition* 26, no. 4 (1998): 791–803.

Layne, S. S. "Some Issues in the Indexing of Images." *Journal of the American Society for Information Science* 45, no. 8 (1994): 583–588.

Lazreg, Cecilia Karpowicz, and Etienne Mullet. "Judging the Pleasantness of Form–Color Combinations." *American Journal of Psychology* 114, no. 4 (2001): 511–533.

Leontiev, Dmitrii A. "The Perception of Art: Psychological Mechanisms, Factors, and Processes." *Journal of Russian and East European Psychology* 38, no. 3 (2000): 45–63.

Leung, Clement H., Simon So, Audrey M. Tam, Dwi Sutanto, and Philip Tse. "Semantic-Based Retrieval of Visual Data." In *Principles of Visual Information Retrieval*, ed. Michael S. Lew, 297–318. New York: Springer, 2001.

Levy, Jerre. "Psychological Implications of Bilateral Asymmetry." In *Hemisphere Function in the Human Brain*, ed. S. J. Diamond and J. G. Beaumont. New York: John Wiley & Sons, 1974.

Lew, Michael S., ed. *Principles of Visual Information Retrieval.* New York: Springer, 2001.

Lew, Michael S. "Feature Selection and Visual Learning." In *Principles of Visual Information Retrieval*, ed. Michael S. Lew, 145–162. New York: Springer, 2001.

Li, John Z., M. Tamer Ozsu, and Duane Szafron. *Query Languages in Multimedia Database Systems.* Technical Report TR95-25. Edmonton, Alberta, Canada: Department of Computing Science, The University of Alberta, 1995.

Li, John. Z., M. Tamer Ozsu, Duane Szafron, and V. Oria. "Moql: A Multimedia Object Query Language." A paper delivered at the 3rd International Workshop on Multimedia Information Systems, Como, Italy, 1997.

Library of Congress Cataloging Distribution Service. *Library of Congress Subject Headings*, 26th ed. Washington, D.C.: Library of Congress, 2003.

Liddell, Christine. "Every Picture Tells a Story—Or Does It? Young South African Children Interpreting Pictures." *Journal of Cross-Cultural Psychology* 28, no. 3 (1997): 266–283.

Light, Richard. *CIMI Tagging Guide for the SGML DTD, Version 1.* CIMI Consortium, June, 1996. Available from http://www.cimi.org/old_site/ standards/ (accessed on April 20, 2003).

Lindeberg, T. *Scale-Space Theory in Computer Vision.* Boston, Mass.: Kluwer Academic Publishers, 1992.

Lindeberg, T., and J. O. Eklundh. "Scale Space Primal Sketch Construction and Experiments." *Image and Vision Computing* 10 (1992): 3–18.

Liu, F., and R. W. Picard. "Periodicity, Directionality, and Randomness: Wold Features for Image Modeling and Retrieval." *IEEE Transactions on Pattern Analysis and Machine Intelligence* 18, no. 7 (1996): 517–549.

Livingston, Kenneth R., Janet K. Andrews, and Stevan Harnad. "Categorical Perception Effects Induced by Category Learning." *Journal of Experimental Psychology: Learning, Memory, and Cognition* 24, no. 3 (1998): 732–753.

Lockhead, Gregory R. "On Identifying Things." In *Percepts, Concepts, and Categories: The Representation and Processing of Information*, ed. Barbara Burns, 93, 109–143. New York: North-Holland, 1992.

Loftus, Geoffrey R. "Eye Fixations and Recogntion Memory for Pictures." *Cognitive Psychology* 3 (1972): 525–551.

Loftus, Geoffrey R., and S. M. Bell. "Two Types of Information in Picture Memory." *Journal of Experimental Psychology: Human Learning and Memory* 1, no. 2 (1975): 103–113.

Loftus, Geoffrey R., and H. J. Kallman. "Encoding and Use of Detail Information in Picture Recognition." *Journal of Experimental Psychology: Human Learning and Memory* 5, no. 3 (1979): 197–211.

Loftus, Geoffrey R., and N. H. Mackworth. "Cognitive Determinants of Fixation Location during Picture Viewing." *Journal of Experimental Psychology: Human Perception and Performance* 4 (1978): 565–572.

Loftus, Geoffrey R., and Jennifer E. McLean. "A Front End to a Theory of Picture Recognition." *Psychonomic Bulletin and Review* 6, no. 3 (1999): 394–411.

Lohse, Gerald L., H. Rueter, K. Biolsi, and N. Walker. "Classifying Visual Knowledge Representation: A Foundation For Visualization Research." A paper delivered at the 1st IEEE Conference on Visualization, San Francisco, Calif., October 23–26, 1990.

Lohse, Gerald L., N. Walker, K. Biolsi, and H. Rueter. "Classifying Graphical Information." *Behaviour and Information Technology* 10, no. 5 (1991): 419–436.

Lohse, Gerald L., K. Biolsi, N. Walker, and H. Reuter. "A Classification of Visual Representations." *Communications of the ACM* 37, no. 12 (1994): 36–49.

Lu, Ye, Chunhui Hu, Xingquan Zhu, Hong-Jiang Zhang, and Qiang Yang. "A Unified Framework for Semantics and Feature Based Relevance Feedback in Image Retrieval." A paper delivered at the ACM Multimedia conference, Los Angeles, Calif., October 30-November 4, 2000.

Lupker, S. J. "On the Nature of Perceptual Information during Letter Perception." *Perception and Psychophysics* 25 (1979): 303–312.

Ma, Y., and B. S. Manjunath. "A Comparison of Wavelet Transform Features for Texture Image Annotation." A paper delivered at the International Conference on Image Processing, 1995.

Ma, Y., and B. S. Manjanuth. "NeTra: A Toolbox for Navigating Large Image Databases." A paper delivered at the IEEE International Conference on Image Processing, Santa Barbara, Calif., 1997.

Machamer, Peter. "Theories of Perception, Art, and Criticism." In *Perceiving Artworks*, ed. John Fisher, 10–22. Philadelphia: Temple University Press, 1980.

Mackworth, N. H., and A. J. Morandi. "The Gaze Selects Informative Details within Pictures." *Perception and Psychophysics* 2 (1967): 547–551.

Macrosson, W. D., and P. E. Stewart. "The Inclination of Artists to Partition Line Sections in the Golden Ratio." *Perceptual and Motor Skills* 84, no. 3, pt. 1 (1997): 707–713.

Madigan, S. "Picture Memory." In *Imagery, Memory, and Cognition*, ed. J. C. Yuille, 65–89. Hillsdale, N. J.: Erlbaum, 1983.

Madigan, S., and Lawrence, V. "Factors Affecting Item Recovery and Reminiscence in Free Recall." *American Journal of Psychology* 93 (1980): 489–504.

Maki, Ruth H., and Sharon Swett. "Metamemory for Narrative Text." *Memory and Cognition* 15, no. 1 (1987): 72–83.

Mandal, M. K., F. Idris, and S. Panchanathan. "A Critical Evaluation of Image and Video Indexing Techniques in the Compressed Domain." *Image and Vision Computing Journal* 17, no. 7 (1999): 513–529.

Mandler, G. "Origins and Range of Contemporary Cognitive Psychology." *Zeitschrift fur Psychologie* 192, no. 1 (1984): 73–85.

Mandler, J. M., and N. S. Johnson. "Some of the Thousand Words a Picture Is Worth." *Journal of Experimental Psychology: Human Learning and Memory* 2, no. 5 (1976): 529–540.

Mandler, J. M., and R. E. Parker. "Memory for Descriptive and Spatial Information in Complex Pictures." *Journal of Experimental Psychology: Human Learning and Memory* 2, no. 1 (1976): 38–48.

Mandler, J. M., D. Seegmiller, and J. Day. "On the Coding of Spatial Information." *Memory and Cognition* 5, no. 1 (1977): 10–16.

Mannan, S., K. H. Ruddock, and D. S. Wooding. "The Relationship between the Locations of Spatial Features and Those of Fixations Made during Visual Examination of Briefly Presented Images." *Spatial Vision* 10, no. 3 (1996): 165–188.

Markey, Karen. "Computer-Assisted Construction of a Guide to Themes and Concepts in Medieval Art and Their Essential Attributes." Ph.D. thesis, Syracuse University, 1981.

Markey, Karen. "Interindexer Consistency Tests: A Literature Review and Report of a Test of Consistency in Indexing Visual Materials." *Library and Information Science Research* 6 (1984): 155–177.

Markey, Karen. *Subject Access to Visual Resources Collections: A Model for Computer Construction of Thematic Catalogs.* New York: Greenwood Press, 1986.

Markkula, M., and E. Sormunen. "Searching for Photos: Journalists' Practices in Pictorial IR." A paper delivered at The Challenge of Image Retrieval, A Workshop and Symposium on Image Retrieval, Newcastle upon Tyne, England, February 5–6, 1998.

Markkula, M., and E. Sormunen. "End User Challenges in Indexing Practices in the Digital Newspaper Photo Archive." *Information Retrieval* 1, no. 4 (2000): 259–285.

Marr, David, and H. K. Nishihara. "Representation and Recognition of Three Dimensional Shapes." *Proceedings of the Royal Society of London, Series B* 200 (1978): 269–294.

Marr, David. *Vision.* New York: Freeman, 1982.

Marshall, Philip H., and Ashton G. Thornhill. "When a Photograph Is Judged Artistic: The Influence of Novelty and Affect." *Visual Arts Research* 21, no. 1 (1995): 71–75.

Marsicoi, M., L. Cinque, and S. Levialdi. "Indexing Documents by their Content: A Survey of Current Techniques." *Image and Vision Computing* 15, no. 2 (1997): 119–141.

Martin, Abigail Leab, ed. *AMIA Compendium of Moving Image Cataloging Practice.* American Society of Archivists, forthcoming.

Martinez, José M., ed. "Overview of the MPEG-7 Standard (Version 5.0)." Requirements Group, 65 pp. Singapore: ISO/IEC JTC1/SC29/WG11, 2001.

McCann, John J. "Color Imaging Systems and Color Theory: Past, Present, and Future." A paper delivered at the Human Vision and Electronic Imaging conference, San Jose, Calif., 1998.

McManus, I. C., and P. Weatherby. "The Golden Section and the Aesthetics of Form and Composition: A Cognitive Model." *Empirical Studies of the Arts* 15, no. 2 (1997): 209–232.

McRae, Linda. "Indexing Images for Subject Access: Controlled Vocabularies in the VISION Project." *Art Documentation* 19, no. 2 (2000): 4–9.

McRae, Linda, and Lynda S. White, ed. *ArtMARC Sourcebook: Cataloging Art, Architecture, and Their Visual Images*. Chicago: American Library Association, 1998.

Medin, Douglas L., and Lawrence W. Barsalou. "Categorization Processes and Categorical Perception." In *Categorical Perception*, ed. Stevan Harnad, 455–490. New York: Cambridge University Press, 1987.

Medin, Douglas L., and John D. Coley. "Concepts and Categorization." In *Perception and Cognition at Century's End*, ed. Julian Hochberg, 403–439. New York: Academic Press, 1998.

Medin, Douglas L., and William D. Wattenmaker. "Category Cohesiveness, Theories, and Cognitive Archeology." In *Concepts and Conceptual Development: Ecological and Intellectual Factors in Categorization*, ed. Ulric Neisser, 25–62. New York: Cambridge University Press, 1987.

Meghini, C., F. Sebastiani, and U. Straccia. *A Model of Multimedia Information Retrieval*. Report B4-21-0998. Pisa, Italy: Italian National Research Council/Istituto Elaborazione dell'Informazione (C.N.R.-I.E.I.), 1998.

Mehrotra, R., and William I. Grosky. "REMINDS: A Relational Model-Based Integrated Image and Text Database Management System." A paper delivered at the Workshop on Computer Architecture for Pattern Analysis and Image Database Management, Miami Beach, Fla., 1985.

Mehrotra, Sharad, Yong Rui, Michael Ortega-Binderberge, and Thomas S. Huang. "Supporting Content-Based Queries over Images in MARS." A paper delivered at the IEEE International Conference on Multimedia Computing and Systems, June 3–6, 1997.

Mehtre, Babu M., Mohan S. Kankanhalli, and Wing Foon Lee. "Shape Measures for Content-Based Image Retrieval: A Comparison." *Information Processing and Management* 33, no. 3 (1997): 319–337.

Mesquita, Batja, Nico H. Frijda, and Klaus R. Scherer. "Culture and Emotion." In *Handbook of Cross-Cultural Psychology*, ed. John W. Berry, Pierre R. Dasen, and T. S. Saraswathi, Vol. 2: Basic Processes and Human Development, 255–297. Needham Heights, Mass.: Allyn & Bacon, 1997.

Messaris, Paul. *Visual Persuasion: The Role of Images in Advertising*. Thousand Oaks, Calif.: Sage Publications, 1997.

Metzger, Richard L., and James R. Antes. "The Nature of Processing Early in Picture Perception." *Psychological Research* 45, no. 3 (1983): 267–274.

Miller, Michael B., and Michael S. Gazzaniga. "Creating False Memories for Visual Scenes." *Neuropsychologia* 36, no. 6 (1998): 513–520.

Miller, R. J. "Pictoral Depth Cue Orientation Influences the Magnitude of Perceived Depth." *Visual Arts Research* 23, no. 1 (1997): 97–124.

Minka, T. P., and R. W. Picard. "Interactive Learning with a Society of Models." *Pattern Recognition* 30, no. 4 (1997): 565–581.

Minsky, Marvin. "A Framework for Representing Knowledge." In *The Psychology of Computer Vision*, ed. P. Winston, 211–277. New York: McGraw-Hill, 1975.

Mishra, R. C. "Cognition and Cognitive Development." In *Handbook of Cross-Cultural Psychology*, ed. John W. Berry, Pierre R. Dasen, and T. S. Saraswathi, Vol. 2: Basic Processes and Human Development, 143–175. Needham Heights, Mass.: Allyn & Bacon, 1997.

Moates, Danny R., and Gary M. Schumacher. *An Introduction to Cognitive Psychology*. Belmont, Calif.: Wadsworth Publishing Company, 1980.

Möckel, W., and C. Heemsoth. "Maximizing Information as a Strategy in Visual Search: The Role of Knowledge about the Stimulus Structure." In *Theoretical and Applied Aspects of Eye Movement Research: Selected/Edited Proceedings of the Second European Conference on Eye Movements*, ed. A. Gale and F. Johnson. New York: Elsevier Science Publishers, 1984.

Morris, M. W., and G. L. Murphy. "Converging Operations on a Basic Level in Event Taxonomies." *Memory and Cognition* 18 (1990): 407–418.

Müller, Wolfgang, Stéphane Marchand-Mailet, Henning Müller, D. M. Squire, and Thierry Pun. "Evaluating Image Browsers Using Structured Annotation." *Journal of the American Society for Information Science and Technology* 52, no. 11 (2001): 961–968.

Mumford, David. "Mathematical Theories of Shape: Do They Model Perception?" A paper delivered at the Geometric Methods in Computer Vision conference, San Jose, Calif., 1991.

Munsell, A. H. *A Grammar of Color*. New York: Van Nostrand Reinhold, 1969.

Murphy, G. L., and D. L. Medin. "The Role of Theories in Conceptual Coherence." *Psychological Review* 91 (1985): 289–316.

Murtha, Susan, Howard Chertkow, Mario Beauregard, and Alan Evans. "The Neural Substrate of Picture Naming." *Journal of Cognitive Neuroscience* 11, no. 4 (1999): 399–423.

Nadler, M., and E. P. Smith. *Pattern Recognition Engineering*. New York: John Wiley & Sons, 1992.

Nagae, Seiji. "Handedness and Cerebral Hemispheric Differences in Memory for Pictorial Organization." *Journal of General Psychology* 121, no. 3 (1994): 227–240.

Narasimhalu, A. D. "Special Issue on Content-Based Retrieval." *Association for Computing Machinery Multimedia Systems* 3, no. 1 (1995): 1–41.

Narumoto, Hiroki Yamada, Tetsuya Iidaka, Norihiro Sadato, Kenji Fukui, Harumi Itoh, and Yoshiharu Yonekura. "Brain Regions Involved in Verbal or Nonverbal Aspects of Facial Emotion Recognition." *Neuroreport: An International Journal for the Rapid Communication of Research in Neuroscience* 11, no. 11: (2000): 2571–2576.

National Library of Medicine. *Medical Subject Headings*. Bethesda, Md.: Medical Subject Headings Section, Library Operations, National Library of Medicine, 2003.

Naveh-Benjamin, M. "Coding of Spatial Location Information: An Automatic Process?" *Journal of Experimental Psychology: Learning Memory and Cognition* 13, no. 4 (1987): 595–605.

Navon, D. "Forest before Trees: The Precedence of Global Features in Visual Perception." *Cognitive Psychology* 9 (1977): 353–383.

Neill, S. D. "The Dilemma of the Subjective in Information Organization and Retrieval." *The Journal of Documentation* 43, no. 3 (1987): 193–209.

Nelson, T. O., J. Metzler, and D. A. Reed. "Role of Details in the Long-Term Recognition of Pictures and Verbal Descriptions." *Journal of Experimental Psychology* 102, no. 1 (1974): 184–186.

Nepal, S., M. V. Ramakrishna, and J. A. Thom. "A Fuzzy Object Query Language (FOQL) for Image Databases." A paper delivered at the International Conference on Database Systems for Advanced Applications, Hsinchu, Taiwan, April 1999.

Ng, R., and A. Sedighian. "Evaluating Multi-Dimensional Indexing Structure for Images Transformed by Principal Component Analysis." A paper delivered at the Storage and Retrieval for Image and Video Databases conference, San Jose, Calif., February 1–2, 1996.

Niblack, Wayne, Ron Barber, William Equitz, Myron Flickner, Eduardo Glasman, Dragutin Petkovic, Peter Yanker, and Christos Faloutsos. "The QBIC Project: Querying Images by Content Using Color, Texture, and Shape." A paper delivered at the Storage and Retrieval for Image and Video Databases conference, San Jose, Calif., February 1, 1993.

Niblack, Wayne, and Myron Flickner. "Find Me Pictures That Look Like This: IBM's Image Query Project." *Advanced Imagery* 8, no. 4 (1993): 32–35.

Nickerson, R. S., and M. J. Adams. "Long-Term Memory for a Common Object." *Cognitive Psychology* 11 (1979): 287–307.

Niemann, H., V. Fischer, D. Paulus, and J. Fischer. "Knowledge Based Image Understanding by Iterative Optimization." A paper delivered at Advances in Artificial Intelligence, 20th Annual German Conference on Artificial Intelligence (KI-96), Dresden, 1996.

Nigrin, Albert. *Neural Networks for Pattern Recognition*. Cambridge, Mass.: The MIT Press, 1993.

Nilsson, Nils J. "Introduction to Machine Learning." In *Draft of Incomplete Notes*, 1996. Available at robotics.stanford.edu/people/nilsson/mlbook.html (accessed on April 20, 2003).

North, Adrian C., and David J. Hargreaves. "Collative Variables versus Prototypicality." *Empirical Studies of the Arts* 18, no. 1 (2000): 13–17.

Noton, David, and Lawrence Stark. "Eye Movements and Visual Perception." *Scientific American* 224, no. 6 (1971): 34–43.

Oakley, J., D. Davis, and Richard Shann. "Manchester Visual Query Language." A paper delivered at the Storage and Retrieval for Image and Video Databases conference, San Jose, Calif., February 2–3, 1993.

O'Brien, Justin, and Alan Johnston. "When Texture Takes Precedence over Motion in Depth Perception." *Perception* 29, no. 4 (2000): 437–452.

O'Connor, Brian C. *Explorations in Indexing and Abstracting: Pointing, Virtue, and Power*. Englewood, Colo.: Libraries Unlimited, 1996.

O'Connor, Brian C., Mary K. O'Conner, and June M. Abbas. "User Reactions as Access Mechanism: An Exploration Based upon Captions for Images." *Journal of the American Society for Information Science* 50, no. 8 (1999): 681–697.

O'Keefe, Elizabeth. "The Future of Anglo-American Cataloging Rules." A paper delivered at the Art Libraries Society of North America 27th Annual Conference,

Vancouver, B.C., Canada, March 27, 1999. Available from www.arlisna.org/Conf_1999/aacr2.htm (accessed on April 23, 2003).

Ogle, V. E. "CHABOT: Retrieval from a Relational Database of Images." *Computer* 28, no. 9 (1995): 40–48.

Ohlgren, Thomas. "Subject Indexing of Visual Resources: A Survey." *Visual Resources* 1, no. 1 (1980): 67–73.

Ohrn, Steven G. *Cataloguing in Context: The African Studies Program Slide Archives.* Bloomington, Ind.: African Studies Program, Indiana University, 1975.

Oldal, Maria. "A Foot in the Door: Adapting Cataloging Standards to Visual Materials." *Art Documentation* 15, no. 2 (1996): 7–12.

Oliva, Aude, and Philippe G. Schyns. "Coarse Blobs or Fine Edges? Evidence That Information Diagnosticity Changes the Perception of Complex Visual Stimuli." *Cognitive Psychology* 34 (1997): 72–107.

Oliva, Aude, and Philippe G. Schyns. "Diagnostic Colors Mediate Scene Recognition." *Cognitive Psychology* 41, no. 2 (2000): 176–210.

Olson, R. K., and F. Attneave. "What Variables Produce Similarity Grouping?" *American Journal of Psychology* 83 (1970): 1–21.

Orenstein, J. A., and F. A. Manola. "Probe Spatial Data Modeling and Query Processing in an Image Database Application." *IEEE Transactions on Software Engineering* 14, no. 5 (1988): 611–629.

Orians, Gordon H., and Judith H. Heerwagen. "Evolved Responses to Landscapes." In *The Adapted Mind: Evolutionary Psychology and the Generation of Culture*, ed. Jerome H. Barkow and Leda Cosmides. New York: Oxford University Press, 1992.

Ørnager, S. "The Newspaper Image Database: Empirical Supported Analysis of Users' Typology and Word Association Clusters." A paper delivered at the 18th Annual Special Interest Group Conference on Research and Development in Information Retrieval (SIGIR), Seattle, Wash., July 9–13, 1995.

Paek, S., C. L. Sable, V. Hatzivassiloglou, A. Jaimes, B. H. Schiffman, S.-F. Chang, and K. R. McKeown. "Integration of Visual and Text Based Approaches for the Content Labeling and Classification of Photographs." A paper delivered at the ACM SIGIR'99 Workshop on Multimedia Indexing and Retrieval, Berkeley, Calif., August 19, 1999.

Paivio, Allan, T. B. Rogers, and P. C. Smythe. "Why Are Pictures Easier to Recall than Words?" *Psychonomic Society* 11, no. 4 (1968): 137–138.

Paivio, Allan. "Dual Coding Theory: Retrospect and Current Status." *Canadian Journal of Psychology* 45, no. 3 (1991): 255–287.

Palmer, Stephen E. "The Effects of Contextual Scenes on the Identification of Objects." *Memory and Cognition* 3, no. 5 (1975): 519–526.

Palmer, Stephen E. "Modern Theories of Gestalt Perception." In *Understanding Vision: An Interdisciplinary Perspective*, ed. Glyn W. Humphreys. Cambridge Mass.: Blackwell, 1992.

Palmer, Stephen E., and Irvin Rock. "Rethinking Perceptual Organization: The Role of Uniform Connectedness." *Psychonomic Bulletin and Review* 1, no. 1 (1994): 29–55.

Palmer, Stephen E., E. Rosch, and P. Chase. "Canonical Perspective and the Perception of Objects." In *Attention and Performance* Vol. 9, ed. J. Long and A. D. Baddeley. Hillsdale, N.J.: Lawrence Erlbaum Associates, 1981.

Panofsky, Erwin. *Meaning in the Visual Arts: Papers in and on Art History*. Garden City, N.Y.: Doubleday Anchor Books, 1955.

Panofsky, Erwin. *Studies in Iconology*. Reprint ed. New York: Harper & Row, 1962.

Papathomas, Thomas V., Tiffany E. Conway, Ingemar J. Cox, Joumana Ghosn, Matt L. Miller, Thomas P. Minka, and Peter N. Yianilos. "Psychophysical Studies of the Performance of an Image Database System." A paper delivered at the Human Vision and Electronic Imaging conference, San Jose, Calif., January, 1998.

Papin, Jean-Paul. "Use of the NAC Eye Mark Recorder to Study Visual Strategies of Military Aircraft Pilots." In *Theoretical and Applied Aspects of Eye Movement Research*, ed. A. G. Gale and F. Johnson, 22, 367–371. New York: North Holland, 1984.

Park, Denise C. "Item and Attribute Storage of Pictures and Words in Memory." *American Journal of Psychology* 93, no. 4 (1980): 603–615.

Park, Y. C., P. K. Kim, F. Golshani, and S. Panchanathan. "Conceptualization and Ontology: Tools for Efficient Storage and Retrieval of Semantic Visual Information." A paper delivered at the Internet Multimedia Management Systems conference, Boston, 2000.

Parker, Elizabeth Betz. *LC Thesaurus for Graphic Materials: Topical Terms for Subject Access*. With an introduction by Jackie M. Dooley. Washington, D.C.: Library of Congress, 1987.

Paulus, D., U. Ahlrichs, B. Heigl, J. Denzler, J. Hornegger, M. Zobel, and H. Niemann. "Active Knowledge-Based Scene Analysis." A paper delivered at the International Conference on Vision Systems, Las Palmas de Gran Canaria, Spain, 1999.

Pavlidis, Theo. "Image Analysis." In *Annual Review of Computer Science*, ed. Joseph F. Traub, Vol. 3, 75–123. Palo Alto, Calif.: Annual Reviews Inc., 1988.

Pavlidis, Theo. "Why Progress in Machine Vision Is So Slow." *Pattern Recognition Letters* 13, no. 4 (1992): 221–225.

Peeck, J., G. Van Dam, and R. W. F. Uhlenbeck. "Incidental Cues and Picture/Word Differences in Recall." *Perceptual and Motor Skills* 45 (1977): 1211–1215.

Pejtersen, A. M. *The Book House: Modelling User's Need and Search Strategies as a Basis for System Design*. Technical Report Risø-M-2794. Roskilde, Denmark: Risø National Laboratory, 1989.

Penfield, W., and L. Roberts. *Speech and Brain Mechanisms*. Princeton, N.J.: Princeton University Press, 1959.

Pentland, A., R. W. Picard, and S. Sclaroff. "Photobook: Content-Based Manipulation of Image Databases." *International Journal of Computer Vision* 18, no. 3 (1996): 233–254.

Petersen, Toni. *Art and Architecture Thesaurus*. 2nd ed. New York: Oxford University Press, 1994.

Petersen, Toni, and Patricia J. Barnett. *Guide to Indexing and Cataloging with the Art and Architecture Thesaurus*. New York: Oxford University Press, 1994.

Petersen, Toni, and Pat Molholt, ed. *Beyond the Book: Extending MARC for Subject Access*. Boston: G. K. Hall & Co., 1990.

Petrakis, E., and C. Faloutsos. "Similarity Searching in Medical Image Databases." *IEEE Transactions on Knowledge and Data Engineering* 9, no. 3 (1997): 435–447.

Pettersson, R. "Interpretation of Image Content." *Educational Communication and Technology Journal* 36, no. 1 (1988): 45–55.

Pezdek, Kathy. "Recognition Memory for Related Pictures." *Memory and Cognition* 6, no. 1 (1978): 64–69.

Pezdek, Kathy, Ruth Maki, Debra Valencia-Laver, Tony Whetstone, J. Stoeckert, and T. Dougherty. "Picture Memory: Recognizing Added and Deleted Details." *Journal of Experimental Psychology: Learning, Memory, and Cognition* 14, no. 3 (1988): 468–476.

Pezdek, Kathy, Tony Whetstone, Kirk Reynolds, Nusha Askari, and T. Dougherty. "Memory for Real-World Scenes: The Role of Consistency with Schema Expectation." *Journal of Experimental Psychology: Learning, Memory, and Cognition* 15, no. 4 (1989): 587–595.

Pham, Binh. "Design for Aesthetics: Interactions of Design Variables and Aesthetic Properties." A paper delivered at Human Vision and Electronic Imaging conference, San Jose, Calif., 1999.

Pizano, Arturo, Allen Klinger, and Alfonso Cardenas. "Specification of Spatial Integrity Constraints in Pictorial Databases." *Computer* 22 (1989): 59–71.

Pommert, A. K., H. Hoehne, Bernhard Pflesser, Martin Riemer, Thomas Schiemann, Rainer Schubert, Udo Schumacher, and Ulf Tiede. "A Highly Realistic Volume Model Derived from the Visible Human Male." A paper delivered at the 3rd Visible Human Project Conference, Bethesda Md., October 5–6, 2000. Available from www.nlm.nih.gov/research/visible/

Potter, M. C. "Short-Term Conceptual Memory for Pictures." *Journal of Experimental Psychology: Human Learning and Memory* 2, no. 5 (1976): 509–522.

Potter, M. C., and E. I. Levy. "Recognition Memory for a Rapid Sequence of Pictures." *Journal of Experimental Psychology* 81, no. 1 (1969): 10–15.

Pylyshyn, Z. W. "The Role of Visual Indexes in Spatial Perception and Mental Imagery." In *Vision and Attention*, ed. R. Wright, 215–231. New York: Oxford University Press, 1998.

Rabitti, F., and P. Savino. "Querying Semantic Image Databases." A paper delivered at the Image Storage and Retrieval Systems conference, San Jose, Calif., February 13–14, 1992.

Raff, Ulrich. "Visual Data Formatting." In *The Perception of Visual Information*, ed. William R. Hendee and Peter N. T. Wells, 177–222. New York: Springer-Verlag, 1993.

Rajaram, Suparna. "Perceptual Effects on Remembering: Recollective Processes in Picture Recognition Memory." *Journal of Experimental Psychology: Learning, Memory, and Cognition* 22, no. 2 (1996): 365–377.

Ramakrishna, M. V., and S. Nepal. *Similarity Query Processing in Image Databases*. 2000. Technical report. Melbourne, Australia: RMIT University, 2000.

Rao, A. R., and G. L. Lohse. "Identifying High Level Features of Texture Perception." *Computer Vision, Graphics, and Image Processing* 55 (1993): 218–233.

Rasmussen, Edie M. "Indexing Images." In *Annual Review of Information Science and Technology*, ed. Martha E. Williams, Vol. 32, 169–196. Medford, N.J.: Learned Information, 1997.

Rawlings, David, Neus Barrantes Vidal, and Adrian Furnham. "Personality and Aesthetic Preference in Spain and England: Two Studies Relating Sensation Seeking and Openness to Experience to Liking for Paintings and Music." *European Journal of Personality* 14, no. 6 (2000): 553–576.

Reed, S. K. "Structural Descriptions and the Limitations of Visual Images." *Memory and Cognition* 2, no. 2 (1974): 329–336.

Reed, S. K., and J. A. Johnson. "Detection of Parts in Patterns and Images." *Memory and Cognition* 3, no. 5 (1975): 569–575.

Rensink, Ronald A. "Seeing, Sensing, and Scrutinizing." *Vision Research* 40 (2000): 1469–1487.

Rensink, Ronald A., J. K. O'Regan, and J. J. Clark. "To See or Not to See: The Need for Attention to Perceive Changes in Scenes." *Psychological Science* 8 (1997): 368–373.

Rentschler, Ingo, Martin Juettner, Alexander Unzicker, and Theodor Landis. "Innate and Learned Components of Human Visual Preference." *Current Biology* 9, no. 13 (1999): 665–671.

Rickman, Rick, and John Stonham. "Similarity Retrieval from Image Databases." A paper delivered at the Storage and Retrieval for Image and Video Databases conferences, San Jose, Calif., February 2–3, 1993.

Rifkin, A. "Evidence for a Basic Level in Event Taxonomies." *Memory and Cognition* 13 (1985): 538–556.

Ritchey, G. H. "Pictorial Detail and Recall in Adults and Children." *Journal of Experimental Psychology: Learning, Memory, and Cognition* 8, no. 2 (1982): 139–141.

Ritchey, G. H., and C. R. Beal. "Image Detail and Recall: Evidence for Within-Item Elaboration." *Journal of Experimental Psychology: Human Learning and Memory* 6, no. 1 (1980): 66–76.

Rock, Irvin. *An Introduction to Perception.* New York: Macmillan, 1975.

Rock, Irvin, and Arien Mack. "Attention and Perceptual Organization." In *Cognitive Approaches to Human Perception*, ed. Soledad Ballesteros, 23–41. Hillsdale, N.J.: Lawrence Erlbaum Associates, 1994.

Roddy, Kevin. "Subject Access to Visual Resources: What the 90s Might Portend." *Library Hi Tech* 9, no. 1 (1991): 45–49.

Rogowitz, Bernice E., Thomas Frese, John R. Smith, Charles A. Bouman, and Edward Kalin. "Perceptual Image Similarity Experiments." A paper delivered at the Human Vision and Electronic Imaging conference, San Jose, Calif., January 1998.

Rogowitz, Bernice E., Thrasyvoulos N. Pappas, and Jan P. Allebach. "Building Bridges between Human Vision and Electronic Imaging: A Ten Year Retrospective." A paper delivered at the Human Vision and Electronic Imaging conference, San Jose, Calif., January 1998.

Romer, Donna M. *A Keyword Is Worth 1,000 Images.* Kodak Internal Technical Report. Rochester, N.Y.: Kodak, 1993.

Roos, Jane Mayo. "Review of Courtald Gallery Paintings CD–ROM." *College Art Association Reviews* (1999).

Rorvig, Mark E. *The Two Domain Theory of Image Collections Searching.* Project ICON working paper, 86-1. Austin, Tex.: Graduate School of Library and Information Science, University of Texas, 1986.

Rorvig, Mark E. "Image Information Retrieval." *Journal of Education for Library and Information Science* 27, no. 3 (1987): 190–193.

Rorvig, Mark E., C. H. Turner, and J. Moncada. "The NASA Image Collection Visual Thesaurus." A paper delivered at the American Society for Information Science 17th Mid-Year Meeting, Ann Arbor, Michigan, May 15–18, 1988.

Rosch, Eleanor. "Principles of Categorization." In *Cognition and Categorization*, ed. Eleanor Rosch and Barbara B. Lloyd, 27–47. Hillsdale N.J.: Lawrence Erlbaum Associates, 1978.

Rosch, Eleanor, and C. B. Mervis. "Family Resemblences: Studies in the Internal Structure of Categories." *Cognitive Psychology* 7 (1975): 573–605.

Rosch, Eleanor, C. B. Mervis, W. Gray, D. Johnson, and P. Boyes-Braem. "Basic Objects in Natural Categories." *Cognitive Psychology* 8 (1976): 382–439.

Rose, T., D. Elworthy, A. Kotcheff, A. Clare, and P. Tsonis. "ANVIL: A System for the Retrieval of Captioned Images Using NLP Techniques." A paper delivered at the 3rd UK Conference on Image Retrieval (CIR2000), Brighton, England, 2000.

Rothenstein, Julian, and Mel Gooding. *The Playful Eye: An Album of Visual Delight*. San Francisco: Chronicle Books, 2000.

Roussopoulos, N., C. Faloutsos, and T. Sellis. "An Efficient Pictorial Database System for PSQL." *IEEE Transactions on Software Engineering* 14, no. 5 (1988): 639–650.

Rowe, Neil C., and Brian Frew. "Automatic Classification of Objects in Captioned Depictive Photographs for Retrieval." In *Intelligent Multimedia Retrieval*, ed. Mark T. Maybury, 65–79. Cambridge, Mass.: AAAI Press/MIT Press, 1997.

Rubin, Edgar. "Figure and Ground." In *Readings in Perception*, ed. David C. Beardslee and Michael Wertheimer. New York: D. Van Nostrand Company, 1958.

Rui, Yong, and Thomas S. Huang. "Relevance Feedback Techniques in Image Retrieval." In *Principles of Visual Information Retrieval*, ed. Michael S. Lew, 219–258. New York: Springer, 2001.

Rui, Yong, Thomas S. Huang, and Shih-Fu Chang. "Image Retrieval: Current Techniques, Promising Directions, and Open Issues." *Journal of Visual Communication and Image Representation* 10, no. 4 (1999): 39–62.

Rui, Yong, Alfred C. She, and Thomas S. Huang. "Automated Shape Segmentation Using Attraction-Based Grouping in Spatial–Color–Texture Space." A paper delivered at the IEEE International Conference on Image Processing, Lausanne, Switzerland, September 16–19, 1996.

Rumelhart, D. E. "Schemata: The Building Blocks of Cognition." In *Theoretical Issues in Reading and Comprehension*, ed. R. J. Spiro, B. Bruce, and W. F. Brewer, 33–58. Hillsdale, N.J.: Erlbaum, 1980.

Rumelhart, D. E., and D. A. Norman. "Representation in Memory." In *Stevens' Handbook of Experimental Psychology: Learning and Cognition*, ed. R. C. Atkinson, R. J. Herrnstein, G. Lindzey, and R. D. Luce, 2, 511–587. New York: Wiley, 1988.

Runge, O. P. *Die Farbenkugel*. 1810. Reprint, England: Bern Benteli, 1973.

Russ, John C. *The Image Processing Handbook*. Boca Raton, Fla.: CRC Press, 1998.

Russell, P. A., J. B. Deregowski, and P. R. Kinnear. "Perception and Aesthetics." In *Handbook of Cross-Cultural Psychology*, ed. John W. Berry, Pierre R. Dasen, and T. S. Saraswathi, Vol. 2: Basic Processes and Human Development, 107–142. Needham Heights, Mass.: Allyn & Bacon, 1997.

Ruth, Jan-Erik, and Kyösti Kolehmainen. "Classification of Art into Style Periods: A Factor Analytical Approach." *Scandanavian Journal of Psychology* 15, no. 4 (1974): 322–327.

Ruthrof, Horst. *The Reader's Construction of Narrative*. London: Routledge and Kegan Paul, 1981.

Sagerer, Gerhard, and Heinrich Niemann. *Semantic Networks for Understanding Scenes*. Advances in Computer Vision and Machine Intelligence, ed. Martin D. Levine. New York: Plenum Press, 1997.

Saint-Martin, Fernande. *Semiotics of Visual Language*. Advances in Semiotics. Bloomington and Indianapolis: Indiana University Press, 1990.

Saito, Miho. "Comparative Studies on Color Preference in Japan and Other Asian Regions, with Special Emphasis on the Preference for White." *Color Research and Application* 21, no. 1 (1996a): 35–49.

Saito, Miho. "A Comparative Study of Color Preferences in Japan, China, and Indonesia, with Emphasis on the Preference for White." *Perceptual and Motor Skills* 83, no. 1 (1996b): 115–128.

Samadani, R., and C. Han. "Computer Assisted Extraction of Boundaries and Images." A paper delivered at the Storage and Retrieval for Image and Video Databases conference, San Jose, Calif., February 2–3, 1993.

Santini, Simone. "Evaluation Vademecum for Visual Information System." A paper delivered at the Storage and Retrieval for Media Databases conference, San Jose, Calif., January 2000.

Santini, Simone, Amarnath Gupta, and Ramesh C. Jain. "Emergent Semantics through Interaction in Image Databases." *IEEE Transactions on Knowledge and Data Engineering* 13, no. 3 (2001): 337–351.

Santini, Simone, and Ramesh C. Jain. "The Graphical Specification of Similarity Queries." *Journal of Visual Languages and Computing* 7 (1997): 403–421.

Santini, Simone, and Ramesh C. Jain. "Similarity Measures." *IEEE Transactions on Pattern Analysis and Machine Intelligence* 21, no. 9 (1999): 871–883.

Saupe, D., R. Hamzaoui, and H. Hartenstein. "Fractal Image Compression: An Introductory Overview." A paper delivered at SIGGRAPH'96, New Orleans, La., August 4–9, 1996.

Scassellati, B., S. Alexopoulos, and Myron Flickner. "Retrieving Images by 2-D Shape: A Comparison of Computation Methods with Human Perceptual Judgments." A paper delivered at the International Society for Optical Engineering (SPIE) conference, San Jose, Calif., Feb. 7–8, 1994.

Schouwstra, Sanneke J., Johan Hoogstraten, Catharina A. Hartman, and Marlies E. A. Stouthard. "Robustness of the Photo Anxiety Questionnaire: Changing the Sequence of Stimuli and Photographs." *Psychological Reports* 78, no. 2 (1996): 447–457.

Schreiber, A. Th., Barbara Dubbeldam, Jan Wielemaker, and Bob Wielinga. "Ontology-Based Photo Annotation." *IEEE Intelligent Systems* 16, no. 3 (2001): 66–74.

Schroeder, Kimberly A. "Layered Indexing of Images at the General Motors Media Archives." *The Indexer* 21, no. 1 (1998): 11–14.

Schyns, Philippe G., and Aude Oliva. "From Blobs to Boundary Edges: Evidence for Time- and Spatial-Scale-Dependent Scene Recognition." *Psychological Science* 5, no. 4 (1994): 195–200.

Sclaroff, Stan, Marco La Cascia, Saratendu Sethi, and Leonid Taycher. "Unifying Textual and Visual Cues for Content-Based Image Retrieval on the World Wide Web." *Computer Vision and Image Understanding* 75, no. 1–2 (1999): 86–98.

Sclaroff, Stan, Marco La Cascia, Saratendu Sethi, and Leonid Taycher. "Mix and Match Features in the ImageRover Search Engine." In *Principles of Visual Information Retrieval*, ed. Michael S. Lew, 259–277. New York: Springer, 2001.

Scott, M. J., and D. V. Canter. "Picture or Place? A Multiple Sorting Study of Landscape." *Journal of Environmental Psychology* 17, no. 4 (1997): 263–281.

Seloff, Gary A. "Automated Access to the NASA-JSC Image Archive." *Library Trends* 38, no. 4 (1990).

Shaari, Ahmad Jelani. "The Interactive Effects of Color Realism, Clustering, and Age on Pictorial Recall Memory among Students in Malaysia." Virginia Polytechnic Institute and State University, 1999.

Shanbehzadeh, Jamshid, Amir Masud Eftekhari Moghadam, and Fariborz Mahmoudi. "Image Indexing and Retrieval Techniques: Past, Present, and Next." A paper delivered at the Storage and Retrieval for Media Databases conference, San Jose, Calif., January 2000.

Shannon, C. E. "A Mathematical Theory of Communication." *The Bell System Journal* 27, no. 3 (1948): 379–423, 623–656.

Sharps, Matthew J., Carla A. Wilson-Leff, and Jana L. Price. "Relational and Item-Specific Information as Determinants of Category Superiority Effects." *Journal of General Psychology* 122, no. 3 (1995): 271–285.

Shatford, Sara. "Describing a Picture: A Thousand Words Are Seldom Cost Effective." *Cataloging and Classification Quarterly* 4, no. 4 (1984): 13–30.

Shatford, Sara. "Analyzing the Subject of a Picture: A Theoretical Approach." *Cataloging and Classification Quarterly* 6, no. 3 (1986): 39–62.

Shen, Heng Tao, Beng Chin Ooi, and Kian-Lee Tan. "Giving Meanings to WWW Images." A paper delivered at the ACM SIGMM 2000 International Multimedia Conference, Los Angeles, Calif., October 30–November 3, 2000.

Shepard, R. N. "Recognition Memory for Words, Sentences, and Pictures." *Journal of Verbal Learning and Verbal Behavior* 6, no. 1 (1967): 156–163.

Simons, Wendell W., and Luraine C. Tansey. *A Slide Classification System for the Organization and Automatic Indexing of Interdisciplinary Collections of Slides and Pictures*. Santa Cruz, Calif.: University of California, 1970.

Slater, Alan. "Visual Organization and Perceptual Constancies in Early Infancy." In *Perceptual Constancy: Why Things Look As They Do*, ed. Vincent Walsh and J. J. Kulikowski, 6–30. New York: Cambridge University Press, 1998.

Small, Jocelyn Penny. "Retrieving Images Verbally: No More Key Words and Other Heresies." *Library Hi Tech* 9, no. 1 (1991): 51–67.

Smeaton, A., and I. Quigley. "Experiments on Using Semantic Distances between Words in Image Caption Retrieval." A paper delivered at the 19th International Conference on Research and Development in Information Retrieval, Zurich, Switzerland, August 1996.

Smeulders, A. W. M., Marcel Worring, Simone Santini, Amarnath Gupta, and Ramesh C. Jain. "Content-Based Retrieval at the End of the Early Years." *IEEE Transactions on Pattern Analysis and Machine Intelligence* 22, no. 12 (2000): 1349–1380.

Smith, Brenda D., Cynthia Miller, Frances Grossman, and Maria Valeri-Gold. "Vocabulary Retention: Effects of Using Spatial Imaging on Hemispheric-Preference Thinkers." *Journal of Research and Development in Education* 27, no. 4 (1994): 244–252.

Smith, Edward E., Gerald J. Balzano, and Janet Walker. "Nominal, Perceptual, and Semantic Codes in Picture Categorization." In *Semantic Factors in Cognition*, ed. J. W.

Cotton and R. L. Klatzky, 137–168. Hillsdale, N.J.: Lawrence Erlbaum Associates, 1978.

Smith, John R. "Quantitative Assessment of Image Retrieval Effectiveness." *JASIST* 52, no. 11 (2001): 969–979.

Smith, John R., and Shih-Fu Chang. "An Image and Video Search Engine for the World-Wide Web." A paper delivered at the Storage and Retrieval for Image and Video Databases conference, San Jose, Calif., February 1997a.

Smith, John R., and Shih-Fu Chang. "Visually Searching the Web for Content." *IEEE Multimedia* 4, no. 3 (1997b): 12–20.

Smith, Linda B., and Diana Heise. "Perceptual Similarity and Conceptual Structure." In *Percepts, Concepts, and Categories: The Representation and Processing of Information*, ed. Barbara Burns, 93, 233–272. New York: North-Holland, 1992.

Soergel, Dagobert. "Indexing and Retrieval Performance: The Logical Evidence." *Journal of the American Society for Information Science* 45, no. 8 (1994): 589–599.

Solso, Robert L. *Cognition and the Visual Arts*. Cambridge, Mass.: MIT Press, 1994.

Sormunen, E., M. Markkula, and K. Järvelin. "The Perceived Similarity of Photos: A Test-Collection Based Evaluation Framework for the Content-Based Image Retrieval Algorithms." A paper delivered at the Multimedia Information Retrieval Systems (MIRA) conference, Glasgow, Scotland, April 14–16, 1999.

Sowa, John F., ed. *Principles of Semantic Networks: Explorations in the Representation of Knowledge*. San Mateo, Calif.: Morgan Kaufmann, 1991.

Spoehr, Kathryn T., and Stephen W. Lehmkuhle. *Visual Information Processing*. San Francisco: W. H. Freeman and Company, 1982.

Springer, Sally P., and Georg Deutsch. *Left Brain, Right Brain: Perspectives from Cognitive Neuroscience*. 5th ed. New York: W. H. Freeman, 1998.

Squire, D. M. "Learning a Similarity-Based Distance Measure for Image Database Organization from Human Partitionings of an Image Set." A paper delivered at the 4th IEEE Workshop on Applications of Computer Vision (WACV '98), Princeton, N.J., October 1998.

Squire, D. M., and Thierry Pun. "Assessing Agreement between Human and Machine Clusterings of Image Databases." *Pattern Recognition* 31, no. 12 (1998): 1905–1919.

Srihari, Rohini K. "Use of Captions and Other Collateral Text in Understanding Photographs." *Artificial Intelligence Review* 8, no. 5–6 (1995): 409–430.

Srihari, Rohini K. "Using Speech Input for Image Interpretation, Annotation, and Retrieval." *Library Trends* 48, no. 2 (1999): 141–156.

Stam, Dierdre C. "Choosing Our Words: Reflections on Authority Control in Art Information Systems." A paper delivered at the Authority Control Symposium, Tuscon, Ariz., 1986.

Stam, Dierdre C. "The Quest for a Code, or a Brief History of the Computerized Cataloging of Art Objects." *Art Documentation* 8, Spring (1989): 7–15.

Stam, Dierdre C. "Shared Access to Visual Images: The Potential of the Web." *Visual Resources Association Bulletin* 23, no. 2 (1996): 63–67.

Stam, Dierdre C., and Angela Giral. "Linking Art Objects and Art Information." *Library Trends* 37, no. 2 (1988): 117–264.

Standing, Lionel, Jerry Conezio, and Ralph N. Haber. "Perception and Memory for Pictures: Single-Trial Learning of 2500 Visual Stimuli." *Psychonomic Science* 19, no. 2 (1970): 73–74.

Stanny, Claudia J., and George F. Weaver. "Effects of Processing Tasks on the Recognition of Pictures." *Bulletin of the Psychonomic Society* 23, no. 2 (1985): 116–118.

Stark, L., and S. R. Ellis. "Scan Paths Revisited: Cognitive Models Direct Active Looking." In *Eye Movements and Psychological Processes*, ed. J. W. Senders, D. Fisher, and R. A Monty, 192–226. Hillsdale, N.J.: Lawrence Erlbaum Associates, 1981.

Stein, Marty. "Panel on Subject Access to Visual Images: The Online Horizon from Where We Stand." A paper delivered at the Art Libraries Society of North America 27th Annual Conference, Vancouver, B.C., Canada, March 27 1999.

Stiny, G., and J. Gips. *Shape Grammars and Their Uses*. Basel, Switzerland: Birkhauser Verlag, 1975.

Stricker, M., and A. Dimai. "Color Indexing with Weak Spatial Constraints." A paper delivered at the Storage and Retrieval for Image and Video Databases conference, San Jose, Calif., February, 1996.

Stricker, M., and M. Orengo. "Similarity of Color Images." A paper delivered at the Storage and Retrieval for Image and Video Databases conference, San Jose, Calif., 1995.

Stuchlikova, Iva, Pavel Kindlman, and Frantisek Man. "Anxiety in Visual Perception." *Anxiety, Stress and Coping: An International Journal* 9, no. 1 (1996): 87–103.

Stumm, Deborah. "When Is a Forest Fire a Bushfire? Towards an Australian Pictorial Thesaurus." A paper delivered at the 13th National Cataloguing Conference, Brisbane, Australia, October 13–15, 1999.

Suzuki, Kotaro, and Rika Takahashi. "Effectiveness of Color in Picture Recognition Memory." *Japanese Psychological Research* 39, no. 1 (1997): 25–32.

Svenonius, Elaine. "Thesauri." In *Automatic Processing of Art History Data and Documents*, ed. Laura Corti and Marilyn Schmitt, 33–48. Los Angeles: J. Paul Getty Trust, 1984.

Swain, Michael J. "Interactive Indexing into Image Databases." A paper delivered at the Storage and Retrieval for Image and Video Databases conference, San Jose, Calif., February 2–3 1993.

Swain, Michael J., and Dana H. Ballard. "Color Indexing." *International Journal of Computer Vision* 7, no. 1 (1991): 11–32.

Swett, Henry A., Maryellen L. Giger, and Kunio Doi. "Computer Vision and Decision Support." In *The Perception of Visual Information*, ed. William R. Hendee and Peter N. T. Wells, 272–315. New York: Springer-Verlag, 1993.

Tadmor, Y., and D. J. Tolhurst. "Discrimination of Changes in the Second-Order Statistics of Natural and Synthetic Images." *Vision Research* 34, no. 4 (1994): 541–554.

Takahashi, Shigeko. "Aesthetic Properties of Pictorial Perception." *Psychological Review* 102, no. 4 (1995): 671–683.

Tam, Audrey M, and Clement H. Leung. "Structured Natural Language Descriptions for Semantic Content Retrieval of Visual Materials." *Journal of the American Society for Information Science and Technology* 52, no. 11 (2001): 930–937.

Tamura, Hideyuki, Shunji Mori, and Takashi Yamawaki. "Texture Features Corresponding to Visual Perception." *IEEE Transactions on Systems, Man, and Cybernetics* SMC-8, no. 6 (1978): 460–473.

Tansley, Robert H. "The Multimedia Thesaurus: Adding a Semantic Layer to Multimedia Information." Ph.D. thesis, University of Southampton, England, 2000.

Tansley, Robert H., Colin Bird, Wendy Hall, Paul Lewis, and Mark Weal. "Automating the Linking of Content and Concept." A paper delivered at the 8th ACM Multimedia Conference, Los Angeles, Calif., October 30–November 4, 2000.

Taylor, Bradley L. "Chenhall's Nomenclature, the Art and Architecture Thesaurus, and Issues of Access in America's Artifact Collections." *Art Documentation* 15, no. 2 (1996): 17–23.

Taylor, Bradley L. "The Effect of Surrogation on Viewer Response to Expressional Qualities in Works of Art." Ph.D. thesis, the University of Michigan, 2001.

Taylor, Robert. "Question-Negotiation and Information Seeking in Libraries." *College and Research Libraries* 29, no. 3 (1968): 178–194.

Thuraisingham, Bhavani. *Managing and Mining Multimedia Databases*. New York: CRC Press, 2001.

Tobias, Jenny. "Apples and Oranges: Juggling Visual and Verbal Reference Queries (Panel Report)." A paper delivered at the Art Libraries Society of North America (ARLIS/NA), San Antonio, Tex., April 6, 1997.

Toglia, Michael P., Philip J. Hinman, Bradley S. Dayton, and John F. Catalano. "The Blocked-Random Effect in Pictures and Words." *Perceptual and Motor Skills* 84, no. 3, pt. 1 (1997): 976–978.

Torre, Diane S. "Keywording for Subject Retrieval: Using Words to Find Pictures." *Visual Resources Association Bulletin* 23, no. 2 (1996): 13–16.

Town, C. P., and D. Sinclair. "Ontological Query Language for Content Based Image Retrieval." A paper delivered at the IEEE Workshop on Content-Based Access of Image and Video Libraries (CBAIVL), Kauai, Hawaii, December 14, 2001.

Townsend, J. T., and F. G. Ashby. "Experimental Test of Contemporary Mathermatical Models of Visual Letter Recognition." *Journal of Experimental Psychology: Human Perception and Performance* 8 (1982): 834–864.

Treisman, Anne. "Features and Objects in Visual Processing." *Scientific American* 255, no. 5 (1986): 114B–125.

Triandis, Harry C., and William W. Lambert. "A Restatement and Test of Schlosberg's Theory of Emotion with Two Kinds of Subjects from Greece." *Journal of Abnormal and Social Psychology* 56 (1958): 321–328.

Tsichritzis, D. C. and F. H. Lochovsky, *Data Models*. Englewood Cliffs, N.J.: Prentice-Hall, 1982.

Tsotsos, J. K. "Image Understanding." In *Encyclopedia of Artifical Intelligence*, ed. Stuart Shapiro. New York: Wiley, 1992.

Turner, James M. "Subject Access to Pictures: Considerations in the Surrogation and Indexing of Visual Documents for Storage and Retrieval." *Visual Resources* 9, no. 3 (1993): 241–271.

Turner, James M. "Determining the Content of Still and Moving Image Documents for Storage and Retrieval: An Experimental Investigation." Ph.D. thesis, University of Toronto, 1994.

Turner, James M. "Comparing User-Assigned Terms with Indexer-Assigned Terms for Storage and Retrieval of Moving Images: Research Results." A paper delivered at the 58th Annual Meeting of the American Society for Information Science, Chicago, Ill., October 9–12, 1995.

Tversky, A. "Features of Similarity." *Psychological Review* 84 (1977): 327–352.

Tversky, A., and I. Gati. "Studies of Similarity." In *Cognition and Categorization*, ed. E. Rosch and B. Lloyd, 79–98. Hillsdale, N.J.: Lawrence Erlbaum Associates, 1978.

Tversky, B. "Eye Fixations in Prediction of Recognition and Recall." *Memory and Cognition* 2 (1974): 275–278.

Tversky, B., and K. Hemenway. "Categories of Environmental Scenes." *Cognitive Psychology* 15 (1983): 121–149.

Tyler, Christopher W. "Eye Placement Principles in Portraits and Figure Studies over the Past Two Millennia." A paper delivered at the Human Vision and Electronic Imaging conference, San Jose, Calif., 1998.

Universal Bibliographic Control and International MARC Programme. *ISBD (NBM): International Standard Bibliographic Description for Non-Book Materials*. 2nd ed. London: International Federation of Library Associations and Institutions, 1987.

Uttal, William R. *On Seeing Forms*. Hillsdale, N.J.: Lawrence Erlbaum, 1988.

Vaidya, C. and J. Gabrieli. "Picture Superiority in Conceptual Memory: Dissociative Effects of Encoding and Retrieval Tasks." *Memory and Cognition* 28 (2000): 1165–1172.

Vailaya, A., M. A. T. Figueiredo, A. K. Jain, and Hong-Jiang Zhang. "Image Classification for Content-Based Indexing." *IEEE Transactions on Image Processing* 10, no. 1 (2001): 117–130.

Vailaya, A., A. K. Jain, and Hong-Jiang Zhang. "On Image Classification: City vs. Landscape." A paper delivered at the IEEE Workshop on Content-Based Access of Image and Video Libraries, Santa Barbara, Calif., June 1998.

Vailaya, A., Y. Zhong, and A. K. Jain. "A Hierarchical System for Efficient Image Retrieval." A paper delivered at the 13th International Conference on Pattern Recognition, Vienna, Austria, August 1996.

Vaina, L. "Visual Texture for Recognition." In *Matters of Intelligence*, ed. L. M. Vaina, 402–427. Dordrecht: D. Reidel, 1987.

Valdez, Patricia, and Albert Mehrabian. "Effects of Color on Emotions." *Journal of Experimental Psychology: General* 123, no. 4 (1994): 394–409.

Van der Starre, Jan H. E. *Access to Museum Catalogues: The Example of Van Eyck*. 1996. Available from www.rkd.nl/pblctns/eyck-e.htm#6 (accessed on April 20, 2003).

Van der Waal, H., L. D. Couprie, E. Tholen, and G. Vellekoop. *Iconclass: An Iconographic Classification System*. 3 vols. Amsterdam: North-Holland, 1985.

Vellaikal, A., and C.-C. Jay Kuo. "Hierarchical Clustering Techniques for Image Database Organization and Summarization." A paper delivered at the Multimedia Storage and Archiving Systems conference, San Jose, Calif., 1998.

Venters, Colin C., and Matthew Cooper. *A Review of Content–Based Image Retrieval Systems. Report to JISC Technology Applications Programme*. Technical report JTAP-054. Manchester, England: University of Manchester, 2000.

Visual Resources Association. *VRA Core Categories, Version 3.0*. Visual Resources Association Data Standards Committee, 7/24/2000 2000. Available from www.vraweb.org/vracore3.htm (accessed on April 20, 2003).

Viviani, Paolo. "Eye Movements in Visual Search: Cognitive, Perceptual, and Motor Control Aspects." In *Eye Movements and Their Role in Visaul and Cognitive Processes*, ed. Eileen Kowler, 353–393. New York: Elsevier, 1990.

Wacholder, Nina, Judith Venuti, Michael Krauthammer, and Pat Molholt. "Accessing and Browsing 3D Anatomical Images with a Navigational Ontology." A paper delivered at Classification for User Support and Learning (11th Classification Research Workshop), Chicago, Ill., November 12, 2000.

Wade, Nicholas. *Visual Allusions*. Hillsdale, N.J.: Lawrence Erlbaum, 1990.

Wakimoto, Koji, Mitsuhide Shima, Satoshi Tanaka, and Akira Maeda. "Content-Based Retrieval Applied to Drawing Image Databases." A paper delivered at the Storage and Retrieval for Image and Video Databases conference, San Jose, Calif., February 2–3, 1993.

Walsh, Vincent, and J. J. Kulikowski. "Introduction: What You See Is Not What You Get." In *Perceptual Constancy: Why Things Look As They Do*, ed. Vincent Walsh and J. J. Kulikowski, 1–5. New York: Cambridge University Press, 1998.

Wang, James Ze, Jia Li, Desmond Chan, and Gio Wiederhold. *Semantics-Sensitive Retrieval for Digital Picture Libraries*. 1999. Available from www.dlib.org/dlib/november99/wang/11wang.html (accessed on April 20, 2003).

Wang, James Ze, Gio Wiederhold, Oscar Firschein, and Sha Xin Wei. "Wavelet-Based Image Indexing Techniques with Partial Sketch Retrieval Capability." A paper delivered at the 4th International Forum on Research and Technology Advances in Digital Libraries (ADL '97), Washington D.C., May 1997.

Watkins, Michael J., and Thomas M. Graefe. "Delayed Rehearsal of Pictures." *Journal of Verbal Learning and Behavior* 20, no. 3 (1981): 276–288.

Weber, R., J. Bollinger, T. Gross, and H.-J. Schek. "Architecture of a Networked Image Search and Retrieval System." A paper delivered at the Conference on Information and Knowledge Management (CIKM '99), Kansas City, Mo., November 2–6, 1999.

Weber, R., H.-J. Schek, and S. Blott. "A Quantitative Analysis and Performance Study for Similarity Search Methods in High-Dimensional Spaces." A paper delivered at the 24th International Conference on Very Large Data Bases, New York, August 1998.

Weibel, Stuart L., and Traugott Koch. "The Dublin Core Metadata Initiative: Mission, Current Activities, and Future Directions." *D-Lib Magazine* 6, no. 12 (2000).

Weiland, Constance. "Indexer Consistency of Images: A Study." Master's thesis, University of North Carolina, 1997.

Weithas, Art, ed. *The Society of Illustrators Twenty-Fifth Annual of American Illustrators*. Vol. 25. New York: Society of Illustrators, 1984.

Werner, H. "Studies on Contour." *American Journal of Psychology* 47 (1935): 40–64.

Wertheimer, Max. "Principles of Perceptual Organization." In *Readings in Perception*, ed. David C. Beardslee and Michael Wertheimer, 115–135. New York: D. Van Nostrand Company, 1958.

Whalen, Paul J., Scott L. Rauch, Nancy L. Etcoff, Sean C. McInerney, Michael B. Lee, and Michael A. Jenike. "Masked Presentations of Emotional Facial Expressions Modulate Amygdala Activity without Explicit Knowledge." *Journal of Neuroscience* 18, no. 1 (1998): 411–418.

White, D. A., and Ramesh C. Jain. "Similarity Indexing: Algorithms and Performance." A paper delivered at the Storage and Retrieval for Image and Video Databases conference, San Jose, Calif., 1996.

White, Hedy, Amanda Morris, and April G. Arthur. "Gender Role Stereotyping in Picture Interpretation." *Journal of Genetic Psychology* 157, no. 1 (1996): 119–120.

White, Murray. "Representation of Facial Expressions of Emotion." *American Journal of Psychology* 112, no. 3 (1999): 371–381.

White, Murray. "Parts and Wholes in Expression Recognition." *Cognition and Emotion* 14, no. 1 (2000): 39–60.

White-Hensen, Wendy, ed. *Archival Moving Image Materials: A Cataloging Manual*, 2nd ed. Washington D.C.: Library of Congress, Cataloging Distribution Service, 2000.

Wilkes, D., and J. Tsotsos. "Active Object Recognition." A paper delivered at the Computer Vision and Pattern Recognition conference (CVPR '92), Champaign, Ill., 1992.

Williams, L. G. "The Effects of Target Specification on Objects Fixated during Visual Search." *Acta Psychologica* 27 (1967): 355–360.

Wilson, Brent Guy. "The Development and Testing of an Instrument to Measure Aspective Perception of Paintings." Ph.D. thesis, The Ohio State University, 1966.

Wittgenstein, L. *Philosophical Investigations.* Oxford, England: Basil Blackwell, 1958.

Wolfe, J. "Visual Attention." In *Seeing*, ed. K. K. De Valois, 335–386. San Diego Calif.: Academic Press, 2000.

Woodley, M. *Crosswalks: The Path to Universal Access?* Getty Research Institute, 2001. Available from www.getty.edu/research/institute/standards/intrometadata/2_articles/woodley/index.html (accessed on April 23, 2003).

Wright, Johan M. von, P. Gebhard, and M. Karttunnen. "A Developmental Study of the Recall of Spatial Location." *Journal of Experimental Child Psychology* 20, no. 1 (1975): 181–190.

Yandle, Ashley. "Comparing User Queries and Archival Indexing of Photographs." M.S. thesis, University of North Carolina at Chapel Hill, 1998.

Yang, Zijun, and C.-C. Jay Kuo. "A Semantic Classification and Composite Indexing Approach to Robust Image Retrieval." A paper delivered at the International Conference on Image Processing (ICIP '99), Kobe, Japan, 1999.

Yarbus, A. L. *Eye Movements and Vision.* New York: Plenum Press, 1967.

Yik, Michelle S. M., Zhaolan Meng, and James A. Russell. "Adults' Freely Produced Emotion Labels for Babies' Spontaneous Facial Expressions." *Cognition and Emotion* 12, no. 5 (1998): 723–730.

Yoshitaka, Atsuo, and Tadao Ichikawa. "A Survey of Content-Based Retrieval for Multimedia Databases." *IEEE Transactions of Knowledge and Data Engineering* 11, no. 1 (1999): 81–93.

Yoshitaka, Atsuo, S. Kishida, M. Hirakawa, and Tadao Ichikawa. "Knowledge-Assisted Content-Based Retrieval for Multimedia Databases." *IEEE Multimedia* 1, no. 4 (1994): 12–21.

Young, Andrew W., Duncan Rowland, Andrew J. Calder, and Nancy L. Etcoff. "Facial Expression Megamix: Tests of Dimensional and Category Accounts of Emotion Recognition." *Cognition* 63, no. 3 (1997): 271–313.

Zadeh, L. A. "A Note on Prototype Theory and Fuzzy Sets." *Cognition* 12 (1982): 291–297.

Zaidel, Dahlia W. "Memory and Spatial Cognition following Commissurotomy." In *Handbook of Neuropsychology*, ed. Robert D. Nebes and S. Corkin, 4, 151–166. New York: Elsevier Science, 1990.

Zaidel, Dahlia W. and A. Kasher. "Hemispheric Memory for Surrealistic versus Realistic Paintings." *Cortex* 25 (1989), 617–641.

Zaidel, Dahlia W., and Peter Fitzgerald. "Sex of the Face in Western Art: Left and Right in Portraits." *Empirical Studies of the Arts* 12, no. 1 (1994): 9–18.

Zarate, Michael A., and James D. Sanders. "Face Categorization, Graded Priming, and the Mediating Influences of Similarity." *Social Cognition* 17, no. 4 (1999): 367–389.

Zhang, Hong-Jiang, and Di Zhong. "Scheme for Visual Feature-Based Image Indexing." A paper delivered at the Storage and Retrieval for Image and Video Databases conference, San Jose, Calif., 1995.

Zhao, W., R. Chellappa, A. Rosenfeld, and P. J. Phillips. *Face Recognition: A Literature Survey.* Technical Report TR4167. Silver Spring, Md.: University of Maryland, 2000.

Zhuang, Yueting, Xiaoming Liu, and Yunhe Pan. "Apply Semantic Template to Support Content-Based Image Retrieval." A paper delivered at the Storage and Retrieval for Media Databases conference, San Jose, Calif., January 2000.

Subject Index

AACR2. See Anglo-American Cataloging Rules 2
AAT. See Art and Architecture Thesaurus
access (images): considerations in choosing systems for, 132–34; levels of, 102. *See also* cataloging; classification; image indexing
active vision, 166–67
aesthetic preferences, determinants of, 61–63; impact of art training, 59–61; origins of, 54, 62; and personality type, 61; theories, 56–57
aesthetic properties, interactions, 58
aesthetic variables, 57–59; and emotion, 63–65
affective computing, 170–71
affective response: and color in images, 170–71; cross-cultural dimensions, 29; and ecological view, 28; to images, 28–30, 64–65, 208, 229–30; presentation effects on, 64; types of, 28. *See also* emotion
AMORE (system), 201n38
amygdala, role in sensory perception, 27–28
Anglo-American Cataloging Rules 2 (AACR2), 73, 103
area, Gestalt principle of, 22
Art and Architecture Thesaurus (*AAT*): analysis, 84–89; application of, 89
art historians, as image users, 122–23, 126, 128–29
art history information, 250–51
art images *See* art objects
ART MUSEUM (system), 155
art, theories of: factors in perception, 59–61; and science, 55
art objects: description, 74–77; fine arts images, attributes of, 219–21; and shape grammars, 152–53; thesauri, 77–94
Association of Moving Image Archivists (AMIA), 116–17
attention: effect of anomalies on, 246; role in visual processing, 26–27
attributes (images): categories in describing tasks, 205–8; categories in sorting tasks, 216–18; definition, 3, 232–34; distribution in thesauri, 81–84, 87–89, 90–91; in fine arts images, 219–21; grouped by levels, 227–28; interpretive, 206–7, 219, 229–30, 251, 254–56; perceptual, 206–7, 222, 229–30; representation of (table), 258; research results, 237–39; in scientific diagrams, 221–23, 226–7; in story of image, 251. *See also* features; interpretation (of images)
Australian Pictorial Thesaurus, 98
authority files, 89, 95–96

basic level objects, 40–41, 42, 213–15
Bayesian methods, 156
Belmont Conference, 85
Benchathlon, 197
Blobworld (system), 188, 201n41
bottom-up processing, in human vision, 19–20
boundary extension effect (memory), 52–53
browsing, 128–29, 134

canonical view, 42, 47
captions, in image retrieval, 172, 173
cataloging: assumptions of, 98; cooperative, 74–75, 104. *See also* access; classification; image indexing.
categorical perception, 43–44; and facial expressions, 29–30; "sensory aesthetics," 62
Categories for the Description of Works of Art (CDWA), 107
categorization: and cognitive processes, 40; and image semantics, 172–74; and physiological specialization, 43; theories of, 40–44. *See also* similarity; classification.

category structure, 213–15
category superiority effect (CSE), 50
CBR. *See* content-based retrieval
Chabot (system), 148, 184
charts. *See* diagrams
classification (images): and aesthetic responses, 54; bias in, 98–99; and cognition, 8; contexts for, 98; process, 69–71; research agenda, 262–64; systematic, 91–92; theoretical basis for, 117–121. *See also* access; cataloging; categorization; image indexing
classification systems, 73–74; for art objects, 74; for images, 96–97; problems with, 74–75
closure, Gestalt principle of, 21
clustering methods, 180; use for, 96
cognitive approach: in experimental aesthetics, 58; in information retrieval, 2
cognitive psychology: perspectives on human image processing, 7–8; and psychology of art, 55–56
color, cross-cultural factors, 64; effect on visual memory, 49–50; impact on emotion, 63–64; machine processing, 146–48; memory for, 15, 51; perception of, 14–15, 28, 58; as retrieval cue, 146–47, 249–50; systems of description, 15, 88
color histogram, 147–48
color space, 200n6
color theory, 63
common fate, Gestalt principle of, 21
composition. *See* aesthetic variables; *See* organization (image content)
compression, 157–59
compromised need, 125
computational theory of perception, 10
Computer Interchange of Museum Information (CIMI), 112
computer science, literature of, 199
concept (definition), 18
concept-based indexing, 6
concept maps, 191
concept organization, 176–77
Conference on Intellectual Access to Visual Resources (Belmont Conference), 85
consistency effect, 33, 52
constructive perception (theory), 10
content-based image retrieval (CBIR). *See* content-based retrieval
content-based retrieval (CBR), 142–44, 146–52; definition, 5; research agenda, 266–67; system requirements, 198
context: and image quality, 141–42; importance in image description, 98, 243; role in image understanding, 68n10; role in visual processing, 25–26, 33, 66, 243
controlled vocabulary, 70–71; steps for consistency, 99. *See also* thesauri
Core Categories for Visual Resources, 107
Courtauld Institute of Art, 121
cross-cultural effects, in aesthetic response, 54, 64
cross-disciplinary research, lack of, 5–6
crosswalks, 111–12
culture, bias in classification, 98–99; effects on pictorial perception, 8, 29, 61
Cypress (system), 154

data communication tools, 111–12
data content tools, 70, 99–104
data representation, 112–14
data reduction, 157–59
data structure tools, 70, 104–11; problems with, 116–17
data value tools, 70–99
database architecture, 182–85
describing tasks (research), 204–5, 224–25
Description Logics, 177
Descriptive Terms for Graphic Materials: Genre and Physical Characteristics Headings, 78–79
details: influence on perception, 47–48; role in image memory, 47–48, 51, 52

developmental stages, in aesthetic perception, 59–61
diagrams, 221–23, 226–27
digitization of images, 141–42, 200n1
direct perception (theory), 10
distance measures, 144–46
distributed indexing, 255–56
documentalists, 2
dual-coding theory, 44–45
Dublin Core, 108–9

ecological view of perception, 8, 28
edge detection, 150–51
emotion: and aesthetic variables, 63–65; category structure of, 44; definition and types, 28; dimensions of, 28; expressed through drawings, 64; impact of color on, 63–64; impact on cognitive processing, 27–30; role in similarity judgments, 60; role in visual processing, 28–30. *See also* affective response
Encoded Archival Description (EAD), 110
entity–attribute–relationship modeling, 127, 190–91, 258–59
evaluation. *See* system evaluation
evaluation measures, 195
Excite search engine, 126
exemplars, 41–42
expectations, role in image understanding, 25–26, 57
experimental aesthetics, 53–55
Extensible Markup Language (XML), 109
eye movements, 30; individual differences in, 34; relation to task, 33; and spatial frequencies, 34–35
eye-tracking, assumptions of, 30; experiments, 30–36

face recognition, 200n18
faceted arrangement, 86
facial expressions: and emotions, 29–30; encoding of, 29; recognition, 29–30, 44
failure analysis, 127
feature analysis, hierarchical model of, 163–64.
feature-based models, 19–20
feature matching systems, 154
"feature model," 165
feature-theoretical approach, 39
features (image), 142–43; definition, 142; hierarchical model of, 180–81. *See also* low level features.
fiction indexing, 253–54
figure–ground, theory of, 21; as indexing guideline, 245–46
fine arts images. *See* art objects
fixations (eye movement), factors affecting, 30; role in memory, 46
focal point, in picture viewing, 31–32
format: effect on visual memory, 48; headings in TGM II, 79
FourEyes (system), 168
Fourier methods, 157–58, 165
fractals, 149, 158
frames (representation), 177
functional view, 105

gender, in image memory, 49
gender stereotyping, in picture interpretation, 38
General Motors Media Archives, 132
genre, headings in TGM I, 78–79
geons, 19
Gestalt theory, 20–24; and creativity, 57; principles (ill.), 22; and similarity, 39, 155–56; and visual variables, 57
Getty Thesaurus of Geographic Names (TGN), 95
global features, 142–43, 150
global processes (perception), 20–25; and aesthetic perception, 57
golden ratio, 61–62
good continuation, Gestalt principle of, 21
ground truth (similarity judgments), 144–46, 194; methods, 268
grouping of features, 164
Guidelines for Subject Analysis of Audiovisual Materials, 101

hemispheric specialization, 13, 61, 62
histograms, 159
historical photograph collections, 124–25, 132
Hulton Deutsch Collection, 121, 124
hypersemantic database model, 185
HyperText Markup Language (HTML), 109

ICONCLASS, 91–94
iconic indexing, 177–78
iconic memory, 44
iconography: as basis for indexing, 118–19, 255; in classification systems, 119; system requirements, 85; thesaurus for, 91–94
iFind (system), 190
image construct queries, 123
image databases. *See* imagebases
image indexing, 129–32; by commercial vendors, 94–95; cognitive basis for, 246–47; conceptual structure for, 229–31; consistency in, 100–101; experiments, 236–37; guidelines for, 101–4; integrated record, need for, 270–71; levels of, 246–47; locus of authority, 242; methods for, 5, 159–60; organizational factors, 114–16; problems in, 72–73, 97–99; process, 69–71; research agenda, 262–64, 270–71; template for, 223–24. *See also* access; cataloging; classification; thesauri
image interpretation, effect of gender, 38
image quality, 141–42
image retrieval, needs in, 198–99; research communities, 5–6, 142–44, 271–72; systems research agenda, 266–67
image search engines, Internet based, 186
image understanding: factors affecting, 25–26; machine methods, 161–62, 164–67; theories of, 36–44. *See also* machine vision; object recognition
imagebases, 181–91; characteristics, 181–82; problems faced by, 181–82, 184–85; versus text databases, 187–88
ImageRover (system), 201n38
ImageQuery (system), 96
images: definition, 3; functions of, 225–26; models, research agenda, 261–62. *See also* picture viewing; art objects
index structures (databases), 159–60
indexing. *See* image indexing
information retrieval, cognitive approach, 2
information theory: and Gestalt principles, 22–23; and picture viewing, 32–33
informativeness: definition, 33; effect on image memory, 50; and eye movements, 34–35; in picture viewing, 32–33, 246
interfaces (image retrieval systems), 272–74
International Affective Picture System, 28
International Standard Bibliographic Description for Non-Book Materials, 104
International Standards Organization (ISO), 158
interpretation (of images): culturally and socially mediated, 203–4; levels of, 119–21. *See also* attributes (images)

Joint Photographic Experts Group (JPEG), 125–26, 158
journalists, as image users, 128. *See also* newspaper image archives

kansei engineering, 201n24
knowledge representation, techniques in image processing, 176–77

Latent Semantic Analysis, 172–73

Latent Semantic Indexing. *See* Latent Semantic Analysis
lateral geniculate nucleus, 12
Library of Congress Prints and Photographs Division, 78–79
Library of Congress Subject Headings (LCSH), 73, 79–80
Library of Congress Thesaurus for Graphic Materials: analysis, 79–84, 135n13; in relation to image attributes, 223–24
limbic system, role in sensory perception, 27–28
literary warrant, 77, 85
local features, 142–43, 150
local processes (perception), 19–20
location (spatial composition), 248–49. *See also* organization (image content)
low-level features: perception of, 14–18; processing, 146–52, 162–64; role in memory, 48–50, 52, 66; and similarity, 39; and visual learning, 172–73. *See also* features (image); visual perception

machine learning, 178–80; of visual concepts, 172. *See also* neural networks
machine vision, 143–44, 147; versus content-based retrieval (CBR), 143–44. *See also* object recognition; image understanding
MARC format, 105; problems with, 105–6
markup languages, 109–10
MARS (system), 154, 189
MAVIS 2 (system), 169, 248
meaning: effect on memory, 46; in images, 43, 224–25, 242; levels of, in images, 119–21. *See also* metaphor
MediaNet (system), 169, 175
memory (visual), 44–45; experiments, 45–48, 208–9; features affecting, 66; role of attention in, 27; semantic memory, 42; spatial memory, 51
mental model, of image system, 223–24
metadata, 104–9, 111–12, 114, 135n1; research agenda, 265–6
metaphor, in images, 43. *See also* meaning
mid-level processing, in human vision, theories, 20–25
motion, perception of, 23, 30, 67
movies. *See* moving images
moving images, cataloging, 116–17. *See also* video
Moving Picture Experts Group (MPEG), 158–59
MPEG-7 (standard), 110–11, 158–59
multidimensional indexing methods, 159–60
multimedia, next-generation systems, 198
Multimedia Retrieval Markup Language (MRML), 186
museum objects. *See* art objects

narrative structure, in video and images, 140
NASA Visual Thesaurus, 96, 127–28
National Library of Medicine, Prints and Photographs Collection, 121
natural language processing: in image indexing, 256; in image retrieval, 172
NeTra (system), 154, 188, 201n41
neural networks, 178–80; in content-based image retrieval, 173–74; and human similarity judgments, 156. *See also* machine learning
neuropsychology, 8
newspaper image archives, 122, 125–26, 130–32. *See also* journalists
noise (in images), 146

Object ID Project, 105
object recognition: machine techniques, 149–50, 162–64; model-based approaches, 165–66; theories of, 19–20, 25–26. *See also* machine vision; image understanding.

object oriented database model, 183–85
object oriented programming: and MARC record, 107; Conceptual Reference Model (CRM), 114
object-relational model, 185
objects: naming, 41, 43; perception of, 25–26; representation, 27; significance, automatic recognition of, 162–64; tools for description, 244
ontologies, 113–14, 259
organization (image content): effects on memory, 51; role in image viewing, 248–49. *See also* location (spatial)
organizational factors, impact on access, 114–16

partitioning methods, 159–60
patterns, preferences for, 62; visual processing, 15–16
percept: definition, 21; in indexing levels, 229
perception: cultural influence on, 8; ecological view, 8; influence of emotion, 30. *See also* visual perception
Photobook (system), 154, 156
physiology, specialization in categorization, 43
PicHunter (system), 156, 174, 189, 196
PicSOM (system), 180
PICTION (system), 172, 177
pictorial space, and figure–ground, 21
PicToSeek, 201n38
picture superiority effect, 45
picture viewing: and neurophysiological response, 29; eye-tracking experiments, 30–36
pixel (definition), 141
placement, physical laws of, 25–26
Point Access Method (PAM), 159–60
pose (composition), 62
Prägnanz, 39
preattentive vision, 12
PRECIS (Preserved Context Indexing System), 257
precoordination (of terms), 79–80, 93
primary subject matter, 120–21, 126
principal component analysis, 157
PROBE (system), 184
prototype theory, 40, 55; use in image retrieval, 176
proximity (Gestalt principle), 21
psychology of art, 9, 53–67; relation to cognitive psychology, 55–56
"Pyramid," conceptual structure for indexing, 229–31

QBIC (system), 153–54, 184, 188
queries (for images), 123–27; basic types, 127; interaction methods, 272–74; for system evaluation, 193–94, 267–68; on the World Wide Web, 130–31. *See also* search behavior
query-by-example (QBE), 188–91
query languages, 190–91, 201n40
query techniques: in content-based retrieval, 160–61; in imagebases, 181–82, 186–91

raster graphics, 141

RDF. *See* Resource Description Framework
reading habits, effect on aesthetic preference, 61
recall experiments (image memory), 46–48
recognition by components (theory), 19
recognition experiments (image memory), 45–46
region growing, 151–52
relational database model, 183
relations, functional and spatial classes, 25–26
relevance feedback, 189–90
REMINDS (system), 184
repeat rate (statistical measure), 210–13
representation, of images in memory, 44–45
research (images): agenda, 259–74; communities, 5–6, 142–44, 271–72; constraints, 5–6
Resource Description Framework (RDF), 109, 112

saccade (eye movement), 30
saliency: as aid to memory, 52–53; definition, 200n19
"Santa Cruz system" (classification), 73
"Savannah hypothesis," 54
scale: and object perception, 24; in machine processing, 164
scene recovery approach, 165–66
scenes: context and object detection, 25–26; description of, 41
schemas, 36–38, 177; and eye movements, 34; and image memory, 51–53; and image understanding, 25; as indexing guide, 247, 252–53, 255; and perception, 38; and works of art, 57, 250–51
schemata. *See* schemas
search behavior, 127–29, 134. *See also* queries
search engines. *See* image search engines
search methods. *See* queries
search process, research agenda, 264–66
search tools, visual, 273
segmentation (of images): by human visual system, 17; machine methods, 163
Self-Organizing Map (SOM), 180
semantic gap, 172
semantic networks, 113, 176
semantic relations: and hierarchical categories, 156; in object recognition and scene understanding, 25–26, 167–70; and similarity judgments, 156
semantic visual template, 169
semiotics, in CBR systems, 169
shape: expressive qualities of, 64; machine recognition, 149–52, 165–66; perception and recognition, 17–18, 50; role of attention in perception, 27
shape grammars, 152–53
shape similarity, 153–54, 155
Show&Tell (system), 172
similarity: cognitive models, 38–44; developmental effects, 43; feature-theoretical approach, 39; Gestalt principle of, 21, 39. *See also* categorization
similarity judgments, 144–46, 155–56; in art, 60; in newspaper images, 144–46
similarity measures, 144–46, 147; subjective, 155–56
SIMPLIcity (system), 168
sketch-based retrieval, 188
sorting experiments (images), 144–45, 215–18, 225–26
spatial frequencies: and eye movements, 34–35; and Gestalt theory, 24
spatial information, and image memory, 51, 66–67
spatial keyword indexing, 249, 273
spatial scale theory, support for Gestalt theory, 24
spectral power distribution, 146
spoken language, as annotation, 172
Standard Generalized Markup Language (SGML), 109
standards, for compression, 158–59
stories: images as, 67, 207–8, 224–25, 251–52; indexing, in images, 252–54
structuralist theory of perception, 19–20
structured annotation, 195, 259
style (artistic), 58, 61
subject heading lists: historical overview, 71–73; versus thesaurus, 79
subject indexing, 71
subjective aspects of images, in indexing, 94, 97–98
symmetry, Gestalt principle of, 22
system evaluation, 191–97, 202n47, 267–69

task, effect on eye movements, 33
template matching, 165
term variability, in image descriptions, 209–13

testbeds (images), 192–93, 267–69
texel, 149
text, annotation in image retrieval, 171–75, 268–69; effect in picture viewing, 32; use in evaluation, 194–95
textons, 16
texture: models of, 15–17, 148–49; machine processing, 148–49; perception of, 15–17, 27, 149; and visual memory, 48
thesauri, 81–97; in commercial systems, 94–95; cultural bias in, 98–99; relationships, 77. *See also* controlled vocabulary; image indexing; visual thesaurus
Thesaurus iconographique: descriptif des représentations, analysis, 89–91
TOKEN (system), 155, 201n42
top-down processing, in human vision, 20–25
transform methods, 157–58
TRADEMARK (system), 155
TREC Video Retrieval Track, 196
"two-domain theory," 178
typologies, for images, 263–64

uniform connectedness, 23
Union List of Artist Names (*ULAN*), 95
user needs, in image systems, 6
user studies (image collections), 121–23
user testing, 195–96

validity, of data, 116
Van Eyck Project, 105, 110
vector graphics, 141
Vesalius Anatomy Browser (system), 96
video: descriptive terms and indexing, 225; indexing, compared to still images, 140; retrieval evaluation, 196. *See also* moving images
viewing time, effect on image memory, 50
viewpoint, as indexing guideline, 105
VIMSYS (system), 154, 184
Virage (system), 154, 184
vision. *See* visual perception
VISION (database), 105
Visual Aesthetic Sensitivity Test (VAST), 60
visual concepts, 168–70, 229–31
visual content, as basis for indexing, 73, 122, 124
visual cortex, 12
visual indexing language, 269–70
Visual Indexing (theory), 12
Visual Information Management Systems (VIMS) Workshop (1993), 198
visual memory. *See* memory
visual perception: attentive processing, 13; as data processing, 11; factors affecting, 65–66; of low level features, 14-18; mid-level processing, 20–25; physiological processes, 12–13; preattentive processing, 11–12, 146; theories of, 10–13, 165. *See also* attributes (images); low-level features; perception
visual preferences. *See* aesthetic preferences
visual similarity, research agenda, 260–61
visual thesaurus, 96, 127–28, 247–48; as multimedia thesaurus, 175
VisualSeek (system), 154
VRA Core. *See* Core Categories for Visual Resources

Wavelets, 158
WebSEEk (system), 174
WebSeer (system), 201n38
WordNet (system), 175

XML. *See* Extensible Markup Language

Author Index

Abbas, June M., 224, 225, 251
Adams, M. J., 49
Aggarwall, J. K., 155
Ahlrichs, U., 176
Aigrain, P., 144
Aks, Deborah J., 62
Albrechtsen, Hanne, 256, 263
Aldershoff, Frank, 174
Alexopoulos, S., 153
Al-Khatib, Wasfi, 140, 142, 162, 184, 201n20
Allebach, Jan P., 170
Allen, Bryce L., 2
Aloimonos, Y., 166
Alvarado, Christine, 153
Amlani, M., 197
Anderson, John R., 8, 19
Ando, Michiyo, 52
Andrews, Janet K., 44
Anstis, Stuart, 17
Antes, James R., 31, 33
Armitage, Linda H., 121, 124, 227
Arnheim, Rudolf, 21, 41, 56, 58
Arthur, April G., 38
Ashby, F. G., 23
Ashley, J., 140, 153, 154
Askari, Nusha, 33, 48, 52
Aslandogan, Y. Alp, 163, 175, 191
Athitsos, V., 168, 201n38
Attneave, F., 22, 23, 200n9
Aumont, Jacques, 4, 13
Austin, Derek, 257
Avison, Margaret, 61
Avital, Tsion, 64

Baca, Murtha, 92, 99
Baddeley, A. D., 44
Baeza-Yates, Ricardo, 189
Bai, Xuesheng, 180
Baker, Sharon L., 253
Bakewell, Elizabeth, 122, 123, 255, 272, 126
Ballard, Dana H., 30, 147, 166
Ballesteros, Soledad, 27
Balzano, Gerald J., 41, 213
Bandopadhay, A., 166
Barbarotto, R., 43
Barber, Ron, 151, 184
Barnett, B. D., 33, 36
Barnett, Patricia J., 89
Barry, Ann Marie, 4, 18, 27, 28, 67
Barsalou, Lawrence W., 3, 44
Barthes, Roland, 4, 204
Bartlett, F. C., 20, 36, 46, 47, 48
Bates, Marcia J., 128
Batley, Susan, 128, 245
Beal, C. R., 48, 50
Beard, David Volk, 141
Bearman, David, 107
Beauregard, Mario, 8
Bechhofer, S., 93, 177
Beck, C., 101
Beck, J., 16, 23
Beckmann, N., 160
Beghtol, Clare, 253, 254, 275n6
Beigi, Mandis, 167, 171
Beilin, Harry, 53
Beiring, E., 20
Bell, S. M., 48, 50
Bellas, Elizabeth, 95
Bellon, Erwin, 151
Belongie, S., 148, 188
Benitez, Ana B., 167, 168, 169, 171, 175, 181, 199, 229,
Beretta, Giordano B., 197
Bergen, J. R., 68n6, 149
Berlin, B., 15, 41, 43
Berlyne, D. E., 32, 54, 250
Berra, P. Bruce, 140, 142, 162, 184, 201n20
Berretti, S., 153, 155, 159, 188, 202n43
Bertino, Elisa, 182
Besser, Howard, 1, 89, 96, 141, 274n2
Betz, Elizabeth W., 78
Beveridge, J. R., 197
Biederman, Irving, 19, 20, 25, 26, 37
Binford, T. O., 197
Biolsi, Kevin, 226
Bird, Colin, 173, 248
Birren, Faber, 14
Bischof, Walter F., 18, 20, 165
Bjarnestam, Anna, 94, 98
Bjorklund, D. F, 8
Black, Max, 10, 17
Blank, Paula, 64
Blickle, T., 20

Bloom, Faye A., 175
Blott, S., 160, 186
Borges, Marilyn A., 49
Bornstein, M. H., 15, 43, 215
Bos, Bert, 112
Bost, Preston R., 50
Boucart, Muriel, 24
Bouman, Charles A., 144, 226
Boyes-Braem, P., 41, 213
Bradley, Margaret M., 27, 29, 28
Brain, Douglas, 62
Brant, Linda, 55
Bray, Tim, 112
Bregler, Chris, 154, 167
Breitenbach, F., 33, 36
Brewer, W. F., 52
Brickley, Dan, 112
Brink, A., 177
Brolio, John, B., 197
Brown, C. M., 166
Brown, J., 215
Brown, P., 256
Bruce, Vicki, 14, 34
Bruner, Jerome S., 8, 10, 40
Brunold-Conesa, Cynthia, 62
Brunskill, Jeff, 221
Buckland, Michael K., 2, 134
Buckner, Randy L., 8
Burnham, Denis K., 43
Burns, A., 28, 29
Buswell, Guy T., 31, 32, 33

Cabeza, Roberto, 26
Caelli, Terry, 8, 18, 20, 154, 165, 166
Calder, Andrew J., 29, 44
Canter, D., 215
Canter, D. V., 226
Capitani, E., 43
Cardenas, A. F., 190
Carnine, D., 8
Carson, Chad, 148, 154, 167, 188
Catalano, John F., 50
Catania, Barbara, 182
Cavazza, M., 169
Cave, Carolyn B., 50
Cawkell, A. E., 5
Chan, Desmond, 168
Chan, Lois Mai, 71
Chance, June E., 45
Chang, Shih-Fu, 145, 154, 156, 167, 168, 169, 171, 173, 174, 175, 180, 181, 186, 191, 229, 240n10
Chang, Shi-Kuo, 177, 186, 187
Chapman, Antony J., 37, 53, 58
Chase, P., 42
Chau, Phyllis M. L., 28
Chellappa, R., 200n18
Chen, Hsin-Liang, 126, 227
Chen, William, 169, 191
Chertkow, Howard, 8
Chijiwa, H., 63, 201n25
Childress, Eric, 70
Chin Ooi, Beng, 174, 175
Chiou, G. I., 179
Chipman, Alison, 257
Chiu, M., 162, 178
Chokron, Sylvie, 61
Christal, R. E., 51
Christiaens, D., 33
Chu, Heting, 5
Cinque, L., 144
Clare, A., 256
Clark, J. J., 11, 27, 36
Clark, James M., 44
Clarke, Sherman, 105
Clore, Gerald L., 30
Cobb, Ronald E., 50
Cohen, Arie, 50
Cohen, Barry H., 51
Cohen, E., 250
Coley, John D., 39
Collantes, James R., 209
Collins, Karen, 124, 132
Colonelli, Christine, 49
Conesa, Jorge, 62
Conezio, Jerry, 45, 49
Conway, Michael, 30
Conway, Tiffany E., 196
Cooper, Matthew, 196
Corballis, Michael C., 12–13
Corbeil, Jean-Claude, 247
Coren, Stanley, 9
Corridoni, J. M., 171
Coss, Richard G., 54
Coulter, M. L., 48
Coulter, R. G., 48
Couprie, L. D., 91
Cox, Ingemar J., 156, 174, 178, 189, 196

Crevier, D., 176
Cromwell-Kessler, W., 111
Crozier, W. Ray, 37, 53, 58
Cupchick, Gerald C., 64, 260
Cuthbert, Bruce N., 27, 28, 29
Cutting, James E., 10

Dalton, John, 221
Dane, William J., 72
Daneels, Dirk, 151
Danko-McGhee, Katherina, 59
Davis, D., 191
Davis, Randall, 153
Davis, Stephen, 112
Davis, W. J., 28, 29
Day, J., 48, 51
Day, Y. Francis, 140, 142, 162, 184, 201n20
Dayton, Bradley S., 50
De Agostini, Maria, 61
De Graef, P., 33
De Houwer, Jan, 28
Dearing, M. F., 28
Deerwester, S., 172
Dekkers, M., 109
Del Bimbo, A., 153, 155, 159, 171, 188, 202n43
DeLoache, Judy S., 42
Deng, D., 180
Deng, Y., 154
Denis, Michel, 49
Denzler, J., 176
Deregowski, J. B., 8, 54
Dervin, Brenda, 242
Detenber, Benjamin H., 64
Deutsch, Georg, 67n4
Dickinson, A., 28
Dill, A., 31
Dimai, A., 148
Dimberg, Ulf, 8
Dobie, Mark, 169
Doi, Kunio, 163
Dolan, Raymond J., 28
Dom, B., 140, 153, 154
Dorling Kindersley, 247
Dougherty, T., 25, 33, 48, 52, 53
Dowe, J., 179
Drabenstott, Karen M., 129
Draper, A., 197
Drucker, J., 269
Dubbeldam, Barbara, 253
Dumais, S. T., 209, 172
Dunlop, Mark D., 128, 174, 201n36
Durgin, F. H., 68n8
Durran, Jennifer, 69, 74, 76

Eakins, John P., 99, 144, 111
Earnshaw, Lynda J., 43
Edelman, G. M., 8
Eklundh, J. O., 201n19
Ekman, P., 28
Eliade, Mircea, 242
Elings, Mary W., 97, 110
Ellis, S. R., 34
Elworthy, D., 256
Enser, P. G. B., 6, 119, 121, 124, 134, 227
Equitz, William, 151, 184
Ester, Michael, 141
Etcoff, Nancy L., 30, 44
Evans, Alan, 8
Evans, Hilary, 72
Eysenck, Hans J., 60

Fagin, Ronald, 189
Faloutsos, Christos, 160, 161, 176, 184, 190
Farley, Frank H., 50
Fechner, G. T., 53
Federmeier, Kara D., 44
Fehr, Dennis E., 53
Fellbaum, Christiane D., 201n30
Feng, W. C., 197
Fernandez, R., 197
Ferrari, Elena, 182
Fidel, Raya, 133
Fidopiastis, Cali, 23
Fierens, Freddy, 151
Figueiredo, M.A.T., 180
Fink, Gereon R., 28
Finlayson, G., 147
Firschein, Oscar, 158
Fischer, J., 176
Fischer, V., 176
Fish, P. R., 100
Fisher, D. F., 33, 36
Fisher, John, 53
Fitzgerald, Peter, 62
Fleck, Margaret M., 154, 167
Flexner, Stuart B., 3

Flickner, Myron, 140, 153, 154, 184
Fodor, Jerry, 45
Forsyth, David A., 154, 167
Foster, D. H., 23
Frankel, C., 168, 201n38
Freedman, J., 46
Freeman, Norman H., 60
French, J. C., 96
Frese, Thomas, 144, 226
Frew, Brian, 174
Friedman, A., 33, 52
Friesen, W. V., 28
Frijda, Nico H., 68n15
Fritz, Deborah A., 136n29
Frois, J. P., 60
Frost, C. Olivia, 76, 129
Fry, Eileen, 76, 85, 97
Fukui, Kenji, 30
Funt, B., 147
Furnas, G. W., 172, 209
Furnham, Adrian, 60, 61
Futterweit, Lorelle R., 53

Gabrieli, J., 45
Gaede, V., 160
Gardner, Howard, 58, 64
Garnier, Francoise, 89, 102, 103
Gary, J. E., 153
Gati, I., 39
Gaut, Britt, 256
Gaut, Philip, 256
Gazzaniga, Michael S., 52
Gebhard, P., 51
Gernsbacher, M. A., 49
Gevers, Theo, 174, 201n38
Ghafoor, Arif, 140, 142, 162, 184, 201n20
Ghosn, Joumana, 174, 196
Gibson, J. J., 8, 10, 67n2
Giger, Maryellen L., 163
Gilbert, Karen Diane, 72
Gill, Tony, 105, 113
Giorgianni, Edward J., 146
Gips, J., 152
Giral, Angela, 122
Girgus, Joan Stern, 9
Glasman, Eduardo, 184
Glass, A. L., 25
Glass, Elizabeth, 97
Glover, J. A., 48
Gluck, M., 42
Goble, C., 177
Goethe, W., 14
Goldman, Alan H., 56
Goldmeier, E., 38
Goldstein, Alvin G., 45
Golshani, F., 254
Gombrich, E. H., 10, 57, 250
Gomez, L. M., 209
Gooch, B., 250
Gooding, Mel, 9
Goodman, , Gail S., 53
Goodman, N., 68n20
Goodrum, A., 126
Gordon, Andrew S., 93, 252
Gordon, Catherine, 121, 126
Gorkani, M., 140, 153, 154
Gottesman, Carmela V., 53
Goude, Gunnar, 60
Gould, John D., 25, 31, 32, 34, 68n16
Graefe, Thomas M., 48
Graham, Margaret E., 99, 111, 130, 144, 269
Graham, N., 17
Gray, W., 41, 213
Green, Christopher D., 62
Green, R. J., 169
Green, Stanford J., 72
Greenberg, Jane, 111
Greenspan, Hayit, 148, 154, 167
Greenwald , Mark K., 28
Gregory, Richard L., 18
Groat, L., 215
Grosky, William I., 159, 177, 182, 184
Grossman, Frances, 51
Grout, Catherine, 113, 105
Gruber, Tom, 113
Grund, Angelika, 92
Gudivada, Venkat N., 142, 144
Guest, Steve, 43
Gunther, Neil J., 197
Gunther, O., 160
Gupta, Amarnath, 140, 148, 154, 157, 160, 161, 163, 170, 184, 187, 199, 200n5, 202n46

Haber, Ralph N., 45, 46, 49
Hafner, J., 140, 153, 154
Hagen, Margaret A., 67n3
Haig, A., 55

Hall, Wendy, 169, 173, 248
Halpern, J. A., 28, 29
Hamel, Cheryl J., 49
Hamm, Alfons O., 28
Hamzaoui, R., 158
Han, C., 151
Han, Kyung-Ah, 156
Handel, S., 16, 17
Hanson, A. R., 197
Hara, Yoshinori, 201n38
Haralick, R. M., 149
Hargreaves, David J., 57
Harmandas, V., 174
Harnad, Stevan, 40, 43, 44
Harpring, Patricia, 95
Harrison, E. R., 42
Harrison, Harriet W., 95
Harshman, R. A., 172
Hartenstein, H., 158
Hartman, Catharina A., 29
Hasegawa, J., 188
Hastings, Samantha K., 128, 129
Hatzivassiloglou, V., 173
Hauske, Gert, 35
Heaps, C., 16, 17
Heemsoth, C., 33
Heerwagen, Judith H., 54
Heidemann, G., 176
Heigl, B., 176
Heise, Diana, 44
Hekkert, Paul, 55, 59
Heller, Wendy, 61
Hellerstein, J. M., 188
Hemenway, K., 41, 214
Hemphill, Michael, 64
Hendee, William R., 14, 18, 67n1
Henderson, John M., 26, 32, 33, 35, 68n13
Herdan, Gustav, 210
Hermans, Dirk, 28
Herz, R. S., 260
Hibler, J. N. David, 127, 190, 196, 258
Hidderley, G. R., 256
Hill, Donna, 72, 101
Hinman, Philip J., 50
Hirakawa, M., 201n32
Hirata, Kyoji, 188, 201n38
Hochberg, Julian, 10, 23, 25, 38, 57
Hoehne, H., 113
Hoffman, Donald D., 18, 23, 19
Hogan, Matthew, 96, 249
Hoge, Holger, 61
Hollingworth, Andrew, 26, 32, 33, 35, 68n13
Holt, Leland H., 49
Homa, Donald, 48
Hoogstraten, Johan, 29
Hornegger, J., 176
Hotelling, H., 157
Hou, T., 162, 178
Hourihane, Colum, 96, 110, 114, 118, 120, 129
Howe, N. R., 193
Hsu, A., 162, 178
Hu, Chunhui, 190
Huang, J., 148
Huang, Q., 140, 153, 154
Huang, Thomas S., 145, 151, 154, 156, 171, 180, 189, 190
Humphrey, N. K., 55
Humphrey, R., 140
Humphreys, Glyn W., 21, 24, 34, 67n1
Hunter, Jane, 114
Hwang, Jeng-Neng, 179

Ichikawa, Tadao, 144, 185, 201n32
Idris, F., 200n7, 143, 147, 157
Iidaka, Tetsuya, 30
Intraub, Helene, 48, 50, 52, 53
Iqbal, Q., 155
Itoh, Harumi, 30
Itten, Johannes, 14, 15, 63
Iyer, Hemalata, 214
Izard, Carroll E., 44

Jagadish, H. V., 146, 153, 184
Jaimes, Alejandro, 168, 173, 181, 229, 240n10
Jain, A. K., 155, 156, 169, 180
Jain, Ramesh C., 139, 140, 144, 145, 148, 153, 154, 157, 160, 161, 163, 170, 182, 184, 187, 190, 192, 195, 197, 198, 199, 200n3, 200n5, 202n46
Järvelin, K., 196
Jaynes, Julian, 13
Jenike, Michael A., 30
Jin, Jesse S., 180
Johansson, Björn, 154
Johansson, Gunnar, 67

Johnson, Carla J., 44
Johnson, D., 41, 213
Johnson, J. A., 51
Johnson, N. S., 51
Johnston, Alan, 23
Jolicoeur, Pierre, 42
Jolion, Jean-Michel, 166
Jolley, Richard P., 43
Jones, Dorothy B., 254
Jones, G. T., 101
Jörgensen, Peter, 96, 249
Joseph, Jane E., 38
Joseph, T., 190
Joyce, Dan, 169
Ju, G., 19
Juettner, Martin, 62
Julesz, B., 16, 149
Jungert, Erland, 186, 187

Kahn, J. L., 23
Kahneman, D., 49
Kaiser, Julius O., 71
Kalin, Edward, 144, 226
Kallman, H. J., 48
Kamel, Ibrahim, 160
Kankanhalli, Mohan S., 150, 152
Kaplan, M., 250
Karlsson, Barry, 8
Karsh, R. B., 33, 36
Kartunnen, M., 51
Kasturi, Rangachar, 197, 200n3
Katayama, N., 160
Kato, T., 155, 170, 188
Kato, Takashi, 26
Katsikis, Mary, 29
Katz, B. F., 58
Kay, P., 15, 41, 43
Keane, Jill, 29, 44
Keefe, Jeanne M., 115
Kehrer, Lothar, 16, 68n7
Keil, F. C., 42, 204
Keister, Lucinda H., 120, 123, 134
Kelly, Brian, 62
Kessler, B., 75
Kim, P. K., 254
Kindlman, Pavel, 30
Kinnear, P. R., 54
Kinsbourne, Marcel, 27
Kirsch, Joan L., 152
Kirsch, Russell A., 152
Kishida, S., 201n32
Kitamoto, A., 176
Klinger, Allen, 190
Kobus, David A., 175
Koch, Traugott, 109
Koffka, K., 23
Kolehmainen, Kyösti, 60
Konecni, Vladimir J., 62
Korf Vidal, Noni, 225
Kose, G., 9
Koskela, Markus, 180, 189
Kosslyn, Stephen M., 33, 42
Kotcheff, A., 256
Krause, Michael G., 98
Krauthammer, Michael, 96
Kreiger, Gerhard, 35
Kristjanson, Arlinda F., 34
Kueppers, Harald, 15
Kuhl, Julius, 30
Kulikowski, J. J., 11
Kumar, S. R., 148
Kummert, F., 176
Kunii, T. L., 183
Kuo, C.-C. Jay, 147, 180
Kurita, T., 155, 170
Kurniawati, Ruth, 180
Kutas, Marta, 44
Kwasnik, Barbara, 209, 215

La Cascia, Marco, 142, 173, 201n38
Laaksonen, Jorma, 180, 189
Lafon, Yves, 112
Lagoze, Carl, 114
Lahlou, Youssef, 185
Laiacona, M., 43
Lambert, William W., 29
Landauer, T. K., 172, 209
Landis, Theodor, 62
Landy, M. S., 17, 149
Lane, Richard D., 28
Lang, Peter J., 27, 29
Lanzi, Elisa, 136n36, 137n47
Larkin, J. H., 222
Lasaga, Maria I., 24
Lassaline, Mary E., 41
Latto, Richard, 62
Lauzzana, Raymond G., 152
Lawrence, V., 49
Lawson, Rebecca, 42
Layne, S. S., 101, 131

Lazreg, Cecilia Karpowicz, 58
Lee, D., 140, 153, 154
Lee, Michael B., 30
Lee, Wing Foon, 150, 152
Lehmkuhle, Stephen W., 22, 32, 51
Leontiev, Dmitrii A., 60
Lepage, R., 176
Leung, Clement H., 127, 172, 190, 196, 253, 257, 258
Leung, Thomas K., 154, 167
Levialdi, S., 144
Levy, Jerre, 13, 46, 50
Lew, Michael S., 2, 168, 169, 201n21
Lewis, Paul, 169, 173, 248
Li, Jia, 168
Li, John Z., 190, 191, 202n41
Li, Wen-Syan, 201n38
Liddell, Christine, 8
Light, Richard, 110
Lindeberg, T., 24, 201n19
Liu, C., 163, 175, 191
Liu, F., 149
Liu, P., 162, 178
Liu, Xiaoming, 169, 175
Livingston, Kenneth R., 44
Lochovksy, F. H., 183
Lockhead, Gregory R., 38, 39
Loftus, Geoffrey R., 12, 25, 32, 33, 46, 48, 50, 246
Lohse, Gerald L., 16, 17, 149, 226, 264
Lorenceau, J., 24
Loui, Alexander C., 168
Lu, Ye, 190
Lupker, S. J., 23

Ma, Y., 158, 188
Machamer, Peter, 9, 54, 55
Mack, Arien, 27
Mackworth, N. H., 25, 32, 246
Macrosson, W. D., 61
Madden, Thomas E., 146
Madigan, S., 48, 49
Maeda, Akira, 176
Mahmoudi, Fariborz, 148
Maki, Ruth H., 25, 52, 53
Malik, J., 148, 188
Malik, Jitendra, 154, 167
Man, Frantisek, 30
Mandal, M. K., 143, 147, 157, 200n7
Mandler, G., 53
Mandler, J. M., 48, 51
Manjunath, B. S., 154, 158, 188
Mannan, S., 35
Mannock, K. L., 127, 190, 196, 258
Manola, F. A., 184
Marchand-Mailet, Stéphane, 191, 194, 268, 195
Marcus, S., 177
Markel, Stephen, 129
Markey, Karen, 100, 118, 119, 120, 121, 122, 255
Markkula, M., 99, 122, 125, 128, 130, 144, 196
Marr, David, 10, 11, 19, 151, 165
Marshall, Philip H., 55, 64
Marsicoi, M., 144
Martinez, José M., 110, 158
Massey, Christine, 64
Massironi, Manfredo, 10
McAlister, E., 23
McArthur, D., 28, 29
McCann, John J., 15, 269
McInerney, Sean C., 30
McKeown, K. R., 173
McKeown, Roy, 136n36, 137n47
McLean, Jennifer E., 12
McManus, I. C., 62
McRae, Linda, 100, 104, 106, 111, 130, 138n58
Medin, Douglas L., 3, 38, 39, 41, 44
Meghini, C., 177
Mehrabian, Albert, 63
Mehrotra, Rajiv, 153, 159, 177, 182, 184
Mehrotra, Sharad, 154, 189
Mehtre, Babu M., 150, 152
Meinecke, Cristina, 16, 68n7
Meng, Zhaolan, 29
Mervis, C. B., 40, 41, 213
Mesquita, Batja, 68n15
Messaris, Paul, 4
Metzger, Richard L., 33
Metzler, J., 48
Mezzanotte, Robert J., 26, 37
Miezin, Francis M., 8
Miller, Cynthia, 51
Miller, Matt L., 156, 174, 178, 189, 196
Miller, Michael B., 52
Miller, R. J., 60

Minka, Thomas P., 156, 168, 178, 189, 196, 197
Minsky, Marvin, 177
Miron, Maria, 62
Mishra, R. C., 68n14
Mitra, M., 148
Moates, Danny R., 37, 243
Möckel, W., 33
Moghadam, Amir M., 148
Molholt, Pat, 78, 85, 96
Moncada, J., 77, 96
Morandi, A. J., 32
Mori, Shunji, 149
Morris, Amanda, 38
Morris, M. W., 41, 214
Moses, John D., 175
Mueller, Hermann, 21
Mukherjea, Sougata, 201n38
Müller, Henning, 191, 194, 195, 268
Müller, Wolfgang, 191, 194, 195, 268
Mullet, Etienne, 58
Munsell, A. H., 14
Murphy, G. L., 39, 41, 214
Murtha, Susan, 8
Myaeng, Sung-Hyun, 156

Nadler, M., 151
Nagae, Seiji, 45
Nair, K., 163, 175, 191
Narasimhalu, A. D., 144
Narumoto, Jin, 30
Naveh-Benjamin, M., 51
Navon, D., 20, 23
Neill, S. D., 242, 274
Nelson, T. O., 48
Neo, Peter, 177, 181
Nepal, S., 186, 189
Ng, R., 160
Niblack, Wayne, 140, 151, 153, 154, 184
Nickerson, R. S., 49
Niemann, Heinrich, 176
Nigrin, Albert, 178
Nilsson, Nils J., 178
Nimmo-Smith, Ian, 29, 44
Nishihara, H. K., 19
Noakes, Anna, 129
Norman, D. A., 37
North, Adrian C., 57
Noton, David, 34

O'Brien, Justin, 23
O'Connor, Brian C., 224, 225, 251, 256
O'Connor, Mary K., 224, 225, 251
O'Gorman, Lawrence, 184, 146
O'Keefe, Elizabeth, 103
O'Regan, J. K., 11, 27, 36
Oakley, J., 191
Ogle, V. E., 148, 174, 177, 184
Ohlgren, Thomas, 74
Ohrn, Steven G., 98
Oja, Erkki, 180, 189
Okada, N., 188
Oldal, Maria, 75
Oliva, Aude, 24, 35
Olson, R. K., 23
Orengo, M., 148
Orenstein, J. A., 184
Oria, V., 190, 191
Orians, Gordon H., 54
Ørnager, S., 122, 125, 128, 130
Ortega-Binderberge, Michael, 154, 189
Ozsu, M. T., 190, 191, 202n41

Paek, S., 173
Paivio, Allan, 44, 45, 49
Pala, P., 153, 155, 159, 171, 188, 202n43
Palmer, Stephen E., 23, 25, 42, 52
Palmer, I. J., 169
Pan, Yunhe, 169, 175
Panchanathan, S., 17, 143, 147, 157, 200n7, 254
Panofsky, Erwin, 117, 118, 122
Papathomas, Thomas V. 156, 174, 178, 189, 196
Papin, Jean-Paul, 31
Pappas, N., 170
Park, Denise C., 48
Park, Y. C., 254
Parker, Elizabeth Betz, 78, 102
Parker, R. E., 48, 51
Parsons, Michael J., 60
Paulus, D., 176
Pavlidis, Theo, 141, 149, 197
Peeck, J., 48
Pejtersen, , A. M., 253
Penfield, W., 13
Penland, J. G., 33
Pentland, A. 154, 188
Perlmutter, A., 28, 29

Perrett, David I. 29, 44
Petersen, Steve E., 8
Petersen, Toni, 78, 85, 89
Petkovic, Dragutin, 140, 144, 153, 154, 184
Petrakis, E., 176
Pettersson, R., 100
Pezdek, Kathy, 25, 33, 48, 52, 53
Pfaltz, J. L., 96
Pflesser, Bernhard, 113
Pham, Binh, 59
Phillips, P. J., 200n18
Picard, R. W., 149, 154, 156, 168, 178, 188, 197
Pierroutsakos, Sophia L., 42
Pizano, Arturo, 190
Pocock-Williams, Lynn, 152
Pommert, A. K., 113
Potter, M. C., 31, 46, 50
Powell, A. L., 96
Price, Jana L., 50
Proffitt, Dennis R., 38
Prophet, William D., 23
Pun, Thierry, 145, 191, 194, 195, 268
Pylyshyn, Z. W., 12

Quigley, I., 175
Quinn, Maria C., 43

Rabinowitz, Jan C., 26, 37
Rabitti, F., 176, 182
Raff, Ulrich, 141, 146, 148, 149, 151, 163, 164
Raghaven, Vijay V., 142, 144
Rahman, M. A., 28, 29
Raichle, Marcus E., 8
Rajaram, Suparna, 48, 49
Ramachandran, V. S., 17
Ramakrishna, M. V., 186, 189
Rao, A. R., 16, 17, 149
Rasmussen, Edie M., 6n1
Rauch, Scott L., 30
Rawlings, David, 61
Reed, D. A., 48
Reed, S. K., 51
Reeves, Byron, 64
Rensink, Ronald A., 11, 27, 36
Rentschler, Ingo, 35, 62
Reuter, Henry H., 226
Reye, David, 154
Reynolds, Kirk, 33, 48, 52
Ribeiro-Neto, Berthier, 189
Richards, W., 19
Richardson, Michael, 52
Richmond, Phyllis A., 71
Rickman, Rick, 179
Riemer, Martin, 113
Rifkin, A., 214
Ritchey, G. H., 48, 50
Ritter, H., 176
Roark, Bret, 55
Roberts, L., 13
Rock, Irvin 11, 23, 27
Roddy, Kevin, 98, 129
Rogers, T. B., 45, 49
Rogowitz, Bernice E., 144, 170, 226
Romer, Donna M., 133
Roos, Jane Mayo, 93
Rorvig, Mark E., 77, 96, 127, 178
Rosch, Eleanor, 20, 40, 41, 42, 204, 213
Rose, T., 256
Rosenfeld, A., 200n18
Rothenstein, Julian, 9
Roussopoulos, N., 190
Rowe, Neil C., 174
Rowland, Duncan, 29, 44
Rubin, Edgar, 21
Ruddock, K. H., 35
Rui, Yong, 145, 151, 154, 156, 171, 180, 189, 190
Rumelhart, D. E., 37
Runge, O. P., 63
Russ, John C., 157
Russell, James A., 29
Russell, P. A., 54
Ruth, Jan-Erik, 60
Ruthrof, Horst, 254
Ryan-Jones, David L., 49

Sable, C. L., 173
Sadato, Norihiro, 30
Sagerer, G. 176
Saint-Martin, Fernande, 13, 14
Saito, Miho, 64
Samadani, R., 151
Sanders, James D., 42
Sanderson, M., 174
Sanfeliz, Aurora, 50

Santini, Simone, 140, 144, 145, 148, 153, 154, 157, 160, 161, 163, 170, 187, 192, 199, 200n5, 202n46
Saslona, Monique, 51
Satoh, S., 160
Saupe, D., 158
Savino, P., 176, 182
Sawhney, H., 140, 153, 154
Scassellati, B., 153
Schek, H.-J., 160, 186
Scherer, Klaus R., 68n15
Schiemann, Thomas, 113
Schiffman, B. H., 173
Schill, Kerstin, 35
Schouwstra, Sanneke J., 29
Schreiber, A. Th., 253
Schroeder, Kimberly A., 72, 132
Schubert, Rainer, 113
Schulman, E., 96
Schumacher, Gary M., 37, 243
Schumacher, Udo, 113
Schunck, Brian G., 200n3
Schwarz, Norbert, 30
Schyns, Philippe G., 24, 35
Sclaroff, Stan, 142, 154, 173, 188, 201n38
Scott, M. J., 226
Sebastiani, F., 177
Sedighian, A., 160
Seegmiller, D., 48, 51
Sellis, T., 190
Seloff, Gary A., 96
Senecal, L., 28, 29
Sethi, Saratendu, 142, 173, 201n38
Shaari, Ahmad Jelani, 49, 50
Shanbehzadeh, Jamshid, 148
Shann, Richard, 191
Shannon, C. E., 33
Sharps, Matthew J., 50
Shatford, Sara, 75, 99, 103, 118, 119, 227, 240n7
She, Alfred C., 151
Shen, Heng Tao, 174, 175
Shepard, R. N., 45
Shima, Mitsuhide, 176
Shu, C., 140
Sickels, W., 28, 29
Silverstein, A., 23
Simon, H. A., 222
Simons, Wendell, 73, 135n4
Sinclair, D., 173
Singh, Manish, 23
Slater, Alan, 44
Small, Jocelyn Penny, 252, 253
Smeaton, A., 175
Smeulders, A. W. M. 140, 148, 154, 157, 160, 161, 163, 174, 187, 199, 200n5, 201n38, 202n46
Smith, Brenda D., 51
Smith, E. P., 151
Smith, Edward E., 41, 213
Smith, John R., 144, 154, 167, 169, 171, 174, 175, 186, 192, 194, 199, 226, 268
Smith, L. J., 28, 29
Smith, Linda B., 44
Smith, Louise, 105, 113
Smythe, P. C., 45, 49
Snelders, H. M. J., 55
Snow, Marily, 1, 89, 96
So, Simon, 172
Soergel, Dagobert, 101
Solso, Robert L., 4, 204, 250
Sormunen, E., 99, 122, 125, 128, 130, 144, 196
Sowa, John F., 137n54
Spink, A., 126
Spoehr, Kathryn T., 22, 32, 51
Springer, Sally P., 67n4
Sprott, Julien C., 62
Squire, D. M., 140, 145, 180, 191, 194, 195, 195, 268
Srihari, Rohini, 172, 177, 192, 194
Stacy, E. W., 25
Stam, Dierdre C., 74, 75, 76, 98, 114, 122
Standing, Lionel, 45, 49
Stanny, Claudia J., 49
Stark, Lawrence, 34
Steele, D., 140, 153, 154
Stein, Marty, 95
Stepnowsky, Mary A., 49
Stewart, P. E., 61
Stiny, G., 152
Stoeckert, J., 25, 52, 53
Stonham, John, 179
Stouthard, Marlies E., 29
Straccia, U., 177
Stricker, M., 148
Stuchlikova, Iva, 30

Stumm, Deborah, 98
Subrahmanian, V. S., 177
Sundaram, Hari, 169
Sutanto, Dwi, 172
Suzuki, Kotaro, 49
Svenonius, Elaine, 71, 77
Swain, Michael J., 30, 147, 168, 195, 201n38
Swett, Henry A., 163
Swett, Sharon, 53
Szafron, Duane, 190, 191, 202n41

Tadmor, Y., 149
Takagi, M., 176
Takahashi, Rika, 49
Takahashi, Shigeko, 63, 68n17
Tam, Audrey M., 172, 253, 257
Tamura, Hideyuki, 149
Tan, Kian-Lee, 174, 175
Tanaka, Satoshi, 176
Tansey, Luraine C., 73, 135n4
Tansley, Robert H., 169, 173, 195, 248
Taycher, Leonid, 142, 173, 201n38
Taylor, Bradley L., 64, 76, 129
Taylor, Robert, 125
Tenenbaum, J. M., 183
Thier, Chuck, 163, 175, 191
Thom, J. A., 189
Thomas, Glyn V., 43
Thomas, M., 188
Thornhill, Ashton G., 64
Thuraisingham, Bhavani, 185
Tiede, Ulf, 113
Tobias, Jenny, 121
Toglia, Michael P., 50
Tolhurst D. J., 149
Toriwaki, J., 188
Torre, Diane S., 104
Torres, Deborah, 129
Town, C. P., 173
Townsend, J. T., 23
Treisman, Anne, 16
Treyens, J. C., 52
Triandis, Harry C., 29
Tse, Philip, 172
Tsichritzis, D. C., 183
Tsonis, P., 256
Tsotsos, J., 162, 164, 166, 176
Turner, C. H., 77, 96
Turner, James M., 99, 100, 118, 119, 225, 240n7
Tversky, A., 39
Tversky, Barbara, 32, 41, 46, 214
Tyler, Christopher W., 62

Uhlenbeck, R. W. F., 48
Unzicker, Alexander, 62
Uttal, David H., 42
Uttal, William R. 8

Vaidya, C., 45
Vailaya, A., 155, 156, 169, 180
Vaina, L., 48
Valdez, Patricia, 63
Valencia-Laver, Debra, 25, 52, 53
Valeri-Gold, Maria, 51
Van Campenhout, David, 151
Van Dam, G., 48
Van der Starre, Jan H. E., 110
Van der Waal, H., 91
Van Laar, Darren, 43
van Wieringen, Piet C. W., 59
Vellaikal, A., 180
Venters, Colin C., 196
Venuti, Judith, 96
Vidal, Neus Barrantes, 61
Viera, Cynthia, 48, 52
Viviani, Paolo, 34

Wacholder, Nina, 96
Wade, Nicholas, 9
Wagner, W., 28, 29
Wakimoto, Koji, 176
Walker, Janet, 41, 213
Walker, John, 60, 61
Walker, Neff, 226
Walsh, Vincent, 11
Wang, James Ze, 158, 168
Watkins, Michael J., 48
Wattenmaker, William D., 38, 39
Weal, Mark, 169, 173, 248
Weatherby, P., 62
Weaver, George F., 49
Weber, R., 160, 186
Weeks, Phillip A., 32, 33
Wei, Sha Xin, 158
Weibel, Stuart L., 109
Weiland, Constance, 100
Weiss, I., 166

Weithas, Art, 204
Wells, Peter N. T., 18
Werner, H., 23
Wertheimer, Max, 21
Weyl, S., 183
Weymouth, T. E., 154, 184
Whalen, Paul J., 30
Whetstone, Tony, 25, 33, 48, 52, 53
White, D. A.,, 160
White, Hedy, 38
White, Lynda S., 100, 106, 111
White, Murray, 26
White-Hensen, Wendy, 117
Whitfield, A., 55
Wiederhold, Gio, 158, 168
Wielemaker, Jan, 253
Wielinga, Bob, 253
Wilkes, D., 166
Willey, Edward V., 53
Williams, L. G., 49
Wilson, Brent Guy, 59
Wilson-Leff, Carla A., 50
Wimmers, E., 189
Winer, Ellen, 64
Winston, A. S., 260
Wisniewski, Edward J., 41
Wittgenstein, L., 4
Wolfe, J., 26
Wooding, D. S., 35
Woodley, M., 137n48
Worring, Marcel, 140, 148, 154, 157, 160, 161, 163, 187, 199, 200n5, 202n46
Wright, Johan M. von, 51

Xu, Guangyou, 180

Yamada, Hiroki, 30
Yamawaki, Takashi, 149
Yandle, Ashley, 132
Yang, Qiang, 190
Yang, Zijun, 147
Yanker, Peter, 140, 153, 154, 184
Yarbus, A. L., 30, 33, 32
d'Ydewalle, G., 33
Yianilos, Peter N., 156, 174, 178, 189, 196
Yik, Michelle S. M., 29
Yonekura, Yoshiharu, 30
Yoshitaka, Atsuo, 144, 185, 201n32
Young, Andrew W., 14, 29, 44
Yu, Clement T., 163, 175, 191

Zadeh, L. A., 176
Zaidel, D. W., 13, 62
Zarate, Michael A., 42
Zetzsche, Christoph, 35
Zhang, Hong-Jiang, 144, 156, 169, 180, 190
Zhao, W., 200n18
Zhi, Zhang, 43
Zhong, Di, 180
Zhong, Y., 155
Zhou, C., 176
Zhu, W. J., 148
Zhu, Xingquan, 190
Zhuang, Yueting, 169, 175
Zobel, M., 176
Zuk, Ilan J., 53

About the Author

Corinne Jörgensen is an associate professor in the School of Information Studies at the Florida State University. Her research areas address issues in the organization of information, the impacts of technology on information seekers and providers, usability of information systems, and users' information-seeking behaviors, with a special focus on users of image and multimedia databases. She is active in both the LIS and computer science communities, serving on program committees for such conferences as Internet Imaging (SPIE), the IEEE Workshop on Content-Based Access of Image and Video Libraries (CBAIVL), and the American Society for Information Science and Technology (ASIST) SIG for Classification Research. Most recently she participated in the development of the ISO/IEC MPEG-7 standard for content description of multimedia, focusing on the issues associated with description of semantic features of images. She has authored or coauthored over fifty publications in the area of image indexing and retrieval and has won four national awards for her research and publications. She guest edited a special issue of the *Journal of the American Society for Information Science and Technology* (September 2001) on "Image Access: Bridging Multiple Needs and Multiple Perspectives."